To James, Warmly to.

AF207740

THE HEART'S OBSESSION

AN INTIMATE BIOGRAPHY OF NEWFOUNDLAND
SONGSTRESS GEORGINA STIRLING

TONIA EVANS CIANCIULLI and CALVIN D. EVANS
WITH A FOREWORD BY MAESTRO KERRY STRATTON

Follow your heart!

Tonia

FLANKER PRESS LIMITED
ST. JOHN'S

Library and Archives Canada Cataloguing in Publication

Title: The heart's obsession : an intimate biography of Newfoundland songstress Georgina Stirling / Tonia Evans Cianciulli with Calvin D. Evans.
Names: Cianciulli, Tonia Evans, 1976- author | Evans, Calvin D., author.
Description: Includes bibliographical references and index.
Identifiers: Canadiana (print) 20190101520 | Canadiana (ebook) 2019014050X | ISBN 9781771177597
   (softcover) | ISBN 9781771177603 (EPUB) | ISBN 9781771177610 (Kindle) | ISBN 9781771177627 (PDF)
Subjects: LCSH: Stirling, Georgina, 1867-1935 | LCSH: Sopranos (Singers)—Newfoundland and Labrador—
   Biography. | LCGFT: Biographies.
Classification: LCC ML420.T723 C565 2019 | DDC 782.1092—dc23

© 2019 by Tonia Evans Cianciulli, Calvin D. Evans

ALL RIGHTS RESERVED. No part of the work covered by the copyright hereon may be reproduced or used in any form or by any means—graphic, electronic or mechanical—without the written permission of the publisher. Any request for photocopying, recording, taping, or information storage and retrieval systems of any part of this book shall be directed to Access Copyright, The Canadian Copyright Licensing Agency, 1 Yonge Street, Suite 800, Toronto, ON M5E 1E5. This applies to classroom use as well.

PRINTED IN CANADA

This paper has been certified to meet the environmental and social standards of the Forest Stewardship Council® (FSC®) and comes from responsibly managed forests, and verified recycled sources.

Cover design by Graham Blair

FLANKER PRESS LTD.
PO BOX 2522, STATION C
ST. JOHN'S, NL
CANADA

TELEPHONE: (709) 739-4477 FAX: (709) 739-4420 TOLL-FREE: 1-866-739-4420
WWW.FLANKERPRESS.COM

9 8 7 6 5 4 3 2 1

We acknowledge the [financial] support of the Government of Canada. *Nous reconnaissons l'appui [financier] du gouvernement du Canada.* We acknowledge the support of the Canada Council for the Arts, which last year invested $153 million to bring the arts to Canadians throughout the country. *Nous remercions le Conseil des arts du Canada de son soutien. L'an dernier, le Conseil a investi 153 millions de dollars pour mettre de l'art dans la vie des Canadiennes et des Canadiens de tout le pays.* We acknowledge the financial support of the Government of Newfoundland and Labrador, Department of Tourism, Culture and Recreation for our publishing activities.

THIS BOOK IS THRICE-DEDICATED:

First, to the memory of GEORGINA STIRLING (1867–1935)
The Newfoundland prima donna opera singer with the astonishing voice and compassionate heart.

Second, to the memory of RON HYNES (1950–2015)
The man of a thousand songs.
Celebrated Newfoundland singer/songwriter whose beautiful song "Marie" helps to bring Georgina Stirling's music and songs into the twenty-first century.

Third, to the memory of BRIAN GORDON EVANS (1959–1992)
My uncle and my singing inspiration (*Tonia Evans Cianciulli*)
and our beloved son (*Calvin and Goldie Evans*)

More Praise for *The Heart's Obsession*

"This lovingly written book opens up for us the fascinating story of one of the most interesting figures in Newfoundland's cultural history, Georgina Stirling. My dear friend Ron Hynes would be thrilled to see this meticulous and detailed tribute to her life and legacy. We are indebted to Tonia Evans Cianciulli and Calvin D. Evans for this welcome contribution to the growing Newfoundland library."
— GREG MALONE, Canadian Impressionist, Actor,
Writer of CBC's The Wonderful Grand Band

"It is clear when you read *The Heart's Obsession* that the life and times of Georgina Stirling have, in many ways, become the heart and soul of Tonia Cianciulli. The book is a compelling account of the work and dedication that it takes to arrive at the top of this demanding artistic career. Passion, drive, and unwavering commitment to the art have always been the hallmarks of success. The 'look back' at Georgina Stirling gives us a chance to 'look forward' with Tonia Cianciulli."
— DEAN STAIRS, Citadel House, Newfoundland Record Label

"*The Heart's Obsession* is a historically educational must-read for any opera singer interested in the history of artists like Georgina Stirling who inspired humanity with their voices."
— MANNY PEREZ, Voice Teacher, Miami Music Classical Music Festival

"Canada has a long history of great opera singers, with names like Vickers, Stratas, Forrester, and Heppner coming to mind. It seems only appropriate that two people with strong ties to Newfoundland and a definite love of opera should tell the magnificent tale of Georgina Stirling, possibly Canada's first prima donna! Well done!" — BRIAN McINTOSH, Canadian Operatic Bass-baritone

"This book of two Newfoundland sopranos fascinates us, as a historical biography of Georgina Stirling, with an interlacing contemporary musical memoir of Tonia Evans Cianciulli. It informs and compels us on many levels, as an endearingly co-authored account by a grandfather and granddaughter in their distinctively individualized voices. *The Heart's Obsession* gathers us in as a highly informing chronicle, juxtaposed with inspirations, aspirations, and insightful observations of a classically trained soprano, joyfully ignited by the flame of her singing Newfoundlander 'ancestor in spirit!'"
— DARRYL EDWARDS, Voice Studies: The University of Toronto,
Artistic Director: The Centre for Opera Studies in Italy, The COSI Connection, & COSA Canada

"As a successful soprano songstress, Tonia brings an intimacy and depth to Georgina's story that only an artist of her kind can. Throughout the past two years, I've had the opportunity to speak with Tonia and see her and her grandfather/co-author perform in the church of Georgina's childhood. Tonia's passion for preserving Georgina's legacy is not only seen in her retelling of the singer's life story. In her remarkable renditions of Georgina's repertoire, Tonia's performance goes beyond tribute and borders on a reincarnation of Twillingate's honoured opera singer. I expect this work will bring a renewed interest to a remarkable woman in my hometown's history."
— KYLE GREENHAM, Twilingate-born Journalist and Writer

Contents

FOREWORD
BY KERRY STRATTON

What is immediately obvious about the blend of Georgina Stirling and Tonia Evans Cianciulli is that they are both sopranos from Newfoundland. It's considerably more than that, however. Certainly that rock in the middle of the Atlantic has taught us that it is the home of song. We expect in her successful artists that we shall find that unbeatable combination of talent, determination, and a great portion of pure heart. We've also grown to realize that they won't stay long when the wide world beckons. These two singers are plainly cut from the same cloth though a century apart, and what the story tells is not only history, but the present. This writer can think of no one better to have penned this biography than Tonia. This is the work of a determined woman telling the story of a sister equally as steadfast, and perhaps it is a distinctly Newfoundland tale, but more likely a story for those who will not be deflected from the course no matter what the challenges. The reader will no doubt come away with new knowledge of yet another underappreciated Canadian, but the real bonus in these pages is that we might leave them with a glimpse of self. In the music world it is rare that any two paths are the same, but what is common among the successful is the ability to create a new way forward. May you read this book with pleasure and see your own path that much better.

Kerry Stratton, Maestro
Conductor and Music Director
Toronto Concert Orchestra and Chorus
Conductor for Wish Opera
Radio Host for the New Classical FM 96.3

INTRODUCTION
by Tonia Evans Cianciulli

THE JOURNEY OF A HEART'S OBSESSION, ALWAYS LEADING US BACK HOME

"Georgina Ann Stirling, you have had a profound impact on my heart and on my life. You've beckoned me home to celebrate my precious Newfoundland roots and to embrace my unique voice. Your untold story has inspired me to awaken your sleeping memory and breathe new life into your legacy and your heart's journey. This story is a duet. We shall be two "nightingales" converging across time and ocean waves as one voice to tell your story."

— Tonia Evans Cianciulli, Newfoundland-born Soprano

WHAT I HAVE COME TO LEARN in a much deeper way these last few years is that we are all on our own unique path, honouring our own unique voices, whether in singing or in our life's individual expression. And while we may have much in common with others with whom we connect in a deep and meaningful way, we are all different. Just as no two fingerprints are identical, there will never be another voice like that of Georgina Stirling. No two voices will ever sound exactly the same, as they come from completely different bodies, of both experience and in the physical, thus emerging from each of us in a tone, colour, timbre, weight, texture, and richness that is distinctly our own.

We are all individually blessed to leave our footprint on the path of life's journey—little pieces of ourselves scattered around for the world to remember us. Throughout this journey I have come to know Georgina in a most beloved way. Georgina had her own special gift that touched her family, friends, and audiences in a miraculous way. She had her own story, her own path, her sorrows, demons, and her own light.

There was a time when I thought I wanted the life of a full-time opera singer—travelling abroad, auditioning, and performing in fully-staged productions with opera companies around the world. I wanted this so desperately that it hurt to imagine this dream not coming true. It looked at one point as if this was the path I was taking. After graduating from the University of Western Ontario with a Bachelor in Voice Performance, I continued training and started auditioning in Toronto and beyond. I had glimpses into the life of an opera singer, performing roles that suited me well at that early point in my career. When I was on stage I felt alive. I was told countless times that if I wanted this as a full-time career I needed to leave Canada and go immediately to Germany or Italy to start auditioning. One particular memory of this very conversation with a conductor nearly broke my heart. It broke my heart because I knew I had a big decision to make. I was engaged to my husband, Frank, and wanted to start a family. While I chose to make having a family my priority, my life has unfolded in its own unique way, bringing what was perfectly meant for me into clear sight—and all in God's perfect timing. At the time I write this introduction, I am finishing my fifth year of homeschooling our two children—Sophia and Anthony. Throughout these years I have been able to dedicate time to consistent vocal training and to create and celebrate myself as a classically trained soprano, actively performing as a professional concert artist. You will discover in the pages to follow how I was led on a journey that has resulted in your now holding this special book, *The Heart's Obsession*, in your hands.

THERE HAS BEEN MUCH LINGERING MYSTERY and hearsay around the life and career of Newfoundland's late Nightingale, Georgina Stirling. I've chosen to share some of my own experiences as a professional singer and the experiences of other industry professionals in order to lend understanding and compassion for the significance Georgina Stirling played in Newfoundland and Canadian music history. I view my role in this book as an interpreter. My in-depth research, professional insight, and embodiment of her and her music have enriched my musical interests as well as my singing. My passion—one I fondly refer to as my heart's obsession—is to revive her memory and repertoire, and help people to see her and her musical life for the rich and beautiful legacy it is.

MY NEWFOUNDLAND ROOTS

My Newfoundland Heart

They can take this Newfoundlander,
From the place I got my start,

But there's one thing they can NEVER take,
My Newfoundland Heart.

A little poem like this one helps,
My heart to take a stand,
To say—though I am somewhere else,
My heart's in Newfoundland.

No disrespect intended for,
My home away from home,
But Newfoundland is where I'm from,
No matter where I roam.

Sometimes it's only once a day,
Quite often it is more,
My heart drifts back to Newfoundland,
And thoughts of life before.
And so I hope the world at large,
Will try to understand,
It's fine in other places but,
My heart's in NEWFOUNDLAND.

— Author Unknown

I WAS BORN ON FEBRUARY 4, 1976, in St. John's, Newfoundland, at the Grace General Hospital. My roots in Newfoundland are strong and plentiful. I am the eldest of four children, all born within three years, and the only child who gets to boast about being a "real" Newfoundlander. The older I get, the prouder I become of my roots. I love to travel and have a deep affection for many of the places I've visited and where I've lived. There is nowhere I feel a more profound connection than Newfoundland. It's in my bones, my blood, and my commitment to its future preservation. As my mother used to say, "You can take the girl out of Newfoundland but, you'll never take Newfoundland out of the girl!" I now take great pride in introducing my own family to Newfoundland and all of its splendour. My husband, Frank

Cianciulli, and our children, Sophia and Anthony, have come to accept Newfoundland as part of their own roots.

My mother was born in Nova Scotia and was raised in Newfoundland. At sixteen she was crowned Miss Teen Newfoundland and placed 8th at the Miss Teen Canada Pageant in Toronto. She graduated from the Grace General Hospital in St. John's as a registered nurse working in neonatal care, emergency, and psychiatry. She is now a real estate broker and owner of Century 21 Millennium, with branches in central Ontario, always ranking in the top ten Canada-wide.

My father, Fred Dyke, was born on Pool's Island, Bonavista Bay. He graduated from Memorial University in St. John's. He rowed in the boat races at Quidi Vidi Lake. Following his passion for Judo, he won seven consecutive Newfoundland Judo championships, three in the Atlantic Provinces, and three Ontario championships. He was inducted into the Newfoundland and Labrador Judo Hall of Fame in 2017. We moved to Ontario when I was very young, when my father was transferred for a new financial job. After a successful business career, he is now a full-time Christian pastor.

Both my parents' accomplishments continue to make me proud and have inspired and encouraged me to be the person I am today.

I have three younger brothers—Philip Evans, Trevor Evans, and Matthew Evans—who are among my best friends in life. They are experts in their various fields and talents and are all raising beautiful families. We all visit Newfoundland frequently and pride ourselves on keeping our roots strong. In fact, two of my bothers, Philip and Matthew, are also immersed in the preservation of Newfoundland arts, architecture, and culture, with a plethora of artistic and historical projects that they have personally seeded throughout their adult lives across Newfoundland. Philip is a principal architect with ERA Architects in Toronto and is the founder of an initiative in Newfoundland called the Culture of Outports, which derived from visits to about twenty-five coastal communities in Newfoundland in 2010 with our grandfather, and which focuses on the renewal of communities affected by enormous changing circumstances, such as the diminishing of fishing and the resources of the sea. Small groups of architects and architectural students visited Newfoundland coastal communities over the following six years to do "design and build" projects focusing on the history and culture of the region and which would capitalize on Newfoundland's rich sense of place, restoring heritage buildings and reorienting communities. Also, on Pool's Island, Bonavista Bay, there are now various art installations overlooking the ocean that my brother Matthew, in collaboration with a four-artist project by CTG Collective, had the honour of organizing and establishing.

Our family's deep roots are spread across Newfoundland, making it both necessary and fulfilling to visit on a regular basis. My maternal grandfather six generations ago, Edward Evans, was a young Welsh warrant officer on a British ship which was doing fishery protection service for Great Britain around the island of Newfoundland and along the coast of Labrador. Around 1840, he met a young Newfoundland woman, fell in love with her, and deserted his ship when he returned the following summer, and they married and settled in the Bay of Exploits, where Edward started a shipbuilding industry that lasted through three generations, for about 100 years. The story of the Evans family is told in my grandfather's book For Love of a Woman: The Evans Family and a Perspective on Shipbuilding in Newfoundland.

My paternal grandfather, Chesley Dyke of Pool's Island and St. John's, became a warrant officer (boatswain or bosun) at the age of twenty-one with the Furness-Withy Shipping Lines of Bowring Brothers, St. John's, sailing on at least four of their large ships to and from the Barbados over a five-year period. At age thirty-five he returned to school and studied navigation, after which he obtained his master mariner's ticket and became a captain of his own fishing and cargo ships. His exploits on the sea have been mentioned in four published books.

These are my family's roots in Newfoundland.

Although life's circumstances may require us to leave the place we call home, it will always remain exactly that. Home. Your first love, where life began, that special and familiar place that remains in your heart always.

No one knew this better than Georgina Stirling, as you will soon discover. It's been an honour and an incredible journey to bring this story to life with my grandfather, Calvin D. Evans. I have been blessed with the example of this beautiful human being in my life. Writing this book with him is a memory and experience I will cherish forever.

We hope that you come to know Georgina Stirling as affectionately and intimately as we have. May she live through these pages in the telling of her journey and the music that she so passionately interpreted.

A DIVINE TURNING POINT

"Once you experience a tragedy in your life, you will hear the tears in your voice."
— Brian Evans, My Late Uncle and Mentor

The first time I heard the sound of my voice was in church on Sunday mornings. From a prideful story my mother likes to tell, I was noted for my natural talent during a solo at a Mother's Day concert at the age of six. Having children of my own who have performed in concerts with me, I have experienced the swell that parents feel when their children share their sweet voices; it's deeply touching. My parents enrolled me in my first voice lessons with Rosemary Hebert, wife of the youth pastor at our church. I knew that I wanted to be a singer. Thinking back when I had entertained other career options that might have seemed more realistic, singing was always on the top of my list; my mind and heart knew no other option. Today, other than the joy of being a mother, nothing else comes close.

The turning point in my life that confirmed my path to become a singer could only be described as a divine intervention. My mother frequently brought me and my brothers to visit our uncle Brian. At the time, he lived in a beautiful Victorian home on the historic Bright Street in downtown Toronto. It was thrilling for us to escape the suburbs, to explore and be part of a city that was alive with such vibrant culture, art, and music. Like many young girls who wanted to be singers, I loved to sing along with the latest hits on the radio. At the time, "Wind Beneath My Wings" by Bette Midler was popular. One evening, I proudly stood in Uncle Brian's living room and belted that song out like the pop singer I wanted to be. Although I was thirteen, his words still echo in my mind today. "Tonia," he said, "you have a pure voice meant for classical and opera music." I sat on the sofa as he energetically told me what my next steps were. That night he sent me home with a CD of the renowned soprano Dame Kiri Te Kanawa, called Ave Maria. This was supposed to ease me into opera? Uncle Brian told me to find a voice teacher in my area who taught classical music and that I was to learn the well-known song "Ave Maria" by Schubert for his upcoming Christmas party. I was ready to toss that CD and the idea of singing in a foreign language!

Two nights later, my mother sat across from me in the piano room, and we listened to that CD. I told her that classical and opera were out of the question—especially in Latin! Didn't she realize how old I was? Clearly, she did, because she played the parent card and told me that I would give it a chance and sing it because my uncle Brian asked me to. Thankfully, she did. They both saw the potential of something in me to which I was blind, simply and understandably because of a lack of life wisdom and perspective. My mom has played a significant role in the nurturing of my musical career. Her influence and support have always been a strong force in my life. I don't take for granted the sacrifices she made for me week after week, driving me to voice lessons, competitions, concerts, and auditions. Most importantly, all the encouraging pep talks to bolster my confidence along the way, all the consoling of my fears and my tears; she believed in me long before I believed in myself. It's a special feeling to see my mom explode with pride and adoration when I sing. She's always told me that even if she were the only one who got to hear me sing, she would be just as proud as if an entire audience heard me. This connection with my uncle was a meaningful experience for my mother as well. Since he didn't have any children, she was touched that he thought of her children as his own.

Brian was passionate about opera. He sang in choirs growing up, attended the Canadian Opera Company every season, volunteered as an usher, and assisted the board of directors in fundraising galas. This qualified him to be as good a coach as any. He sincerely had my best interests in mind and delighted in the fact that I was fulfilling one of the biggest dreams of his life, which also became the biggest dream of my life.

That same year, I took regular classical voice lessons and started learning to sing in Latin, Italian, German, and French. My first classical voice teacher was a dear woman, Judy Harmsworth, in Toronto. She gave me the gift of a strong and lasting base for technique, which still guides me well. Dedicated to seeing her students thrive, she enrolled us in provincial competitions and travelled with us. Her support helped me gain the confidence to get up there and perform, no matter the outcome.

I absolutely fell in love with opera. I spent countless hours with Uncle Brian. When it came to artistic sensitivity and portraying the emotions, he was an impeccable coach. As a young girl, I could not fully grasp these complex emotions, and he helped me develop insight into the psyche of these characters to perform music of such depth and, often, heartache.

Over and again I would sing an aria or Italian art song for Brian and he would play me examples of the operatic greats while pointing out the inflections in their voices. His favourites included Pavarotti, Montserrat Caballé, Jesse Norman, Kathleen Battle, Kiri Te Kanawa, and above all, Maria Callas. Maria Callas was Brian's favourite. This legendary opera soprano is instantly recognizable and famous for the pure emotion in her voice and the intensity of the characters she portrayed. Maria Callas was the final element that converted me to opera. I became obsessed with her. I read books on her and watched her interviews and all her performance videos. She opened my mind to the world of grand opera.

Opera is predominantly sung in Italian, German, and French, and sometimes English. Subtitles will help if you are in a theatre; however, if you are listening to a concert or a recording, the singer's voice is the key to unlocking the emotion to the listener. Much of Brian's work with me was developing this ability to show the emotion of a piece without verbal translation. Out of Brian's mouth one day came a phrase that I will never forget: "Once you experience a tragedy in your life, you will hear the tears in your voice." I had no idea his comment was foreshadowing something that would mark my life and my voice forever. Two years later, Uncle Brian died of a terminal illness at the young age of thirty-three. I was devastated. It created a void in my life, and I couldn't help but feel abandoned in my operatic journey. At eighteen I had lost one of the most significant people in my entire life. This tragedy is what gave me the tears in my voice. When I sing, it's a true honour if someone shares that they wept without knowing a single word, that it helped them recall the sentimental memories of someone they lost. Or it lifted their spirits. This is one aspect that makes singing so fulfilling, and a sign that I am living my purpose. I often joke about this, but it's true: if I can bring someone to tears, I've done my job.

This is the power of the human voice and its dramatic expression of the heart and soul. Heartbreak, despite its pain, can be channelled into something of service and meaning. Georgina Stirling and I relate on heartbreak. I felt a soul connection to her because she too experienced great loss in her life at a young age. It put the tears in her voice and shaped her to be Newfoundland's greatest soprano.

INTRODUCTION
BY CALVIN D. EVANS

IT IS A GREAT PRIVILEGE TO be able to work on a major project with a grandchild. I am enormously excited and grateful to be collaborating with my granddaughter, Tonia Evans Cianciulli, on this book, which is designed to honour the Newfoundland prima donna opera singer Georgina Ann Stirling.

I previously had the opportunity to work with my grandson Philip Evans, Tonia's brother, on the Newfoundland Culture of Outports project and the writing of two books on Newfoundland master shipbuilders. In yet another book which I am writing, our other grandchildren have already expressed an interest in contributing ideas and critiques.

One can only be mightily grateful for grandchildren.

But the focus at the moment is on Tonia and her expressed desire to revive the repertoire of Newfoundland's prima donna soprano of the nineteenth and early twentieth centuries. The person and the story and the songs and the music of Georgina Stirling are now relevant to the twenty-first century.

When Tonia was a little girl and we would visit occasionally from Guelph and Edmonton and Montreal, she would resist going to bed at night until the last adult had turned in. I took up the challenge on one occasion and began to tell her invented "birdie stories" in the hope that this might help her to settle down. It did. Birdies in these stories are not birds but bird-like creatures that talk, develop relationships with other creatures in the forest, and do a variety of interesting and magical and challenging things and have a unique life of their very own. My last recollection of telling the four siblings a birdie story was when they were in high school and they *demanded* a story during one of our visits. It ended in eruptions of laughter, a bit of embarrassment, and some precious memories. The birdie stories may have somehow fired the imagination of the young Tonia, and when she was a student at university, her first time away from home for an extended period, she phoned and asked me if I would write down a few of the stories so that she could read them at night just before going to bed and thus have a restful night. It worked.

In her very early years, Tonia assiduously compiled and jealously guarded a stack of what she called her "important papers," and occasionally she would blurt out "I got an idea," and she was off to shuffle her papers and initiate yet another event in which she often included her three young brothers. It was an indication of her boundless creativity.

Tonia did an inspired writing shortly after her uncle Brian, our son, died in 1992. Brian had coached her in the appreciation of opera, of which he was extremely fond and about which he had become very knowledgeable, took her to several opera performances in Toronto, and taught her the importance of discipline in her singing and performances. Tonia, in that inspired piece of writing, reflected on the incredible influence that her uncle Brian had on her life. It was a kind of thank-you letter.

I routinely weep when I hear Tonia sing, especially to a large audience, and most especially in churches. Perhaps the formal setting has something to do with it. But there is something else—her singing is so heart-expressive that every performance connects us with Brian in a very special way and reminds us of the care he took with Tonia to challenge her and help her to cultivate that expressive voice. We become more aware of Brian's presence whenever Tonia sings.

CHAPTER ONE
BY CALVIN D. EVANS

THE NEWFOUNDLAND SETTING

ON THE ROUGH, ROCKY COAST OF NEWFOUNDLAND, with riotous waves crashing against the solid rocks, many a voice has been shaped and honed to carry its message clear and far—from the rough voices of fishermen and mariners conveying a life-saving communication in a storm, to the melodic softness of the distinctive Newfoundland accent, and to the sweet sounds of island singers reflecting their quiet happiness or their unrestrained joy.

One of these sweet singers originated in Twillingate on April 3, 1867 (the year that Canada became a nation), and her love for and connection with the sea was evident from the very beginning. Her name was Georgina Stirling. She lived and played and frolicked and sang at the edge of the sea and gave voice to the melody that filled her young heart.

From about 1730, Twillingate was a centre of trade for both the Labrador fishery and the shore fishery and, along with Fogo, served as a business centre for British merchant firms in the fish, fur, and seal trades. Added to these was the lumber trade from the Exploits and Gander rivers. Even in 1843, when Dr. William Stirling, Jr., arrived in Twillingate, the town bore the distinction of being known as "Capital of the North" and "Metropolis of the North," and soon after it became a major mercantile town serving Notre Dame Bay and had its own customs centre, where ships registered their cargoes for the export of many products. By 1843, Twillingate was a flourishing fishing and commercial centre with a population of about 3,600 people, and shortly after Georgina was born in 1867, the population had more than doubled in size. Since regular travel to and from Twillingate was afforded by boat, ship, and coastal steamer, the town could hardly have been described as remote. In 1924, with the construction of the Notre Dame Bay Memorial Hospital, it became a significant regional health centre.

Georgina lived close enough to the sea on Twillingate's North Island to be lulled to sleep with its myriad sounds and to be startlingly awakened by its occasional fury, to be stirred and even frightened by its stormy, gloomy character. These fears often involved the dangers associated with "those who go down to the sea in ships." The Stirling house fronted toward the northeast, and Burnt Island was too far away to serve as a natural barrier to the fierce winds on stormy days, yet it helped to quell the raging sea, thus offering a kind of breakwater for ships anchored in the spacious harbour. Across the harbour lay the South Island, and along the shore to the northwest lay the rocky shore that led to Paradise, Wild Cove, and Long Point lighthouse, with the incredible vistas of the sea that still inspire every visitor.

The harsh conditions of wind and sea and ice and snow will frighten some girls but produce in others a sense of adventure and daring that enables them to rise to any challenge. Georgina seems to have been in that latter group. A writer in England, sometime after 1896, in describing Georgina's early life, wrote these words: "Such latitude and freedom were permitted to her that although the daughter of a physician of considerable standing in his profession, she has been known when but a mere child to go twenty miles from land with a rope and a knife to kill her seal and tow it home in triumph." Undoubtedly, she and others her age would have been accompanied by adults who would have helped in the kill, but the words show the daring spirit of this young woman.

I asked an expert Twillingater, Eric Waterman, for a comment on the winds in the area where the Stirling house was located. He commented that the prevailing winds are westerlies, and added further: "From May to September, the winds are generally west and southwesterlies. From October to December they are generally east to northeast to north. From January to April they are generally northeast to north to northwest." The seasonal symphony of winds added to the sounds that Georgina integrated into her panoply of precious sounds.

Georgina and her sisters would have followed footpaths to visit their cousins, the Peytons, in Back Harbour. Here the ocean is generally civil, even tranquil, unless there is an onshore wind. Back Harbour faces Twillingate Bight and the open ocean to the west and the northwest. As the young girls followed the footpaths, they would journey on beyond Back Harbour to Murray's Cove and Davey Button's Cove. Then they would traverse back toward Back Harbour Beach and on toward Battrick's Island, following the beautiful crescent-shaped harbour.

Here in Twillingate, amidst the myriad sounds of the sea, there are sweet and lasting memories of Georgina Stirling—but also dark secrets about the tragic loss of her talents that may lie forever buried, that may never be fully revealed. She rocketed quickly to the dizzying heights of her professional career, but plummeted even more quickly to the greatest depths.

Georgina's life was divided into two periods of thirty-four years each—1867 to 1901, years of joy and jubilation, and 1901 to 1935, years of despair, depression, and ever-approaching death from cancer. As there had been a period of grief and mourning with the tragic loss of three or probably four little brothers and her mother, Ann (Peyton) Stirling, during the first period, there was also an interlude of quiet contemplation, contentment, and even triumph, after she had settled at home in Twillingate for the final years.

We now know that the Stirlings had three sons, and possibly a fourth son, in addition to the seven daughters. The first son had died as an infant about seventeen years before Georgina was born, the second son died with complications from measles at three years of age, and twelve years before Georgina was born, the third son died from typhoid fever at about ten years of age, when Georgina was about seven years old. Amy Louise Peyton writes of a son who died as a toddler by accidental drowning, and claims that his name was entered in the Stirling birthday book as Peyton. All of these tragedies were followed by the death of Georgina's mother in 1882, undoubtedly as a direct result of these tragic happenings in her beloved family. It is hard for us, perhaps impossible, to imagine what this poor mother, Ann Stirling, endured in losing all three or four sons. She had raised seven promising and gifted daughters, but all her sons were taken by untimely deaths. Her heart must have been irreparably broken.

The care and supervision of Georgina, still only fifteen years old, fell to the lot of the older sisters—Lucy, Rose, Kate, and Janet. The burden of the grief at their mother's death must have been especially hard for Georgina at just fifteen years of age.

Georgina herself, after her mother's untimely death, hardly had time to grieve naturally before she was whisked away to a life of formal academic and musical training in a foreign environment, and then to a life on the stage. She was not yet ready for the larger world when she was taken away from Twillingate by her sister Kate to continue her music studies, as well as other academic studies, in Toronto. This program of studies would have been carefully researched and approved by Georgina's adoring but befuddled father, Dr. William Stirling, who was, himself, still grieving over the bewildering loss of his sons and wife.

It should be noted that there is a headstone marker in St. Peter's churchyard cemetery giving the names of three Stirling sons only, so it is possible that there were only three sons born before 1874, and that Ann Stirling had a fourth son born *after* the third son died in that year (say 1875 or 1876), and after the headstone marker had been erected. Perhaps this, then, is the son who tragically drowned. Appendix Three discloses more definitive information on all of the Stirling children.

Georgina's father had provided much of her musical inspiration, he with the violin and she at the piano. By arranging for her to go so quickly to the musical life in Toronto, he undoubtedly thought he was doing the very best thing for his daughter. The required training for her musical gifts was no longer available in Twillingate, but the required motherly support and direction that this young woman still needed at the age of fifteen and a half years would now be forever absent. There must surely have been an artificial quality to this new life, divorced as it was from every familiar and familial support on which she had depended for so many years. Did anyone really appreciate what this young woman had endured? Was she able to share what Anne Morrow Lindbergh in her book *Gift from the Sea* called "the wilderness of the mind" with anyone? The record is silent. We can only speculate. Perhaps her despair and depression in the later tragic years were linked to what had happened in these early formative years. Despair does not issue in rational action. Fame is a fickle friend.

The amazing and tragic story of Georgina Stirling—or as she also was variously known, Miss Georgie, Twillingate Stirling, Mademoiselle Marie Toulinguet, Madame Toulinguet, Nightingale of the North, the Florence Nightingale of Newfoundland, Newfoundland's Nightingale, the Terra Nova Nightingale, the Songstress of Newfoundland—still draws tourists from far and wide to this spectacular coastal town. It is eminently worth the visit.

Gary L. Saunders in his book *Doctor Olds of Twillingate* writes on page 58: "Twillingate, Toulinguet—a lovely name for a town and its pair of islands, seven miles from heel to prong with nothing between them and Greenland but a waste of ocean. One would be hard pressed to find a more weatherful place. Wind . . . forever sighing along the wall, keening under the eaves, driving boats to harbour, lashing the sea feather-white, riming the windows with salt. The sky . . . benign and sparkling one minute, drizzling the next, prone to celebrate with extravaganzas of lemon, orange and magenta before the day goes down to velvet dark. The sea . . . mutable as quicksilver, its distant rote the bass accompaniment of all life here."

This extravagant, complex statement captures the myriad complexion of Twillingate, Toulinguet. It calls forth the ever-changing moods that comprise this unique town.

CHAPTER TWO
BY CALVIN D. EVANS

GLIMPSES INTO GEORGINA'S EARLY YEARS

TWILLINGATE DEVELOPED A VIBRANT MUSICAL COMMUNITY from its early beginnings. The Church of England congregation was able to attract directly from England clergy and teachers who had a great interest in developing education and its ancillary disciplines such as singing, dramatic presentations, and skills with musical instruments. The Methodist Church also attracted English clergy, and these had similar interests and skills. Because Twillingate had developed as a commercial centre from its very early days, it attracted many professional people, again mostly from Great Britain, and these brought with them, especially the women, skills in organ and piano playing and singing and the dramatic arts that gave a special character to the community.

Maymie (Roberts) Hewlett, who grew up in Twillingate from 1898 and became an organist in the North Side Methodist Church, commented in a 1969 interview that "Twillingate was the home of good music and talented singers." Organists and pianists were talented, and choral music was performed at a high level. Georgina Stirling declared later in life that she had never heard better male voices than in Twillingate, and that Mrs. Minnie Maley, one of the church organists and soloists at the Methodist Church, would have "topped the world" if she had had the training that Georgina had during her singing career. Maymie Hewlett rhapsodizes about "the glorious nights of singing" during Christmas and the carolling through the streets of the town. Choirs were well-trained and sang selections regularly from such musical pieces as Handel's *Messiah*, including the "Hallelujah Chorus."

Dr. William McCleery Carrington Stirling, Georgina's father, graduated from the University of Edinburgh, Scotland, in 1839 after four years of medical studies. In Edinburgh's records he is classed as "ex-America Septentrionale," which is the Latin way of saying simply "from North America." It is believed that he worked with his father, Dr. William Archibald Stirling, at Harbour Grace for a time and that he arrived in Twillingate in 1843. However, Dr. Stirling's obituary, which appeared in the *Twillingate Sun* on April 19, 1890, raises another possibility as to what he may have been doing for part of the years 1839 to 1843. The obituary reads: "Dr. Stirling matriculated at the University of Edinburgh *and other colleges noted for the education of students in the honorable profession of medicine."* (italics mine) Did he stay on in Scotland or go to England for further postgraduate studies, or did he go to the United States following his return to Newfoundland for advanced studies? That possibility must now be considered.

The elder Dr. Stirling had been practising medicine at Harbour Grace since 1808 and was especially highly regarded in that town and in Conception Bay generally. Dr. Stirling, Jr. is believed to have moved to Twillingate in 1843, and in 1844 was appointed coroner for the

Stirling Family photo album (Courtesy of Bruce Manuel and Brent English)

District of Fogo, which included the jurisdiction of Twillingate. On October 31, 1845, he signed a fourteen-year lease with John and Robert Slade, merchants, for property "on the Southside of Twillingate . . . property formerly occupied by the late Andrew Pearce Esquire." The yearly rent was "fourteen pounds in the currency of Newfoundland." In 1846, Dr. Stirling married Ann Peyton, daughter of John Peyton, Jr. Peyton had been appointed district magistrate in 1836 and had moved to Back Harbour on Twillingate's North Island at that time, gradually withdrawing from a long business career. Dr. Stirling and his bride settled at Front Harbour on the South Island of Twillingate and lived there until about 1851–53, at which time they moved to the North Island and, according to some sources, bought the large double house that had been built by the Murphy brothers after they had completed the construction of St. Peter's Church in 1845. Robert and John Slade, merchants, are thought by some sources to have owned this home first, and they may have sold it to Dr. Stirling about 1851–53. It should be noted, however, that Maymie (Roberts) Hewlett of Twillingate noted in her journal that "the Stirling house . . . (was) first built by two brothers from England, one died and the other sold the house to a young medical doctor from Harbour Grace . . . Dr. William Stirling . . ." Dr. Stirling may have bought the house on North Island at the time when his aging parents (his father having become blind by this time) moved from Harbour Grace to Twillingate and lived with them in the large double house. The precise date of their move is unknown, but it is estimated by authoritative sources that the move of the elder Stirlings occurred between 1851 and 1853. Dr. Stirling, Sr., died at Twillingate in 1858, and Mrs. Emma Stirling died in 1863.

If the Stirlings remained on South Island until 1851–53, then four or possibly five of their children would have been born there. A growing family provided an additional reason for purchasing a much larger house and may have precipitated the move.

Men of the stature of Dr. Stirling brought special gifts of music, especially with the violin, piano, organ, and the flute, and probably also the bagpipes, as a much-later letter from Kate Stirling affirms. Dr. Stirling nurtured in his children a love of music and of performance that was demonstrated in the family from very early years. There is no evidence that Georgina's mother played a role in the family's music except through encouragement of her children in the art. The Peytons do not seem, in the early years, to have demonstrated either facility or skill in music, but that certainly came in the later generations.

Dr. Stirling would have brought the violin with him when he came to Twillingate about 1843, and undoubtedly the flute. Amy Louise Peyton portrays the Stirling family as lighthearted, funloving, socially gregarious, and party-oriented—all traits which they had apparently inherited from the senior Dr. William Stirling of Harbour Grace. As founding president of the Benevolent Irish Society at Harbour Grace in 1814 (an Irish Protestant among Catholics), Dr. William Stirling, Sr., was a leader and encourager of Irish music and "good times" at their social events.

THE STIRLING HOME IN TWILLINGATE was the scene of elegant dinner parties, and family members were skilled at entertaining their guests. Eleanor Cameron Stockley, who wrote the musical *Georgie*, called the Stirling home "a house filled with love and music." It probably was not long before the Stirling children (seven daughters) were involved in the entertainment of the adult guests, using the two pianos, the violin, and the flute. Though daughter Georgina became the noted singer in the family, she was not the only musical one. All the daughters were very probably skilled in the piano and later the organ through formal musical instruction by experts in the town. The first piano in the home was purchased for Lucy (Lucinda), the eldest daughter, who was born about 1847. Rose (Rosetta), the third daughter, is known to have participated in a dialogue entitled *Council of the Gods* in the Dorcas Society Concert of 1888 as

"Ceres," though it is not known if this was a spoken or sung dialogue. Janet also had developed musical skills, and her sister Kate encouraged her in this pursuit, as later letters attest. Amy Louise Peyton writes about the Stirling sisters: "There was a light-hearted side to their personalities; the love of a merry tune and a great flair for lively entertainment, dinner parties and gala times. It was their grandfather Stirling who was said to be 'the life of the good times.'" All the sisters in their growing up engaged in community concerts and dramatic events, and Kate Stirling demonstrated a gift for the arts at an early age. Though most or all of the sisters were undoubtedly trained in the piano and organ, none excelled in the way Georgina did.

Georgina was the daughter who showed most promise in music and singing at an early age. Most of her early training would have been under the tutelage of her father, but at a young age she would have been trained in playing the piano, the organ, and singing in choirs and performing solos as her teachers became aware of her developing voice. Rev. Robert Temple was appointed to St. Peter's Church in 1877, when Georgina was just ten years of age. Mrs. Hannah Temple, a native of Norfolk, England, was an accomplished musician and became the organist at St. Peter's Church and also Georgina's music teacher beginning when Georgina was about ten years of age. The Temples' daughter, Carrie, was about Georgina's age, and the two girls soon became good friends. Carrie also was musically gifted, and this helped to form a strong bond between the two girls. Georgina demonstrated such unusual musical skill at both singing and instrumental performance under Mrs. Temple's tutelage that Dr. Stirling bought a second piano for the home, this one for Georgina. Magistrate Berteau moved to Twillingate in 1880, and his family included four girls in their teens—Frances, Minnie, Mary, and Dely. These six girls along with the three daughters of the Justice of the Peace, J. B. Tobin—Gertie, Lizzie, and Minnie—became fast friends and participated in many concerts, singing and acting together.

Georgina as a little girl, possibly three or four years of age (Courtesy of Bruce Manuel and Brent English)

Such was Georgina's skill at the organ that she became a church organist before she was fifteen years of age. The *Twillingate Sun* commented on Georgina's first public performance on the organ with the words ". . . she gave the instrumental performance in a delightful manner, elicited the hearty encomiums of the hearers."

Left: Georgina Stirling at Twillingate at about age eight (Courtesy of Archives and Special Collections, Memorial Libraries)
Right: Georgina Stirling at about ten or twelve years of age, at Twillingate (Courtesy of Archives and Special Collections, Memorial Libraries)

The Stirling sisters for a time attended a private school at Tickle Point, Twillingate, probably in the mid-1870s. Tickle Point is the extreme southwest point of land on the North Island of Twillingate and takes its name from Shoal Tickle, which almost naturally joins the North and South islands. The word "tickle" is used in Newfoundland to define a narrow saltwater strait, often between islands. Writing about these years in 1980 to 1984, Maymie recollects some of her mother's stories: "She told me that Kate Stirling pierced her ears. She placed a cake of soap underneath the lobe of the ear, sterilized a darning needle, and the tiny hole was made, and she could wear earrings. The hole was still there at age eighty-six years." Maymie was wrong about Kate's age; Kate died at age eighty-two in 1941. She probably heard the story from members of the Golden family, Kate's American descendants, who visited Maymie from the United States in 1980 and visited again in 1984. One of them was Ann (Stirling) Putzki. During the latter visit the Golden family met both Amy Louise Peyton and Hiram Silk.

The newspaper *Twillingate Sun* offers some insights into the activities of the Stirling family and particularly the Stirling sisters for the period 1880 to 1886. For example, in July–August 1880, it published the results of the high school exams—midsummer examinations. Georgina was only thirteen years of age at the time, so it seems curious that she is listed as being in high school. She was an average student, as shown by the following results. In geography she obtained a mark of sixty-five out of a possible ninety. In history she obtained 106 marks out of a possible 150. In scripture she gained forty-eight out of a possible 103 marks, a failure that must have disappointed her clergy and music teacher, Reverend and Mrs. Robert Temple. In arithmetic Georgina gained fifty-three marks out of a possible seventy, so this was her best subject.

A DIVERSION FROM THE *TWILLINGATE SUN* reports is necessary at this point because of newly revealed letters written by Kate Stirling to her father in 1881 from several mining sites on the Baie Verte Peninsula—specifically Betts Cove, Tilt Cove, Little Bay, and Hall's Bay, the first of these letters written on March 2, 1881. The discovery of copper ore had made Betts Cove one of the most prosperous mines in Newfoundland through the late 1870s and up to the mid-1880s. Kate must have been sent there (probably in the fall of 1880) for the

Kate Stirling, Georgina's sister, undoubtedly in Chicago, 1883–1885 (Stirling family)

specific purpose of reporting on mining operations to her father, who was an active investor in the mines. It also demonstrated the enormous confidence that Dr. Stirling had in his twenty-two-year-old daughter. This information has been shared with us by Jeff Golden of Minnesota, Kate (Stirling) Putzki's great-grandson.

In order to develop a better understanding of Georgina, it is necessary to gather as much information as we can about her sisters. Kate Stirling's letters provide a great deal of new and valuable information that sets the record straight on several topics and fills many gaps. By March 1881, Kate was living at Betts Cove with Mr. and Mrs. Sheppard (though she refers to them in several letters, she never provides first names). Mr. Sheppard was the manager of the copper smelter works at Betts Cove. The Sheppards were from England, and appear from Kate's letters to have been very prosperous, and eventually returned to England. In the 1891 England and Wales Census, when Janet Stirling is a visitor at their home, William Sheppard's occupation is given as Colliery Proprietor. At that time they had four female servants, but their occupations are not stated.

It is just possible that the reason Kate was living with the Sheppards may have been because Dr. Stirling had already met them in his visits to the mining sites and viewed them as a suitable couple to provide both accommodations and friendship to his daughter. The connection to this family may have been related to Dr. Stirling's medical studies at the University of Edinburgh, or perhaps to a prior Scottish connection to the Stirling family. Some sources have stated that the original Stirling family "had come to Newfoundland from Ireland by way of Scotland." Added to this is the fact that Catherine C. M. Sheppard was born in Motherwell, Scotland, and that two of their children seem to have had a Glasgow birthplace, as stated in the England and Wales Census.

In that same letter of March 2, 1881, Kate informs her father that she has talked to Mrs. Sheppard about Janet going to England, "because Mrs. Sheppard knows about the costs of getting to London." Kate demonstrates here her care and planning for the future of one of her sisters. In an April 27 letter, Kate describes how she and the Sheppards escaped a major fire that damaged the house they were occupying. At the end of the letter she gives her personal assessment of the couple: "I never met anyone I like better than I do Mr. & Mrs. Sheppard." At that time the couple had a small boy who was just beginning to talk. Kate was so impressed with the boy that she writes, "He is really one of the finest little children ever I saw." One can empathize with such a statement from a young woman who had lost at least three young brothers, and almost certainly four. Her friendship with the Sheppards lasted, because her letter from Chicago on November 24, 1883 (two and a half years later), informs her father, "I had a very kind and long letter (last week) from Mr. & Mrs. Sheppard inviting me to England." Obviously, by this time the Sheppards had left Betts Cove and returned home. Kate was the Sheppards' first choice for the visit to England, but since she was now settled in Chicago and loving the city, she encourages her father to allow Janet to visit the Sheppards in her place. That visit appears to have been postponed, possibly for as long as ten years.

Kate was still corresponding with the Sheppard family as late as June 29, 1889, as stated in her letter to her father. Since no letters of Kate's can be found after 1889, it is assumed that the correspondence continued. In that same letter, Kate writes, "I also gave them Georgie's London address." This is startling news. How is it possible that Georgina had a London address in less than a year after leaving Twillingate to go to Italy? It now seems certain that Dr. Stirling must have had prior contacts in London and Georgina may have been using their address for forwarding of mail. These may have been the same people to whom Lucy was "sent abroad" after the tragic jilting on her planned wedding day. This would have been about 1870, when Lucy was twenty-three years of age.

The 1891 England and Wales Census shows William P. Sheppard and Catherine C. M. Sheppard with three sons—Samuel aged seven, John aged three, and Geoffrey aged a few months. There is no mention of the older boy, so it appears either that he had died or more probably been away at school, at the age of twelve or thirteen years. The 1901 Census also seems to show their children away from home and at school, with a Glasgow birthplace mentioned; by that time the older boy would have been about twenty-two, Samuel seventeen, and John thirteen. The three boys named in the 1891 Census were stated as having been born in County Leicestershire, which may have been true for only the two youngest. William Sheppard was in 1901 aged forty-seven, and Catherine was aged forty-two.

We will meet Catherine Sheppard later in connection with Georgina's 1891 audition with Madame Mathilde Marchesi, the acclaimed voice teacher in Paris, and also in connection with Janet Stirling's nursing training in London. Three, and possibly four, of the Stirling sisters appear to have maintained contact with the Sheppard family.

TO RETURN NOW TO THE EVENTS detailed in the *Twillingate Sun* for 1882. The issue of June 16, 1882, reported that "Mrs. Dr. Stirling has been very unwell for a few weeks. Dr. Simms of St. John's and Dr. Malcolm of Fogo came on a professional visit to see her." The daughter Eleanor (Stirling) Winsor came home from Burin, Newfoundland, and spent the summer with her mother, and Susan (Stirling) Temple came from White Bay to be with her mother while she waited for her first child to be born. Mrs. Stirling died on August 9 at fifty-nine years of age. Her death was especially devastating for the sisters who remained at home.

An incident described in the September 1, 1882, issue of the *Twillingate Sun* demonstrates the compassion of the Stirling girls and their readiness to come to the aid of someone in need. This incident happened just three weeks after their mother died. The report reads: "Dog attack. A little boy about six years old, under the guardianship of Mrs. Henry Newman on his way to school yesterday morning, was knocked down and severely bitten by a dog. It happened opposite the residence of Dr. Stirling and the Misses Stirling, seeing his danger-ous predicament, speedily ran to his rescue. He was taken to their house where he received proper treatment from the skillful hands of the doctor. Had it not been for the timely assist-ance rendered, the attack on the little fellow by the ferocious animal might have been fatal. The dog was shot soon afterwards." All five of the Stirling sisters, including Georgina, aided in the rescue of this little boy.

On September 22, 1882, Kate and Georgina Stirling were among the passengers on the steamer *Plover* from Twillingate to St. John's. Their sister Eleanor (Stirling) Winsor was taking them to her home in Burin for a holiday, and to help them deal with the grief caused by their mother's recent death. Ann (Peyton) Stirling died on August 9, 1882, her death at-tributed in large part to the accidental drowning of her very young son. Kate and Georgina may have stayed in Burin for a few weeks and were probably back in Twillingate before the end of October.

From Kate Stirling's letters it is now clear that she and Georgina almost immediately began preparations for a trip to Toronto, where Georgina would begin music and academic studies at the very beginning of 1883. Dr. Stirling would have been fully involved in the plan-ning for this event and would have felt comfortable in assigning the duty of settling Georgina at school in Toronto to his very responsible and well-organized daughter Kate. This new scenario contradicts and corrects a previously suggested timeline. Kate and Georgina would have arrived in Toronto by mid-fall of 1882, and Kate would have made arrangements to register Georgina at school and for her boarding at the same school. The facilitator in all of these Toronto arrangements was Mrs. Jessie Murray, who is believed to have been the wife of Dr. Stirling's attorney, George Murray, in Toronto. The first school that Georgina attended was "Miss Champion's School." This was one of several boarding and day schools for young ladies in Toronto during the late 1800s.

The diligent research of Jeff Golden has identified this particular school. In two Toronto directories for 1878 and 1879, this school is listed under the name "Misses Champion's and Berthon's School." These two single women teachers were named Elizabeth Champion and Sidonia Berthon. In the Toronto Census for both 1881 and 1891, the two single teachers are listed as living together at the same address. There are also two references in Kate Stirling's let-ters to this school. There were other such schools listed in Toronto newspapers, such as Miss Isabella F. Mathieson's, Miss Dupont's, and Mrs. Hunt's. Young ladies would have boarded at these schools and taken classes from various "masters" who would visit the school, and the students would be taken to classes in other venues according to their specialty and interests. With Mrs. Murray's capable guidance, Kate would have made all suitable arrangements for Georgina, knowing that Mrs. Murray would keep a watchful eye on all proceedings.

Kate may well have remained in Toronto until Georgina began attending classes in early January 1883, and then Kate travelled to Chicago to find work. She had relatives there; her father's brother George Stirling and his wife, Maria, ran a boarding house in the city. Kate's March 3, 1883, letter states that "some weeks ago I answered an ad and got a clerical job in Mr. Dean's office." Kate's first day on the job was February 15, so she very probably had arrived in Chicago by mid-January. This same letter mentions that Georgina is in school at Toronto and "I shall go up to Toronto this summer. Georgie will need fixing up. I expect she will spend some of her midsummer holidays at Macgraths." The McGraths lived in Springfield, Ontario, just outside London. Kate's March 29, 1883, letter to her father states: "She (Georgie) is now at Erindale spending her Easter holidays . . . she says she is getting on well with the music." Kate's letter of September 19, 1883, notes that "Georgie has gone back to school again. She enjoyed the holidays very much." Dr. Stirling had been away from Twillingate for the entire summer of 1883 and during that time made at least one visit to Toronto, to see his musically talented daughter.

In a letter dated August 6, 1884, Kate states, "Very soon Georgie and I shall have been away from home two years. It does not seem so long to me. I have been at Mr. Dean's twenty months." Twenty months at Mr. Dean's takes her back to January 1883; she may have been interviewed for the job in January but began work the following month.

Allowing for travel time, getting Georgina settled in Toronto, etc. would mean that Kate and Georgina very probably left Twillingate in mid-fall 1882 and arrived in Toronto early enough to have completed all arrangements for Georgina well before Christmas. Undoubtedly, Mrs. Murray would have played a large role in these arrangements, and the sisters would have spent Christmas together in Toronto. We must remember that Georgina was still only fifteen and a half years old in mid-fall 1882.

TO RETURN ONCE AGAIN TO THE INCIDENTS written about the Stirling sisters in the *Twillingate Sun*: Here we encounter a most curious matter. Keep in mind that these excerpts were not transcripts from the newspaper, but edited and summarized writings posted to the

Internet. The following must surely be an error. One excerpt notes that sometime during 1883 (a date is not provided), Georgina and her cousin Nellie Peyton were bridesmaids at the wedding of Annie, daughter of Thomas Peyton, to William John Scott, Jr., of St. John's. William Scott was employed in Twillingate by Messrs. Waterman & Co., merchants. We know from Kate's letters that Georgina was in Toronto for the summer, that Kate had visited her there during the summer, and that Dr. Stirling himself visited Georgina in Toronto sometime during his summer away from Twillingate. So, the *Twillingate Sun* or the person who contributed the edited excerpt made the error. It was probably Janet who was the bridesmaid, certainly not Georgina.

Henry James Morgan affirms in his book *Canadian Men and Women of the Times* (Second Edition, 1912) that Georgina "was educated . . . (at the) . . . Toronto Ladies' College." This college was located at 60 Gloucester Street and existed only for a short time under that name (possibly for only 1885 and 1886) and had previously been known as the Young Ladies' Boarding and Day School. Amy Louise Peyton concluded that "Miss Georgie's stay at the College was also short . . ." It is possible that the precursor to the Toronto Ladies' College may have been Miss Champion's school.

The *Twillingate Sun* makes no mention of Georgina or the other Stirling sisters during 1884 or 1885, but it should be noted that the newspaper's issues for these two years are incomplete. Only February to April and November to December 1884 exist, and only June, July, and October are available for 1885. It must be taken into account also that this newspaper never missed an opportunity to mention Georgina and other members of the Stirling family whenever anything newsworthy occurred.

By 1883 the two married sisters, Eleanor and Susan, had already left their home in Twillingate. Lucy, Rose, and Janet remained at home in Twillingate, it seems. The newsworthy sister, Georgina, was in Toronto, and this would certainly account for a lack of mention in the local newspaper.

There is a story that Titus Manuel, a Twillingate carpenter who is known to have worked in Toronto, built a house there for the Stirling girls to live in. One source relates an intriguing story that Georgina and Kate were living in Toronto with "three maids." We know now that Kate did not remain in Toronto after getting Georgina settled but moved to Chicago very early in 1883. Amy Louise Peyton, in her interview by Hiram Silk of CBC Grand Falls, dismisses the idea of Titus Manuel building a house for the Stirling sisters in

Toronto, and she is undoubtedly right. We will discover later in Hiram Silk's interview with Maymie (Roberts) Hewlett, Georgina's "best friend" and near neighbour during the years after Georgina returned permanently to Twillingate, that Maymie remarked about Toronto "while they were studying there" and also affirms the story about Titus Manuel building the house in Toronto for the Stirling sisters. This information would seem to have come directly from Maymie's conversations with Georgina, but it may simply have been hearsay around Twillingate. Maymie's reference to "they" affirms that Georgina was accompanied by at least one sister, and this may be accounted for by the fact that Georgina and Kate left Twillingate in the late fall of 1882 to travel to Toronto, that they were in constant contact with each other after Kate moved to Chicago, that Kate played a large role in concert with Mrs. Murray to care for, encourage, and support Georgina through the process of getting settled, and that Kate eventually moved to Chicago.

A corner of Georgina Stirling's rose garden in Twillingate. Maymie Roberts's house is visible in the background. (Courtesy of Vaughn Harbin)

IT IS IMPORTANT TO MAKE A few comments about the sisters who remained in Twillingate through the period when Georgina was in Toronto. It seems clear from Kate's letters to her father that all three sisters were at home through the three-year period, and we now present information that locates them there.

On March 29, 1883, Kate writes, "I suppose this morning you are all going to church at St. Peter's—Eleanor at Burin, Susie at St. Pierre, Georgie at Springfield with the Mcgraths & I alone in Chicago. How we are all scattered." This statement strongly implies that the three sisters—Lucy, Rose, and Janet—were at home. The reference to Georgina means, I think, that during March break from school, Georgina had been invited to spend the week with the McGraths at Springfield, Ontario. The McGraths were very probably friends of the Stirling family.

Lucy was the eldest sister, and the tragic experience of being jilted on her planned wedding date left her a broken woman who constantly needed sisterly support. Apart from occasional visits with her sister Susan at Saint Pierre and her sister Eleanor at Burin, Lucy seems to have gravitated toward her sister Janet, who eventually offered her the strong sisterly support she needed, arranged for her to take the job that Janet had in Chicago when Janet returned to Twillingate to care for her dying father, and then arranged for Lucy to join her in London, England, to work in her nursing station for several years.

Janet, in the years after Kate and Georgina left Twillingate, appears to have been unable to decide what she wanted to do with her life. Kate knows the worth and the potential of this sister and expresses both her concern and her encouragement in her letters. Kate, in her letter of November 24, 1883, writes, "I sent Janet some music & she never got it but very likely it is now resting peacefully in the office at Twillingate." Is she trying to stimulate Janet's interest in something worthwhile? On March 27, 1884, she writes, "Your letters this mail are quite distressing to me. Janet is full of rubbish about Charlie Newman and yours about mistakes in Georgie's Account." Did Janet have a beau of whom Kate did not approve? And Kate seems to be chiding her father about his concerns with Georgie's expenses in Toronto. On April 21, 1884, Kate writes, "You will see in my last letter to Janet all about Georgie's complaining of being ill." No specifics could be found about this particular ailment.

Georgina Stirling possibly taken during her vocal training in Paris, and maybe at her Paris debut in 1893 (Courtesy of Archives and Special Collections, Memorial Libraries)

On September 6, 1884, Kate writes, "I hope Janet has gone to St. Pierre. She certainly requires a change of some kind." On October 1, 1884, she writes, "Had a letter from Janet last week. She does not seem to be very favorably impressed with St. Pierre." In that same letter, she pleads with her father, "Let Jan go to visit the Sheppards in England. It may be a new start for her. If she remains in Twillingate much longer she will be another old maid." On November 18, 1884, Kate writes very directly to her father, "After you are gone . . . if Lucy, Rose and Janet are not married, they will very probably have to help themselves in some way, and they will find it no easy task."

These are the words of a young woman who knows what she wants and is unafraid to chide her other sisters, even though two of them are older than she is. In a letter of December 13, 1885, Kate writes, "Janet says Lucy has gone to Susie (at Saint Pierre) for the winter and that you are also thinking of sending Rose somewhere. The household this winter will be a small one."

In spite of Kate's pleading, Janet appears to have remained in Twillingate until the summer of 1887, when she, Georgina, and their father spent about three months touring the Maritime Provinces, and from the recordings in her father's notes, it appears that Janet assisted him in writing his notes and recording his business transactions and helping to make arrangements for their travels. When father and daughters reached Nova Scotia on the homeward trip, Janet left them and went to Chicago, planning to spend the winter there, visiting Kate, who was by now married to Paul Putzki, the artist. She became employed as a housekeeper and companion to an elderly gentleman and remained in Chicago until June 1889, when she returned to Twillingate to care for her father, who had become seriously ill. At that point she arranged for her sister Lucy to come to Chicago and take her job. We tried without success to determine whether Janet did her nurse's training either in Toronto, when Georgina was studying there, or in Chicago, after she went there in 1887. We have concluded that she did her nursing training in England after her father had died in April 1890, when she went to England to meet the Sheppard family. We will discover later in this chapter the details of her nursing training in England.

From the few references made to sister Rose in several family letters, it seems that she also remained in or near Twillingate during the years 1882 to 1888. In the December 13, 1885, letter, Kate notes that ". . . you are also thinking of sending Rose somewhere." Having three grown sisters at home may have caused certain friction, and Rose seems from several other communications to have been an aggravating and quarrelsome sister. Perhaps Dr. Stirling's plan to send Rose away came to nothing. What may Rose have been doing in Twillingate? In several of Hiram Silk's CBC interviews, which we will read about later, Rose is portrayed as "the most educated" sister in that she had experience working in the Grenfell Hospital at St. Anthony and had training and experience as a schoolteacher. If the latter is true, where would she have taken her teacher training? The first provision for teacher training in Newfoundland was made after the 1858 Act for the Encouragement of Education was enacted. This provided for an apprenticeship program through which first each electoral district, and later each district board, was permitted to send two students to the academies in St. John's for specific training in teaching methods. They were called pupil-teachers, were tested by a board of examiners, and their training could last up to three years (while they were teaching in a classroom setting), with half-yearly examinations, and then they would be graded as first, second, and third grade and paid accordingly. Being the daughter of a prominent physician and having been taught in excellent schools in Twillingate would have qualified Rose for such an appointment. Having qualified for the profession, Rose would likely have stayed at home and taught in one or more of the Twillingate schools. Having spent much time in St. John's in her early years may account for Rose's frequent trips to the city even after she returned permanently to Twillingate in early 1914.

In consideration of Maymie (Roberts) Hewlett's assertion that Georgina and Rose were "studying together" in Toronto, we must allow the possibility that Rose may have spent perhaps a year in Toronto, possibly between 1883 and 1885, upgrading her skills at the Toronto Ladies' College, or its precursor, while Georgina was studying with Carl Martens. This is not a strong argument, but it is a possibility. Maymie seldom made serious mistakes in recall, but no one is infallible.

Rose Stirling, aged sixty, is listed in the 1911 English Census records as being a teacher and a boarder in a household in Southborough, Kent, England, near where her sister Susan (Stirling) Temple was living. This would have followed Rose's more than twenty years living and working in Italy. She is affirmed by several reliable sources to have been an English governess to the Royal Family in Italy, but it is more likely that she worked with families of the Italian nobility, as we shall see later.

In spite of the claim that Rose was "the most educated" sister, this surely seems not to be the case. Georgina deserves that honour. She had two and a half years of music and academic training in Toronto, two years in Florence, Italy, two years of training in Paris, and took private lessons from Charles Santley in England over a two- or three-year period in connection with many concert tours.

WE RETURN NOW TO GEORGINA and her music and academic studies in Toronto. It appears that she began her studies at Miss Champion's school in January 1883 and continued in this school until at least 1884, when her curriculum was broadened and deepened, as we shall see presently.

Georgina was already quite proficient in playing the piano and the organ as well as in what might be called junior or introductory voice training when she arrived in Toronto, so it is assumed that training in these disciplines continued at a higher proficiency and that she would have expanded her proficiency in stage presence, acting, and related disciplines. Amy Louise Peyton states in an interview with Hiram Silk of CBC Grand Falls that the phrase "thrice-gifted daughter" in the testimonial which was presented to Georgina at St. John's in 1895 at the Grand Farewell Concert referred specifically to her skills as "actress, singer and pianist."

The formal-looking picture of six young ladies which appears on page 59 of Amy Louise Peyton's book is claimed to be a picture of Georgina "while attending school at Toronto." In her October 6, 1981, letter to her nephew Robert Walter Parsons, Amy Louise writes about this picture: "On an old photograph of her (Georgina) of about 16 or 17 years old, taken in Toronto, what looks like a school picture, on the back is written lobby this word is a bit obliterated, but which looks like cantab, so I wrote to Cantab College, 287 Russell Hill Rd. but did not receive an answer." It seems more likely that "cantab" may have been part of the word "cantabile," which refers to music characterized by an easy, flowing singing style. The picture may well have been of a select small singing group taken in the lobby at the college which Georgina was attending in Toronto. Her singing teacher at that time may have been Mrs. Bradley.

We noted earlier that there has been some difference of opinion about whether Georgina was away from Twillingate and presumably living in Toronto for as much as two full years. Georgina had become re-engaged with the musical and cultural life of her community and church by January of 1886. From the data presented earlier and what will now follow, we can confidently state that Georgina was away from Twillingate for two and a half years: from the late fall of 1882 until at least the summer of 1885. She began her studies in January 1883 and concluded them probably in the early summer of 1885.

Thanks to a collection of invoices which we discovered at the Memorial University of Newfoundland's (MUN) archives in the summer of 2018, we now have a reasonably clear idea of both the later period which Georgina spent in Toronto and what she was studying there. The invoices do not cover the period that Georgina spent at Miss Champion's school. They cover the period September 6, 1883, to June 30, 1885, and it cannot be determined if the set of invoices is complete. Some may well be missing. But they do cover a period of twenty-two months. Specifically, they cover "tuition of Miss Stirling," organ lessons by L. H. Wood at 182 Richmond St. West, by Blowers (?) at Carlton St. Church, and "Organ Lessons and Church Lessons."

It is clear from the invoices that Georgina's program of studies from at least May 1884 was supervised by Carl Martens, a graduate of the Royal Conservatory of Music in Lepsic (Leipzig), Germany, and his music school was located at 414 Church Street. He is noted in one invoice to be a "Teacher of the piano, violin and theory of music." Carl Martens would almost certainly have been teaching Georgina piano and theory of music and coordinating her organ lessons with city church organists. She was so well schooled in the organ that he suggested that one practice per week would be sufficient. Mrs. Murray of 297 Jarvis Street, Toronto, "in account with Carl Martens," seems to have played the role of coordinator of Georgina's academic program of studies from the time that Georgina enrolled in the Carl Martens school. This is the same Mrs. Murray whom we encountered earlier in Kate Stirling's letters. As Mrs. Murray had exercised supervision over Georgina's studies in Miss Champion's school, she continues that supervision at Carl Martens's school. Mrs. Murray submitted invoices to Kate Stirling in Chicago, who sent them to her father in Twillingate, and Dr. Stirling paid the school directly.

Emma Abramowicz, a planner with ERA Architects in Toronto, helped us with research into Carl Martens's proficiencies. The *Canadian Encyclopedia* refers to Martens as "part of a small cadre of musicians who were building Toronto's serious music industry through the 1880s . . . and was one of the Ontario music teachers included on a committee to form an examiners board." Martens was a composer of music, a promoter of chamber music, and played both viola and piano for the Toronto String Quartette from 1884 to 1887. In a book published in 1886 entitled *Industries of Canada: Historical and Commercial Sketches of Toronto and Environs*, it is stated that "As a teacher and composer of music, the position he occupies is almost a unique one. He was educated at Hamburg, and at the Leipsic Conservatory under the famous Carl Reinecke. Arriving in Toronto some six years ago, Mr. Martens has perhaps a larger number of pupils than any other music teacher in the city. He adopts the Italian method of vocal culture, which, while it produces the natural possibilities of the voice, refines and cultivates it."

Carl Martens's invoices are for tuition and sheet music. The named sheet music pieces are: Flower Song, Lange; Lila Stanchezza; Czerny Exercises; 30 Sonatinas; Scotson Clarke, 15 marches; Gloria in Excelis; Silver Trumpets; Cufas Ainmatne; Roman March; and March of Israelites.

We return to Kate Stirling's letters for a clear picture of what was happening with Georgina during this period of 1883 to 1884. Kate reassures her father from the beginning of 1884 about Mrs. Murray's care and supervision of Georgina. In her January 5, 1884, letter, Kate praises Mrs.

Murray for the way she handled "a church matter" for Georgina. "I don't know of anyone who takes as much interest in another as Mrs. Murray does in Georgina. I know very few of us would look after a stranger as well as she does." On May 8, 1884, Kate wrote about Mrs. Murray taking control of a mischievous Georgina, and then wrote, "Certainly, she (Georgie) is alone but Mrs. Murray has watched and cared for her I'm sure just as carefully as Mama would have done." What a tender reference to a caring mother as Kate reflects on the past and the loss of a mother and its effects on the family! (As an aside, this is the only reference to what the Stirling daughters called their mother—Mama. Their favoured word for their father was Papa.)

Mrs. Murray would have facilitated Georgina's transition from Miss Champion's school to the Carl Martens school. Georgina may have been attending classes at both schools for part of the time, depending on the subjects. Georgina appears to have been enrolled and boarding at Miss Champion's school for the first year and a half. In the summer of 1884, letters exchanged between Kate and her father, with input from Mrs. Murray, considered the possibility of Georgina moving to Chicago for the next school year because she was unhappy in Toronto. The decision was left to Kate as she examined the difference in costs and appropriate schools and living accommodations; she finally decided that living expenses and an education in Chicago would be too expensive. The cause of Georgina's unhappiness in Toronto seems to have been with the "group schooling" at Miss Champion's school. Georgina had won several awards in English and scripture at the school, but Dr. Stirling expected even more. Kate decided that the conduct of the girls at this school constituted impediments to Georgina's contentment and academic progress. Mrs. Murray must have offered to have Georgina board with her, oversee her lessons, and assure that she was given more individualized instruction.

On September 6, 1884, Kate writes to her father, "Now about Georgie's future, I have decided as I think best to let her board and study with Mrs. Murray and, of course, have her different masters. I am quite sure that she will do better away from all the other girls." Later in the same letter, she reiterates these points to her father: "Now you understand I think it good to accept Mrs. Murray's last offer of boarding Georgie and teaching her some branches. Then she can have her Masters &c for various other studies. I think Mrs. Murray will teach her and see that her other teachers do their duty."

The major changes proposed by Mrs. Murray and agreed to by Kate are reflected in Kate's letter of October 1, 1884, written from 206 State Street in Chicago, to her "Dear Papa" in Twillingate. In it she gives the details of Georgina's progress in her studies. She quotes from Mrs.

Murray's letter: "I am glad to say that Georgie seems quite interested in her studies and happy. I hope this pleasant state of things will last. She spends <u>four hours</u> & sometimes more a day in music practice. She has begun singing with Mrs. Bradley & is much pleased both with her teacher & her prospects of singing. Her organ practice is arranged, she gets her first lesson next Saturday. Martens thinks one lesson a week should suffice, as she is pretty well drilled in the theory. We have made a beginning at French and History & she is to have some special instruction from a good teacher in Arithmetic. I will write from time to time & will prompt Georgie to keep up her correspondence as she should. She is going to write from copies you sent her."

Kate had developed a beautiful handwritten style and was obviously attempting to coach Georgina in copying this style. Georgina had recently visited Kate in Chicago, spending more than two months with Kate during the summer, and before the beginning of the fall term in Toronto. Kate continues in her letter: "When here, I made Georgie write a little every day & I found she could copy my handwriting nearly exact. Her own writing, at best, was very scratchy and uncharacteristic, so I thought it better, as she found it so easy, to let her adopt my style. Of course, there are many little peculiarities which she need not follow."

There is a note written across the upper left corner of Kate's letter covering part of her introductory two first lines, obviously by Dr. Stirling, and in handwriting strikingly like that of Kate's. "Rec'd Oct. 11 with 2 others by mail from Kate, all replied to in one letter. Oct. 14th, 1884." This was typical of the meticulous record-keeping of Dr. Stirling. Georgina's letters to her "Papa" and to her sister Janet are also strikingly similar in style to that of Kate's and their father. It would appear Dr. Stirling had coached his daughters in his handwriting style.

Though Georgina would have taken piano instruction from Carl Martens, it was always the organ that she preferred. In a letter dated August 10, 1884, while Georgina was spending the summer with Kate in Chicago, Kate writes to her father in Twillingate, "Georgie puts her whole soul into the organ." Kate assures her father that she thinks more highly of Georgina's organ playing compared to the piano.

We have assumed that Georgina was sent to Toronto for music, vocal, and academic studies, but we now wonder, based on Kate's letters, whether vocal studies were emphasized as much as music studies, particularly advanced organ and piano lessons. There seems to have been no emphasis at the Carl Martens school on vocal training. Mrs. Murray, in June of 1884, had suggested to Kate that she was prepared to take Georgina in for a few weeks "on condition that she will do some study with me & perhaps continue her music lessons, also *I would select a singing teacher and let her have a term to see if her voice is worth cultivating."* (italics mine) It would appear that at that point Georgina's singing voice was judged to be unremarkable. Apparently, the singing teacher was not engaged until the fall of 1884, as is reflected in Kate's letter of October 1, where she quotes Mrs. Murray as saying that she had engaged Mrs. Bradley as Georgina's "new singing teacher." Whether "new" can be interpreted as meaning a second teacher cannot be determined. Georgina may well have been a "late bloomer," and perhaps it was under the tutelage of Mrs. Bradley that Georgina's voice was roused and nurtured and matured into the astonishingly beautiful voice it would later become.

The "printed edited manuscript," which we will examine later, affirms that even in 1887, after she had returned to Twillingate from Toronto, "she was receiving an education to fit her for the position of an organist." This is when the new governor of Newfoundland "accidentally heard her sing" and was "enraptured with her voice" and insisted that she be sent away "to study singing." Amy Louise Peyton writes about Georgina in or about 1879, when she was twelve years old, that, "Her singing ability was surprising, and the quality of her voice showed great promise." Yet all references to her musical ability seem to emphasize unique proficiency at the organ and piano.

It is important, therefore, to consider Kate's comments. In her letter of March 29, 1883, Kate writes, "She (Georgie) has been to hear Nilsson sing & as she wished it so much I thought you would not object to such a luxury for once. I asked her what she thought of her singing & she says she never could imagine such music coming from a human being." We cannot be sure that at that point she was already enrolled in the Carl Martens school, but she certainly had the passionate desire to hear the famous Swedish soprano, Christina Nilsson, sing (Nilsson was visiting Toronto at the time and sang there on March 7, 1883); Georgina was only two and a half months into her studies), and her passion to hear the singer was enough to persuade her reluctant sister to spend a little extra money for a ticket to the event. Now, in the letter, Kate defends her decision to their father. It seems most likely that this was Georgina's first exposure to operatic singing and the whole culture of opera. Christina Nilsson is credited with revitalizing the opera genre by uniting her stunning vocal techniques with a stylish stage performance. Georgina was entranced.

Georgina spent more than two months with Kate in Chicago during summer break 1884, and Kate makes no mention in her letters about Georgina's singing abilities or expression. The long summer was a sufficient period for Kate to become aware of Georgina's various interests and talents. In her letter of October 1, 1884, she had quoted Mrs. Murray as writing, "She (Georgina) has begun singing with Mrs. Bradley & is much pleased with her teacher & her prospect of singing." When Kate returns from a visit to Toronto in April 1885, she writes to her father in a letter dated April 24, "I find Georgie the same old Georgie but much improved. I think you will all be very much surprised to hear her sing. I had no idea she had such a beautiful voice."

When I first saw the reference to "the same old Georgie," I was inclined to take it as a somewhat negative comment, but I think that would be a mistake. It may be understandable coming from a very responsible sister who is eight years Georgina's senior and who may have been impatient with the antics of an eighteen-year-old, but from Kate's other letters there is another, and much more positive, way of interpreting it. Within six weeks of starting her new job in Chicago, on March 29, 1883, she writes to her father about the girls in the office being very kind to her, and says, "Grace Jackson is very like Georgie in her manner, always saying something to call forth a laugh." On February 13, 1884, Kate writes, "Georgie writes me every week. Her letters are very amusing. On the marriage question, she is very eloquent. When I get her letters, is about the only time I ever have a good laugh." This probably refers to both sisters' feelings about their three single sisters back in Twillingate—Lucy, Rose, and Janet—whom Kate remarked in another letter to her father that she expected would all become "old maids." On July 3, 1884, about Georgina, Kate wrote, "She is certainly very witty, and it is very easy for her to remember anything where the ridiculous comes in." While Georgina was visiting Kate in Chicago for the summer of 1884, Kate wrote to her father, "You should hear her telling some of her school stories. I laugh sometimes till I am weak," and again, "You should hear her talking. I have hardly stopped laughing since she came." When Eliza LeMessurier came from Newfoundland for a visit, Kate wrote, "When she and Georgie got started, I put my fingers in my ears. Just like a clock wound up. I would not take a fortune and go down town with the two." Eliza was very probably a daughter of John LeMessurier, Dr. Stirling's lawyer in St. John's, and whose correspondence regarding the mines at Betts Cove, Hall's Bay, and others, we found at the Memorial University archives.

Georgina's wit and sense of humour continued and undoubtedly became more refined, and we will note in one of her letters from Florence, Italy, in 1890 that she writes to her "Papa" in Twillingate, "I make myself also agreeable at the rehearsals telling funny stories, etc.—so that the people are always glad to see me."

Within three or four months of Kate's "discovery" of Georgina's "beautiful voice" during her visit to Toronto in April 1885, Georgina would be back in Twillingate, and within two years the Governor of Newfoundland would have heard her sing and been "enraptured with her voice." *See Appendix Two for a full transcript of Kate Stirling's letter of October 1, 1884.*

KATE HAD BEEN REQUESTED BY HER FATHER, Dr. Stirling, to be the liaison between himself and Mrs. Murray on all affairs pertaining to Georgina's musical and academic education. She plays a very proactive role in this process. Her letter of October 8, 1884, to her father states, "As regards the changes we have made for Georgie, I am very glad you approve of it. I feel sure it is for her good. She seems very happy . . ."

For a seventeen-year-old in Toronto, Georgina was permitted certain freedoms in travelling, and that may have been conducive to her changed happiness. In March 1883, Georgina travelled on the train alone to Springfield, Ontario, just outside London, to visit the McGraths, probably family friends. Georgina's Christmas travel in 1883, her Easter travel in 1884, and her summer visit with Kate in Chicago in 1884, all appear to have been done unaccompanied. She must have felt both family support and a sense of growing up.

One other comment on Mrs. Murray: In Kate's letter of January 5, 1884, she writes to her father, "I had some good talks with Mrs. Murray about Georgie and Rose." Rose was almost surely at home in Twillingate, so what could the "good talks" have been about? My guess is that Mrs. Murray was pondering Georgina's future and the possibility of advanced vocal training in Europe. She could not possibly travel to Europe alone. Lucy would not have been a suitable travel companion as she was still dealing with her own brokenness and needed sisterly support herself. Kate was nicely settled in Chicago and loved the city and was looking to the future. If travel to Europe was necessary in future, Rose would have been the most suitable candidate as a chaperone. She was fifteen years older than Georgina, she had experience working in a hospital, training and experience as a teacher, and would herself be eminently employable in a new country once Georgina became sufficiently independent.

Yet another word about Kate Stirling's continuing activity in Chicago: Kate was a proactive person, and ready at age twenty-four to make her own way in the world. Chicago represented adventure, opportunity, and new horizons for daring people. Kate visited her uncle George and aunt Maria occasionally and lived with them for about five months in 1884.

She lived most of the time in the first year or two with Horace and Annie Phillipps, who seemed to have had a connection with Toronto.

Kate had a previous interest in art and showed real promise in colouring and tinting photographs but appears not to have had any formal instruction in the art. In her January 5, 1884, letter she writes, "When first in Chicago, Horace and I went to an Artist who had advertised for help but we did not approve of his Terms, so gave up the idea." These words seem to confirm Kate's early interest in art. This is where Mrs. Murray again comes to the rescue, this time for Kate and not for Georgina. In late 1883, Mrs. Murray suggested that Kate undertake art training in order to become eventually a china painting teacher as a career. The idea appealed to Kate, and she wrote in her January 5 letter, "I am in favor of painting, but I should never have given it a second thought had not Mrs. Murray suggested it and offered me her help." We are not told what this "help" meant—it may have been more than encouragement. In her letter of February 14, 1884, Kate states that she has begun lessons and writes, "On Monday I am going to take my first lesson in Porcelain painting . . . my object in making a beginning while I still have my situation (the clerical job with Mr. Dean) is to see whether I really have a talent for it. My teacher is considered the finest porcelain painter of Flowers and Birds in Chicago." Her teacher was Paul Putzki, so Kate's talent was not limited to porcelain painting. In 1886 she married her teacher.

Lucy Stirling, while visiting her sister Kate (Stirling) Putzki in Chicago, 1887 and later (Stirling family)

There is a significant gap in Kate's letters (letters missing), and the next communication to her father was on June 29, 1889. From this letter we learn that Janet has already returned to Twillingate to care for their ailing father. She writes, "I am more than thankful that Janet is again with you." Lucy would by that date have been in Chicago, caring for Mr. Kerby. In anticipation of her first child's birth in September, Kate states to her father, "I hope to be able to have Lucy for a week or two in September. Of course I will pay her way here and back." That would have been from Chicago to Indianapolis and return. The Putzkis were there, having been invited by Mrs. Benjamin Harrison so that Paul could teach china painting to Mrs. Harrison and her friends. In Kate's letter of October 25, 1889, she details to her father how close she came to dying with the birth of her stillborn son in September; she had not expected to survive the ordeal. She praised her sister Lucy in these grateful words: "Lucy was very good to me & I shall not forget it when she needs a friend in any way." She also mentioned their preparations for the planned move to Washington, DC, in the following year. Benjamin Harrison would by then be the president of the United States, and Mrs. Harrison would have invited the Putzkis to move to Washington and teach painting classes to her friends at the White House.

Following 1889, no letters of Kate can be found until 1938, when she visited Twillingate for the final time. But the Putzki family had come to Twillingate, probably in the late summer or early fall of 1895, and stayed until sometime in 1886, living in the Stirling house. A third child, William Stirling Putzki, was born to them on January 14, 1896, and baptized at St. Peter's Church on April 12. It cannot be determined whether they arrived after Georgina and Janet had left Twillingate in the early part of September 1895, and whether they had left Twillingate before Georgina and Lucy returned from England in the summer of 1896. During the Putzki year-long visit to Twillingate, Paul Putzki produced many beautiful watercolour paintings of the Stirling house, the Peyton houses at Back Harbour, of various Twillingate scenes, and of Exploits Harbour. Several of these paintings still grace the homes of local residents. Paul Putzki is also reported to have painted an entire china service set, and this is said to be in Twillingate still.

WE DO NOT KNOW EXACTLY WHEN GEORGINA returned to Twillingate from her two and a half years in Toronto. She probably would have left Toronto following the conclusion of the 1885 first term, likely after the end of June. From Kate's letter of October 1, 1885, we know that Georgina was at home in Twillingate, since Kate writes to her father, "Tell Janet and Georgie I will write next week." By January of 1886, Georgina would have already spent several weeks of preparation for various concerts taking place at Christmas and major events to occur in the new year. Detailed programs for three of these musical events early in the new year in which Georgina plays a significant role are listed on pages 195 and 196 of Amy Louise Peyton's book. The newspaper *Twillingate Sun* immediately resumes its coverage of Georgina's music activities and refers to other members of the Stirling family.

Shortly after arriving back in Twillingate, Georgina became involved under the direction of Rev. Mr. and Mrs. Temple in many church and community activities. She superintended and taught in a Sunday school at Crow Head, three miles away, and it is believed that she rode there every Sunday on horseback, because Dr. Stirling makes reference to "the side saddle for Georgie's use." She was probably taken there by horse and sleigh in the winter. She also became a regular organist at St. Peter's Church, was requested to do many piano performances, and she sang solos and participated in duets. Her training in Toronto had honed her natural skills, and she now gained increasing confidence and poise through these many activities in her hometown.

By January–February of 1886, the *Twillingate Sun* resumes comments about the Stirling sisters at Twillingate. On January 9, the *Sun* informed its readers that "It is intended to hold a Bazaar, early in October 1886 for the purpose of procuring funds to re-shingle, paint and re-seat St. Peter's Church. Contributions in money, useful or fancy articles for the above will be received by the following ladies:" Then, among others, appear the names of Miss R. Stirling (Rose) and Miss G. Stirling (Georgina).

On January 30, 1886, it was announced that "The first Tea Meeting of the season . . . took place" at the North Side Methodist Church, and the *Sun* noted: "It is needless to say that Miss Georgie Stirling who presided at the organ accompanied with much taste." The full program for this "Tea Meeting and Service of Song" is printed on page 195 of Amy Louise Peyton's book and elaborates on Georgina's contribution. "*Eva* a musical service compiled and arranged from *Uncle Tom's Cabin*. Musical illustrations by organist Miss Georgie Stirling (age nineteen years)." A note at the end of the program asserted: "During the description of the funeral scene the *Dead March in Saul* was played with organ and drum accompaniment." It is assumed that Georgina was the organ accompanist. The *Twillingate Sun* added, "We suppose this was the first service of song ever given in Twillingate." Georgina's proficiency at the organ was now being recognized outside her own St. Peter's Church, and it is heartening to see her willingness to contribute to the broader Christian community. At a festival concert in February 1886 and an Easter tea and entertainment in April 1886, Georgina again plays a prominent role in the musical offerings.

On April 24, 1886, the *Sun* announced the March 9 wedding in Chicago, USA, of Kate Stuart Stirling to Paul Adolphe Putzki, Artist of Altwasser in Schlesien, Germany.

When the steamer *Hercules* arrived in Twillingate from St. John's on November 20, the *Sun* reported that "two Misses Stirlings" were passengers, as well as Rev. Mr. Pittman. The latter was Rev. A. Pittman, who became a minister at the Methodist Church and would do special readings at several of the concerts where Georgina would be singing and playing in Twillingate. His name appears in several of the programs from 1886 to 1892.

While they were in St. John's, the two sisters (one of whom was almost certainly Georgina) must have made a special purchase. In Dr. Stirling's meticulously kept record book, there is an entry for December 14, 1886, with an invoice received from Job Brothers Co. of St. John's for "payment of tea and **a ladies seal cap**." We noted earlier that Georgina had "gone to the ice" to hunt seals, so it seems certain that the "ladies seal cap" was for her and would be used at the seal hunt in March 1887. Perhaps she had outgrown an earlier cap! Georgina was a bold, venturesome young woman.

Following a marriage ceremony held on December 25, 1886, at the North Side Methodist Church, Misses G. Stirling and Helen Scott were among the guests who were afterwards entertained at the residence of the magistrate William J. Scott. Georgina was included among the honoured guests to be entertained rather than to be entertaining others. This must have been in recognition of the growing popularity of Georgina, who was still just nineteen years of age.

Georgina remained in Twillingate from mid-1885 to 1888, and the programs on pages 197 to 198 of Amy Louise Peyton's book provide details about two of the singing and instrumental engagements in which Georgina played a prominent role in 1888—the Church of England Temperance Society and the Dorcas Society concert. Georgina was often singled out for praise in the pages of the *Sun*, as in the review of the Dorcas Society concert, where it was noted that ". . . we may be excused if we make mention of Miss Georgie Stirling who seemed to actuate the whole, and whose talents as vocalist, accompanist or prompter were in requisition the whole evening."

Sometime before May of 1887, Georgina and Janet persuaded their father, Dr. Stirling, to accompany them to Halifax, Nova Scotia, where their friend Minnie Tobin was graduating from Mount Saint Vincent College with "academic honours." The Stirlings were away for three months, spending some time in St. John's before visiting "the neighbouring provinces."

After Georgina and her father arrived home in Twillingate, a letter was sent from John W. Cowan, president of the Albert Railway, to Dr. Stirling. He must have heard Georgina sing while the Stirlings were visiting the area. He wrote, "'Where are the friends of my youth?' still lingers in my ears. Are you conscious of her rare gift? She's an artist and you should send her to Italy, depend upon it she would repay you in a very short time." A recommendation from yet another source for advanced vocal training for this talented young Georgina! Mr. Cowan must have been either a visitor to Twillingate previously or had worked there, because he ends his letter with, "Remember me kindly to Mrs. Lethbridge and any other old friends who are likely to recollect me."

Janet parted from her father and Georgina somewhere in Nova Scotia and travelled to Chicago to visit her sister Kate (Stirling) Putzki, intending to spend the winter there.

While still in Twillingate, Georgina's schedule of musical events continued with great support from her beloved community, and this gave Georgina the courage to dream bigger and consider a possible career in opera. Dr. Stirling accordingly made arrangements to send Georgina to Europe to study voice at an advanced level.

In the document which we referred to earlier in this chapter, written in England some-time after 1896, an interesting insight is given the reader about Georgina Stirling at about this period in her life. The British Governor of Newfoundland from 1887 to 1889, Sir Henry Arthur Blake, "on one of his frequent trips round the coast" (very probably his first trip), is said to have "accidently heard her sing. He was enraptured with her voice, and insisted upon her friends permitting her to study." There is an error in the manuscript when it refers to the governor as Sir Edward Blake. The manuscript continues, "At this time she was receiving an education to fit her for the position of an organist."

One cannot help wondering why there was such a long period of time between the completion of Georgina's studies in Toronto (say June 1885) and the decision to send her to Europe for advanced vocal studies near the end of 1888—three and a half years! Dr. Stirling appears to have been responsible for delaying a decision to send Georgina away again, on the grounds that he would be "losing" another of his children. Was he reluctant to send his precious youngest daughter so far away? Was he persuaded that she had a sufficiently gifted voice? Would he have preferred that she stay at home and be a church organist and choral dir-ector for community musical activities? Did the losses he had suffered, his wife and three (or four) sons, play a role in such a slowly developing decision? Georgina had left home within two or three months of her mother's death and lived in Toronto for two and a half years with-out a visit home to Twillingate, and in that time her father saw her only once, during a visit to Toronto in 1883. It seems natural that he would want her to remain at home, especially in view of his own deteriorating health. He must have thought he would never see her again. This may explain the heartfelt nature of Georgina's letters to her father and her determination to share every detail of her life abroad. Dr. Stirling lived for only about fifteen months after she left for Europe.

But the decision to send Georgina away was made. Undoubtedly the persuasive words of men like the British Governor of Newfoundland and Dr. Stirling's old friend, John W. Cowan of New Brunswick, played a major role in the decision. One wonders also about the role that Mrs. Murray of Toronto may have played through Kate and perhaps directly with Dr. Stirling.

Georgina's sisters Rose and Lucy helped her to prepare for the exciting adventure to Italy. Georgina and Rose travelled from Twillingate to St. John's on the steamer *Conscript* on October 22, 1888. The *Twillingate Sun* entry reads, "Among the passengers per *Conscript* who embarked here this morning was Miss G. Stirling, youngest daughter of Wm. S. Stirling Esq., M.D., who goes to St. John's *on route to Italy*. (italics mine) This young lady is endowed by nature with no ordinary degree of musical talent, and being desirous of excelling in the art of music, she has decided to take a thorough course of studies from first-class Italian professionals, who are renowned all the world over for their proficiency in the musical art. Miss Stirling has many amiable qualities, and by her genial disposition is a general favorite, and will be greatly missed in the community, especially by many of the poor, to whom it was her delight to administer deeds of kindness. We wish our young friend a safe and speedy journey across the Atlantic and every success in the future. Miss Rose Stirling accompanied her sister as far as St. John's." The newspaper was in error, since Rose went all the way to Italy with Georgina.

On November 17, 1888, they left St. John's on the vessel *Peruvian* for Liverpool, England. The *Twillingate Sun* had mistakenly affirmed that Rose had accompanied Georgina only as far as St. John's, and Amy Louise Peyton unintentionally repeats the error, but Dr. Stirling had arranged for Rose to accompany Georgina to Europe, as we shall discover later from letters that Georgina writes to her father from Italy. Georgina was only twenty-one years old, and going to Europe was entering a very different world. Rose was indeed with Georgina, and thus began Rose's "more than twenty years" or twenty-eight years in Europe. *See Appendix Three: The Children of Dr. William C. Stirling and Ann (Peyton) Stirling as compiled by Milton Anstey.*

CHAPTER THREE
BY TONIA EVANS CIANCIULLI

A SPARK IGNITES THE FLAME

"Destiny awaits. It is always an adventure. It drives us past the pain of life to the purpose of living. There's more going on in your life than just you. At moments that I felt the least adept, I have known there is a force between my wings for which I could take no credit. There was a perfect timing I could not explain. There was a person I could never have schemed to meet. There was an opportunity I could never have orchestrated on my own."

— T. D. Jakes, Pastor, Author, and Filmmaker

THE MORNING AFTER SAYING FAREWELL to 2016, I sat on the sofa with my coffee, rubbed the sleep from my eyes, and reflected on the previous year. I chatted over Facebook Messenger with my dear cousin Jody Locke about the year on which we had just written our final pages. With a clean slate for the year ahead, we wondered what it might possibly hold for us. This particular conversation was the spark that ignited the flame.

Jody was born and raised in Newfoundland and now lives in Portugal with her daughter, Lauren. We have always lived with miles and oceans between us but have remained in close contact as we share the pursuit of our life's wishes and journeys. We both have a fondness for beachcombing in search of treasures from the sea, most importantly, heart rocks. This particular morning, we were discussing her ever-growing portfolio of rock art creations that were now overtaking her apartment . . . and my desire to bring my lifelong passion of opera into my life in a more poignant way. Being the proud Newfoundlander that Jody is, she suggested I explore my "Newfoundland roots." I had no clue what that would look like or where to begin. From enough past experience, I know that the moment an intention is put in motion, the wheels start turning, and people and things start coming together to conspire toward your dreams becoming reality. This particular journey will reveal proof of the incredible synchronicities and coincidences that began to arise, confirming for me that God has had His Hand on a unique vision for my life, far greater than I could have imagined for myself.

Thinking about Jody's suggestion, I remembered a book that my grandparents gifted me in 1993: *Nightingale of the North* by Amy Louise Peyton. It was about the late Newfoundland opera singer and soprano Georgina Stirling, born in Twillingate in 1867. She was also known affectionately to her international audiences as Marie Toulinguet. I had been so obsessed with the life and music of Maria Callas, "La Divina," that I figured I had no extra mental capacity for this Newfoundland Nightingale. I was simply not meant to read Georgina's story at that time. What I did not realize until years later was that while that book sat patiently waiting for me, the music of Georgina's life started making its way into mine in a way that would connect our hearts and paths forever.

I decided to take this long-forsaken book off the shelf and see what it might spark in me. I was instantly intrigued. I read it with great excitement and appreciation for what this young girl from the commercial and fishing outport of Twillingate, Newfoundland, had accomplished out of the pure desire to follow her operatic dreams! This was no small feat in the 1800s in Newfoundland, when most women and children busied themselves with household chores and tended to duties common to growing up in a fishing outport. Several women in my own family line in Newfoundland held occupations that were connected with the sea, and many of their sisters were proudly known as shipowners. Georgina had other dreams. She was a true trailblazer, paving the path for those who came after her.

The more I read, the more I realized that much of the repertoire Georgina performed abroad and at home across Newfoundland was similar to mine. I wrote a list of the specific opera arias, oratorio, sacred solos, and well-loved songs that she and I had in common. What a thrill it was to see how they started to fill the page! It quickly became obvious to me that there was so much more than our musical repertoire that united us provincial songbirds, born over 100 years apart (109 years to be exact).

I shared my excitement with Jody about all the coincidences, events, and even relatives of ours that connected us with Georgina over the span of all those years between. The first significant connection was that my great-grandmother, Jody's grandmother, Minnie (Waterman) Locke, grew up in Durrell, Twillingate. As a young mother, later living in Botwood, she brought her children back to Twillingate for summer vacations in the 1930s and heard Georgina sing on more than one occasion, thus making Georgina a meaningful figure in our family history.

I connected the fact that Georgina was born in 1867—the same year that Canada became a nation—and we were in 2017, the year Canada was celebrating its 150th birthday! I wanted to honour both Georgina Stirling and Canada for their 150th by creating a poignant program of music along with historical facts and affectionate stories as a special tribute concert. I wrote a detailed proposal with my intentions for this dedication concert and called the Newfoundland churches that Georgina had filled with her remarkable voice. My hands were shaking as I pressed the numbers, and my voice trembled when I introduced myself to perfect strangers. Thankfully they all spoke with such welcoming affection.

I was starting to see all the pieces miraculously fall into place as I continued to "fan the flame." As the first concerts quickly approached, I was busy with training vocally, fine-tuning my repertoire, and other concert-related details. As fate would have it, I was introduced to a significant song that would greatly impact the telling of Georgina's story. I was on the phone with Newfoundland singer/songwriter and photographer Chris LeDrew, whom I had been referred to in my search for a photographer for the concerts. I told him about the scope of my project, and he asked me if I had heard of the song *Marie*, written by the late Ron Hynes, Newfoundland's folk hero. I got in touch with Ron's manager, Charles MacPhail, who then sent me a recording and the lyrics. Sadly, it was hard to make out some of Ron's words because he had undergone chemotherapy during his illness, thus taking a toll on his voice. He still managed to bring such beauty to this tribute and so poignantly told the story of Marie Toulinguet that would forever change my life. I fell in love with the song immediately. I travelled to St. John's that May with my family, making it all the more special. When I met pianist Evan Smith to rehearse the concert, he came up with a breathtaking piano arrangement for *Marie*, on the spot, in place of the original guitar accompaniment.

After performing that first Nightingale concert in St. John's in May 2017 at Gower Street United Church, I was approached by a kind and generous gentleman named Bert Riggs. Bert had been the head of Archives and Special Collections at Memorial University from 1989 to 2015 and had attended school with my mother in Grand Bank, Newfoundland, when they were preteens. Bert told me that the archives had recently received a large number of Stirling family files, not yet catalogued, and that he would be happy to arrange for me and my grandfather to look through the materials. He notified Colleen Quigley of Archives that we would be visiting and to have these files available to us the next day. What a treat! I never thought I'd be as excited to go to a library as I was that day. Opening the file boxes was like opening a treasure trove that allowed us to understand and look into Georgina's life in a whole new way. I remember looking at my grandfather many times that day and thinking, *He's like a kid in a candy shop!* As a librarian, he was truly in his element. This was the defining moment in which we agreed that another book must be written about Georgina. We found documents, letters, and receipts that corrected old rumours and revealed new facts and stories. This was just the beginning of the people who started to come forward with more pieces of information to help create a fuller picture of Georgina's life.

In August that same year, I travelled back to Newfoundland to perform at Faith United Church in Northern Arm and at St. Peter's Church in Twillingate, the latter being Georgina's home church. Being met with great enthusiasm and interest, I knew this was just the beginning of my "heart's obsession"—my deep connection to Georgina.

The seeds I had planted in 2017 were all starting to germinate. My interest in bringing Georgina's memory into the twenty-first century continued to grow. I refined my concert program with the support of my friend, musician Pandora Topp. Pandora has studied and performed concerts based on the life of Edith Piaf for twenty years, so her experience was an invaluable asset to this work. Together we fleshed out the order and content of the program so that the audience would be musically carried throughout the journey of Georgina's life. The narrative that was originally read by me was now to be performed by my grandfather as part of our dramatic presentation. Also lending repertoire suggestions and support as I further developed this program was my mentor, maestro Kerry Stratton. I was overcome with goosebumps, and sometimes tears, as I came closer to finalizing the transitions throughout the program, weaving song and narrative, to tell Georgina's story.

Along the way, my writing took a back seat to training and performing. I know my grandfather was eager to receive more chapters, but I knew I was not yet ready to write them. As a performer, I needed to gain more wisdom and insight, which came over the course of that year. They enriched my perspective on Georgina's life and career in a distinct way. Performing these concerts, I was obtaining a more focused education that I could only have received by living and breathing the music she sang in the places she sang them.

The week I departed for the 2018 Nightingale Sings tour across Newfoundland, I performed a concert of operatic arias and duets with the Toronto Concert Orchestra under the baton of Maestro Kerry Stratton, with mezzo-soprano Beste Kalender, at Toronto's Casa Loma for an audience of over 1,200 people. This concert for me was one of challenging and significant operatic repertoire. I made every effort to ensure that it was a vocal success. And it was. I came home that night absolutely delighted. I sat enjoying the success of the night with a glass of wine and my family. My husband slid a package across the kitchen island to me. Just when I thought I couldn't be any happier, I was thrilled to learn I had been awarded a circulation and touring grant from the Canada Council for the Arts for my Nightingale Sings concerts for which I was departing the next morning. I was full of excitement to share this news with the audiences of Newfoundland. Along with my grandfather and Newfoundland-born pianist Jason Locke, we performed our concerts in St. John's at Gower Street United Church, at St. Paul's Anglican Church in Trinity, and finally, in Twillingate at St. Peter's Anglican Church. Those ten days in Newfoundland were full of research, interviews, meetings with publishers, rehearsals, concerts, and video shoots. We stopped along the way to take in the extreme beauty of some of our favourite spots in Newfoundland at Middle Cove Beach, Bonavista, Dungeon Provincial Park, the magnificent harbour of Trinity, and of course visiting as much family as we could manage.

Returning from Newfoundland with much buzz and excitement created around the Nightingale Sings concerts and our new book, I was engaged to perform this very concert program in Ottawa at Southminster United Church, in Wasaga Beach at the Wasaga Beach United Church, and in Miami at the First United Church. The year came to a close with extreme gratefulness and an uplifting Christmas concert at Islington United Church, which included many elements of Georgina's repertoire along with my grandfather's touching narrative. Throughout all of this I had been deepening my connection to Georgina. With each concert grew my confidence, not only as a concert performer but in striving to become an expert on "everything Georgina." It was then that my writing on Georgina's musical life and career started to flow out of me. I finally felt within me the insight and knowledge necessary to bestow, upon you, Georgina's story.

CHAPTER FOUR
BY TONIA EVANS CIANCIULLI

BECKON ME HOME

"And so I'll cast my leaving shadow and I'll be Canadian. But distance won't decide what matters to the Hard Rock's loving son. And when I'm thinking of St. John's I'll bring her closer with a song. I don't know where I'm going but I know where I belong."
— Alan Doyle and Russell Crowe, Lyrics, "Where I Belong"

THE OLDER I GET, THE MORE sentimental I become, and I feel the pull to return "home" to Newfoundland more frequently with my own family, to visit our many relatives. It doesn't matter how many times we go back; the feelings attached to home never dim. Nostalgia guides me every time to make a stop into the local store for homemade bread, snowballs, and gingersnaps. I love a leisurely stroll down Water Street, stopping in at the endless number of knick-knack shops, and grabbing a coffee and treat at Rocket Bakery. Almost every night ends with me cozy in my flannel pyjamas, watching old movies with my aunt Lucy, my favourite of all, *Magnificent Obsession*, with Rock Hudson.

What really starts tugging at my heart the moment I step off the plane are my visits to Middle Cove Beach. It's a very special place for me. As a child, my parents brought my three brothers and me down to Middle Cove to watch the capelin roll in. What a sight! Most times now we will head down there with Aunt Lucy, the kids, a bag of wood and newspapers for a beach fire, some Tim's coffee, and a bucket of Mary Brown's chicken. My kids make up games to play for hours, throwing, piling, and sorting rocks. They hop from rock to rock across a tiny river that trickles nearby. They let the waves try to catch them along the shore with their pants rolled up past their knees. It's a simple kind of fun that has become a lost art these days. It is magical when the sun starts setting and all the tiny campfires along the beach illuminate the sand and pebbles. Some days we will simply grab a plastic container to collect rocks and just go there to "be." These rugged beaches and landscapes hold a special magic with treasures all around. A safeness and sense of peace wash over me when I get close enough to hear the waves crashing. I usually get the kids situated and then walk down over the beach to sit myself as close to the waves as possible without getting wet. I sit down and nestle my bum into the stones, and I am immediately taken hostage by the sea. I listen for the wisdom I come in search of. Time freezes, and the usual mental clutter that seems to produce its own relentless waves starts to fade from my mind. Everything becomes drowned out by the waves crashing in toward me; then the waves boast a new sound as they exhale while dragging and turning over thousands of stones with them as if to prove their might in case one had forgotten. There is a power and a certainty that comes with these waves which have lived here for millions of years. There is a grandeur that makes me feel so small in a world where our ego can feel so large. It chops me back to size and makes me realize just how insignificant all my worries and anxieties really are. It speaks a special wisdom just to turn inward and trust. It is confirmation that just as the waves will always be there, so will home; sometimes I just have to search from within to find it, feel it, and sense it.

Whenever I sit for this symphony of sounds, I have such a great urge to layer in my own melodic lines of song. I sing to the ocean, and it provides a safe audience, one which doesn't judge any sounds it hears; it just accepts my offering and keeps playing and improvising along with me. Although I have sung for audiences on many stages, I have a strange insecurity to sing at liberty around my natural surroundings, as if I am singing my intimate thoughts, fearful of others judging. But when I sing for the ocean, I can sing any thought or feeling that surfaces, and they are taken into its arms and held safely without judgment.

The only other thing that steals my attention on these beaches is my endless search for heart rocks to add to my ever-growing collection. Keeping my eyes down while the ocean continues to play, I run my hands along the stones, turning them over in a more careful way to search the layers of stones so that I don't miss any that could be hiding out of plain sight.

It is no coincidence that about ten years ago I found my first heart rock on a beach in Newfoundland—Michael's Harbour, to be exact, the very beach where my dear cousin Jody spent her summers. On that same trip home, my grandmother's sister, Aunt Florence, more commonly known in the family as Aunt Fussy, gifted me my second heart rock that she had found one day on a beach walk. In a sense, I treasure my heart rocks more than fine jewels. They all hold a specific story, a memory of when and where I found them. By the time they are discovered and picked up, they've all endured a tumultuous journey of being shaped into their smooth or jagged heart shape by waves, chaos, persistent friction, or sudden crashing.

Finding hearts has become a sort of obsession in my family, you could say. In fact, I exchange weekly, sometimes daily, images of discovered hearts with many of my cousins, aunts, step-sisters, and sister friends. Maybe you will start finding them, too.

Hearts have become a sign for me—a confirmation that I am on the right track and following my own heart, even on days when I feel lost. These hearts have also led me back home to the beloved place where I was born, for a new passion that would take my life by storm.

GEORGINA'S HEARTFELT WELCOME

"If light is in your heart, you will find your way home."
— Rumi

THERE MAY NEVER BE ANOTHER OPERA singer who knew the power of the sea, its moods and personality, better than Georgina. When I arrived for the first concert that I performed in Georgina's Twillingate, I walked arm in arm with my mom down the long gravel road from St. Peter's Church to the cemetery at Snelling Cove. My kids ran ahead as I stood at the double white gates of Georgina's gravesite for the first time. I felt a wave of goosebumps break out over my entire body. This was a significant moment that I had been waiting for with great anticipation. As I knelt down to lift up the white painted steel stake to open the gates, my mother grabbed my arm and said with excitement, "Tonia, look!" What do you think was in the centre of this rugged path that ended at these gates and waited for our entry? A perfectly shaped heart rock! We erupted with disbelief and delight. It was as if Georgina was waiting for us, welcoming us with an open heart to her final home overlooking her Twillingate.

The kids continued to run on excitedly ahead of my mom and me toward a white wooden gate that led beyond the gravesite and onto a picturesque pebble beach. My mom and I walked ceremoniously on the gently worn grassy path down the centre of the cemetery toward Georgina's grand granite headstone. It was a very special moment. I began to imagine what it was like to be Georgina walking toward the sea, inhaling the smell of the salt air, hearing the cries of seabirds and the sound of crashing waves. I looked out as far as I could see, wondering what had been on the other side of that ocean for her. I stood and stared at her monument reading the adoring stage names by which she had been known.

In Memory

of

GEORGINA STIRLING

MLLE MARIE TOULINGUET

PRIMA DONNA

DIED

APRIL 21, 1935

AGE 68 YEARS

SONGSTRESS OF NEWFOUNDLAND

THE NIGHTINGALE OF THE NORTH SANG

FAIRER THAN THE LARKS OF ITALY

SHE ENTERTAINED ROYALTY BY THE SWEETNESS OF HER VOICE

AND THE POOR BY THE KINDNESS OF HER HEART

ERECTED BY AN ADORING PUBLIC

IT JUST SO HAPPENS THAT MY GRANDPARENTS, Calvin and Goldie Evans, and my great-grandparents, Minnie and Gordon Locke, were present on the beautiful sunny day of July 19, 1964, for the unveiling of this special monument in dedication to Georgina's memory. What a thrill it was to be standing where they were to honour the Nightingale of the North so many years ago!

When I got home from that first trip, I received a package in the mail. Irene Pardy, a community member who attended my performance, sent us photocopies of newspaper clippings with my grandparents and great-grandparents standing by Georgina's monument among a large crowd of long-adoring fans. This was another significant event that connected my family to Georgina.

As our wandering and wondering continued, I felt Georgina was walking alongside me, showing me around, introducing me to the shores she so intimately knew and loved her entire life. Closer to the water, I looked down and saw a smooth round pebble with a splash of water on it in a perfect heart shape. My mother and I kept shaking our heads in disbelief. Georgina was guiding me.

No one will ever know the deep secrets or mysteries of Georgina's heart that lay to rest with her by the sea. I was determined more than ever to share the impact she was having on me. When I sang that first time in Georgina's church at St. Peter's Anglican, I became aware of the fact that her voice once filled these soaring ceilings and bounced off the same stained glass windows that my voice now explored. Bringing me closer to this realization was singing Ron Hynes's *Marie* for her in her home church. As I sang the opening words, "Twillingate's a million miles away," I felt sentimental and moved. Tears welled up in my eyes as I continued to sing this hauntingly beautiful melody. I thought, *Oh, Georgina! You've got my full attention. I'm standing where you stood. I'm singing where you sang. I am humbly at your service to share your story and your heart with all who will listen.*

Tonia Evans Cianciulli at Twillingate. St. Peter's Cemetery with Georgina Stirling's monument in the background. Taken during the *Nightingale Sings* concert of 2018. (Megan White Photography)

CHAPTER FIVE
BY TONIA EVANS CIANCIULLI

GEORGINA'S TWILLINGATE
—HER VOICE, HER SEA, AND HER FAMILY

LET me be
Where the sea
Ceaselessly
Washes o'er
Pebbly shore.

There I find
Buoyant mind
When the wind
Doth combine
With the brine
Making sound
All around
Like a song
For the strong.

Company
For the free
There I see . . .
Let me be
By the sea!

— A. C. Wornell, "The Old Salt's Request"

MY SECOND TRIP BACK TO TWILLINGATE was in August 2018 for the final of three Nightingale Sings concerts across Newfoundland. I sat at a window table in Georgie's Restaurant with the owner, and new friend, Deborah Bourden. As we both have a love and fascination for "all things Georgina," our conversation was one of wonder, surmising, and a shared desire to discover the truth. Deborah pointed to the government wharf, just steps from her restaurant, and remarked that whenever Georgina came home to Twillingate from performances abroad, the wharf would be full of community members, family, and friends to welcome her back home with pride. I was transported in my mind to what it must have been like to stand at the edge of that wharf. Georgina boarded a grand steamer ship from that very wharf with trunks full of personal belongings, setting sail on a voyage to continents unknown. Her dreams were lofty. There must have been an overwhelming sense of anticipation and joy bubbling up from within as she embarked on this adventure. How did she feel when she looked back over her shoulder to watch her Twillingate slowly disappear from her sight? When she departed for her first trip to Europe, her voice had only fallen on the ears of familiar audiences and shores. She was soon to be heard by an entirely new world. The birthplace of opera: Italy. Did Georgina, at the young age of twenty-one, realize that she was one of a small company of women of that time to have the opportunity and the courage to reach for a dream so rare and momentous, and that she would also be considered a trailblazer in her time? I think she did but was gracious and humble in her pursuit.

Another Ron Hynes song that touched me was "Away." Tears rolled down my face the moment I first heard it. I couldn't help but think about Georgina as I listened to Ron's touching lyrics. In describing his song "Away," Ron commented that as much as it's a love song between a man and a woman, it's also a song about the love Newfoundlanders have for their home and the heartache they feel when they have to leave "her." History saw many Newfoundlanders leave their beloved homes and families to travel across the ocean in search of work in the eighteenth and nineteenth centuries, to what was referred to back then as the "Boston States." Ron so poignantly portrays these emotions in this short but haunting melody. In my mind, I reflected on Georgina standing on the ship for the first time, with her trunk, as the coastal boat pulled away from her Twillingate wharf. At the young age of sixteen, she travelled to Toronto after losing her mother and four young brothers. Although Georgina was sailing toward the start of great dreams, I was sympathetic to what heartache she had already endured at such a young age as she sailed . . . away.

AWAY

So well I remember the morning that I sailed away,
And turning one last time I threw a kiss to her,
She smiled to me from the cold edge of the water.
I turned my face to the wind and the tears followed,
That night I dreamed that I lay beside her,
Clinging to her like a child to its mother.
And when I awoke the cold lay claim to my heart,
Knowing full well as I whispered her name,
I never would smile upon her sweet face again.
And well I remember the morning that I sailed . . . away.

— Ron Hynes

EXCEPT FOR AN OCCASIONAL RIDE BY HORSE and carriage in the summer and by horse and sleigh in the winter, people would have walked everywhere in those early days. Georgina, during walks with her sisters, would have revelled in every changing view of the surrounding landscape. The sisters walked occasionally from their home near St. Peter's Church on North Island to St. Andrew's Church on South Island to assist with concerts and musical and dramatic events, and also to visit friends. They walked to Wild Cove and Crow Head and even on occasion would have undertaken the long and rigorous walk to Long Point to enjoy the dramatic coastal views. The roads changed over the years from footpaths to carriage tracks, but the marvellous views remained the same. And then there were the well-worn trails over the hills to Back Harbour with its quieter waters and beautiful, restful beaches. In winter the sisters observed the coastal ice and skated and played games on its flatter surfaces. In the spring they practised the dangerous art of "copying" on ice, jumping from one pan of ice to another and sometimes even falling into the icy waters and being rescued by their friends. They saw the seals arrive on the ice in early spring and watched the men as they went out to hunt the seals and bring back juicy morsels for their dinner tables. They watched the icebergs arrive, most floating along slowly well off the coast, but many coming to shore and grounding and gradually melting as the weather warmed. They enjoyed watching a variety of coastal seabirds, and in summer the arrival of flocks of songbirds. They swam in the vigorously cool coastal waters and enjoyed the buoyancy of swimming in salt water.

The coastal beaches furnished a treasure trove of finely shaped and variegated coloured stones. Many of these were carried home to occupy a prominent place in transparent dishes on the tops of bedroom bureaus. Most Newfoundland mothers in the coastal communities (outports) of Newfoundland routinely took their children to the beaches to search for "lucky rocks" or finely shaped stones, perhaps even for heart rocks. A "lucky rock" is a rock or stone with a hole all the way through it so that a string can be pushed through and tied so the treasure can be hung in a prominent place in the house, usually in the kitchen, to "bring luck to the house." Once the practice had been taught to the children, they were often sent to the beach on occasion to find these lucky rocks. This may have been a diversion on the part of the mother so that she could have some quiet time in the midst of a busy day, but once the practice was thoroughly learned, children would initiate their own searches, delighting in returning with treasures.

There was something magical in learning such practices, a custom passed down through generations of coastal dwellers. I've grown up seeing these beach and sea treasures on display in precious family dishware on coffee tables and bureaus throughout my great-grandmother's, grandmother's, and my own mother's home. This tradition has indeed been passed down through the generations, and in my home now are my own prized possessions on display that my children and I have found along our own journeys from coast to coast. Georgina's mother, Ann Peyton, would have been taught this ritual by her own mother. I can imagine her helping her seven daughters thread their own rocks to display. These family outings to the beach deliver both a sense of accomplishment and genuine pleasure, adding a magical element to many a day and establishing a lovely family tradition.

Luckily, Georgina's voice did not fall through the cracks and go unnoticed, and the ocean waves weren't her only audience. She was born into the perfect family and setting for her unique voice to be heard across the globe. Her voice was a gift, but it was honed and delicately sharpened by many factors. Her father shared this passion and also enjoyed playing music in their home. He fostered and encouraged all of his daughters' musical talents, providing several musical instruments and voice and music training at St. Peter's Church and by several community music teachers.

Georgina was born by the edge of the sea and spent her first sixteen years breathing in its cold breezes, listening to its pleasant and harsh sounds, tasting its salty spray, and touching its exhilarating texture. The sea was alive for her because it provided her food and her transportation, triggered her dreams, and fashioned her playground. News from faraway places came regularly to her home community, because Twillingate was considered for many years "The Capital of the North," and even "The Metropolis of the North," and was a home to visiting ships from foreign lands and the site from which local ships carried their cargoes of fish and oil and berries and lumber to exotic locations.

What was Georgina like as a young girl growing up in Twillingate? Two incidents in her life reflect the daring, venturesome character of the young Georgina.

One incident involves a winter trip home from Back Harbour, where she had been visiting her Peyton cousins. She was pulling her sleigh when she reached the top of Church Hill, and she decided to ride the sleigh down the hill at top speed. As she neared the bottom of the hill, she suddenly lost control of the sleigh, and it went off the road to her left and she ended up in a snowbank by the cemetery fence. An elderly man who had been walking up the hill ran to her rescue and asked if she was hurt. "No," she replied, "but I got one hell of a flice." This was the Newfoundland way of saying that she had experienced a rough-and-tumble upset.

The second incident is described in a professionally edited but apparently unpublished paper, written in England sometime after 1896 by a woman who was visiting Paris that year, and who met Madame Mathilde Marchesi, the acclaimed voice teacher, who described Georgina's marvellous singing voice. The author describes how Georgina as a young girl, went twenty miles from land on the ice with other sealers, carrying her rope and knife, and killed her seal and towed it home. This reflects the venturesome character of Georgina at that age.

Georgina's father, Dr. William C. Stirling, was known for having a love and passion for music like his father before him, and despite his serious profession, he had a light, jovial side and a generous and compassionate heart for helping others. Georgina grew up inspired by this ex-

Georgina Stirling's voice teacher in Paris, the young Madame Mathilde Marchesi (Courtesy of Vaughn Harbin)

ample, and it set the tone for her life and for her unique brand of service to others. Dr. Stirling was the great encourager on whom his daughter had come to depend for much of the development of her early career, enabling her natural and God-given talents, pre-paving her artistic path with a confidence from the most significant man in a young girl's life—her father.

Georgina's mother, Ann Peyton Stirling, was a real society woman with a wardrobe of elegant gowns and bustle dresses of the period with hoops and ruched trimmings and lace. Georgina grew up in a home of churchgoing parents and was raised to socialize with influential people hosted in her parents' home. Georgina's parents were well-respected members of their community and were well-known for hosting lavish dinner parties and gatherings in their home as Georgina and her sisters grew up. Also present in the Stirling home were two pianos, a violin, and a flute which their father had purchased during the girls' young and impressionable years. The love of music, and also entertaining and hosting, was passed down to Georgina, for which she became well-known around Twillingate later on in her adult life. Georgina and her sisters grew up with a natural and early desire to explore and express themselves musically.

Being raised in a home where music would have commonly filled the rooms along with the sights and sounds of delicate linens, clanking monogrammed silverware on fine china, crystal glasses and the chatter of guests coming and going from the Stirling home, set the stage on many levels for Georgina. The elements of a sturdy, hard-working, no-fuss Newfoundland upbringing along with her family's cultured and musical influences provided a harmonious counterpoint in creating the traits of both the woman and artist Georgina was so well-known and adored for being.

Georgina had the talent and technique to impress an audience with operatic glory. Her treasured repertoire while growing up and on return trips home to Newfoundland was dominated by music of the heart, connection, and community. Opera is certainly a genre of music that can intimidate and overwhelm its listener at first. Besides its many foreign languages, it can come with a sense of royalty and prestige; many people might quickly judge that opera is just not for them or that it's too fancy or conservative. Some fall in love with it immediately, and some come to love it over time, gradually acquiring a taste for it. Since acquiring the taste for opera at a young age, after first being resistant, I have been passionate about bringing opera to a younger, broader audience. By discovering the wide range of repertoire, venues, and functions that Georgina performed over the course of her life, it is evident that she was also passionate about sharing her love of opera and classical music in a way that invited her audience in, welcoming and enveloping them into its majestic sounds with open arms.

Georgina was said to have "performed with poise." In getting to know Georgina and seeing photographs of her, I feel the words "poise," "grace," and "humble" best suit her demeanour and stage presence. I believe her authentic nature was felt by audiences regardless what genre of music she performed or for whom she performed it.

Georgina was a storyteller. One can learn a lot about a singer from the type of repertoire they choose. In studying the music that Georgina chose for her concert performances, it is obvious that Georgina had a strong connection and pull toward singing music that really spoke to her heart, her culture, her love of the sea, and that stirred her soul as well as the hearts and souls of her audiences—the real "tear-jerker" sort of repertoire, such as "The Holy City," "'Tis The Last Rose of Summer," or "The Murmuring Sea."

As you will soon see more intimately, the repertoire Georgina chose throughout her career were testaments to her and her humanness. She was living the life of a professional opera singer abroad and also used her skills as an opera singer technically and emotionally as a vehicle to transport her audiences no matter where she performed. The magic that an opera singer possesses can bring an audience to another place in time, to drag feelings of pain, desire, or excitement out of listeners without having to verbalize it: it comes out of them through a deep sigh of relief, a flooding of tears, a burst of laughter, or a body full of goosebumps. An opera singer can also be viewed as an enchantress, a storyteller, and a healer of sorts. Georgina was this. Indeed, it is apparent, based on reports of her performances and the way her audiences and public adored her, that this was Georgina. She was not in this profession to simply show off a fireworks type of display of operatically sung notes; if this were so, her programs of music would be full of flashy operatic arias to impress and wow her audiences. Her programs instead are mainly filled with a broad selection of arias, sacred solos, hymns, and traditional songs that all seem to have the same underlying themes and heartfelt undertones. Songs of heartache, songs of her love of the sea, songs of home, songs of pleading for forgiveness, songs of trusting in God.

A place of great significance for Georgina was her church in Twillingate, St. Peter's Church of England, one of the oldest wooden churches in the province. Walking the grounds, I felt the presence of Georgina with such majesty, with a view of the ocean and Burnt Island and a narrow dirt road that leads to its cemetery and Snelling Cove along the ocean shore. Georgina was baptized in this church; she performed often as an organist and singer, and returned regularly to this church throughout her career and life. It was in St. Peter's where

Georgina was then finally welcomed back into her Father's arms as her simple handmade wooden casket covered in white velour was carried down the aisle on April 25, 1935.

When she was about ten years of age, Georgina started music instruction with Mrs. Temple, the wife of Rev. Robert Temple of St. Peter's Church. Georgina showed great promise in her musicality but also pleasantly surprised her teacher and parents with her great singing ability, a rare gift. Adding to her sense of confidence as a young musician, beyond her sturdy upbringing surrounded by strong and confident women of purpose and a partnership with ever-changing nature and the sea, was that of playing and singing music in church throughout her childhood, while forming great bonds with the other children of her neighbourhood who grew into their teen years sharing a passion for music and often performing at various community events.

Just before Georgina turned fifteen years of age in February of 1882, she was singled out and mentioned in the *Twillingate Sun* for her remarkable singing as well as playing of the organ: "It is needless to say, that Miss Georgie Stirling, who presided at the organ, accompanied with much taste." She was playing the organ at St. Peter's Church on a frequent basis, and before long she was being asked to perform solos, to sing in duets, and to take leading roles in concerts. Georgina was listed as one of the earliest organists of St. Peter's Church before she even turned fifteen years of age. Soon she was being invited to participate at other churches in the town, to play the organ, and to perform in concert programs, fundraisers, and social gatherings. Georgina's praises were being acknowledged more and more often in the *Twillingate Sun*, and it was clear that the people of Twillingate looked forward to hearing her perform in church. Filling the church pews week after week, the press often noted people's "disappointment at not being able to procure a seat" during performances, thus beginning their great sense of pride around their Nightingale, Georgina.

Tragically, this was the same year that Georgina's mother died at fifty-nine years of age, an event that deeply saddened and impacted Georgina and her sisters. It is said that Georgina's mother never fully recovered from the drowning of her young son; such devastating events often precipitate a ripple effect that can torment and break the hearts of those left behind. These are the types of heartache that leave an internal wound that never quite heals—a wound that no one can see on the exterior but is always with us, sometimes lying dormant until triggered by a scent, a song, a sentiment. I recall my father and my aunt Lucy mentioning their younger brother, Edward, drowning in Pool's Island, Bonavista Bay. The phrase they remember, "Poor li'l Edward," rings through my mind, a phrase they would often hear their mother, my grandmother Elsie Dyke, repeating over and over to herself. In 1935, Edward was five years old. He drowned in a cove about two hundred feet from their house in only about three feet of water. Aunt Lucy said she had never heard her mother or father talk about it, but one statement she remembers her mother saying often was, "If it wasn't for Aunt Lizzie, I would never have made it." My father remembers his mother telling him that she saw her husband down in Squid Cove standing on a rock next to their house and heard him shouting out to God, "You gave him to me, now why did You take him from me?" They never knew their oldest brother, Edward, but they feel strongly that he was always a part of their lives, known to each one of them as "Poor l'il Edward."

Georgina would have been only about seven years old when her brother William died of typhoid fever at the age of ten. Her younger brother, Peyton, tragically drowned when he was a toddler, when Georgina was about nine years of age. At such a vulnerable time in a child's life, to experience such tragedies as these first-hand, also seeing her mother suffer from such great loss and depression, would most likely have caused her to internalize these experiences and use these great sorrows to fuel her own musicianship, being the compassionate and empathetic soul and musician she was. It is for this reason, I believe, that she had such an emotional impact on her audiences whenever she performed, often bringing people to tears not only with her music but with her generous heart and willingness to connect on such an authentic level. In an effort to identify with Georgina and the thoughts and feelings she must have had and struggled with, I reaffirmed in myself that I have viewed the traumas in my own life as the prerequisite for my purpose and sense of duty and of service as a singer.

Within about three months after Georgina's mother had died, in mid-fall of 1882, Georgina left her beloved home of Twillingate and travelled to Toronto, Ontario, to begin a two-and-a-half-year program of intensive training in voice, advanced organ instruction, and other musical studies, as well as involvement in a variety of other academic subjects. Having recently lost her mother, leaving home and family and friends, and adapting to a foreign environment, must have been very difficult for a fifteen-and-a-half-year-old. In Toronto she did vocal studies under the direction of Carl Martens, a graduate of the Royal Conservatory of Music in Lepsic (Leipzig), Germany, and singing lessons under Mrs. Bradley, and other studies which were supervised by Mrs. Jessie Murray, the coordinator of Georgina's studies. Studying music and fine arts in a more formal setting gave Georgina a whole new confidence in her performance and in the technical aspects of music theory and history. In fact, in March of 1883, while Georgina was studying, she persuaded her sister Kate to provide money to purchase a ticket to see the famous Swedish soprano Christina Nilsson perform in concert at the Horticultural Gardens of Toronto. Kate wrote to her father hoping he would not object to such a "luxury." In the book *Golden Thoughts at Ingleside* by Hattie M. Perkins Leland, this very concert was reviewed, expressing how much the audience was enchanted by Christina Nilsson's performance, saying, "but it is in the wonderful pathos and bird-like purity. . . . The great Nilsson is not only full of all womanly sympathies, but combines a full round of the rarest musical gifts as well—and one listens to this peerless songstress whose voice combines majestic power and melodious full-ness—a tenderness and sympathy of tone which thrills and captivates all hearts—an exquisite sweetness and pathos which demonstrates that it is a noble, true hearted woman that is singing . . ." Georgina told Kate after the performance that she could never have imagined such music coming from a human being. This is a true expression of appreciation from an aspiring singer, and Kate confirms later, in a letter to her father after she had made a visit to Toronto in 1885, that "he would be very much surprised to hear her (Georgina) sing." She writes, "I had no idea she had such a beautiful voice." It seems that Georgina's studies of piano, organ, and music had come to encompass her studying of voice to a much grander extent. Perhaps Georgina, after hearing the possibility of what heights she could achieve with her own talents, embraced this desire inside herself to an even greater extent.

When Georgina returned home to Twillingate after just a couple of years, she was warm-ly greeted as a more mature musician. No time was wasted in putting Georgina's talents and abilities to good use, and Georgina was encouraged to take a teaching position for a Sunday school about three miles from her home, in Crow Head. She was loved by the children of her Sunday school, and this would have been a first glimpse of Georgina's inspiring the love of sacred music and hymns in the young children she taught and guided both before embarking on an international career and upon her final return to Twillingate, and immersing herself again in her community. Georgina would go on to prove that she possessed a voice that was deserving of international acclaim, but never did she forget from where it came and never did she put herself on a pedestal above others.

An acknowledgement of the musical maturity that Georgina displayed after her return to Twillingate from studies in Toronto was the comment in the *Twillingate Sun* in early 1888: "It would be invidious were we to attempt to praise any one singer more than another, where each did their part so well, but we may be excused if we make mention of Miss Georgie Stir-ling who seemed to actuate the whole, and whose talents as vocalist, accompanist or prompt-er were in requisition the whole evening . . ." Georgina had achieved a mature level in musical accomplishment and leadership which the entire community gladly acknowledged.

Being born and raised in Twillingate established in Georgina a humble and family-oriented nature, a meaningful and strong base of education for a budding musical career, gratitude for the simple joys in life, a healthy respect and relationship to the ocean, and she would spend a great deal of time crossing the oceans of the world, and the forming of a hearty and affectionate personality, paired with the voice of an angel, that would take the world by storm, having them fall in love with her one performance after another. The unique magic that Newfoundland, but most particularly Twillingate, possesses had been instilled within the heart and soul of Georgina, and she would carry this magic across the ocean to share with and influence the world.

CHAPTER SIX
BY CALVIN D. EVANS

GEORGINA OFF TO EUROPE
—HER CAREER IS LAUNCHED

WHEN GEORGINA AND ROSE LEFT ST. JOHN'S on November 17, 1888, arriving at Liverpool about ten days later by steamship, where did they go from there? It has generally been understood that Georgina went directly to Paris, France, but that is not so. Newly gathered evidence makes it clear that Georgina travelled directly to Italy and spent the first two years there, studying, as one writer puts it, "under the greatest professors of the age," before moving about two years later to Paris to study under the acclaimed Madame Mathilde Marchesi.

In addition to what was written at the end of the previous chapter, let us review the evidence for the "Italy first – Paris second" case. Henry James Morgan in the first edition of his book *Canadian Men and Women of the Time* writes that Georgina "received her musical education in Italy, and *afterwards* (italics mine) studied French opera in Paris, where she made her debut in 1893, eliciting high encomiums from the musical critics." Morgan's first edition of the book was published in 1898 when Georgina was at the very height of her career and is more likely to be accurate than later sources. In the second edition of his book, published in 1912, Morgan changes his wording thus: "Georgina studied for her profession in France, under Mad. Marchesi, and in Italy, made her debut in grand opera, Paris, 1893." While the wording is not a direct contradiction of what Morgan said in 1898, it does give that impression. It is of interest also that although Newfoundland did not become a province of Canada until 1949, Morgan includes Georgina as a Canadian in both the first edition of his book in 1898 and in the second edition published in 1912.

Edward B. Moogk, writing of Georgina in his 1975 book *Roll Back the Years*, states that Georgina's father "sent her to study singing in France and Italy," thus reversing the order that Henry James Morgan had given in 1898. Moogk appears to be much more casual in his brief assessment of Georgina, so one would more likely accept Morgan's order of things in his first edition.

Despite what Amy Louise Peyton has written about Madame Marchesi's school of music in Paris, she was unable to place Georgina specifically among the thirty pupils who were being schooled there between 1888 and 1891. The "singing engagement in Italy" to which Amy Louise refers on page 74 seems to have been a continuation of, or more likely a result of, her studies in Italy, rather than the result of the audition of May 29, 1890, mentioned on page 73. There is no connection made between the two events. What Amy Louise conjectures as Georgina's return to Paris "to resume her studies with Madame Marchesi for the year 1891–92" was undoubtedly her beginning with Madame Marchesi (page 76), and the *Twillingate Sun*'s reference (page 77) on April 2, 1892, to Georgina's upcoming "second appearance in the operatic world" was very probably a reference to her intended debut in 1893. Curiously, however, the *Theatrical Whip* of

Milan, Italy, was quoted in the *Weekly Record* of St. John's, Newfoundland, on September 13, 1890, as saying that Georgina was "new to Italy, but . . . has sung with much success in various foreign theatres . . . possesses a magnificent voice and sings with much feeling. The managers were fortunate in securing her for their theatre to sing the important part of Azucena for the coming season." This comment seems to imply that Georgina was training elsewhere in Europe (but likely not in France, or certainly not with Madame Marchesi)—or possibly elsewhere in Italy but unknown at the time to the writer.

The fact that writers have accepted the sequence of events suggested in Amy Louise Peyton's book has given rise to some extravagant statements such as Paul Butler's in the *Evening Telegram* of October 16, 2004: "By late fall (1888) she (Georgina) was wandering the boulevards of Paris with their lively Renoir bustle." It would be almost three years before Georgina wandered these boulevards. It is important to establish the correct sequence of events.

The "coming season" referred to earlier must have covered 1890–91, since Roger Neill in his book

Georgina and her sister Rose in Florence, Italy, 1889 or 1890 (Courtesy Bruce Manuel and Brent English)

Divas: Mathilde Marchesi and Her Pupils writes: "Georgina is said to have made her debut as Azucena in *Il trovatore* in Milan in 1891." In the appendices of his book, however, Neill gives estimated start dates for the various students at the École Marchesi in Paris, and the date given for "Marie Toulinguet (Georgina Ann Stirling, sometime Twillingate Stirling, Canadian sop)" is given as 1889. "Sop" is, of course, the abbreviation for soprano. It cannot be determined how Neill settled on this date, but a note is added: "all dates are *estimated start dates.*" (italics mine). Neill sometimes gives the impression of being casual in his comments, as well as dismissive in his judgments on many of Marchesi's pupils, so that date might just as easily be 1891, since he mentions no source. As elsewhere in his book, especially in the section on Georgina Stirling, he obviously follows the timeline suggested by Amy Louise Peyton.

Classroom at École Marchesi in Paris where Georgina Stirling took voice training
(www.voice-talk.net)

Roger Neill also states that when Georgina returned to Europe following her visit to Twillingate and St. John's in 1892, she went not to Paris but to Florence, where she "continued her vocal studies . . . with Luigi Vannuccini, and by 1895 she was in London studying with

Charles Santley and appearing in occasional concerts, including one in the Queen's Hall for the benefit of the Carmelite Church in Kensington. The following April (1896?) she sang in a Santley Concert at the Leinster Hall in Dublin." Neill offers no sources for these statements. Dublin was the home of Georgina's friend, Marie du Bedat.

Neill doesn't seem to realize that he is contradicting himself with the assertion that Georgina is "estimated" to have begun her studies with Madame Marchesi in 1889 and the counter-assertion that "Returned to Europe (after the summer of 1892 in Newfoundland), she *continued* her vocal studies in Florence with Luigi Vannuccini . . ." So here the facts begin to emerge with the certainty that Georgina spent about two years in Florence, Italy, doing vocal studies with Luigi Vannuccini and only then (very probably in 1891) began studies with Madame Mathilde Marchesi.

Georgina and Rose would have arrived in Florence in late 1888, perhaps just before Christmas. They sailed from St. John's on November 17, 1888, on the vessel *Peruvian* and would have arrived at Liverpool, England, about November 28 if they had a smooth cross-

ing. They may even have spent some time in England, perhaps even Christmas, and then would have crossed the English Channel and travelled by steam railroad lines to Florence, Italy. They would not have done much shopping in Liverpool, as one might expect, because these were penurious young women, responsible spenders, as Georgina's letters to her father clearly indicate.

Georgina's studies with Vannuccini would presumably have begun at the very beginning of 1889 and lasted through to late 1890.

Thanks to a serendipitous moment in the life of a very perceptive real estate agent in St. John's, Chris O'Dea, in September 2018, we now have the proof from Georgina's own pen that she and her sister Rose went to Florence, Italy, in late 1888. Chris O'Dea is the husband of Mar-

Georgina Stirling at Russel and Sons studio in London, England, sometime between 1893 to 1896 (Stirling family)

garet (Baird) O'Dea, who is the daughter of Elmo and Eleanor Baird, whose interview (in 2018, by me) appears in Appendix Six of this book under the section entitled "Witness of Georgina's Cousins." While dealing with a client, Karen Stirling, who lives in both St. John's and the United States, and who wished to sell some of her Newfoundland property, Chris mentioned that he and his wife had just returned from Twillingate, where they attended an operatic concert to honour Georgina Stirling, and learned that the opera singer who staged the concert and her grandfather were writing a new book about Georgina. Then Chris posed the question: Are you possibly related to that Stirling family? She *is* related, and during that conversation she stated that she had copies of letters which Georgina and her sisters had written to their father, Dr. William Stirling in Twillingate, and would you be interested in seeing these and possibly passing them on to the people who are writing the new book about Georgina? Chris *was* interested, and this is how the letters came to us. These letters were discovered in Washington, DC, in 1976. The letters include three which were written by Georgina from Florence, Italy, in December 1889 and February and March 1890. In Florence, Georgina was sharing an apartment with her sister Rose and pursuing her vocal studies with the famous Italian teacher Luigi Vannuccini.

The letters from five of the Stirling sisters, along with a few other documents, were sent to the Stirling family in Newfoundland when the man who had found them in 1976 discovered a website that the Stirling family had mounted several years previously. The documents were faithfully indexed and catalogued, and Chris O'Dea and Karen Stirling shared them with us in October 2018. We are enormously grateful to these generous people for sharing this material with us, and we share only relevant excerpts in this book.

There are no letters from sister Susan (Stirling) Temple among the documents found in Washington, DC, and none from Kate (Stirling) Putzki. It appears that a member of the Putzki family had carefully preserved this amazing collection of Kate's many letters dating from 1881 through to 1889, understandably with many gaps and then a few letters dating from 1938, regarding the settlement of affairs connected with the Stirling house and estate at Twillingate, and it is from this incredible collection that Jeff Golden has graciously been sharing with us excerpts that fill many gaps, correct many earlier-drawn false conclusions, and help us to establish a reliable trail of events during those crucial years. Until she was about seventy-eight years of age, Kate faithfully returned to Twillingate to visit her sisters, Georgina and Rose, and provided financial assistance to Rose in the later stages.

Letter from Georgina to her sister Janet in London, England. Most likely written in the summer of 1891, and following her incredibly successful audition with the acclaimed voice teacher Madame Mathilde Marchesi in Paris (Courtesy of Archives and Special Collections, Memorial Libraries)

This material found in Washington, DC, in 1976 was almost certainly brought from Twillingate in 1938 by Kate (Stirling) Putzki, when she and her daughter-in-law, Eleanor Putzki, wife of Dr. Paul Putzki, visited the Stirling home following the death of Rose Stirling in November 1937. How sad and difficult it must have been for Kate to make that final visit! She was now the last surviving sister of the Stirling clan. The elegant Stirling house was full of memories for her, and she would have wept silently as she sorted through old letters, documents, and keepsakes that had lovingly been preserved. She carried much of it back to her home in Washington, DC. And we, today, are the beneficiaries of her wise action.

As a direct result of finding these letters, we have confirmed a conclusion we had drawn earlier, and of which we are now certain, pertaining to the sequence of Georgina's vocal training in Europe—about two years or so with Vannuccini in Florence, then to England, where she engages briefly in the concert circuit, then to Paris for two years of study with Madame Marchesi, and then back to England, where she studies with Charles Santley and becomes more heavily engaged in the concert scene.

Jeff Golden, Kate (Stirling) Putzki's great-grandson, and Maymie (Roberts) Hewlett, Twillingate, 1983. Note Maymie's piano, which she played frequently for Georgina to sing. (Courtesy of Jeff Golden)

What a beautiful, tender, thoughtful letter Georgina writes in December 1889 to her father, who is now ill at Twillingate, and being cared for by his daughter Janet. How he must have delighted to receive such a heart-expressive communication from this special daughter! Her long letter begins with her strong statement about the political situation in Newfoundland, the treatment of "our poor fishermen," then she shares details about her voice training with Vannuccini, draws a musical notation showing the range of her present voice compass, assures her father that she and Rose are spending their money wisely and carefully, talks about Rose's drawing lessons, compares the Italian winter weather with that in Newfoundland, and comments on their learning to play card games with the locals, which she disdainfully dismisses as playing for money, "and there is no <u>play</u> in them."

Georgina's well-balanced character shines through in this letter; she pours out her heart to her beloved "Papa," reassures him on every subject, shows her fierce spirit when she comments on the poor treatment of animals for whom she has the greatest sympathy, and informs him that they will soon move to more comfortable lodgings in a house closer to town.

Georgina's sister Janet is obviously at home in Twillingate at the time of the first letter, where, as Georgina suggests, she could explain the musical notation to her father. It is virtually certain that this letter is simply missing a line or two, since the connecting theme between this and what seems to be a partial separate letter could be the card-playing and the winning of "several pennies."

Notice in this letter Georgina's use of the Shakespearean word "dear" to mean expensive, and her use of the word "find" to mean providing for themselves. This was a typical use of these words in Newfoundland at that time.

See Tonia Evans Cianciulli's Chapter Seven under subheading "Georgina's Training and Repertoire with Luigi Vannuccini" for a full transcript of the first part of Georgina's first letter from Florence.

The second letter, dated February 28, 1890, is short, and she apologizes to "My dear Papa" for not writing because she has "hardly had time to eat and drink, practicing for so many concerts," and says that she lightens the atmosphere at her rehearsals by "telling funny stories, etc." She then tells her father that "My son Cosimo (her cat) sends his love." She had referred to Cosimo in the first letter as "she," but it is almost certainly the same cat.

Georgina's third letter is longer, and it deals mostly with her participation in many concerts, having to sing with an orchestra for the first time, sharing her large bouquets of flowers with her friends after each performance, her master's plan to send her to Milan to study dramatic, and her intended debut "*in the autumn, I believe in Milan.*" (italics mine) She closes the letter with "much love to all my sons. . . . My Italian son is in the country for a week." She was remembering her cats back in Twillingate, and a friend in the country had obviously volunteered to look after Cosimo for a week, perhaps because of Georgina's busy schedule.

This third letter, written on March 28, 1890, almost certainly did not reach Dr. Stirling before his death on April 10 of the same year. *See Appendix Four: Transcripts of the Conclusion of Georgina's First Letter and the Two Last Letters from Florence, Italy, 1889–90.*

AMONG THE LETTERS FOUND IN WASHINGTON, DC, in 1976, there are five letters from Eleanor (Stirling) Winsor to her father, and two letters from her husband, Reverend A. S. H. Winsor, to Dr. Stirling, but these are inconsequential for our purposes since they deal mostly with parish matters in Manitoba and Minnesota, with occasional mention of correspondence received from the Stirling sisters, and Dr. Stirling's decision to give the power of attorney to his daughter Eleanor in November 1889. Amy Louise Peyton indicates that the Winsors had three children, a son and two daughters, so it is curious that in these letters there is no mention of any children.

There are three letters from Janet Stirling among the "find" of materials. The first is dated September 13, 1887, and begins with an inquiry as to whether Georgina and her "dear Papa" have arrived back in Twillingate from the three-month trip the three of them had taken to the neighbouring provinces. Janet had now been in Chicago for three weeks, and it is not possible to determine whether this is her first visit or simply the first time she has met Paul Putzki, Kate's husband. It is very probably her first visit to Chicago. Kate and Paul had been married in March 1886. Janet comments thus to her father about Kate's husband: "I find Paul a very fine man, as kind and good to Kate as can be . . . his industry and perseverance knows no bounds, he never loses a minute, and as Kate is of the same mind, they are pretty sure to rise and not fall . . . life runs smoothly with them." Janet informs her father that she has not yet found "a situation," and Kate and Paul want her to spend at least a month with them before she begins to look for work. She writes further, "I am sure I shall succeed as well as many others when I do try; females working for themselves here is so utterly different from an English place." Janet has learned through her sister Eleanor's letter that their eldest sister, Lucy, is in Saint Pierre with another sister, Susan Temple, "though it is no more than I expected." The tragically jilted sister cannot seem to settle anywhere.

The reference to "an English place" may seem curious. From a reference in Kate Stirling's letter of March 1, 1883, a light is shed on this phrase. When she was interviewed for an office job with Mr. Dean, he realized that she was not an American, and Kate responded, "No, I suppose you would call me English as I live in an English colony." Newfoundland was Great Britain's oldest colony, and there was still considerable pride attached to that reality for most Newfoundlanders.

The second letter is dated October 26, 1887, begins with "My dear Papa," and deals at some length with the difficulty of finding work in Chicago. She has obviously not yet completed her nurse's training, so this means that she did not do so at the Toronto General Hospital during the years that Georgina was doing vocal studies there. Neither does her calendar in Chicago for 1887 to 1889 allow for time to complete nurse's training there, which points to later nursing studies in England.

In this second letter, Janet states that she had placed advertisements in the paper and was following up on these. She notes, "As my experiences are few, my looks and manners have to go a long way." This seems to mean that she was seeking general work.

In her letter, Janet then inquires about Georgina. "How is Georgie's arm and side, Papa, and does she complain of the worries? Now? Look after her well Papa, she is the baby, you know, and let her have all the innocent amusements she can, trouble will come soon enough. Kate joins with me in love and kind Regards to all especially Mrs. Hodge. Yours affectionately, Janet." Since we do not have a response from Dr. Stirling, we do not know the nature of Georgina's ailment. The words with question marks were impossible to decipher. Was the injury that Georgina had sustained related, I wonder, to the prior sealing season? That was the year for which the "ladies seal cap" had been purchased.

Janet's third letter from Chicago is dated December 31, 1888, and Dr. Stirling's notation on the letter reads: "Recd Feb. 8, 1888 & answered Feb. 9." This letter is an example of a responsible daughter "taking her father to task" for his misunderstanding of Janet's intention for inviting Lucy to move to Chicago to be with her and Kate, and friction in the home at Twillingate between the two sisters, Lucy and Rose, and the father's frustration in how to deal with it.

By this time, Janet is working, as a housekeeper and companion, with "an old gentleman 'Canadian' James Kerby Esq . . . a man of large means . . . his business is on the Board of Trade," and whose wife and daughter have died and whose son had to be placed in an insane asylum. She calls him "a very sad man."

Then Janet launches carefully but firmly into a kind but very forthright check on her father. I think she and her sister Kate were the only daughters who might dare to do so, and these two are not ordinary young women. Janet writes: "Now then Papa for a word or two on your last letter dated November 30th which reached me a week ago. I am sorry you do not see the sensibility of my reasoning as regards Lucy, when I wrote that letter encouraging Lucy to come to Chicago. It was done in answer to a very miserable lesson of ??? and before I had had the trial or (of?) being an American housekeeper which I find simply means a general servant. In fact, you are asked if you can do the washing and ??? as a rule. From such degradation I wished to save Lucy after my experience. (This must have referred to Janet's previous job, CDE). I am younger and can better put up with that sort of treatment than she, and if I offered to do the work and let the allowance that <u>you give me</u> for dress go towards her support at Susie's (their sister Susan, at Burin, CDE)—the least—I think you could have done was to supply the extra ten or fifteen pounds. I understand that my dress money is 20 pounds a year and I am very well sure that Sus would not have asked more than thirty or thirty-five pounds for her board at the most which would have been only ten or fifteen pounds more. I did not say <u>under the circumstances</u> that Dr. Stirling's home was the proper place for his eldest daughter. I think quite the opposite; and I cannot help what expense you have been to, on account of other members of the families (family's?) bad conduct. You never had to do anything of the kind for me and I don't expect Papa that ever you will, since I have been here I have never wasted time or money in doing nothing. I tried over and over again for nearly five months to get employment and only as, you see, succeeded within the past two weeks . . . when I wrote that letter to Lucy, I could not see (say?) should Lucy go where we could both stay while we were finding situations, and <u>I have said so</u> And <u>will end the subject by saying so again</u>, that if Lucy and Rose cannot live together peaceably & Lucy has to go, it is your duty as her father with ample means to do so, to support her where she can be comfortable and not send her out to work. I should say my doing so is sufficient. I am sorry Papa if I have again made you angry with me. Nothing but duty and consideration would make me write as I do."

Janet closes her letter with general comments about other family members and friends and promises her father that she will send more papers (newspapers) for his perusal, and then, "I shall be careful as regards postage in the future." He seems to be a generous but demanding parent. She had begun her letter with "My Dear Father." She now signs it "Your loving child, Janet." Contrast that with the opening and closing of her first letter—she is a brave soul.

What could possibly have been meant by "other members of the family's bad conduct"? Surely not one of the seven daughters, at this early stage! Perhaps it was a member (members?) of his extended family to whose financial rescue Dr. Stirling may have come. See the next paragraph in connection with one of Lucy's letters from Saint Pierre for a possible explanation of Janet's anger or frustration with a family member.

We have discovered two letters that Lucy Stirling had written from Saint Pierre to her father, Dr. Stirling, one dated October 30, 1887, and the other on November 28, 1887. These letters shed light on the reason why Janet had "taken her father to task." In the first letter, Lucy asks her father for money "to pay my passage to Chicago" because she has concluded from correspondence with Janet that work was available there and Janet has started a new job even though she has "not had time to give it a fair trial." It seems that Lucy should have waited until Janet had concluded "a fair trial," because Janet soon informs her that the work would be too hard for a woman of Lucy's age. Lucy then writes very strictly to her father: "Please after reading this do not be angry nor please do not discuss contents with such a one at St. John's, Rose Stirling." When I first read that harsh sentence, I thought that perhaps Lucy was speaking of her sister Rose, but on reflection I think not. There is, in fact, a letter from Rose Cheyne Stirling of St. John's, who had visited her uncle, Dr. Stirling, at Twillingate and on January 4,

Georgina Stirling, taken at Duxhurst Colony Farm, Surrey, England (Stirling family)

1888, wrote him a letter about her sea voyage and thanked him for his kindness to her. Was the "kindness" a gift of money to finance her sea voyage, and something to which both Lucy and Janet took strong exception in view of the legitimate needs of his own daughters?

Lucy's letter of November 28, 1887, acknowledges receipt of her father's cheque for $200 but notes that she has received another letter from Janet discouraging her from coming to Chicago at present, that her father's cheque will be returned, that she will "follow Janet's directions to the letter," and that she has enough of her own money to return home to Twillingate for the winter should that be necessary.

I mention these facts about Janet and Lucy because these are the two sisters who later located to London, England, and were available to and supportive of Georgina in the years of her greatest need. Lucy, the sister who was broken from having been jilted on her wedding day, was "mothered" by Janet into years of productive work at the nursing home in London, and the two of them together ministered to Georgina on her return from Milan in 1901, and

Janet then moved with Georgina to the Duxhurst Colony as a nurse in late 1905 or early 1906 and probably stayed with her until the death of Lady Somerset in March 1921. Janet then returned to the nursing station for a while and moved to an apartment in Surrey after her retirement.

FROM GEORGINA'S THIRD LETTER WE KNOW that she was being sent to Milan in May 1890 to study dramatic. A letter from Rose in Florence dated in error April 11, 1889—the year should be 1890, as we shall see presently—provides more detail. Rose states, "Vannuccini has decided for us to go to Milan for 3 months, as he says Georgina must take Dramatic lessons from a master he knows there; there is no master for Dramatic in Florence like there is in Milan and he says every good renowned singer always studies Dramatic there, so of course must she also. Vannuccini will be going to London about the same time for 3 months as he did last summer. The journey from here to Milan is not far, you can go in a day and it does not cost much."

Rose reports on Georgina's progress: "Georgie is getting on well with her studies. Her master Vannuccini is very pleased with her progress and says she is going to be a good artist. She has done wonders the last few months. She sang at a sacred concert on Wednesday, it was given in one of the churches for the benefit of the (blind) and it was crowded, and they were very pleased with her voice and some of the best judges of music were there, indeed they liked it so much that it is to be repeated again next week. She sang the (contralto) solos, and another of Vannuccini's pupils sang the (soprano) but she had studied with him for 4 years and Georgie has not been for more than 18 months with him, and yet they all say that Georgie did the best. She will send you one of the programs and one of the papers that were posted up all over the city with her name printed on it."

The reference to the eighteen months is important in establishing that the date on the letter should be 1890 and not 1889. November 1888 to April 1890 would have covered the eighteen-month period.

Rose continues: "I think she is more pleased with her success for your sake than her own, for she always says to me, 'Won't Papa be proud of me someday.'" Then Rose informs her father of the military and the cavalry bands in the city and reminds him that he was always "so fond of hearing a good band . . . because you used to talk so much of the bands you used to hear in Scotland."

Georgina curtsies before the Royal boxes during what some sources say was her performance before the Italian Royal Family, possibly in Milan (Courtesy of Sylvia Ficken, Newfoundland artist, 1981)

Rose closes her letter with this paragraph: "Georgie is going to write Janet a few lines also. She studies so much that she has not much time for anything else. I do all the marketing, cooking, etc. I have learnt enough Italian for that and still do a little drawing. I shall soon send you another sample of my drawing and painting."

The very sad reflection about this letter is that it would never reach Dr. Stirling. He died the day before Rose wrote her letter.

IT IS FITTING AT THIS POINT to share the information from the *Twillingate Sun* about Dr. Stirling's death at Twillingate and his provision through his Last Will and Testament for his seven daughters.

On April 12, 1890, the *Twillingate Sun* reported Dr. Stirling's death. "We sincerely regret to announce the death of our highly esteemed and deeply lamented friend W. Stirling Esq.

MD which occurred on Thursday April 10th inst. at his residence, North Side. Though very weak and feeble for a considerable length of time, yet his decease was rather unexpected and sudden. His end was emphatically peace—no suffering—no pain—but a gentle falling asleep. We understand that Dr. Stirling was in his 74th year, and on the whole has been remarkable for a healthy constitution, and freedom from any sickness of a serious nature . . . we respectfully offer our sincere sympathy to the relatives of the deceased."

A promised longer eulogy appeared in the *Sun* on April 19, 1890. He was buried on Sunday the 11th inst. at St. Peter's Cemetery, "attended by the largest concourse of the inhabitants it has ever been our lot to witness in Twillingate." The eulogy justly and fairly pays homage to a rare man who literally gave his life for the people of Twillingate and area for forty-seven years. He did not just practise medicine. He practised healing and caring and compassion amongst a people who loved and respected him, and he had returned that favour in kind.

Dr. Stirling's Last Will and Testament provided generously for his seven daughters. The document had been drawn up on May 14, 1889. The four-page, beautifully handwritten Last Will was the work of the local stipendiary magistrate, Francis Berteau. Dr. Stirling named his unmarried daughters as Lucinda Stirling, Rosetta E. C. Stirling, Janet M. Stirling, and Georgina A. Stirling. The married daughters were named as Susannah P. Temple, Eleanor E. Winsor, and Kate S. Putzki. The three married daughters inherited $200 annually and their father's professional testimonials and selections of their choice from his extensive library. The four unmarried daughters were also to receive $200 annually as well as his lands, dwelling, and contents, including his medical library and surgical effects. Dr. Stirling had large investments in the Tilt Cove copper mines and other mines in that area, in mining properties near Springdale, as well as investments in the Dominion of Canada (and possibly in gold mines in Nova Scotia), and in the United States through his son-in-law, Reverend Alfred E. S. Winsor, who was living in the United States in the 1880s.

Dr. Stirling owned properties on both North Island and South Island in Twillingate. There is a reference to Thomas Peyton conducting a survey of property on South Island in 1906 on Georgina Stirling's behalf and handwriting her name on the document. Kate (Stirling) Putzki also sold a piece of property in Twillingate in order to provide financial assistance to her sister Rose; this was almost certainly after Rose returned from England in early 1914 and more likely later, perhaps after Georgina had died. Dr. Stirling had purchased property in Wild Cove, and it is believed that he owned other properties in Twillingate. He also owned a considerable number of properties in St. John's. The Stirling family in Newfoundland have reported that after Dr. Stirling realized some good financial returns from his mining endeavours, he began to purchase and resell properties in the St. John's area, particularly in what at that time would have been regarded as the suburbs. He also acquired several pieces of property in the Quidi Vidi Lake area.

Dr. Stirling, Jr., had also been named as the executor of his father's Last Will and Testament written on December 24, 1857—Dr. Stirling, Sr., died on August 11, 1858. Maymie (Roberts) Hewlett stated in one of her interviews in 1969 that, as late as 1967, she had received a letter from a lawyer who was settling the Stirling estate and wished to know if any members of the family were still living. At that point, the last of the Stirling sisters had died, Kate (Stirling) Putzki—and perhaps her family members inherited what remained of the estate. This, as well as the testimonies of local residents, would seem to contradict the assertion that the Stirling sisters of Twillingate were living in poverty in their last days. The sisters may have been at times "cash poor," but they continued to receive money from some sources, as Maymie testified (she kept Georgina's accounts and did her banking).

The two sisters, Georgina and Rose, appear to have wanted to keep things in the house as they had always been; therein was their security. Georgina was recorded as having given away "a lot of things, beautiful things." They were raised to be careful with money, and they demonstrated this on a daily basis—except for Rose's propensity to feed her cats the very best of meats in the later days. There were many people in Twillingate who maintained that the people of the community would not have countenanced the Stirling sisters being in want. Many of the servant helpers worked without pay, asked for none and expected none.

Dr. Stirling would have estimated the likely average lifespan of his daughters in assessing the annual amounts to be assigned, and it must be considered that he felt that the income from his considerable investments would provide for their needs as long as they lived. He also had the benefit of knowing how much it had cost to support his unmarried daughters in getting their education or their start in life from about 1880 to the time of his death in 1890.

One can appreciate the financial burden which Dr. Stirling carried with four unmarried daughters and their growing needs. Maymie (Roberts) Hewlett had stated that Dr. Stirling had allotted a special amount to Lucy because of her heartbreaking experience of having been jilted on her planned wedding day, and it was reported that she "lived in luxury" in the old Stirling home when she returned from England in 1904 and until her death in 1913. Rose may have been the most financially independent because of revenue from her teaching jobs, and Georgina assures her father in one of her letters from Florence that they are being very careful about spending the money he has given them, and that Rose is "spending her own money to buy her art/drawing supplies." Yet Lucy, Rose, and Janet appear to have lived at home in the Stirling house until 1887 and 1888 respectively, when they were aged forty, thirty-six, and twenty-eight. Janet refers in her letter from Chicago in 1887 to an allowance for "dress" that her father gives her and suggests that he can take that and give it to Lucy to pay her "board" at their sister Susan's in Saint Pierre. Georgina's two and a half years of study in Toronto would have been a substantial expense on her father, and then there were the additional years of study in Florence and Paris and England. By the latter years, of course, Georgina would at last be earning money. Dr. Stirling was a wise man and a generous father, and it was only through his considerable investments that he was able to attend to the substantial needs of his four single daughters. Security for the three other daughters was in their marriages, and Dr. Stirling's further generosity was evident through his Last Will and Testament.

A curious matter occurs in Dr. Stirling's Last Will and Testament. Georgina's name is first recorded as Georgina A. Stirling, and following this it is written twice as Georgiana A. Stirling. One can only assume that it was an error on the part of the magistrate, who would have been accustomed to hearing the name Georgie. In other records, Georgina's name is recorded as Georgina, Georgina A., and Georgina Ann. The latter is almost certainly the accurate form of her name. The records of St. Peter's Church were destroyed in the fire at the rectory in 1913, so we cannot be absolutely sure how her name was recorded in the baptismal register. It is worthy of note that John Peyton, Jr., had a sister in England whose name was Susan Georgianna Peyton; in that case the name was spelled with a double "n."

Now we can return to Georgina's and Rose's letters from Florence, Italy.

WE KNOW ALSO FROM GEORGINA'S THIRD LETTER that her grand debut was being planned for the autumn of 1890, and she believed at that point that it would be in Milan. From the *Weekly Record* of St. John's, Newfoundland, which was quoting the *Theatrical Whip* of Milan for August 12, 1890, we know that Georgina had secured a position with an unnamed theatre in Milan for "the coming season," which would have taken her into the spring of 1891. Curiously, the *Theatrical Whip* of Milan had stated that Georgina "was new to Italy." She was most likely new to the writer.

Georgina would likely have made her first trip back to England from Italy probably in the late spring or early summer of 1891, and Rose would have stayed on in Italy, by this time being located in Naples, employed as "a governess," very likely with families of the nobility. We will provide more details on this later.

Henry James Morgan writes in his 1898 first edition that Georgina was "now a member of the Grand Italian Opera Concert Co." An Internet search did not identify any specific information about this organization, but it is known that Grand Opera emerged in Italy in the first half of the nineteenth century, being dominated by composers such as Rossini, Donizetti, and Bellini and replacing the very conservative attitude in previous Italian opera.

WHY WOULD GEORGINA have gone to Florence for voice training? It is doubtful that Dr. Stirling would have known specifically about Madame Marchesi in Paris and would have been looking for a suitable venue for his talented daughter to pursue her voice studies. Dr. Stirling would have been acquainted with young Philip Anstey of Twillingate. Philip Anstey was Georgina's schoolmate at Twillingate; he "had been abroad" (very likely to Italy) sometime after graduating from high school, returned to Twillingate, and married his sweetheart, who died shortly afterwards in the same year (1897), after which Philip went to (or returned to) Italy and is reputed by his family "to have sung before Royalty." Philip's was one of the male voices about which Georgina had rhapsodized to her best friend, Maymie Roberts, after her return to Twillingate in 1929. Philip's family members claim that he was in Italy during the years that Georgina was there, 1897 to 1901. We will learn more about Philip Anstey later in the book.

As referred to earlier, John W. Cowan of Hillsboro, New Brunswick, also strongly encouraged Dr. Stirling to send Georgina to Italy after he had heard her sing during the summer of 1887. He wrote to Dr. Stirling of her "rare gift" and stated that she is an "artist."

It seems that the most likely reason why Georgina went to Florence for advanced vocal training is that she may have been recommended by Carl Martens, her music teacher during her two and a half years in Toronto. In Georgina's 1889 letter to her father from Florence she twice mentions Mrs. Murray, who seems to have been Carl Martens's coordinator of music studies and other academic studies for Georgina. She was now writing to Georgina every two weeks, giving her good practical advice about the kinds and costs of living accommodations, and sending her copies of Toronto newspapers. Mrs. Murray was an encourager for Georgina.

Georgina returns to England, very probably in the spring of 1891, following two years of vocal training with Vannuccini and an extended "singing engagement" in Milan. In England, she engages in the concert circuit with Charles Santley and Narciso Vert for some time and is then encouraged to go to Paris to audition before the acclaimed voice teacher Madame Mathilde Marchesi.

The occasion for Georgina's undated letter from Paris to her sister Janet was her just-completed audition with Madame Mathilde Marchesi. Madame Marchesi had stated to Georgina following the audition, "Yours is a voice the world is waiting for and you will be a great, great woman." Georgina's effusive reception by Madame Marchesi is expressed excitedly in the letter to her sister. The letter was most probably written sometime in mid-1891. A reference was made in the letter to Dr. Stirling being dead. He died on April 10, 1890. *See Tonia Evans Cianciulli's Chapter Eight for a full transcript of Georgina's letter to her sister Janet regarding the audition with Madame Marchesi.*

THE DOCUMENT THAT WE HAVE CALLED a "printed edited manuscript" was found in the Memorial University of Newfoundland Archives in August 2018. This document is printed on one long page, has sixty-eight lines, and bears the marks of a professional editor in both left and right margins, with a note at the top left side stating "rough proof. Portrait." The printed title at the top is "Miss Georgina Stirling." It was obviously written to be published in a journal or newspaper, and meant to recognize and praise the vocal talents of this accomplished young woman from Twillingate. The manuscript clearly states that Georgina went directly to Florence, Italy, for vocal studies.

This short "printed edited manuscript" was written sometime after 1895, in which year Georgina's medical advisers in England had recommended "a six weeks' rest and a trip somewhere," according to the *Evening Telegram*. She had evidently "overtaxed her powers." Not unexpectedly, she elected to return to Newfoundland and take a rest at Twillingate. She arrived toward the end of July and did not leave for England until early October. At St. John's in October, she participated in a series of concerts, all for charitable causes, giving at least eighteen concerts in a sixteen-day period, culminating in a Grand Farewell Concert on October

4. Coming off a six-week rest, this undoubtedly overtaxed her powers yet again. Neither the St. John's audiences, eager to welcome their sweet songstress, nor Georgina, herself, demonstrated wisdom in maintaining such a frenzied calendar of events. Georgina could not say no to the burgeoning requests.

The "printed edited manuscript" refers to this period incorrectly as "a six month rest" and states that after her return to England she "once more fell ill." There is no corroborating evidence of this second period of illness, but, if it happened, it was probably as a result of exhaustion from the St. John's marathon.

The writer of this "printed edited manuscript" would have had to be a person with considerable knowledge of and familiarity with the world of opera and music who had a particular fascination with the person of Georgina Stirling, having done the research which ranges from Italy to France to England and Germany and then to Newfoundland. The writer obviously had access to Madame Mathilde Marchesi, the world-renowned operatic teacher, who may have supplied much of the biographical material about Georgina. The writer enjoyed a facility in French and conversed in that language with Madame Marchesi and knew about Georgina's two years of vocal training in Florence, and her debut there at the Opera House in Borgo. *See Appendix Five for a transcript of the "Printed Edited Manuscript."*

ALL EFFORTS TO DETERMINE WHEN JANET STIRLING located to London, England, to begin her nursing practice had ended in uncertainty until a chance search of the Internet provided the answer. We had assumed that she did her nursing training either in Toronto, when Georgina was studying there in 1883 to 1885, or in Chicago, when she was living there from 1887 to 1889. This was not so. As early as September 1884, Kate had suggested in a letter to her father, "Let Jan go to visit the Sheppards in England." This was the well-to-do English family with whom Kate had lived in Betts Cove, Newfoundland, at the mining site in 1881, and who kept in contact with her after she moved to Chicago in early 1883, by which time they appear to have returned to England. Janet may have visited the Sheppards sometime in 1885 or 1886, but that is just a supposition. She lived and worked in Chicago from mid-1887 to June 1889, when she returned to Twillingate to care for her dying father. Sometime after Dr. Stirling died on April 10, 1890, Janet went to England. Amy Louise Peyton suggests that it was "around 1890." We know from the England and Wales Census of 1891 that Janet was a visitor at the home of the Sheppards in Ibstock, Leicestershire County. We have been unable to determine what kind of work she was doing in England, but after having worked for at least two and a half years in Chicago, it is most likely that she was gainfully employed in England.

Now we have discovered, with the help of Professor Lynn McDonald, a Florence Nightingale specialist at the University of Guelph in Ontario, an entry in the London Metropolitan Archives for Janet Stirling, which reads as follows:

"Janet Stirling, age 31, on entry to the Nightingale School in 1896, a special probationer, paid 52 pounds sterling (they received extra training and did less work), was Sister of the Female Operating Theatre in 1899, left to begin nursing home, and then worked for the Queen Victoria Jubilee Nurses; described in the Probationer's Register as a colonial from New Brunswick. In 1899, Nightingale was notified that Miss Stirling was on the sick list. Nightingale saw her probationer's diary in 1896 . . . she routinely looked at these but no information that they met."

Some of this is Professor McDonald's interpretation of abbreviations and acronyms which we found in a Names List published by J. Abbott of the University of Guelph several years ago. There is at least one error in the entry, and there could be more. Janet was not a colonial from New Brunswick, as we already know. We have authenticated her birth year as 1861, so she would have been thirty-one in 1892. J. Abbott's Names List says that Janet was thirty-five in 1898, but she would have been thirty-five in 1896. So there still is some uncertainty about when Janet entered nursing studies at the Nightingale Training School and Home for Nurses, which was part of St. Thomas' Hospital, one of London's most famous hospitals, and which was located directly across the River Thames from the Palace of Westminster.

Janet would have entered the Nightingale Training School with possibly two and a half years of home care experience in Chicago, possibly six months of experience caring for her dying father at Twillingate, and possibly between two and four years of work experience in England. As a "special probationer" she paid a fee, indicating that she was from a prosperous background.

The England and Wales Census for 1901 lists Janet Stirling as head of the household at 14 Bulstrode Street, Cavendish Street, London West, which was the location of her nursing home. It gives her age as thirty-five, which is incorrect; she was forty. They "estimated" her birth year incorrectly as 1866. Lucy was listed at age fifty, but she would have been fifty-four. Janet had a second nurse on staff who also lived at this address. She was Eleanor G. Perry, aged thirty-two, and also a graduate of the Nightingale Training School and Home for Nurses. She had left the training school in 1901 to do private nursing at "Soho Square." This must have been when Janet hired her to work at 14 Bulstrode Street. Janet maintained this address until at least 1923, which is probably about the time when she retired.

Janet's facility at 14 Bulstrode Street is variously called in the records a "nursing station" and a "surgical home." One source called it "a fashionable nursing home on Harley Street, London," and another characterized it as "a convalescent home for unwed mothers." Yet another source referred to Janet as "a Nursing Sister who worked in London for more than thirty years." At some point, Janet arranged for sister Lucy to join her from Chicago, where she had been working. This sister, who had been so broken by being jilted on her planned wedding day, was "mothered" into several years of productive work as the housekeeping matron of Janet's nursing home. In the summer of 1901, Lucy wrote to Georgina in Milan, noting on her postcard, "Four patients in now and another coming tonight with a doctor from Harley Street to attend him." It is affirmed that Harley Street physicians regularly visited the nursing station. It was to this facility that Georgina came for rest and recuperation in the fall of 1901.

Thought to be Janet Stirling, Georgina's sister, at her graduation from Nursing School in London, England (Stirling family)

One question remains: How could a young "colonial" woman have afforded to do nursing training at one of London's most famous hospitals and then, within a few years of graduation, set up a nursing station in the heart of London, near the prestigious Harley Street, and hold it for almost thirty years? Janet would have used the inheritance from her father's Last Will to pay the fee required from those who could afford it, but I expect the generosity of the Sheppard family once again came to the aid of another Stirling sister in helping Janet to establish her nursing station. Mrs. Sheppard was from Scotland, and the fact that Dr. Stirling had done his medical studies at the University of Edinburgh would likely have given Mrs. Sheppard a sympathetic connection with the Stirling sisters as well as a desire to assist Janet financially. She may also have helped to finance Georgina's vocal training with Madame Marchesi in Paris, since Georgina wrote her a letter of thanks following the very successful audition with Madame Marchesi.

TO RETURN TO GEORGINA'S RAPIDLY DEVELOPING CAREER. In late June 1892, Georgina and her sister Janet sailed to Newfoundland and stayed until fall, Georgina participating in concerts both at Twillingate and St, John's, in order to provide aid and assistance to many of the people who had been devastated by the Great Fire of July 1892 at St. John's.

Georgina returns to England in the fall of 1892 and, soon after, travels to Paris to continue her studies at École Marchesi. She completes her studies through the next season, makes her debut in Paris in 1893, and returns to England. She makes yet another brief visit to Newfoundland in the summer of 1893, returns to England to re-engage in the concert circuit, travels to Germany to do a series of concerts there, and possibly to do more vocal training, and then returns to England, again to the concert scene. Details are scarce during this period, but she re-engages with Charles Santley and Narciso Vert and expands her field with other managers and sponsors.

It is probable that Georgina began voice studies with Charles Santley soon after her return to England following her debut in Paris in 1893, and the period of study may have continued through 1894 and even into 1895–96. If so, it is most likely that the voice studies and the appearances on the concert circuit overlapped. The "printed edited manuscript" indicates that after Georgina had completed her studies with Madame Marchesi and made her Paris debut in 1893, she "sang for Vert and Santley." It was apparently during this period that she visited Germany. We have few other details of her activity in 1893 and 1894. Amy Louise Peyton's book reflects this lack of detail, though she states on page 85, "During the next summer of 1893, Miss Georgie visited Newfoundland again and performed at the Methodist College Hall in St. John's." Georgina did not again visit Newfoundland until the summer of 1895.

Charles Santley was a British opera and oratorio star and was considered, in his time, to be the most accomplished male concert singer. He trained in vocal studies in Milan under Gaetano Nava from 1855 to 1857, making his debut in Milan in the latter year, and then returning to London, where he had an eminent twenty-year career in opera and oratorio before concentrating on the concert circuit from the 1870s onwards. Santley thus became Georgina's third voice teacher, after Luigi Vannuccini and Mathilde Marchesi—her fourth teacher, if we consider Carl Martens and Mrs. Bradley, as we should. Georgina continued to do concerts in England for Santley and also for the leading agent in London, Narciso Vert. Vert was a famous concert manager and agent in London and was described by author Christopher Fifield as "A Veritable Napoleon of Managers" who sponsored "a high-quality stable of artists including some of the most famous and able musicians."

According to the *Morning Post* of London, Georgina sang at a concert for the Carmelite Church in the Queen's Hall on May 29, 1895, with Charles Santley and five other artists. The Queen's Hall was the principal concert venue in London and seated 2,500 people. She is known to have sung also in London at Mademoiselle Pozzio's matinee on June 27, 1895. In that same month she sang at Henry Richard Bird's concert at Kensington Town Hall. On July 3 she appeared at Signor Tito Mattei's concert at the Queen's Hall. These were somewhat lesser lights in the concert management world, except for Signor Mattei, who was a distinguished concert manager and a popular pianist, presenting his concerts at the Queen's Hall, the Queen's Concert Rooms, and Hanover Square. His concerts were noted as being "presented under the most distinguished patronage of Signor Tito Mattei."

Georgina must have left London immediately after these concerts for her 1895 visit to Newfoundland with her sister Janet. On her return to London from Newfoundland in 1895, Vert offered her "no less than three engagements for oratorio" which, it is said, she was unable to accept. This was occasioned by the second bout of illness referred to above in the words she "once more fell ill," and was almost certainly connected with exhaustion from the eighteen concerts she presented at St. John's in a sixteen-day period.

During late March and early April of 1896, the *Freeman's Journal* of Dublin, Ireland, states that "Miss Georgina Stirling, Soprano" was present at a Grand Afternoon in aid of a Charitable Purpose. It was noted that she "kindly volunteered" her services for the concert, and that Mr. Santley and Miss Kathryne Tennien, contralto, were singers at the concert. On April 8, 1896, the concert at the Leinster Hall in Dublin was covered more fully and named "Miss Georgina Stirling (soprano) who is a native of Newfoundland" as the first artist of the concert.

On April 28, 1896, Georgina "made her first London appearance at the Portman Rooms at Mr. Santley's concert. This function was a huge success. Miss Stirling made a great impression on the public, and as a result she has secured a multiplicity of engagements for the next four seasons." This comment may refer to Georgina's acceptance of a two-year engagement with the New Imperial Opera Company in New York under the direction of Colonel J. Henry Mapleson, because Mapleson was directly involved in the opera scene in England and was undoubtedly recruiting for his new company while on his way back from an extended visit to Italy.

It may be useful at this point to do a brief summary of the contents of the "printed edited manuscript" in order to trace Georgina's activities. It is difficult to keep the calendar straight and accurate on the events referred to in the manuscript. This is what I propose as a timeline: Georgina goes to Italy in the late fall of 1888; she studies voice with Luigi Vannuccini in Florence from 1889 to 1890 and makes her debut there at Borgo in the autumn of 1890 (or in June 1891); she does an engagement in Milan, which takes her through to the spring of 1891; she then returns to London, where her sisters Janet and Lucy are living and working; the three women referred to in Georgina's undated letter from Paris to her sister Janet in London collaborate to arrange an audition for Georgina with Madame Marchesi; Georgina goes to Paris probably in the summer of 1891, accompanied by two of the women, for the audition; the audition with "the greatest teacher in the world" is a stunning success, and Georgina is accepted for the initial thirteen-month training period at the École Marchesi.

The "printed edited manuscript" begins with the words: "In 1892, where we were in Paris, Madame Marchesi, a celebrated teacher of singing, directed our attention to a charming young lady who had just finished her lesson. . . . The young lady of whom she spoke was Miss Georgina Stirling." This scenario also fits with the date of her Paris debut in 1893.

Another significant insight from the manuscript: Of the three women who played a key role in Georgina's trip from London to Paris for the audition with Madame Marchesi—Mrs. Parish, Miss Hadley, and Mrs. Sheppard—only Mrs. Parish and Miss Hadley accompanied Georgina to Paris. Miss Hadley went to the audition with Georgina because Mrs. Parish had become ill. When the successful audition was reported to Mrs. Parish, she immediately offered to finance a second year of studies for Georgina with Madame Marchesi after the initial thirteen months were concluded. Mrs. Parish was obviously the lady in charge as well as being a lady of considerable means. A third lady, Mrs. Sheppard, also seems to have played a role in setting up the audition, because Georgina in her letter to Janet states that "I am going to write Mrs. Sheppard a nice letter of thanks tomorrow. Please tell her all."

Catherine C. M. Sheppard, whom we met earlier, had been a friend of Kate Stirling since 1881, and became a staunch friend of Janet Stirling through Kate's encouragement. Janet may have visited the Sheppards in England prior to the beginning of her nurse's training there in 1890. Janet was visiting them when the England and Wales Census was taken in 1891. The Sheppard family lived at Church End, Ibstock, in Leicestershire County. By 1901, Janet's nursing home was located at 14 Bulstrode Street in London, but the friendship between Mrs. Sheppard and Janet Stirling was a firm and lasting one, and Mrs. Sheppard appears to have played a significant role in setting up Georgina's audition with Madame Marchesi and, perhaps, arranging for Mrs. Parish and Miss Hadley to accompany Georgina to Paris.

Georgina had stated in her undated letter to her sister Janet that at her audition with Madame Marchesi: "Now Mme Melba the great Australian singer was there listening . . . Melba came forward and shook me by the hand and told me I had a grand, grand future before me. She also said the same to Miss H."

In the "printed edited manuscript" the writer states, "Madame Melba has proved a most kind friend throughout the whole of Miss Stirling's career, and Miss Stirling is particularly grateful for the interest thus taken in her."

The writer of this manuscript was an enthusiastic promoter of Georgina's vocal gifts and talents. Witness this quote after Georgina's successful performances at Charles Santley's concert at the Portman Rooms: "This was the more gratifying as Miss Stirling at this concert was a stranger in a strange land relying solely on her vocal abilities, and with not a friend present in the audience to give her countenance. She deserves success, for she is a plucky woman to come among us to try her chances."

Then the writer ends the manuscript with a daring recommendation for others to invite Georgina to perform at their functions. "We have heard that Miss Stirling accepts engagements for 'At Homes,' concerts, etc. If this be so we have no doubt her services will be constantly in requisition. Those who desire a successful 'At Home' could not fail to achieve society distinction for themselves if they secured the services of this most accomplished singer. She is equally proficient in Italian, French or English . . ."

The writer was obviously an English person, proficient also in French, familiar with Paris, with easy access to Madame Marchesi, involved in the music and opera scene in London, and eager to promote the career of the rising young opera star, Georgina Stirling.

CHAPTER SEVEN
BY TONIA EVANS CIANCIULLI

GEORGINA'S EARLY VOCAL TRAINING, BEHIND THE SCENES

"Technique is the basis of every pursuit. If you're a sportsman, or you're a singer . . .
you have to develop a basic technique to know what you're doing at any given time."
— Joan Sutherland, Australian Soprano (1926–2010)

AS AN OPERA SINGER, I'D LIKE to invite you behind the scenes of vocal pedagogy to give you a small glimpse of Georgina's world. Singing is a journey of mastery as well as a journey of self-discovery. It's a spiritual process of peeling back the layers and "getting out of your own way." It's making a commitment to yourself to become a lifelong student of an art form that lives and breathes through you. The voice of a singer grows with them along the course of their life. It expands, matures, and is fed by the emotional depth of their life, deepening in vocal richness. In his book *The Naked Voice: A Wholistic Approach to Singing*, Stephen Smith explains an Italian phrase, "*Come va il canto, come va la vita*" (as singing goes, so goes life). A singer can become subjected to the strong opinions of many teachers, colleagues, coaches, and conductors. It's the responsibility of a singer to take this advice, feedback, education, and training into consideration, and to sing what feels true and safe for their voice. It's a gift to treasure and protect. Some days it feels like a gift, and on other days it can feel like a curse. Unless one is a singer, one can never fully grasp the strings that come attached to having this gift. There comes a great responsibility in being a singer to nurture their voice physically, technically, and emotionally. The training is largely technical. It's also an art that has psychological dimensions.

Receiving a strong and solid basis for vocal technique is important for any singer who is going to have a serious career, most especially for that of an opera singer. It is the foundation on which everything else is built. A singer who does not take vocal training seriously may be able to achieve some level of success based on pure talent. If not properly developed, over time this star potential can quickly fade, and the singers who were once riding the coattails of their competitors could very well pass them based on dedication, consistency, and integrity.

Talent is important when it comes to singing, but it must be followed up with an attitude and dedication similar to that of any serious athlete. Singing is very much considered athletic in nature, and just like any sport or practice, consistency and building a solid base are major components. Just like an athlete must have warm muscles to run a race or skate a competition, a singer must also warm up her/his vocal equipment. Even at a level of enjoying sports for fun or going to the gym to exercise for overall health, the body must be warm to avoid injury. Someone who sets out with a goal to run a marathon, half-marathon, or even a five-kilometre run would not be expected to "just do it." A runner would set out on a concise plan to work up to the goal. Everything has its order and duration of time for which to practise before moving on. And if runners or athletes were to take a break in their training, they would experience a challenge in rebuilding to where they had left off; a singer will experience this exact same obstacle.

All good singing teachers will start their students with beginner's exercises, scales, and manageable repertoire for their appropriate level. Just as a runner would not start out running a full marathon, young singers will not start out singing or performing repertoire that is beyond their initial skill and maturity level. Just as one runner's body may be built to run long and steady distances and another runner's body may be built for fast and short sprints, some singers are meant to sing fast, high, and flexible repertoire, and some are more suited to heavier and slower repertoire. When singers first start studying with a new teacher, they are assessed by that teacher throughout a series of exercises. They'll sing through a few options of repertoire to get to know where their voice comfortably sits, what habits they may have already developed, and what technical ability they may already poses. Depending on the age and development, the teacher can assess the type of voice they might develop into long-term.

An opera singer's vocal range and classification is referred to as "fach." The word is pronounced by rhyming it with the name of the classical composer Bach. This German-originated system classifies our exact vocal type according to the colour of our voice, the range and weight, and so on. Some singers can sit between vocal fachs, giving them a broader range of repertoire. A voice type can certainly change over the course of one's career and can become more flexible and agile with proper training. It can deepen and expand with age and maturity. Women can especially notice a change throughout pregnancy and after childbirth with the expansion of their rib cages, for example, and just becoming more in tune with their body during a time of great change.

The major voice classifications, from highest to lowest, are: soprano, mezzo-soprano, contralto, countertenor, tenor, baritone, and bass. Singers become known by their particular voice type. Opera companies keep an updated list of which fach current singers fall under for casting various roles each season. For the most part, it is important for singers to stay within this voice type to prevent overextending their voice within a role that might be too demanding on their unique vocal makeup. Unfortunately, some companies might depend on a singer to perform roles and repertoire they may not be ready to sing. This was a lot more common in the era Georgina was performing, thus increasing the risk of damaging a singer's voice before it has had the chance to naturally mature. Based on the information we have been able to recover, we will soon see a bigger picture of Georgina's vocal instruction, range, and repertoire as filled in from what we now know about her studies, performance, and from her personal letters.

The first time I sang for my uncle Brian, he had the sense that my voice was meant for classical music and that I would be a soprano. It was then up to my voice teacher to professionally assess my vocal range, type and level of ability. During my first classical voice lesson with Judy Harmsworth, she had me warm up with simple scales and breathing exercises and then had me sing through a few simple things to get an idea of my level and musicality. Thinking back to how green and naive I was, makes me laugh. That's was why I was there, to be trained. Mrs. Harmsworth told me I needed to be prepared to sing age-appropriate repertoire and to be patient with the voice and, above all else, to learn how to breathe properly to support and project the voice without forcing the sound. We started with the Royal Conservatory graded repertoire and the Schirmer's Library of Musical Classics: *Twenty-Four Italian Songs and Arias of the Seventeenth and Eighteenth Centuries*. The songs in this book were by such composers as Bonnocini, Gluck, Geordani, Scarlatti, Monteverdi, etc. This was the very first book of songs that my Uncle Brian gifted me. Inside the cover Brian wrote: "*Tonia, you have the ability to fulfill your dream as well as mine. Love, Uncle Brian xo.*" He put little pencil check marks next to his favourite songs he wanted me to sing. The first one was "Caro mio ben" by Giordani. He played for me Luciano Pavarotti's version from *The Pavarotti Collection* CD, released in 1986. Goosebumps! Classical singers of Georgina's time started singing this type of music as well; appropriate songs composed and compiled to introduce singers into the world of classical and opera in a healthy and elegant way.

GEORGINA'S TRAINING AND REPERTOIRE
WITH LUIGI VANNUCCINI

"A bird is born with that voice and he never tries to push it, otherwise he loses it."
— Luciano Pavarotti, Italian Tenor (1935–2007)

GEORGINA'S VOCAL TRAINING started in St. Peter's Church in her hometown of Twillingate. She expanded this training during her early studies in Toronto, but Europe was where Georgina was immersed in a serious study of vocal pedagogy.

Georgina's first taste of formal operatic training began in Florence, Italy, in 1891, with a well-respected and well-known teacher, Luigi Vannuccini. Italy was the birthplace of opera and the home of many renowned classical and opera composers. In fact, Vannuccini was close friends with the famous composer Rossini. What was thrilling about training and performing in Italy and across Europe in those days was that many of these composers were premiering their famous works, often for specific celebrity singers of the day. Georgina had her first peek into the historical bel canto technique by the great master, Vannuccini.

During almost two years of study with Luigi Vannuccini, from the beginning of 1889 to the end of 1890, Georgina began to lay the foundation from which to launch her European training, studies, and performing. Vannuccini came from a family with a rich classical and operatic history, influencing his own performance and training of students. He started his training with his own father, Ernesto Vannuccini, who had been a voice teacher of the great soprano Adelina Patti. Luigi Vannuccini was experienced in directing operas from his work between 1848 and 1873 in the Theatre of La Pergola, schooling great singers. He composed sacred music and was a concert pianist. He also held a diploma in violin from the Conservatory in Florence. Vannuccini, according to Wikipedia, "published a collection of *Solfeggi* taken from the best Italian vocal tradition." *Solfeggi* is a musical term to describe a method of singing on specific syllables in order to help first learn a melody, also known as sight-singing, or to syllables on which to sing vocal exercises. This is an important skill for singers to have so that they can learn music without the assistance of a piano or someone singing the melody for them. Georgina would have been required to learn and master this skill while she studied with Vannuccini. This and her natural piano and organ skills would have assisted her in learning music at a rapid rate.

Studying with an accomplished singing teacher and someone as influential as Vannuccini, Georgina would have established a good foundation and had valuable exposure and experience. Vannuccini's violin training would have also been an element of expression in training as a wonderful instrument for the singer to try and emulate. I have often been told in voice lessons by a number of teachers to imagine the legato line of a violin with the bow remaining in smooth contact with the strings. Another helpful analogy of the violin is the resonant sound that it produces. As a singer, this resonance comes from the vibration within our mouth and nasal cavities. If we are properly "placing" the tone, we get a vibrant quality that carries out over the piano or orchestra to our audience. As singers we can feel this resonance in our face and head, a sort of "spinning of sound," if you will. A lot of singing is psychological and metaphorical, but by thinking of a particular instrument or by the gesture of a fluttering hand, we can produce the sound we're aiming to achieve. Without this resonance, the sound is flat and does not carry. The vibration of sound adds richness and fullness to the tone. As stated in an article on Luigi Vannuccini by voice-talk.net on June 30, 2010, one of Vannuccini's American students and "an influential pedagogue who interviewed leading European teachers of the period," Frederick W. Root, wrote of him: "Vannuccini's method was very simple and consisted mainly in keeping the pupil's attention directed to the region of the eye and the nose in forming tones."

In a column from Werner's *Voice Magazine* published in September 1890, on page 238, an "American student in Florence, Italy" (giving no name), writes of his experience with Vannuccini, coincidentally during the same year that Georgina was studying with him. The article is titled "Avoid Vannuccini" and outlines his experience with Vannuccini, having gone to see him for problems with "vocal strain from long misuse." This student wanted to "begin at the beginning with a master. I had heard much of Sig. Vannuccini and decided he was the man I needed." The American student gives some explanation on his lesson routine in the article: "At the first lesson I sang a few scales and sustained notes, then he gave me a song for next time." He continues to explain his frustration. "I studied hard upon the song, expecting that we should get to work in earnest at the next lesson. But the next lesson was the same—a few scales, the old song, then a new one. And so it always was, new songs on new songs; one which I had sung much at home, though never to my satisfaction, was tossed aside as 'much too easy for you now,' and in a month I was ready to begin opera. My lesson now consisted of ten minutes of scales and fifty of opera, if, indeed, my voice did not give out before, and many a time I have left his room hardly able to utter a sound. This was his method. My voice was strained and needed careful treatment. He had me sing without a rest for an entire hour from the first lesson. I did not know how to produce my tone properly; with practically no instruction he put me on the most difficult music. Before I could sing a scale with comfort, to say nothing of grace, I was ready to sing opera and have him say 'bravo,' and compliment my rapid progress. Then he put me in a concert to sing a piece, at the end of which I was always exhausted, and said, 'you can sing it so easily there is no need for you to try it with me.'" The student remarks that he had been told, "None but foreigners ever study with him, the Italians never." Finding it "strange that the natives didn't care to avail themselves of their 'greatest,'" he had "met other students, former pupils who had been with him for three months, six months, a year, two years, and had found at last, with anger and grief as I now did, that they had been throwing their money away, or worse, buying positive injury."

Reading this pupil's submission, I can sense his frustration. The best musicians and performers do not always make the best teachers, and vice versa. Also, one teacher's approach might work magic for one singer and not be successful at all for another. Because everyone explains and understands in their own unique ways, voice teachers are not one size fits all. In speaking to a number of singers and teachers, one could be met with absolute confusion, because two singers who produce a similar result can have different mental images and technical instructions taking place in their minds on how to successfully achieve their desired results.

Had Georgina's experience with Vannuccini been similar to that of the American student? Obviously we cannot judge how qualified a teacher Vannuccini was based on one student's experience, and the research on Vannuccini is limited in comparison to the wealth of information there is on Georgina's next teacher, Madame Mathilde Marchesi. I wonder how much guided voice training Georgina was receiving in comparison to learning and performing the substantial operatic repertoire she was singing at the young age of twenty-two to twenty-three. Performing frequently in operas and concerts, some with orchestra, would have been a big demand on her voice at that young age.

Based on letters Georgina wrote to her father, she spent a great deal of time practising on her own. In a letter on December 1, 1889, she makes reference to being "nearly finished the opera of Don Sebastiano & after repeating it, will commence a new one." She also writes that she would be "unfit for any kind of society. I have got so used to the solitude now that I never wish to speak to anyone outside of our own gates. I would be in splendid training now to make a nun."

In a letter of February 28, 1890, Georgina apologizes for not writing in such a long time, and then writes "for the last month and a half I have had hardly time to eat and drink, practicing for so many concerts. . . . On Sunday I am singing in another concert—this time the Coutralls—all the people compliment me & tell me I have a most beautiful voice & with more study will become a great artist. . . . I have two practises & one lesson this evening so have only time to say good bye with much love to all. Georgie." One month later, on March 28, 1890, she mentions more concerts in which she is singing, one in particular for the "Violinista Torricelli" (a female child prodigy concert violinist who was known as Metaura Torricelli-Pente, 1867–1893, she "concertized to great acclaim in both the U.S., including New York and Boston, and in Europe, including three performances in Russia as a soloist with the St. Petersburg Philharmonic."). (www.vialibri.net) "I also sang pretty well that night, but was not very well, so did not do as well as I should have done." Then she writes, "The week after next I sing at another concert & next week 'Holy Week' I sing the Contralto solos in a Stabat Mater to be given in the Spanish Chapel of Santa Maria Novella. Then I shall sing for the first time with an orchestra. I do not know how I shall get on I am sure because singing with fifty or sixty instruments is quite different to singing with a piano or organ."

The Stabat Mater was set to music by a number of composers, some of which include Palestrina, Vivaldi, Domenico, Scarlatti, Pergolesi, and Rossini. "The title comes from its first line, Stabat Mater dolorosa, which means 'the sorrowful mother was standing.'" (Wikipedia) "It is a 13th-century Latin poem exploring the sorrows of the Virgin Mary as she watched her son Jesus dying on the cross." (www.medium.com 1000 Years of Classical Music, July 4, 2016) It is not known which Stabat Mater Georgina performed. Pergolesi's Stabat Mater, written in 1736, which is an extremely popular one, is approximately forty-two minutes long and is written for soprano and contralto, violin I and violin II, viola and basso continuo, which consists of cello and organ. It's an incredibly moving body of work that Pergolesi wrote when he was dying of tuberculosis at the young age of twenty-six years, taking the listener on a very moving and poignant journey. The Stabat Mater starts with a duet between soprano and contralto and then moves throughout with alternating solos and duets between the two singers.

We are fortunate to have this particular letter of Georgina's to her Papa. Her letters show such personality, her dedication, passion, and commitment to her studies. As a singer, I was especially excited to see her outlining her progress and vocal range to her father. The sketching illustrates her broad vocal range from the G (G3) below middle C to a high D above the staff (D6).

Villa Piagga (sic Piaggia)
Via Castelle
Rosso San Gerevasio
Florence Italy
Dec 1st 1889

My dear Pa
I must now commence a long letter for your delectation. I am very glad indeed to see by the Montreal papers that the Thorburn party are defeated. My feelings are entirely with the fishermen, for really when you visit other countries and see how the working classes are treated it makes the blood boil to think of our poor fishermen, "who work harder I believe than any men under the sun" being subject to the rule of

> *(page 2)*

a few men whose policy is to make money out of the people and spend it in some other country. Even here where people are so poor, no master would dare swear at his men, if he did probably before next day he would have a knife in his heart. Today is Sunday, but not a very cheerful one; wind is blowing hard, and the mountains are covered with snow. I was so cold practising in the salon that Rose and I brought out the piano in the kitchen, it being warmer on account of the little fires for cooking. It looks so funny to see the piano out here amongst the pots and pans. My cat (Cosimo) very often lies in my lap whilst I am practicing, when

> *(page 3)*

I sing pretty quietly and not so high she does not mind but when I take a <u>very high</u> note (such as this) she jumps up and sticks her head as far as she can in my mouth, to see what has gone wrong down my throat. I never saw anything so funny. I am now nearly finished the opera of Don Sebastiano & after repeating it, will commence a new one. The compass of my voice now is nearly three octaves. If you do not understand Janet will explain. We have only 19 more days to stay in this dreadfully cold house, when we shall move a little farther in town, which will be better in every

> *(page 4)*

respect. I am sure living like we do so far from our fellow creatures makes me one & stupid and unfit for any kind of society. I have got so used to the solitude now that I never wish to speak to anyone outside of our own gates. I would be in splendid training now to make a nun. Nowadays a great thing in a singer's success is, to make herself agreeable and liked, if you cannot do that, it does not matter how well you sing, you will never gain a footing with the public. As you advise me I keep always in mind the fact that there is but a short time before wherein to complete my studies.

(page 5)

Honestly I try to do my best but I know the sum of money you give me, is a large slice out of your income, but as soon as I commence to earn I will pay back every cent. Remember Mrs. Murray said it would cost no more for Rose & I to live in rooms & find ourselves than for me to live in a Pensione at six francs or one dollar & 20 cts a day, which is the cheapest you could possibly get & would come to eight dollars & forty cts. a week. That amount Rose and I live on, sometimes it may be a shilling more or less. Rose takes two drawing lessons a week for which she pays two shillings (of course out of her own money),

(page 6)

then there are brushes, pencils, paper & rubber to buy, these things are not dear here, compared to England & America but still drawing materials are expensive everywhere. I consider she draws very well, considering she never did any before. The people of the villa often remark how much better in health she looks, & realy (sic) to me she looks ten years younger & has a splendid appetite which never varies indeed. I must say we both enjoy excellent health & spirits very seldom having any disagreements which last longer than five or ten minutes. Dec 4th. Yesterday evening I went to my lesson at Vannuccieu's ? it was his sixty first birthday.

(page 7)

I wish you could have seen the magnificent show of flowers in his room, sent by his various pupils & friends. One very large basket made of gilt wicker work, & filled with the rarest flowers I admired very much, it stood as high as our dining room mantle piece at home, the handle also being covered with flowers. Mrs. Murray writes me every two weeks also sending paper from Toronto, what a good kind woman she is & never forgets a promise. She tells me she has written to Jan asking her to try & get a boy & send her. I should think there are many boys in TGate who would be glad of the chance, they would have a good home & kind master & mistress. By this time you are

(page 8)

no doubt getting on into the middle of winter. Here tonight, it is blowing as <u>hard</u> as I ever heard it do at home. Am sorry to hear Mrs. Berteau is so ill, would not total change of scene put her right again? I hope by this time you have received your violin strings & find their answer?, remember they are a complete set, first, second, third & fourth string. I can easily send you some more if they are not the right kind. Dec 5th. Last night we spent the evening at the big villa & amused ourselves by playing a game of cards, called twenty-one, can't say it was interesting, all their games are just meant to play for money, there is no <u>play</u> in them. Rose & I both

Note: The letter ends abruptly on page 8 in the middle of a sentence. For an explanation, see Appendix Four, which contains what we now believe is the continuation of this letter, and for full transcripts of Georgina's other two letters from Florence.

DURING THE TWO YEARS THAT GEORGINA was studying with Vannuccini, she sang a lot of contralto repertoire and heavier, dramatic roles that would not be recommended for a young singer. There is great danger of damaging and shortening the lifespan of a voice when a singer is performing repertoire they are not vocally mature enough for or causes them to continuously strain. Renowned Canadian tenor Richard Margison explains this well in an interview with *Vancouver Classical Music*: "There are a lot of young tenors who are possibly seduced into major roles by their glamour, and are now facing crisis in their careers. I am certain that they try to move into big roles too fast. This is the one problem with the art form today: everyone wants a visual with young attractive singers in the big roles, but this does not square with how long it takes to build up the infrastructure to perform these roles. . . . I think the voice is like a great red wine; it must spend years in the cask before it actually matures. Opera is an art form, is about voice, and not about stunningly beautiful young people with ultimately short vocal careers."

Stephen Smith, in *The Naked Voice*, uses Maria Callas as an example in his chapter on vocal fach. When addressing a singer's audition repertoire, Smith writes, "Consider the following scenario: A woman comes into an audition and lists the following arias—The Habanera from *Carmen*, 'Vissi d'arte' from *Tosca* and 'Je suis Titania' from *Mignon*. The judges will likely think she has a multiple personality disorder and has no idea who she really is. Carmen is a sultry, dramatic mezzo role, Tosca is a fiery, dramatic soprano, and the *Mignon* aria is sung by a coquettish high coloratura. All three roles represent completely different fachs, and no one would imagine the same person singing all three appropriately." Maria Callas was a thrilling singer to witness. Her versatility in repertoire, character conviction, and fierce passion on and off stage made her one of the most famous divas of all time. In an article called "Maria Callas: Voice of Perfect Imperfection" (www.npr.org), published February 15, 2010, Lynn Neary explains, "Callas' ability to sing such a wide range of roles was one of the things that led to her meteoric rise. But critic Conrad Osborne says it also contained the seeds of her vocal decline. Callas' voice was already starting to fail her by the time she was in her 40's—quite young for an opera singer."

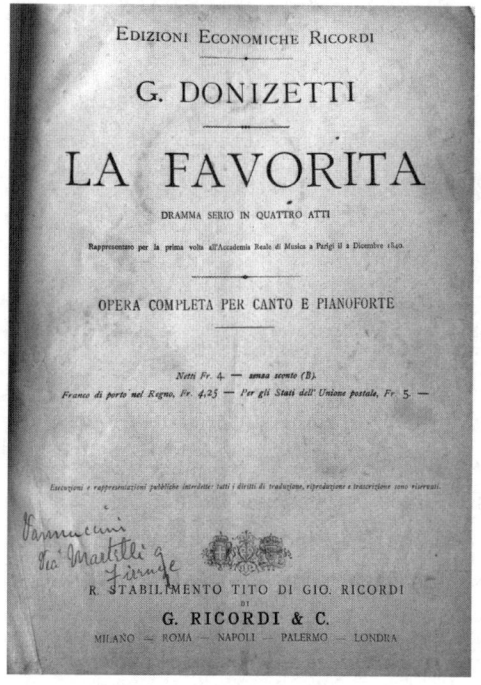

Georgina's *La Favorita* score by Donizetti. Luigi Vannuccini's address is written on the cover. (Author photo)

In analyzing Georgina's repertoire, I cannot help but think that this, too, might have been a similar perfect storm—repertoire demands, performance and career demands, and her unique set of difficult circumstances to contend with, while being far from home and family.

In an unpublished article we found in the Stirling family files at the Memorial University Archives in St. John's, referred to elsewhere in this book as a "printed edited manuscript," it is confirmed that Georgina studied with Vannuccini for two years, from the beginning of 1889 to the end of 1890. This is further confirmed in Georgina's own recently discovered letters which were shared with us by both Karen Stirling and Chris O'Dea of St. John's, letters which were originally found in 1976 in Washington, DC, as Calvin Evans will explain in greater detail. The unpublished article has official editorial markings and states: "permission being given her to study singing, *hey presto*, away flies the lady to Florence, where she studied for opera under Vannuccini. After a time, she made her debut at the Opera House at Borgo, in San Donini, just outside Parma, where she sang in 'Trovatore' (by Giuseppe Verdi) and 'La Favorita'" (by Gaetano Donizetti). The role of Azucena from Verdi's opera *Il Trovatore* was indeed part of Georgina's repertoire, as she had been shown to include the arias on her concert programs as well as having performed it as mentioned above.

In Roger Neill's book *Divas*, he claims that the role of Azucena "seems unlikely;" however, we now know that Georgina did in fact perform the role. What he also mentions as unlikely was Georgina's scheduled debut at La Scala in Milan, to perform *Il Trovatore*, which I believe was based on Amy Louise Peyton's uncertainty or limited knowledge expressed in her book. Mentioned in the *Weekly Record* of Newfoundland on September 13, 1890, is a quote from a newspaper in Milan called the *Theatrical Whip*, where they mentioned the previous month, on August 12, "Miss Stirling of Twillingate, Newfoundland is the name of a young mezzo-soprano and contralto, assoluta artist, new to Italy, but who has already sung with much success in various foreign theatres. Miss Stirling whom we have had an opportunity of hearing, possesses a magnificent voice and sings with much feeling. The managers were fortunate in securing her for their theatre to sing the important part of Azucena during the coming season." In *Roll Back the Years*, a book by Edward B. Moogk, he says, "Marie Toulinguet made her debut at La Scala in Milan, with the Italian Royal Family in attendance." His book was published eight years prior to Amy Louise Peyton's in 1975. Prior to both of these, in an article titled *"Newfoundland Singer Won International Fame"* by the Saskatoon *Star-Phoenix* on July 10, 1963, it is stated: "Marie Toulinguet SANG AT LA SCALA. She sang at La Scala opera house in Milan before the Italian royal family." We then hear in the tender interview of Georgina's dear friend, Maymie (Roberts) Hewlett, by Hiram Silk of CBC Grand Falls in 1969, that Georgina did perform at La Scala in Milan. In the interview Maymie speaks of ". . . her first appearance in Italy in La Scala House in 1897–98." The date is incorrect. It may have been in 1891, after her debut in the fall of 1890 at Borgo, when she secured an engagement for "the coming season" in Milan, or more likely in 1898–99, after she had finished her engagements at Venice and Chioggia.

Looking back at the photographs which I took while on one of our visits to the Memorial University Library, I noticed one was of Georgina's copy of Donizetti's opera score *La Favorita*, a Ricordi edition of this opera for voice and piano. Inside the front cover in cursive writing is: "Vannucinni, Via Martelli a Firenze." Via Martelli is a street name, and Firenze is the Italian name for Florence, so this is most likely the address where Georgina went for her voice lessons with Vannuccini.

Georgina was fully immersed in the world of music and performance. She developed consistent and independent study habits regardless of her repertoire demands. She was being applauded by her audiences, with positive feedback, constantly being presented with "beautiful baskets of flowers at these concerts." She showed her humble and considerate nature through her letters to her father as she tells him, "The morning after the concerts I always divide my flowers among my friends because I can never find enough vases to put them in," and, "Nowadays a great thing in a singer's success is, to make herself agreeable and liked, if you cannot do that, it does not matter how well you sing, you will never gain a footing with the public. As you advise me I keep always in mind the fact that there is but a short time before wherein to complete my studies." Georgina was a conscientious young woman with a great respect for her craft. She showed appreciation to her father by sharing with him the details of her musical development. She knew he would be proud as the most supportive and loving admirer of her talent.

In the final letter Georgina sends to her father from Florence, which sadly he does not receive before his death, she shares with him that, "My master has decided that—I am to go to Milan to study Dramatic. If I can manage it I should be there by the 1st of May. . . . In the autumn I am to make my grand debut in opera, I believe at Milan." When I realized that Dr. Stirling would not have been alive to receive this wonderful letter from Georgina, telling him about her concerts, flowers, and moving on to Milan to further her studies and success, it broke my heart. I couldn't help but put myself in her position, knowing she posted that letter and that it didn't make it to him in time. What loss she had experienced already by the young age of twenty-three. This loss and heartbreak would have to find expression somewhere; I believe it went into her music, embedded deeply in her voice, touching her audiences, as we soon shall see.

At the completion of her engagement in Milan, which probably occurred in the spring of 1891, Georgina went to London, England, and became engaged with the concert circuit through the advocacy of men such as Charles Santley, the renowned British baritone, and Narciso Vert, the "manager extraordinaire," both of whom arranged concerts for her. Georgina made such an impression on three women in her audiences that they arranged for her to travel to Paris and have an audition with the world-renowned vocal teacher, Madame Mathilde Marchesi. Two of the women, Mrs. Parish and Miss Hadley, travelled with her. Mrs. Parish generously volunteered to finance the second year of her studies. It meant a great deal to Georgina to have the support of these women, making it possible for her to be introduced to Marchesi, profoundly impacting the course of her journey!

Prior to Georgina travelling to London and then to Paris to meet Marchesi, a letter is sent from Rose to her father, Dr. Stirling, while the two sisters were still in Florence. This telling and dear letter is from the recent collection discovered in the Washington house and shares more about Georgina's training and performing in Florence under Vannuccini. The girls are all understandably worried about their father's health, and feel the emotions of being so far away from him at a time like this, but delight in sharing all of their wonderful experiences, knowing it would mean a great deal to him. Having lost their mother already at such young ages, and saddened now that they may lose their father, their letters are all that connects them during this uncertain time. Dr. Stirling must have cherished the thought of knowing his daughters were together, living such rich experiences of music and culture. I am touched by Rose's description of how Georgina was working with such dedication and that she is motivated by how proud her father will be: "Won't Papa be so proud of me someday." I am certain he was already proud of her and that his heart ached to feel an ocean of space between them.

Florence
April 11th 1890

My dear Papa

Last mail we received letter from come (someone?) telling us that you had been very sick again but that you were a little better when she Janet wrote and her letter was dated (Ash Wednesday). I do hope by the time you receive this that you will be well again. It made Georgie and I both very sad to think of you ill so far away from us both. I do hope God will spare you till we both come home again.

Georgie is getting on well with her studies. Her master Vannuccini is very pleased with her progress and says she is going to be a good artist. She has done wonders the last few months. She sang at a sacred concert on Wednesday, it was given in one of the churches for the benefit of the (blind) and it was crowded and they were very pleased with her voice, and some of the best judges of music were there, indeed they liked it so much that it is to be repeated again next week. She sang the (contralto) soloes and another of Vannuccini's pupils sang the (soprano) but she has studied with him for 4 years and Georgie has not been for more than 18 months with him, and yet they all say Georgie did the best. She will send you one of the programs and one of the papers that were posted up all over the city with her name printed on it. I think she is more pleased with her success for your sake than her own, for she always says to me won't papa be proud of me someday.

I often wish you could see Florence it is so beautiful and some of the villas and the gardens in the country are lovely beyond anything you could imagine with profusion of fruit and flowers and vegetables. And then you are so fond of hearing a good band and every day the Military Bands play through the principal streets, the calivy (sic) pass close by our house every morning with the band playing in front, it always makes me think of you because you used to talk so much of the bands you used to hear in Scotland.

The weather is getting beautifully warm now indeed it is as warm now as we have it in Newfoundland in August. Vannuccini has decided for us to go to Milan for 3 months as he says Georgie must take Dramatic lessons from a master he knows there, there is no master for Dramatic in Florence like there is in Milan and he says every good renowned singer always studies Dramatic there, so of course she must also. Vannuccini will be going to London about the same time for 3 months like he did last summer. The journey from here to Milan is not far you can go in a day and it does not cost much. You must still address your letters to

> *Miss Stirling*
> *Via Pancani No 2*
> *Piano 2nd*
> *San Gallo*
> *Florence, Italy*

until we send you our address from Milan which we will do as soon as we get to be settled there and the Lady of the house here has promised to send on any letters to Milan to us as soon as they reach here until you get our other address.

Georgie is going to write Janet a few lines also, she studies so much that she has not much time for anything else. I do all the marketing, cooking, etcra. I have learnt enough Italian for that and still do a little drawing. I shall soon send you another sample of my drawing and painting. Now must say good bye for the present with hearty wishes that you may now be quite well again and with much love to you and Janet. I remain your loving child, Rose

CHAPTER EIGHT
BY TONIA EVANS CIANCIULLI

GEORGINA MEETS MADAME MATHILDE MARCHESI

"There are no shortcuts to any place worth going."
— Beverly Sills, American Opera Singer (1929–2007)

I HAD HEARD OF THE SWEET and enthusiastic letter Georgina wrote to her sister Janet from Paris (cir. 1891). During our visit to St. John's in May 2017, I had the distinct honour of holding and reading a copy of that original letter. Holding this piece of history was a privilege. I was able to witness Georgina's effusive and excited expression of having auditioned before the great Madame Mathilde Marchesi.

Madame Mathilde Marchesi (1821–1913) was one of the world's most renowned voice teachers who greatly impacted the world of opera. Her name is synonymous with the bel canto technique and training that Georgina becomes schooled in. I am struck by the significance of Georgina having been a pupil of Marchesi, ranking among the top talents of her era. Our dear Georgina from Twillingate, Newfoundland, made it to Paris to study with the "Great Mathilde Marchesi" and brilliant composers of the day as she gained international fame.

Reading Georgina's letter connected me to her as a singer and the rich history which was being unpacked before my eyes. Singers know the thrill of having a greatly respected teacher applaud their voice. I could feel Georgina's excitement coming off the page as I read it.

Avenue Victor Hugo 100
Champs Elysees
Monday Night

My dear Jan,

I am glad to be able to give you <u>great, great news.</u> Yesterday morning "Sunday" Miss Hadley and I (Miss Parish being ill) went to Marchesi the great Teacher to have my voice tried and the verdict given. Well Jan we were ushered into a grand Salon with a smaller Salon opening off, at Eleven in the morning. The <u>big</u> salon was full of persons waiting to have their voices tried. In the <u>small</u> Salon a Young lady was singing—we could hear all that was said. After she had finished, Marchesi gave her opinion, Well Jan she abused her voice up & down. Sent her away—Also she tried two others and her verdict was not good of anyone. As you may imagine how nervous I commenced to feel. Now <u>Mme Melba</u> the great Australian singer was there listening. You should just have seen their faces when I sang, they were more than Enraptured, Jan. I never dreamed of such a success. Oh if Papa had only been alive to hear it. Melba came forward and shook me by the hand and told me I had a grand, grand future before me. She also said the same to Miss H.

Marchesi said my voice was a true Mezzo Soprano of the <u>highest order</u> and a voice that has been lost for many years—she said My dear Young Lady <u>"Yours is a voice that the world is waiting for & You will be a great, great woman."</u> Well I was nearly paralyzed with pleasure and Miss H nearly cried, fancy Jan <u>such praise from</u> her, the greatest Teacher in the world. She <u>knew nothing of me</u> and I went to her unintroduced & dressed shabbily so I think we may believe she gave an unbiased opinion. Mrs. Parish was so pleased that she begged me to spare us expense and if I wished to study a year beyond the thirteen months that Marchesi demands to do so and it will be a great pleasure to her to pay for it. Jan she is more than kind to me, here they treat me like a princess—I am going to write Mrs. Sheppard a nice letter of thanks tomorrow. Please tell her all.

Georgie.

THE WORLD OF AUDITIONING

"You should just have seen their faces when I sang, they were more than Enraptured, Jan. I never dreamed of such a success. Oh if Papa had only been alive to hear it. Melba came forward and shook me by the hand and told me I had a grand, grand future before me."
— Georgina Stirling, Newfoundland Soprano

AUDITIONING IS A WHOLE WORLD unto itself. The nerves that singers or perform-ers feel when they are being auditioned are different from those of a performance. Many performers agree that auditioning is its own art form. There is a different pressure felt when a singer auditions for a new teacher, an opera company, or a conductor; even more so if there are other singers present to witness the audition. One can imagine the emotions, excitement, and pressure Georgina must have felt when she first sang for this well-known and respected voice teacher, Mathilde Marchesi, in Paris, thousands of miles from home.

Reading Georgina's letter, I recalled some of my own significant auditions. During my first year at the University of Western Ontario, away from home for the first time, young, naive, and inexperienced, I auditioned for the opera that was to be produced under the direction of Brian McIntosh. Brian is a Canadian bass-baritone who enjoyed an international career which started in Germany, taking him to major opera companies around the world. He was the first to take a chance on my ability and potential as a first-year student in the voice department. Shortly after my audition I saw my name listed to perform the role of Jenny Diver in Benjamin Britten's *The Beggar's Opera*. I remember skipping my way home across the campus bridge to call my mother in excitement. It was the early confirmation I needed that I was on the right path. Brian McIntosh has become a close mentor and teacher of mine.

I imagine that singing for my voice teacher, Manny Perez, in Miami, felt similar to what Georgina had felt. I already knew that he was well-known and respected for training excep-tional voices, singers who are now thriving on opera stages of the world. When I walked into his studio, I immediately took note of the Maria Callas oil and canvas painting that hung over the grand piano. My eyes drifted around the room at all the opera posters, photographs of masters of opera such as Joan Sutherland, Montserrat Caballé, Maria Callas, Luciano Pavarotti, and Mirella Freni, to name just a few. I knew I was in a special place, and I felt the excitement of new possibilities in my voice. The "butterflies" in my stomach started to take flight.

How I found myself there that day reminded me of opportunities that presented themselves to Georgina along her journey to meet her own influential voice teachers. I had attended a fundraiser in Fort Lauderdale one evening with my husband, for the "Symphony of the Americas" that our friends George and Sally Borg were hosting. There were live musicians serenading the guests as we mingled, and I found myself in deep conversation with Maestro James Brooks-Bruzzese while indulging in some red velvet cheesecake and a glass of red wine. George asked me to perform a few pieces with the musicians, to which I quickly replied, "Absolutely not!" I explained that I did not feel comfortable singing in front of their guests because I was not vocally warmed up and also offered the excuse that my voice would not do well after cheesecake and wine. I'll never forget what George said. "Shyness will get you nowhere, dear!" I took that as a sign, and within a few minutes I found myself singing some of my favourite arias for the guests. The maestro shook my hand afterwards as he said, "You never know what will happen when you share your gift like that." That very week I got an email from the artistic director telling me they'd like to refer me to sing for Manny. This was an event that shifted the trajectory of my vocal development and artistry.

During Georgina's singing career, she experienced many of these same events and feelings. In *Divas*, Roger Neill references in many sections the audition experiences of various students who went to "try" their voices for Madame Marchesi. It's amazing to think that the great Australian soprano Nellie Melba was present in the room when Georgina auditioned for Marchesi. Georgina must have experienced intense excitement and nervousness while singing; however, it would have been a great confirmation that she was in good hands and company singing among the celebrity singers of her era. For a singer, finding a teacher they greatly respect and connect with is in a sense a spiritual experience. As singers, our voices are our most prized possessions; we long desperately to find the magic key that unlocks our most self-expressed voice and inner diva! Our teacher's role is to guide and inspire us with their knowledge and experience in transforming our gifts into exactly what they are meant to be.

As stated in Nellie Melba's memoirs, described in Roger Neill's book, "Melba wrote that she was not alone with Marchesi for her audition. Rather, she waited her turn to sing in a classroom filled with already-accepted pupils. Georgina's letter confirms this as well. The room was described as 'a great saloon with polished oak floor. There was hardly any furniture—three or four chairs, some benches against the walls and a grand piano. The mantelpiece was covered in photographs, and there were life-sized photographs in frames on the walls.'" In a black and white photograph of École Marchesi in Roger Neill's book we can see the ornate frames on the walls containing what look like photographs of great composers and opera divas, grand curtains, a beautiful chandelier in the centre of the room, and picture frames covering the entire piano top. It was at 88 rue Jouffroy, École Marchesi, that Marchesi taught her pupils lessons in the bel canto vocal technique, languages and diction, music theory and history, and style for singers who wished to embark on a career in the opera houses or as concert singers.

I NOTICED IN GEORGINA'S LETTER, in which she described the first time she sang for Marchesi, that Marchesi referred to her as a mezzo-soprano, "Marchesi said my voice was a true Mezzo Soprano of the highest order." It is my assumption that if Georgina were singing a lot of mezzo-soprano repertoire during her early instruction with Vannuccini, this is the music she would have offered to sing for Marchesi. In an audition setting, singers arrive vocally warmed up and ready to perform a selection of contrasting arias that represent various languages and styles within their voice type. These arias are sometimes referred to as "party pieces," arias that we are confident about performing under pressure and that show the best qualities of our voices. As mentioned in Rose's letter above, we understand that Georgina was singing contralto and mezzo-soprano repertoire as directed by Vannuccini. She refers to another pupil who sang the soprano solos as she had been with Vannuccini for four years, much longer than Georgina's eighteen months. Perhaps Vannuccini gave the soprano solos to pupils who had some seniority in the studio. Also, Georgina was still in the early stages of developing her technique and range.

In William Vennard's book *Singing: The Mechanism and the Technic* he states: "I never feel any urgency about classifying a beginning student. So many premature diagnoses have been proved wrong, and it can be harmful to the student and embarrassing to the teacher to keep striving for an ill-chosen goal. It is best to begin in the middle part of the voice and work upward and downward until the voice classifies itself." Over the course of my own career, I have personally known many mezzo-sopranos who have made a complete repertoire switch to soprano and vice versa. One of the well-known examples in the opera world of this sort of scenario was soprano Joan Sutherland, known to her opera audiences as "La Stupenda" ("The Stupendous One"). This world-renowned soprano, with enormous vocal range and strength, actually started her career as a mezzo-soprano. In her book, *The Autobiography of Joan Sutherland: A Prima Donna's Progress*, she describes growing up listening to her mother, mezzo-soprano Muriel Alston Sutherland. She shares: "As she was a mezzo-soprano, I worked very much in the middle area of my voice. . . . I even picked up her songs and arias and sang them by ear." Assuming she was a mezzo-soprano like her mother, it wasn't until Sutherland started performing in Australia that she was persuaded to explore her upper range. Sutherland became one of the most famous bel canto coloratura sopranos to ever live.

Once Georgina started her private instruction with Marchesi, she would have been able to better assess the range, capabilities, and future development of her voice. As we see from watching her voice mature and progress, Georgina would soon be performing more soprano roles and repertoire. I have enjoyed detailed discussions regarding the progression of Georgina's vocal technique and repertoire, as well as the documented reviews and written descriptions of her vocal range and quality, with several respected professionals. Although I am a soprano myself, and have sung much of Georgina's repertoire, I wanted to search beyond my own experience to understand Georgina's voice and development based on the research to which we have gained access. Lending their expert opinions and experience to this topic, I am grateful to voice professors Darryl Edwards (University of Toronto), Brian McIntosh (University of Western Ontario), voice teacher Manny Perez (voice teacher, Miami Music Classical Music Festival and board member of Florida Grand Opera), colleague Dann Mitton (M.Mus., DMA in voice performance specializing in vocal pedagogy), and Stephen R. Clarke (chair of the board of *Opera Canada Magazine*). There seems to be a consensus among these experts that while Georgina may have started out singing mezzo-soprano repertoire in her early training and career, it is obvious that her broad range justifies the transition to lyric soprano repertoire throughout her training with Mathilde Marchesi. We will discover later that Georgina flourished in the lyric soprano repertoire during her Scalchi Opera Company tour across the United States, in Italy, and beyond.

GEORGINA'S TREASURED "NORMA" SCORE AND THE WORLD OF BEL CANTO

"It is a way of music, but it is a very hard training . . . the bel canto is definitely the schooling, so if you don't have the bel canto, you cannot sing any opera, as a matter of fact."
— Maria Callas, Greek Soprano, Performed the Role of "Norma" Ninety Times

IT'S 2:07 A.M. ON A WEEKNIGHT and I can't sleep. I lay awake running Italian lyrics in my head to the famous duet "Mira, O Norma" from the tragic opera *Norma* by Bellini for the concert with the Toronto Concert Orchestra. I think back to my visit to the Queen Elizabeth II Library at Memorial University. While sifting through the Stirling family files, I was delighted to hold Georgina's *Norma* opera score, now nearly 200 years old. Uncle Brian frequently played *Norma* for me during many of our opera-centred visits, along with the famous aria "Casta Diva" sung by Maria Callas. Oh how I would have loved to hear Georgina sing this aria! We will see later that she stunned audiences with it on her America tour.

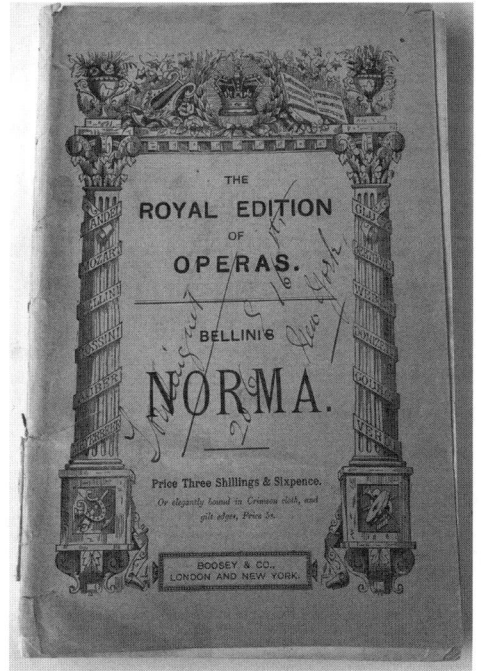

Georgina's music scores were in similar condition to scores of my own: well-loved with pencil markings to note such things as breath marks, vowel reminders, stage directions, dramatic intent, etc. I broke the dead silence with a burst of laughter in the library's archival room when I noticed an old rusted hairpin stuck into one of the pages of her scores and a squashed fly near the bottom of the same page! I think my grandfather, having been a librarian, was a little embarrassed his granddaughter was breaking the number one rule of the library, but when I showed him the reason, he was overcome with "contained" excitement.

Georgina's *Norma* score with "Toulinguet" written on front cover (Courtesy of Archives and Special Collections, Memorial Libraries)

Singers have an intense relationship with their music scores. Flipping through the pages of an opera score or anthology of music, images flood one's mind with the sounds and feelings of portraying their character. This is a unique experience for an opera singer. One of Georgina's songbooks had a pencil drawing of a "dory" boat inside the back cover. Seeing this image showed me just how great a relationship and fondness she had for her upbringing in Newfoundland.

Inside one of Georgina Stirling's opera scores, one of her hairpins and the dead fly! (Author photo)

The opera *Norma* by Bellini is one of the most famous examples of a true bel canto opera. How fitting that one of the very few opera scores left of Georgina's is the tragic character Norma. She was the daughter of a high priest who secretly broke a vow of chastity and gave birth to two sons of Pollione, a Roman proconsul and enemy of her father. The famous aria Norma sings, "Casta Diva," demands a strong and exact technique, vocal flexibility, and broad range. Norma sings and prays for peace and to spare the life of her lover, Pollione, against Roman defeat. The duet Norma sings with Adalgisa (the unknowing mistress to Norma's husband, Pollione, who then becomes a welcomed friend in a time of distress) is "Mira, O Norma" and comes with its own technical challenges of multiple contrasting sections, extreme emotions, dynamics, contrasting tempi combined with tongue-twisting Italian lyrics, and lasts more than eight minutes. This kind of repertoire is what we opera singers would refer to as "a big sing." Georgina performed this duet many times, one in particular at a concert in St. John's at St. Patrick's Hall with her friend, mezzo-soprano Marie du Bedat, "Ireland's Nightingale," on a return trip home from the United States during the summer of 1897. We'll see later how this Irish Nightingale and Georgina developed a close friendship.

In the last few years I've revisited much of the bel canto repertoire and the nuances of the technique. When I started training with Manny Perez in 2016, he suggested I sing more bel canto repertoire while I was fine-tuning my breath control, legato lines, flexibility, and "allowing" my high notes instead of forcing them. He often says, "Singing is not made, it's al-lowed. As a singer you need to learn the art of allowing," another example of how the art of singing and life can meet on common ground.

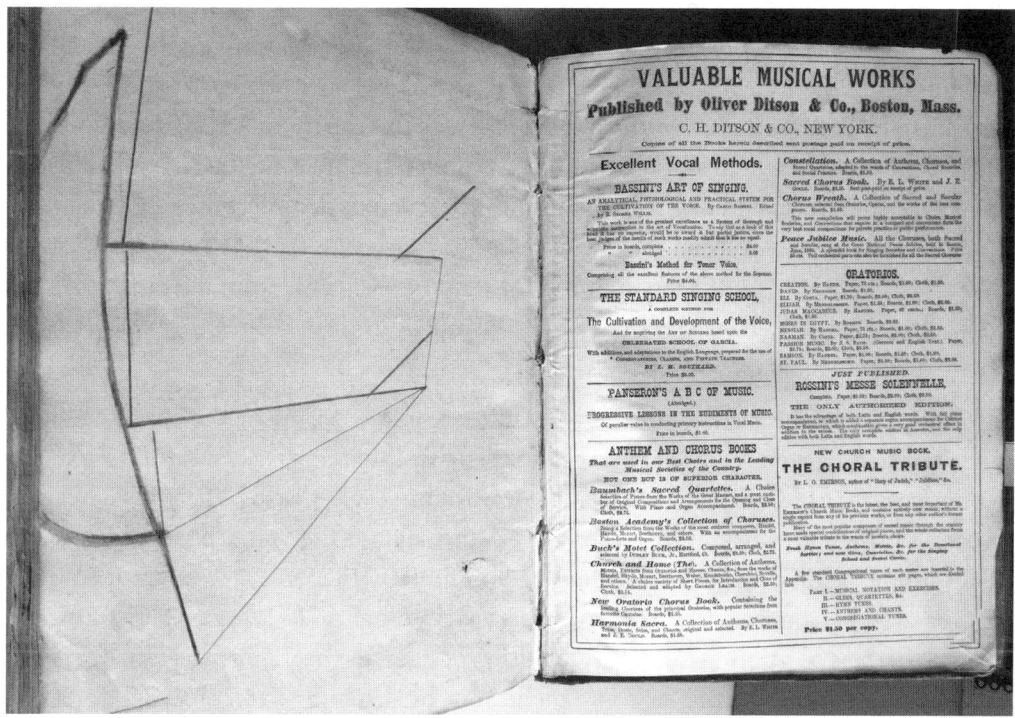

Sketching of a two-masted schooner inside one of Georgina Stirling's songbooks
(Author photo)

I was first introduced to bel canto during my musical training at the University of West-ern Ontario. "Bel canto" translates as beautiful singing, and it is a familiar term among opera singers. However, the term bel canto goes beyond just beautiful singing. It's a style, a way of singing that values smooth and effortless legato lines throughout the entire vocal range, keep-ing the upper ranges light, flexible, and penetrating with ethereal and florid vocal lines. It is also an Italian method of training the voice. It was first introduced in the seventeenth century and is most famously associated with the repertoire of composers Bellini, Rossini, and Doni-zetti. Maria Callas, praised for her bel canto technique, describes this type of singing exquis-itely: "The way the violin plays, the voice must play, you strive to become a real musician, the main instrument of the orchestra," as if the voice has the exact same flexibility as a stringed instrument in the orchestra and will often be featured as a solo line all on its own. Roger Neill confirms this in his book: "It focused initially on a solo melodic line together with sparse chordal accompaniment, either from orchestra or keyboard. Arias especially demanded that singers—in particular sopranos (in the earlier times) castrati—demonstrate their extreme agility and virtuosity, not only in rapid runs and trills, but also in improvised ornaments and embellishments. The way in which singers could float above the instruments with gymnastic ease came to be described as *coloratura.*" It is because of this intricate and calculated yet sensitive and delicate approach to singing that the bel canto technique and the training it involves are so integral. Maria Callas further explains, "the bel canto is definitely the schooling. If you don't have the bel canto, you cannot sing *any* opera, as a matter of fact." Perhaps some singers would disagree with this, but keep in mind this strong belief came from the mouth of a soprano who received sixteen curtain calls for performing the role of Bellini's *Norma* in Chicago for her American debut on November 1, 1954.

Also, praising the benefits of the bel canto technique for his success was the wildly famous Russian baritone Dmitri Hvorostovsky. In an interview with the *New York Times* he comments that the missing link to his vocal training was that of "the classic bel canto approach to singing, which cultivates evenness throughout the voice, pliant legato phrasing and nimble agility. The bel canto heritage profoundly influenced Russian opera in the mid-to-late 19th century . . . cultural overseers viewed bel canto as some elitist European influence that was corrupting the earthy tradition of Russian vocal music." Dmitri goes on to share how he learned the art of bel canto on his own by "listening to recordings of great Italian singers from the early 20th century." ("The Power of a Russian Birthright" by Anthony Tommasini, March 30, 2008)

In his book *Great Singers on Great Singing*, Jerome Hines interviews Luciano Pavarotti. He quotes Pavarotti as saying, "It took me six years of study . . . and one must be convinced of its importance from the first day . . . never change ideas. You know, the first five or six months it is very depressing because it does not come out right, and you become cyanotic, red in the face. Then some students begin to think this approach is wrong, and then they try the other way, but it will never bring them security of voice." As advanced and talented as Pavarotti was, he credits singing the "light, high, elegant roles" of the bel canto composers for contributing to the lasting health of his voice. He used them as "medicine, limbering-up exercises for his performances . . . I try to keep my voice like it is, no bigger than what it is, with agility, with rhythm and fresh accents."

The testaments of these artists and historians speak to the great impact that the bel canto technique had on the world of opera. Madame Marchesi was an integral part of the development and longevity of this technique, reaching worldwide.

Marchesi was close friends with many of the famous composers of her day, including Massenet, Mendelssohn, Gounod, Liszt, and Verdi. In Marchesi's book, *Marchesi and Music: Passages from the Life of a Famous Singing Teacher*, she affectionately mentions many of these composers, remarking: "Apropos of Monsieur Massenet, I want to say that he has always shown deep interest in all young persons who were studying to be artists, whether it was for the lyric stage, for concerts, or as instrumentalists. And he has ever been a devoted friend and earnest adviser of those who came to Paris from abroad. Hundreds of instances could be sited of the unstinted help he has thus given them as well as to his compatriots; and this was true, too, of our other illustrious and distinguished friends Ambroise Thomas, Gounod, Delibes, and Benjamin Godard, all whom were French composers, as they were 'masters' among musicians" (page 291). She explains her close relationship with Charles Gounod: "On the 15th of October, 1893, the musical sustained an irreparable loss in the death of Charles Gounod, and personally I lost in him a devoted friend. I am very fond of his light, flowing melodies, for they appeal to the heart, and are admirably suited to the human voice. No singer has, and never will have, to strain his or her vocal chords when studying Gounod's compositions, but too many have already done so with the music of Wagner and his disciples. . . . Gounod was struck down with apoplexy as he was reading over and correcting his 'Requiem,' his last work. He passed away a few hours afterwards" (page 288).

In Marchesi's memoirs she shares a thrilling moment when Verdi telegrammed her to "share his box with him" at the Opera Comique, at the Paris premiere for what was his final opera, *Falstaff*. At the time, Verdi was eighty-two years old and still ran his own rehearsals. He had been known to attend Marchesi's studio for salon concerts and presentations. Verdi died in January 1901 in Milan at the age of eighty-seven. This was sad news for all who knew him, worked with him, and loved his music. That same month, Georgina's friend and colleague, opera singer Tomasso Boyd, writes to her from England, upset at the news of Verdi's death. Georgina would have been privileged enough to have met and sung for Verdi during her time with Marchesi.

Through Marchesi's connections, Georgina was fortunate to have known and worked with many of these composers first-hand during her time at École Marchesi. Georgina performed in one of Gounod's Masses (which one is not known), accompanied by Gounod himself on the organ, in about 1892. Roger Neill states the dates incorrectly in his book, relying on the limited information that Amy Louise Peyton had provided, saying it was in 1889; however, we know she was still in Florence at this time.

GEORGINA'S BEL CANTO TRAINING WITH THE GREAT MATHILDE MARCHESI

"May this work, which I look upon as my last of the kind, add to the important results that I have obtained from forty-two years of application of my system."
— Mathilde Marchesi, German Mezzo-soprano, Renowned Teacher and Author of the Bel Canto Technique (1821–1913)

THERE IS A WEALTH OF INFORMATION available on Madame Mathilde Marchesi and her technique. From her numerous books and information on the Internet I've been able to get a clear sense of Georgina's training and experience during her time in Paris. As we've seen, anyone who is familiar with the world of opera knows Marchesi's name. Indeed, it established a foundation for generations of healthy singing by opera singers across the globe. Vocal pedagogy was taken very seriously in Marchesi's studio, and she took only students whom she deemed as "star quality" and who were serious about the profession. Georgina was deemed to be one of these "stars," as Marchesi effusively remarked to Georgina, "Yours is a voice that the world is waiting for and you will be a great, great woman!"

During Georgina's course of study in Paris with Marchesi, Newfoundlanders back home continued to hold great pride in their Nightingale. I wonder if they truly grasped the depth of what their provincial songstress was experiencing at the time. She lived the thrilling life that all opera singers dream of experiencing, training with the composers of the time. Among many of her honours was one such night on February 27, 1892, at the 88 rue Jouffroy studio, when Georgina participated in a matinee performance to honour the centenary anniversary of one of the famous bel canto composers, and a valued friend of Marchesi, Gioachino Rossini. This occasion is mentioned in Amy Louise Peyton's book and is confirmed by Roger Neill as being in March. However, Neill explains the grand occasion in greater detail as he pulls from the memoirs of Marchesi, "For Marchesi this was clearly a special event, attended by a long list of aristocratic and artistic guests." (*Divas*, page 308) When word got back to Newfoundland about the occasion, the *Twillingate Sun* was all too proud to share the news with the headline "Noted Amongst the World's Greatest Singers":

"The many friends of Miss Georgina Stirling, youngest daughter to the late much respected Dr. Stirling, will be pleased to hear that this talented young lady has recently been one of the performers on two select occasions in Paris, as will appear from extracts which we take from late numbers of the Paris Galigani Messenger, which came to hand this mail. She is ranking amongst the world's most famous singers and from time to time is very highly complimented in the leading newspapers of Paris as well as in Italy, where she has undergone a thorough course of training under the most eminent and distinguished professors of the age. Miss Stirling has lately been visiting Paris and displaying her talented and cultured voice before audiences composed of the best society."

Madame Mathilde Marchesi, acclaimed voice teacher in Paris, with whom Georgina Stirling trained from 1891 to 1893 (Encyclopedia Britannica)

Shortly after, in the *Twillingate Sun* on April 2, 1892, Georgina is greatly applauded for her progress abroad. "It will greatly interest the readers of the Sun to hear that Miss Georgina Stirling, youngest daughter of the late Dr. Stirling is making rapid progress in the musical world. She possesses a magnificent voice of rare quality, power and longness and it is predicted a very brilliant future lies before her. Miss Georgina Stirling is at present studying with Madam Marchesi, the finest teacher of singing in Europe and it is expected she will make her second appearance in the operatic world in the course of a few months."

Marchesi was not only a well-educated voice teacher with broad performance experience to draw from, but also a savvy businesswoman for her period. It was Mathilde's desire to have a career on the operatic stage; in fact, when Mathilde accompanied her husband, Salvatore, to Berlin in 1852 to perform in Rossini's opera *Il Barbiere di Siviglia*, Mathilde stepped in to perform the role of Rossina when the soprano was ill and not able to perform. She received rave reviews for her performance; however, her husband, Salvatore, was not in agreement with her having a career in opera. She continued performing in concert halls instead of theatres and forged ahead in developing her influential career as one of the most famous voice teachers.

Georgina singing on an operatic stage with accompanist
(Courtesy of Sylvia Ficken, Newfoundland artist, 1981)

Having books published about her technique and vocal exercises ensured Marchesi a broader reach for her technique and guidelines for an opera singer's lifestyle, and she set the stage for her female pupils to experience a longer and healthier career. One of her core books, greatly valued by students and teachers of opera, is called *Bel Canto: A Theoretical & Practical Vocal Method*. Originally published in 1970, this invaluable reference for singers includes many of the vocal training exercises that Marchesi had spent her career developing and teaching in her studio as well as several pages on a "Practical Guide for Singers."

While the technique that was passed down to Marchesi had not been documented, it can be traced back 100 years before her to Nicola Porpora (1686–1768), and the bel canto technique made its way to Manuel Garcia II in Paris, who was the teacher of, and who greatly influenced, Marchesi. It wasn't until the nineteenth century that the bel canto technique really started to flourish and become established through the instruction, development, and documentation of Marchesi, who was the product of those masters before her, creating and presenting a technique that would stand the test of time. Marchesi found the approach of Garcia II methodical and thorough, with the repetition of scales, arpeggios with the metronome to stay exact and in time, using what she learned from him and the addition of her own changes to reflect what she had learned from her own experience in singing; this developed into her own unique method, particularly in the training of female operatic divas. Before starting her own studio, Marchesi assisted Garcia II in his vocal studio with several of his students; he is quoted as telling Marchesi that she was "born to teach." It is interesting to know that it was Marchesi's teacher, Garcia II, who invented the laryngoscope. This was a huge advancement in medical science and of great benefit to singers. Now they were able to see their vocal chords while they were functioning and to monitor their health. In my research on all three of these teachers and their methods, I discovered that they shared a slow and steady approach to mastering the art of opera singing to ensure longevity and vocal health.

Vocal health and lifestyle were of utmost importance to Marchesi. She outlined many of her guidelines for singers to follow in her vocal method books. She approaches every aspect of being a singer in an effort to ensure a career of longevity as an opera singer. She is known for having divas who had long-lasting and healthy careers. If there was any fatigue or strain, they were instructed to take long periods of vocal rest. Georgina had been instructed to take six weeks of vocal rest at one point from taxing singing engagements in London, England, and travelled home to rest in Twillingate.

Marchesi strictly advised her students against inappropriate repertoire for their vocal fach. Just like Maria Callas dared to sing the heavy operatic music of Wagner, so did Georgina's colleague Nellie Melba. Against Marchesi's instruction, Nellie shares in her memoirs her deep regret in singing this repertoire, making it crucial to rest her voice for several months. "I had long wanted to sing the role of Brunnhilde in *Siegfried*, in German. In Paris I had mentioned to Madame Marchesi this desire, always to be met with a horrified expression and great fluttering of hands, as though I had threatened to cut my throat. I was well aware that Brunnhilde was not by any means an ideal role for me. . . . From the moment when the curtain went up and I began to sing, I knew that Madame Marchesi had been right and I had been wrong." This was during the 1896–97 season on December 30 at the Met in New York. Fortunately, Nellie Melba had a thriving and international career once she rested and healed.

In Marchesi's bel canto method book, and echoed in Roger Neill's book, are the signature elements of Marchesi's method and what produced and influenced an impressive number of famous operatic divas, well after Marchesi's time. Marchesi writes, "An attractive appearance, the gifts of the musician, quickness of conception, and the power of representation . . . a good ear, a sound and rich voice of extended compass, added to an ardent desire to become an artist." She was firm in her opinion that becoming a professional opera singer took time, just as with an instrumentalist, and she did not agree with young singers taking a few months of training and then appearing in public as "accomplished songstresses." She was known for having very few amateur students and would only entertain this if the students promised to train as if they were professionals.

Her ambition was "that each of my pupils shall leave my school a good opera-singer, a good concert-singer, or a good teacher." She believed in her pupils being educated in musical history and languages, French, German, and Italian. Georgina was already educating herself in languages, practising her Italian while she was in Florence with Vannuccini. She sweetly explains to her Papa, "Do you know, I think my spelling gets worse every day and I account for it in this way, the difference in the pronunciation of the letters of the alphabet in Italian to the English, & of course all day long, I am practising Italian. . . . I am sending you an Italian Almanac for 1890. I hope you will understand it. (Dom, Sunday) (Lun Monday) (Mar Tuesday) (Mer Wednesday) (Gio Thursday) (Ven Friday) (Sab Saturday). In full they are Domenica, Lunedi; Martedi; Merdcoledi; Gioredi; Venerdi; Sabato. I would have sent you an English one, but it was impossible to get a small one."

Marchesi proposed guidelines for her prized pupils about their lifestyle that included healthy eating and to "abandon" such activities as "bicycling, rowing, dancing, long walks, reading late at night, singing too soon after meals, exposure to excessive heat or cold, too frequent theatre parties or social gatherings."

Marchesi believed in half-hour voice lessons but repeated a few times within a week, over time building up the singer's stamina to be able to sing for longer periods of time. She also believed that singers are able to learn much by listening to other students sing. Marchesi managed her school in a way that supported this method, as singers would often be present during other performers' lessons and auditions, as we saw in Georgina's case. There is always a great deal we can learn about our own voice, our craft, and navigating repertoire simply by listening to another singer work through exercises or music.

Marchesi's vocal training was approached in "baby steps," a slow and steady manner, progressively building on exercises and technical mastery. She did not want to overwhelm her pupils with too many demands when first developing their voice and technique. Her bel canto "vocalises" were focused exercises sung on a variety of vowels instead of text. This would help students as they mastered breath control, vocal freedom, navigating of coloratura passages, embellishments, and the flexibility necessary for performing a variety of repertoire. These "vocalises" are short and often quite beautiful in order to keep a student inspired while not overtaxing the voice. She gave instructions to keep the voice free from tension when singing legato lines, "avoiding jerkiness and forced effort" and relaxing the jaw. Other exercises focused on properly supporting the voice with diaphragmatic breathing and extending the length of phrases. Perfecting the pure Italian vowels was also important. She strongly believed that "training a voice before the age of sixteen or seventeen is a sin, and may spoil many good voices before their normal development." Marchesi held firm to the belief that learning to be a good singer takes time and patience before having a career.

Mathilde Marchesi knew that being a professional opera singer meant to *always* be a student of the art of singing, relying on the supportive ears and knowledge of trusted teachers and mentors. "That one can study singing by one's self is a delusion." The training and refining of a singer's voice never ends. Even "the best" opera singers who enjoy worldwide fame still check in with voice teachers and trusted colleagues to ensure a healthy and enjoyable experience while they're physically performing and throughout their career. Encountering a new role for an opera singer will mean having to navigate through a new set of unique requirements of that character's emotional and technical aspects.

Soprano Renée Fleming in her book *The Inner Voice* reflects on the importance of a singer having the continued support of a voice teacher, emotionally and vocally. In forming a special bond with our teachers, we come to rely on them as a sounding board in more ways than one. Renée recalls a time she called her voice teacher, Beverly Johnson, with whom she continued a strong connection for many years, to sing a troubling note for her over the phone. She said, "'You know I'm having trouble with this note. Can I sing it to you over the phone?' and she always knew how to fix it. When I was especially nervous, she wrote me notes and e-mails that kept me on track." This is a common experience. Georgina would not have been able to take advantage of connection in this sense once she started performing abroad, away from her teachers. Renée goes on to explain why the need for singers to check in is especially important: "I can't remove my ears from my body and place them in the back of the room for a vocal check. What we hear while we're singing just isn't true, so we are always dependent on someone we trust to take the role of our 'outside ears.'" Further technological advancements have allowed singers to have Skype lessons with our teachers. This has been of particular help for me in situations when I am not near my voice teachers and need a quick check-in or lesson. I'll often have Skype lessons with Manny in Miami while I'm home in Toronto or traveling, and at times I've emailed a practice session recording to my teachers or coaches for confirmation or assistance in trouble spots. Although nothing can take the place of having lessons in the physical with our teachers, these have become invaluable tools for singers to rely on during times away or on the road.

In my own consistent training and retraining of my voice, I have learned to be joyfully submissive to my group of trusted teachers and their training methods. It excites me to feel and hear the results of being a student of the voice, knowing that I'm building a reliable technique. From their support I have learned to understand and trust the inner workings of my singing voice and my "inner voice."

Marchesi shares her motto on the final page of her memoirs: "Faith, Labor and Perseverance." She then leaves her reader with the following sentiment. "I am now, and shall always be, the public's most obedient servant, as I am, in a humble but very earnest way, the friend of every student and artist, old or young. God helping, we need none of us have any fear; and as I have always been profoundly in love with my art, so shall I ever by fond of my profession." (*Marchesi and Music*, page 301) Georgina had a great master, mentor, and encourager in Madame Marchesi.

WHAT'S IN A NAME? HOW "MARIE TOULINGUET" BECAME

"A rose by any other name would smell as sweet."
— Shakespeare (1564–1616)

THE VOICE OF GEORGINA ANN STIRLING sounded sweet and touching, no matter the name she was called. She was known throughout Newfoundland and across Europe by a variety of names such as: Mlle. Marie Toulinguet, Nightingale of the North, Twillingate Stirling, the Florence Nightingale of Newfoundland, the Songstress of Newfoundland. These names were bestowed upon her by her adoring public. When did it begin and why?

Since studying the life and music of Georgina Stirling, I've had to explain her many names as I use them interchangeably, as Georgina Stirling or Marie Toulinguet. They are two distinctly different names; if you didn't know, you would assume they were different people. This fascinating tradition would have been considered quite an honour for her. A common practice of Mathilde Marchesi's back in the nineteenth century was to release her pupils onto the opera stages of the world with an appropriate stage name—a sort of branding that would give them more credibility, status, and memorability. This practice began much earlier with a few of Nicola Porpora's "celebrity" students, and Marchesi continued this branding of professional opera singers; for example, Dame Nellie Melba was born Helen Porter Mitchell and was given the stage name of "Melba," a name associated with her hometown of Melbourne, Australia. One of Marchesi's North American sopranos, born as Florence Brimson in Newmarket (very close to Toronto, Ontario), was given the stage name "Florence Toronta." Georgina's mezzo-soprano friend Marie du Bedat became known as "Ireland's Nightingale." Georgina Stirling herself was named after the French form of her hometown's name —Toulinguet—and because Twillingate was in the Bay of Notre Dame, translating to Bay of Our Lady: Mary—Marie. Georgina thus became "Marie Toulinguet." A bit confusing in Georgina's case, but it is interesting to know the origin of her famous stage name. This practice is no longer common in the world of opera, but it is popular among contemporary musicians when branding a performer.

Marchesi went beyond taking her promising students and training their voices. She equipped them with their public identity and also helped them transition into their professional status by arranging for them to perform at student concerts, auditions, events, soirees, and for agents and opera house managers. Many sought Marchesi's recommendations of singers for such opportunities as concerts, events, and roles in opera houses, since she had a reputation for having the most impressive female prima donnas on her roster of talent.

Regardless what her public called her, Georgina Stirling was well-loved and adored throughout Europe, the United States, and her beloved Newfoundland. In the nineteenth century it was not uncommon for opera singers to achieve celebrity status with high regard in the public eye. Marchesi produced a wealth of these "celebrity" prima donnas.

Georgina was showered with constant and enthusiastic recognition for her gifts and talents and given bouquets of flowers, precious gifts, letters, and poems of adoration and pride. She continued to remain humble, kind, and down to earth. I believe she was especially conscious of her humanness, and often found the pressure and expectations challenging and overwhelming.

We were grateful to receive a photograph of the original *Twillingate Stirling* testimonial that Georgina was gifted during her 1895 "Grand Farewell Concert" in St. John's. It is printed in gold lettering on a blue satin background. It beautifully expresses the audience's adulation of Newfoundland's sweet songstress, capturing what she symbolized to her province. The cozy, scratchy sounds of a record playing Puccini's famous soprano aria "O mio babbino caro" introduces Maymie (Roberts) Hewlett's interview with Hiram Silk, CBC Radio, *Sights and Sounds*. She tenderly reads this testimonial to Hiram. Maymie says, "Miss Stirling gave me this before she died and told me the circumstances under which she received it, when she came back to Newfoundland to give her first performance. It was presented to her as a token from Newfoundland to Twillingate Stirling." Maymie then proceeds to read it in its entirety.

The first letter of each line, read downwards, spells the name Twillingate Stirling.

Thrice gifted daughter of the ice-bound coast
Whose voice, enchanting, spell bound, holds in thrall,
In coming years, through growing honours fall
Like sunbeams on the sea; be it still our boast,
Let others hear thy peerless voice and sing
In language choice and eulogy unfeigned,
Not though in prose and verse thy praise they ring,
Giving thee tribute rightfully attained,
And echoing thy tuneful fame afar,
To wider worlds: but not 'neath friendlier star:
Even theirs cannot exceed the warmth we bring.
Sweet songstress, of our hearts' deep gratitude
That thou art true to homeland and the shores
In which the voice, that now melodious pour
Rich stores of harmony was endued
Life's griefs to assuage and ease the chastening rod
Illustrious patriot: songstress without peer
Newfoundland hails thee, and in song sincere,
Gives thanks to thee and grateful praise to God.

TO BE PRESENTED WITH THIS DECORATIVE and resplendent testimonial on October 3, 1895, must have touched Georgina deeply as an extreme honour, as confirmation of her musical talents, and as recognition of whom she had become. Whatever name or title we attribute to our dear songstress, she was indeed very special.

While we're on the topic of names, I can't pass up the opportunity to share Georgina's adoration for pets. She loved to affectionately name them after famous musicians and teachers. Prima donnas have been noted over the course of history to have furry companions. I would think having the unconditional love of a pet makes the lonely times and stress of a career in the spotlight easier to cope with. This common trend started back before our Georgina was with

Marchesi. Impresario Colonel Mapleson of the New Imperial Opera Company refers to this trend in his memoirs and highlights one of Marchesi's star prima donnas, Ilma di Murska, of Croatia. "Every prima donna has generally a parrot, a pet dog, or an ape, which she loves to distraction, and carries with her wherever she goes. Ilma di Murska, however, traveled with an entire menagerie. Her immense Newfoundland dog, Pluto, dined with her every day. A cover was laid for him as for her, and he had learned to eat a fowl from a plate without dropping any of the meat or bones on the floor or even on the table cloth. Pluto was a good-natured dog, or he would have made short work of the monkey, the two parrots, and the Angora cat, who were his constant associates." (Roger Neill, *Divas*, page 53)

Greek soprano Maria Callas had pet poodles, named "Pixie" and "Djeddas," that would howl when she vocalized, and she had to leave them outside the room when she sang. And the great Italian soprano Renata Tebaldi was known for bringing her poodle, "New," to work with her at the La Scala Opera House. It appeared on stage

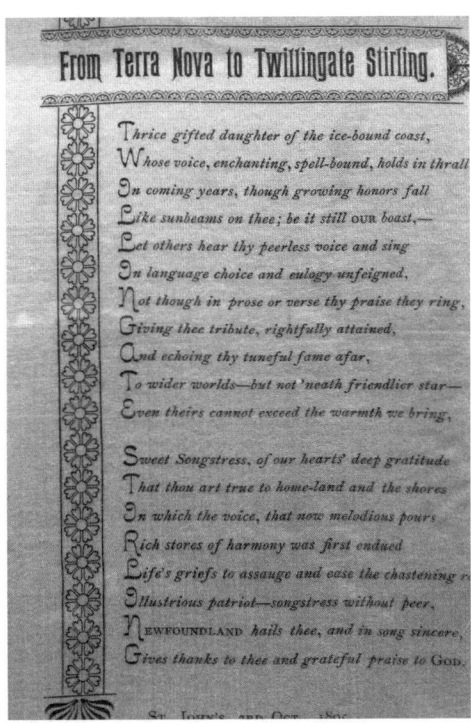

Photograph of the original Twillingate Stirling Testimonial presented to Georgina Stirling in St. John's, Newfoundland, on October 3, 1895, at her Farewell Concert. Maymie (Roberts) Hewlett reads this in her interview with Hiram Silk. (Courtesy of Bruce Manuel and Brent English)

with her in operas at the Metropolitan Opera, for example, when she sang the role of Musetta in *La Boheme*. Her poodle, too, howled along with her in the dressing rooms while she warmed up.

One of the well-known photographs we have of Georgina was taken in Milan in 1891 with her two cats, "Cosimo" and "Marchesi." It was beautifully restored and colourized by Gerard Nash in St. John's. Georgina obviously named one cat affectionately after her dear teacher Mathilde Marchesi. We cannot be certain who Cosimo was named after; however, after doing a little research, I found the Italian composer Cosimo Bottegari (1554–1620), a Florence-born composer. With Georgina having spent much time in Florence, studying the works of many Italian composers, it's possible that this is how her cat received his name.

Georgina Stirling in flamboyant costume. Place and date unknown. Featured in the *Advertiser*, Grand Falls, Thursday, December 22, 1966. Article by Hiram Silk. (Stirling family)

Georgina refers to her cats in her letters and speaks of them with great affection to her father, at times referring to them as her "sons." While her cats couldn't howl along with her, we see in one of her earlier letters that "Cosimo" becomes curious when Georgina is singing her high D's! In the first house they lived in at Florence, Georgina was not too proud to have crawled up under a house to rescue a sick dog, bringing it into the house to feed and care for it. She was not shy about expressing her anger and heartbreak at people who mistreated these innocent animals, and she wrote home to her Papa the following:

"For some time past the dog of the gardiner (sic) has been ill. The young signor told me last night that he saw him out in the yard dying, & that he had not eaten anything for some days. After Rose & I came into our house, I put on my coat and went down to look for him in the yard, I found him under an old part of the house not able to move, so I brought him up & gave him some warm bread & milk, & kept him in <u>on purpose</u> all night, this morning he seems much better than he did. I would love to flogg all the people who ill treat dumb beasts. When I am rich I shall found an asylum for poor cats & dogs. I think I like them better than I ever did & of course everyone laughs at me, but I don't mind."

While Georgina was living in Europe, she was gifted a sleek black dog whom she also named "Marchesi." When Georgina returned to Twillingate, she had five cats, one of whom was named "Felix." One could assume that he was named after the composer Felix Mendelssohn. Another of her family pets was her dog "Chip," whom she had trained to patiently wait until she placed a small piece of toast on his paw. She had a pet pig "Garibaldi," named after a famous Italian general who is reputed to have had a Newfoundland dog. "Garibaldi" roamed freely in and out of the house alongside Georgina, and she took him for walks on a leash in the town. She allowed her neighbour's two dogs to sleep in the Stirling house on cold winter nights, and she named them "Whisky" and "Brandy," most likely because they were of light and dark brown colours. She even had two cockerels in the house. Her generous nature toward pets and animals over the course of her life also speaks to her loving nature.

CHAPTER NINE
BY TONIA EVANS CIANCIULLI

GEORGINA TAKES THE UNITED STATES BY STORM

"In one's brain and one's soul lies the power to do almost anything. I believe that the psychological phenomena we hear so much about are nothing but undiscovered forces in ourselves."
— Sofia Scalchi, Italian Mezzo-soprano (1850–1922)

ON FRIDAY, NOVEMBER 9, 2018, we started our drive from Toronto to Miami with the kids to start our fifth winter of homeschooling. As my husband drove, I watched the highway signs as we made our way through North Carolina. I was reminded of a newspaper article declaring Georgina as "the greatest dramatic soprano in the whole world" as she toured across the United States.

I reflect as if I'm travelling along with Georgina in spirit on her American tour. This is great inspiration for writing. Madame Sofia Scalchi was a renowned Italian contralto with a newly formed opera company. Georgina embarked on tour with the Sofia Scalchi Opera Company in 1897, taking her across the United States by train.

"Newfoundland's clever operatic artist, Miss Stirling, or as she is better known on the stage abroad, Mlle. Marie Toulinguet, is filling a thirty weeks' engagement with the Scalchi Opera Company, as the prima donna soprano. In company with Marie du Bedat, Miss Stirling made her debut on the 18th of October last and has been travelling from place to place on the American continent ever since."
— St. John's *Daily News*, February 21, 1898

"Mlle Toulinguet has been declared the greatest dramatic soprano in the whole world. Her voice is of grand quality and as an artist she ranks with the best operatic stars in

the musical firmament. Mlle. Toulinguet is a native of Newfoundland and was edu-
cated in Italy and is also one of the prize pupils of Marchesi."

— The *Raleigh*, North Carolina, January 1898

The *Anaconda Standard Sun* in Montana, December 26, 1897. "Associated with Scalchi is Mlle. Toulinguet, said to be the greatest dramatic soprano in the world." (newspapers.com)

GEORGINA MADE A CONSIDERABLE IMPRESSION on Sofia Scalchi and was chosen as the "prima donna soprano" of her touring company. She was a versatile singer with a charismatic personality that impacted audiences across the nation. It is no exaggeration to say that wherever she went, she "stole the show." The year prior to joining the Scalchi tour, she made a stunning impression. The *Anaconda Standard* in Anaconda, Montana, had written: "Mlle Toulinguet, who at the head of the Mapleson forces last year, created a sensation by her magnificent singing and wonderfully powerful voice of which she possessed."

The other reputable singers listed on tour with Georgina were tenor Signor M. Guarini, baritone Signor A. Alberti, tenor Thomas McQueen, and mezzo-soprano Mlle. Marie du Bedat, Ireland's Nightingale, Georgina's friend. The singers were accompanied by Signor V. Galli, the musical director.

The *Wilmington Messenger* of Wilmington, North Carolina, on Saturday, October, 23, 1897 states:

"On Tuesday October 26th, at the opera house, the world renowned Sofia Scalchi and Marie Toulinguet, together with one of the strongest companies of operatic artists that have ever gone on the road in this country, will appear here. To those who have heard the great contralto her singing will never be forgotten. Her strong rich voice and grand delivery and her splendid diction have made her the model for all the singers who are yet to be heard. (Adelina) Patti in her palmiest days had to share the triumphs with this contralto, and even the great singers of the European opera houses were placed as second to this most experienced artist and the favorite of the public on two continents. Scalchi today is the model of a great artist. For fifteen years she has held the great first place in all the world as the greatest in her line, and we are to have her in at least one of her favorite operatic roles. Aside from this one of the greatest sopranos of the country, Marie Toulinguet, will make her first appearance here on this occasion. Toulinguet made an immense and unexpected hit with the great Colonel Mapleson's Imperial Opera Company, and it is only owing to the fact there will be no grand opera worthy of the name in New York this season that both Toulinguet and Scalchi will be heard in other cities of the country."

Madame Sofia Scalchi, the acclaimed contralto, with whose opera company Georgina toured through the United States in 1897–98 (Painting in Light/flickr)

THIS QUOTE SPEAKS TO HOW SKILLED, respected, and far-reaching an artist was Sofia Scalchi. Georgina was among incredible talent and was singled out for her own.

The Arkansas newspaper wrote: "Certainly nothing more tender and withal sweeter than Mlle. Toulinguet's voice in song is often heard. The world will never tire of her voice." Also, "Mlle. Toulinguet undoubtedly achieved the triumph of the evening, if gauged by the spontaneity of applause, and the verdict of Little Rock's music loving element will be that she takes the highest rank as a soprano."

The *Savannah Press* caught the flavour of Georgina's relationship with the sea when it commented: ". . . Mlle. Toulinguet won her way with her listeners, particularly when to an encore she sang The Last Rose of Summer treating the beloved air with great delicacy and feeling. Her voice is strong, clear and sweet, and makes one think of the sparkling waves, the fresh cool winds, through the pine forests of her island home."

Undoubtedly these comments reflected the listeners' association of Georgina with her origin at the edge of the sea. Georgina continued to take the United States by storm with her delightful performances. The *Charleston News* of South Carolina said: "Mlle. Toulinguet sings faultlessly and without the least effort. Her high notes are as clear as a bell and her range seems unlimited. She had to sing three times before the delighted listeners would let the performance go on."

The *St. Joseph Herald* of Missouri on Tuesday, January 25, quoted, "We are able to hear one of the greatest sopranos in the world, Mlle. Toulinguet, who is said to be the best dramatic singer on the lyrical stage. She is from Newfoundland and has already made a great career for herself in Europe. She has only sung one season in America and that was last year with the Mapleson Imperial Grand Opera Company, when she created a sensation. Her voice is at once very strong and very sympathetic, and has been pronounced by critics as being wonderfully like that of Mme. Parepa. Mlle Touliguet will sing in the opera and also in the concert part of the programme." Mme. Euphrosyne Parepa-Rosa (1836–1874), to whom Georgina was compared, was a British opera soprano who made her operatic debut in London, England, in 1867; she also toured successfully in America for several years. Tragically, she fell ill at the young age of thirty-seven and died.

Some of these quotes are taken directly from www.newspapers.com. These archived newspaper articles followed the successful Scalchi tour, outlining repertoire sung by the five singers that made up the troupe. It was fascinating to discover the large number of cities they covered in only a few months on tour. Madame Scalchi, in an interview with the *Leavenworth Times* in Leavenworth, Kansas, on January 20, 1898, describes their experience and undertaking by saying, "I started on this tour at Norfolk, Virginia, sixteen weeks ago, and have sung in all the large cities of the south and as far north as Vancouver. We are now on our road east, and will, when the tour is concluded, have been thirty-five weeks in making a most successful tour. Yes, travelling is very tiresome, but with the elegant train service that you have in this country it is not as monotonous as it might be."

Until recently we had information confirming that Georgina's Canadian travels had been limited to musical studies in Toronto and an opera performance in Montreal. We assume that a Montreal appearance could only have been with either the New Imperial Opera Company or with the Scalchi tour, but this cannot be verified. We discovered the Scalchi Opera Company, after a performance in Seattle on December 20, 1897, made its way over to the Vancouver Opera for a one-night-only performance on Friday, December 24. The *Vancouver Daily World* noted at the Vancouver Opera House, "One Night Only," listing Mlle Marie Toulinguet as "a famous artist'" assisting Sofia Scalchi. Her name is in large font below Scalchi's stating that she is, "The renowned prima donna soprano, late of the Imperial Opera Company."

My research also revealed more of the repertoire that Georgina was hailed for performing. During operatic concerts like these, audiences love to hear the classic crowd-pleasers that showed off the vocal abilities and personalities of each singer.

Georgina performed opera arias, duets, and also ballads that resonated with her as an artist and spoke to her family roots and culture. These ballads were quoted as being sung as concert encores. "It was not alone Scalchi who pleased the audience. Encores were asked and freely given, that of *The Last Rose of Summer* by Mlle Touliguet being especially sweet and effective" (*Greensboro Telegram* on Thursday, October 21, 1897). The *Kansas City Journal* of Missouri on Thursday, January 20, 1898, makes reference to Georgina's concert music, saying, "Mlle. Toulinguet the great soprano, who was the featuring artist of the Mapleson Imperial Opera Company last year, will sing some of her favorite old English songs, as well as some of the most popular of the grand opera numbers." The *Butte Miner* of Butte, Montana, on January 1, 1898, says, "Her voice has exceptional range, and her high notes are as clear as a bell. *The Green Isle of Erin*, which the lady gave in response to a hearty and determined encore, gave her an opportunity to show her easy control of a rarely sweet voice."

Singing opera with equal parts passion and poise, Georgina performed with great command the arias of such renowned composers as Verdi, Gounod, Puccini, Bellini, Van Weber, and Handel. As quoted in the *Anaconda Standard*, Thursday, December 30, 1897, "Scalchi will appear in a regular concert programme and will give one or two acts of grand opera presented with full scenery, costumes, and paraphernalia, etc. It will be an event to have an act of 'Faust' and 'Trovatore' with a cast like this and with Scalchi in the chief roles. Associated with Scalchi is Mlle Toulinguet, said to be one of the greatest dramatic sopranos in the world."

The *Greensboro Telegram* advertises the entire program of operatic favourites sung by the five singers in their newspaper on Wednesday October, 20, 1897. On Saturday evening at G.F. College Chapel in Greensboro, North Carolina, the program showed Marie Tou-linguet singing:

> *Ah, forse lui*, "La Traviata" by Verdi
> *Chi mi frena in tal momento* (Act II Finale), "Lucia di Lammermoor" by Donizetti

> Second Act of "Il Trovatore" by Verdi with Marie singing the lead role of "Leonora"
> *Casta Diva*, "Norma" by Bellini

> *Bella figlia dell'amore* (Act III Quartet), "Rigoletto" by Verdi

OTHER GRAND OPERA REPERTOIRE performed by Marie Toulinguet while on tour include: the soprano part of Rossini's *Stabat Mater* scored for four vocal soloists, as quoted in the *Austin American-Statesman* in Austin, Texas, and on Tuesday, November, 30, 1897, the Second Act of the opera *Martha*, a romantic comic opera by Friedrich von Flotow, with Georgina singing the lead soprano role of "Martha." She sang the lead soprano role of "Leonora" in the Fourth Act of *Il Trovatore* by Verdi, and the Third Act of *Faust* by Gounod, singing the role of "Marguerite." These opera excerpts were reported by several newspapers, including the *Anaconda Standard* in Montana, advertising for the upcoming concert in their paper on Sunday, October 17, 1897, the *Los Angeles Times* on Thursday, December, 9, 1897, the *Seattle Post-Intelligencer* on Monday, December, 20, 1897, the *Nebraska State Journal* on Sunday, January 9, 1898, the *Kansas City Journal* on Thursday, January 20, 1898, and the *Star Tribune* in Minneapolis, Minnesota, on Sunday, February 6, 1898.

DRAMA BETWEEN DIVAS

"It's all very easy at the onset. When a singer's commencing her career, everybody has kind things to say about her, everybody encourages her, and there is nothing for her to worry about. . . . But when she has made her reputation, then her troubles begin. So much more is expected of her . . ."
— Lola Beeth, Austrian Soprano, Pupil of Mathilde Marchesi (1861–1904)

WOULD THE GENEROUS PRAISE AND SINGLING OUT that Georgina was receiving in the newspapers become a problem between the two divas? Drama between divas can be very real and is a topic that's been highlighted in the opera world. The newspapers almost exclusively spoke in great detail about only Sofia Scalchi and Georgina Stirling, simply listing the other four singers by name. Often accompanying the newspaper articles were sketch drawings of Scalchi and Georgina. It became evident from the outpouring of the positive press coverage Georgina was receiving throughout the tour that the operatic world was being moved by the "Newfoundland magic" she brought with her everywhere she went. The *Paris News* of Texas quotes: "To Mlle Marie Toulinguet a majority of the audience were doubtless more indebted than to any other member of the company. Her first appearance was in an air from *Traviata* and her voice was as sweet as a lullaby and soothing enough to calm the most boisterous wave on the ocean."

Georgina was constantly gaining public adulation, and this may have been the cause of a growing friction between her and Madame Scalchi. Sofia Scalchi was the main "diva" but could have grown jealous of Georgina's paise. The favourable reviews came fast and furious. Did this create a friction that ended Georgina's involvement with the tour?

There are reasons why female singers have become known as "divas" or "prima donnas" and why opera is famous for its fiery temperaments and personalities. This behaviour can result for a number of reasons: competition over roles, age insecurities, who gets more press coverage, even who has the "better gown," or "who appears first in a program."

During Georgina's career abroad, and even before, competition between opera singers was alive and well. An article on www.independent.co.uk called "Whine, women and song: the bitter rivalry of Handel's divas," written by Arifa Akbar, on Monday, April 28, 2008, recounts the well-known story about the dramatic battle between two Italian star divas in 1726: Francesca Cuzzoni and Faustina Bordoni. Performing for the high society of Britain, these leading ladies made life interesting for Handel and other composers, as they "spent much of their careers battling each other for the lion's share of the audience's applause." These two divas were known as the "rival queens." Another example: "During one steaming night in June 1727, their personal and professional rivalry exploded into a fight on stage of the King's Theatre, in Haymarket, in front of the Princess of Wales. The two women reportedly tore off each other's 'coiffs' and hurled abusive insults in Italian before being escorted from the stage."

More modern examples of this are the stories told about world-famous soprano Kathleen Battle, who was fired from the Metropolitan Opera. Making the front page of the *New*

York Times on April 4, 2016, an article written by Michael Cooper reports that twenty-two years after being fired by the Metropolitan Opera Company, Kathleen Battle "will return to the Met next season to sing a recital of spirituals." Ms. Battle was said to have been fired by the general manager at the time, Joseph Volpe, for "unprofessional actions during rehearsals." The article goes on to list the stories about the diva that were circulating: "divalike behavior and rudeness toward colleagues, including demands that other singers leave rehearsals when she was singing, not to look at her mouth during duets, arriving late, leaving early or not to show up at all."

Mathilde Marchesi's studio was comprised strictly of female voices making the competition for roles fiercer. There would have been plenty of opportunity for jealous encounters and competitiveness. Roger Neill lists a few examples of this type of interaction between Marchesi's pupils throughout his book *Divas* and notes that, "The usual course of events, acted out previously between several pairs of Marchesi pupils, is that prima donnas start out resentful of each other and gradually build up implacable hostility."

The opposite seems to have happened between Georgina and Marie du Bedat. Their friendship may have begun as early as 1894 in England on the concert tours with Charles Santley, which included Dublin, Ireland, Marie du Bedat's home. The friendship continued in New York during their time with Colonel Mapleson's opera company. Georgina then took Marie back home to Newfoundland in June 1897 to perform concerts together at St. John's and to enjoy a summer holiday together in Twillingate before touring with the Scalchi Opera Company. These two Nightingales had a healthy relationship based on mutual respect. I feel this relationship was possible based on a few reasons. With Marie du Bedat being from Ireland and Georgina's Irish roots and culture, this would have given the two singers common interest on which to connect. Georgina was a compassionate and down-to-earth person, an easy friend to be with. Also, the two singers were of different voice types, soprano and mezzo-soprano, so this would have created no direct competition of roles or repertoire.

Roger Neill also commented on the positive notices that Georgina was receiving as the prima donna soprano despite the fact that Scalchi was the star attraction. This could very well have been on Scalchi's mind for some time and then come to a head, resulting in Georgina's abrupt release in February of 1898. "Mlle Toulinguet, the prima donna of the Scalchi Opera company, made her last appearance with the company tonight in this city, and leaves for New York tomorrow. . . . In an interview tonight she stated that she would bring suit against Mme

Scalchi Concert Company.

What will undoubtedly be the event of the season in the eyes of those local theater-goers who prefer musical entertainments of the higher order will be the appearance at Ming's opera house Dec. 30 of the Scalchi Concert company, composed of the following eminent art-

MLLE. MARIE TOULINGUET.

ists: Mme. Sofia Scalchi, prima donna contralto; Mlle. Marie Toulinguet, prima donna soprano; Mlle. Marie du Bedat, mezzo-soprano; Thomas McQueen, tenor; Signor A. Alberti, baritone; Signor C. Gnarro, musical director.

Madame Sofia Scalchi is undoubtedly the greatest living contralto and an artist of the first magnitude. She needs no introduction to those familiar with her long and successful career.

Mlle. Toulinguet, the dramatic soprano of Col. Mapleton's Imperial Opera company last year, will make her first appearance outside of London, New York, Boston and Philadelphia with the Scalchi company. Mlle. du Bedat was a member of the great Imperial Opera company last season, this being her first appearance in America. As one of the principal artists of the Royal Carl Rosa Opera company for three years she achieved a great success in England. Signor Alberti made his first appearance in America last season as principal baritone of Col. Mapleson's Imperial Opera company. His success is a matter of record.

The concert will consist of the third act of Faust, the second act of Martha and the fourth act of Il Trovatore.

Scalchi for the balance of the money due on her contract (and) . . . that she had been getting notices over Mme Scalchi and thought her dismissal was due to jealousy."

Neill goes on to give his own opinion of Georgina being "dispensed for her services," claiming it may have been because Georgina was having a problem with alcohol. At this point in Georgina's career, given her consistent and numerous rave reviews by audiences and press, I don't consider this conclusion valid. If Georgina were overindulging in alcohol to an extent that she was fired, she would not have had the physical or vocal strength and clarity of voice to produce such quality performances, especially considering the type of demanding repertoire she was performing.

In Scalchi's aforementioned interview with the *Leavenworth Times*, she addresses the fact that there were rumours that her own voice was declining. "Despite her vigorous protest to the contrary, Mme. Scalchi's voice has lost much of its old-time sweetness and power, but there is much left to charm and delight the lovers of music." And, "In answer to a query that it had been reported that her voice had lost much of its former strength and sweetness, she said: 'Many critics of music and singers of note think that in writing a criticism they should say things that are not true about stars, and then the critic would be called an almost learned man in music because he had used a pen dipped in gall and malice. They said my age had affected my voice to such an extent that my old friends would not recognize it. You know that is not true. My voice today is more agreeable than ever before. I have over twenty grand operas in my repertoire. I do not sing in any other but my native tongue, which is the one most preferred

The *Independent-Record*, Montana, December 20, 1897. Highlighting Marie Toulinguet, "the dramatic soprano of Col. Mapleson's Imperial Opera Company last year, will make her first appearance outside of London, New York, Boston and Philadelphia with the Scalchi company." (Article found on newspapers.com)

by the opera-loving people.'" This interview was published on January 30, 1898. The last posted article mentioning Georgina with the Scalchi Opera Company that I was able to find was
February 21, 1898, from the *Neenah Daily Times*, Neenah, Wisconsin. Georgina would have
left or been released sometime between February 21 and March 6, 1898.

Could it be that all of this triggered something in Sofia, making her feel insecure of her
rank and talent? The *Daily Arkansas Gazette* on Sunday, November 14, 1897, quoted: "But
with due deference to a star of such magnitude as she (Sofia Scalchi), the treat of the evening
was furnished by Mlle. Toulinguet, prima donna soprano. It is the soprano of a great artist,
and none sweeter has been heard on the local stage. Mlle. Toulinguet undoubtedly achieved
the triumph of the evening. If gauged by the spontaneity of the applause, the verdict of Little
Rock's music-loving element will be that she takes the highest rank as a soprano."

Despite the fact that Scalchi and Georgina had different voice types, thus causing no
direct competition for roles, Georgina was making the headlines in bold print right next to
Scalchi, garnering greater adulation. Georgina was thirty-one years old during this American
tour, and Scalchi was forty-eight. It is possible that Scalchi's fear of the natural process of
an aging voice before her audiences could have caused her to feel insecure with the young
and fresh voice of Marie Toulinguet. Scalchi had retired from her career at the Metropolitan
Opera Company in 1896 prior to her final American tour. It is understandably a sensitive and
delicate matter for an opera singer, and other artists in fields where age can affect their overall
performance ability and length of career, to come to terms with the end of a performance
career. Perhaps this was weighing on Scalchi's mind.

Roger Neill writes, "While Scalchi was billed as the star attraction, Marie (Georgina)
attracted consistently positive notices in the press and the apparent result was that she was
abruptly fired in St. Paul (Minnesota) in February 1898." Neill continues by adding this comment from a source which he unfortunately does not name or date: "Mlle Toulinguet, the prima
donna of the Scalchi Opera Company, makes her last appearance with the company tonight in
this city, and leaves for New York tomorrow . . . in an interview tonight she stated that she would
bring suit against Mlle Scalchi for the balance of money due on her contract (and) . . . that she
has been getting notices over Mlle Scalchi and thought that her dismissal was due to jealousy."

The *Davenport Sun* on March 13 writes that Georgina "has quarrelled with the great
contralto and left the company." Georgina was no wilting violet, and her Irish temper probably guaranteed that she would not hold her tongue if she felt she had been wronged. It

is typical of many of Neill's insensitive and dismissive comments about several of Madame Marchesi's students that he then insinuates that the reason for Georgina's dismissal may have been "her problem with alcohol." Neill then appears to blame Amy Louise Peyton for identifying Georgina's problem as "alcoholism" then saying, ". . . it may well have been alcoholism that triggered both her dismissal by Sofia Scalchi and forced her later retirement." No proof. Simply insinuation. That double-edged conclusion is unacceptable in view of information that we will reveal later.

From what we now know and from what Roger Neill seems to have unfairly concluded from Amy Louise Peyton's book about Georgina's drinking problem, which came much later, we may be on much more accurate grounds to surmise that there was more likely a battle going on between Scalchi's ego (as well as her personal life) and the effusive praise which had been accorded to Georgina in the press, which resulted in Georgina being "let go."

TEMPERS MAY HAVE BEEN FRAYED for other reasons at this point. Count Lolli, Madame Scalchi's husband, had been absent from the tour in 1897–98, and Madame Scalchi had stated to a newspaper that, "He had matters of state to attend to at home." However, they divorced in 1898, leaving one to wonder if she were carrying a heavy burden throughout the whole of that tour.

It makes more sense to conclude that Georgina left the Scalchi tour on her own account. Maybe we will never know the whole truth behind this development. However, the facts seem to present a case in favour of Georgina.

GEORGINA IN NEW YORK AND WASHINGTON

"Learn all there is to learn, and then choose your own path."
— George Frideric Handel

PREDATING GEORGINA'S AMERICAN TOUR with the Scalchi Opera Company, she had been in New York in 1896 and Washington in early 1897. The British impresario James Henry Mapleson was an influential and integral figure in the nineteenth-century world of opera. He was "snapping up" and engaging many of the top opera singers of the day for his productions and helping them in the development of their operatic careers. Sofia Scalchi was herself employed by Colonel Mapleson for many seasons early in her career. Many of Colonel Mapleson's other prima donnas were, not surprisingly, star pupils of Mathilde Marchesi's studio, such as the Croatian-born soprano Ilma di Murska, who was one of Marchesi's first celebrity prima donnas, the Hungarian soprano Etelka Gerster, American soprano Emma Nevada, and the world-famous Madrid-born Adelina Patti.

Before Mapleson's days of showcasing and management of great operatic talent and productions were over, he engaged Marie Toulinguet in his New Imperial Opera Company in New York at the Academy of Music. She made her debut with them in October of 1896, making an incredibly favourable impression on the audiences of New York City. The *New York Recorder* hailed Marie Toulinguet as "an artist such as we have not had in this country for many a year. Her voice is of tremendous power with a sympathetic quality that fairly thrills." And the *Boston Globe* reported, "Such a voice one hears only once in a lifetime. She held her audience spellbound."

It was during Georgina's time with Colonel Mapleson's company that she was united with the Irish mezzo-soprano Marie du Bedat. They were both engaged by the New Imperial Opera in New York and later moved on to the Scalchi Opera Company to tour together once Mapleson's company folded due to the fierce competition with the Metropolitan Opera Company. "I cannot fight Wall Street," the defeated Colonel Mapleson lamented.

These two Nightingales would have experienced such disappointment with the folding of Mapleson's company while they were only partway through the opera season. Opera seasons will generally start in September of a calendar year and continue into the next year until May. The operas seasons would have been scheduled at least a year or two in advance with the singers engaged to fill the roles. This would have left the Newfoundland and Ireland Nightingales searching for engagements.

Thankfully, Georgina was kept busy gaining experience and garnering reviews while engaged with the Boston Symphony Orchestra, singing with them in Brooklyn and Washington. The *Washington Times* on Wednesday, January 20, 1897, speaks to the third concert of the season with the Boston Symphony Orchestra. "As usual the theatre was crowded with cultured and hence appreciative auditors and the concert was received with the customary enthusiasm which Mr. Emil Paur and his players invariably inspire. The program varied in character, presenting selections from the works of Mozart, Weber, Handel, Bizet and Liszt, and there was a measure of novelty in the appearance of a vocalist with the orchestra, the first time this season." The article goes on to list the musical excerpts performed by the symphony and then ends by commenting, "Miss Marie Toulinguet was the soloist. Her voice is a well-rounded soprano of power, but exceeding sweetness in legato passages and pleasing vibrato on organ notes." Her selections were an aria from Weber's rarely given *Xerxes* and a more familiar aria from *Freischütz*. The opera *Der Freischütz* was written by the composer Carl Maria von Weber. It does not say which aria from *Freischütz* that Georgina sang; there are two soprano roles in this opera, and no mezzo-soprano characters. She would have sung an aria of either the character Ännchen or Agathe. The *Xerxes* (the Italian pronunciation: *Serse*) aria to which they refer was "Ombra Mai Fu," which was composed by Handel, not Weber, a typo in the newspaper. In the online Boston Orchestra archives I came across a copy of the Boston Symphony's Third Concert of the Season, which took place on Tuesday evening, January 19, in Washington in their 1896–1897 season. It was thrilling to see "Soloist, Miss Marie Toulinguet" in print on their program. Georgina would have taken great advantage of using her emotional capabilities to impact her audience with these two beautiful solos to stand out amongst an evening of symphony.

Handel's "Ombra Mai Fu" was one of the first popular soprano arias I sang. It speaks to the sheltering branches from storms and winds, never to disrupt one's peace. I imagined this as a metaphor for Georgina's strong Newfoundland roots and the way they sheltered her and protected her along her amazing yet often trying journey. "Tender and beautiful fronds of my beloved plane tree, let fate smile upon you. May thunder, lightning, and storms never disturb your dear peace, nor may you by blowing winds be profaned. Never was a shade of any plant dearer and more lovely, or more sweet."

Boston Symphony Orchestra

Columbia Theatre, Washington.

Sixteenth Season, 1896–97. Twelfth Season in Washington.

Mr. EMIL PAUR, Conductor.

Third Concert, Tuesday Evening, January 19, At Eight.

PROGRAMME.

Wolfgang Amadeus Mozart — Symphony in G minor (Koechel, 550

  I. Allegro molto (G minor) - - - - - - - 4-4
  II. Andante (E-flat major) - - - - - - 6-8
  III. Menuetto: Allegro (G minor) - - - - - 3-4
    Trio (G major) - - - - - - - 3-4
  IV. Finale: Allegro assai (G minor) - - - - 4-4

George Frideric Handel — Air, "Ombra mai fu," from "Xerxes"

Karl Maria von Weber — - - - Overture to "Oberon"

Intermission.

Georges Bizet - - Entr'actes and Ballet Music from "Carmen"

Karl Maria von Weber - - - - Aria from "Freischütz"

Franz Liszt, Scene in the Tavern (Mephisto Waltz), from Lenau's "Faust"

Soloist, Miss MARIE TOULINGUET.
(3)

Program shows Georgina Stirling's appearance as soloist with the Boston Symphony Orchestra, January 19, 1897. "Marie Toulinguet." (Courtesy of Leon Levy BAM Digital Archive)

When the Boston Symphony Orchestra wrapped up their season in Washington with a program of Wagnerian music, the *Evening Star* on Wednesday, March 24, 1897, reviewed the soloists from the symphony's season, a total of five concerts, which had been declared "of the very highest order, and fully merited the strong following it enjoyed. . . . The soloists provided by the orchestra were as a rule, of the first-class and were received with every mark of favor. They were Miss Marie Toulinguet, Teresa Careno, Mr. Martinus Sieveking and Mr. Ben Davies. This array of both music and soloists leaves the music lovers of Washington in a most pleasant anticipation of the treat which will be given them next season by this estimable organization."

Although Georgina's time in the United States brought some of the disheartening aspects of a musical career, it was full of adventure and valuable performance experience. Georgina was closing that chapter with an overwhelming number of rave reviews, establishing "Marie Toulinguet" as one of the leading international prima donnas. Carrying forth these experiences and credentials, Georgina returns to Italy as a favoured songstress among composers and audiences.

CHAPTER TEN
By Tonia Evans Cianciulli

MARIE TOULINGUET RETURNS TO ITALY BY DEMAND

"Believe me, I worked hard, so hard that I never really had a life of my own in all the years I was singing. You also have to be somebody who is willing to suffer, to feel the pain that goes with all of it."
— Rosa Ponselle, American Soprano (1897–1981)

GEORGINA HAD BEEN WILDLY SUCCESSFUL during her time in the United States with Colonel J. Henry Mapleson's New Imperial Opera Company, the Boston Symphony Orchestra, and the Sofia Scalchi Opera Company. The *Boston Globe* in 1897 said, "Such a voice one hears only once in a lifetime." The *Philadelphia Times* commented, "The astonishing voice of Mlle. Toulinguet came as a revelation. It is the grandest soprano we have heard since Parepa's day." This would have been a great honour for Georgina, placing her in the class of Euphrosyne Parepa, the renowned British soprano who, with her husband, Carl Rosa, was largely responsible for introducing opera to America in cities and towns where opera had never been presented.

While she was still engaged in the concert circuit in London, Georgina had been recruited by Colonel Mapleson as the prima donna soprano for two years in his opera company. In 1896, Colonel Mapleson was on his way back from an extensive visit to Italy, where he had been expanding and deepening his repertoire of Italian music. He was gathering ideas for the designing of costumes and stage sets when he stopped in London, where he had spent many years on the concert circuit. Georgina was well-experienced in Italian opera and was ideal for the leading role of soprano. In Colonel Mapleson's company, her singing "astonished" New York audiences and "held them spellbound."

When the New Imperial Opera Company folded in mid-season under strong competition from the Metropolitan, Georgina was engaged by the Boston Harmony Orchestral Society and finished the season with them in the spring of 1897. During this period the Orchestral Society also presented concerts in both Washington and Brooklyn. Presumably Georgina's sister Kate Putzki and her husband, Paul, attended the Washington concerts; they had been living in Washington since 1890. The only extensive press coverage found for Georgina during this period covered a minor role in the opera *Andrea Chenier*.

Georgina had become a favourite of the public, and now with an international reputation as a soprano, she was in a position to choose the path forward. After finishing her time with the Scalchi Opera Company, she journeyed to New York and then to Italy. She entered what could only be described as the pinnacle of her career. It began with an invitation to Venice.

Amy Louise Peyton quotes the newspaper *Daily News* of St. John's but unfortunately does not provide a date. We may assume that this article was published in the early fall of 1898 and that the cablegram from Madame Scalchi to which it refers had been sent to Georgina by midsummer. The cablegram clearly confirms the excitement Georgina had brought to the Scalchi tour during 1897–98 and that Madame Scalchi had come to terms with what the audiences and the press had adored about Georgina. I feel this is good enough evidence to silence Roger Neill's conclusion that Georgina had a problem with alcohol. If alcohol had been problem, Madame Scalchi would not have invited Georgina to return to this high-calibre and well-respected company. The *Daily News* reports: "The many friends and admirers of Marie Toulinguet (Miss Stirling) will rejoice to know of recent success in Italy. About a month ago, a cablegram reached her from Madame Scalchi requesting her to proceed to New York to enter into a season's engagement. This tempting offer was promptly declined by Miss Stirling who preferred to remain in Italy where better opportunities were offered for advancement in her profession."

Georgina had been invited back to Italy during the summer of 1898, accepting the lead soprano role of "Bice" in Errico Petrella's opera *Marco Visconti*, in Venice. The Venice newspaper *Adriatic* recorded, "The favourite of the public is without a doubt the prima donna Marie Toulinguet, who sustained the most difficult part of Bice in the most splendid manner and who is constantly applauded, if alone for her dramatic genius. She sings with great passion and sentiment and her voice shows to great advantage in the high notes. It is much to be hoped that the new opera *Absolum* will have such an interpreting artist."

What comes next for Georgina is an honour that any opera singer sees as a dream come true. Confirming her international success and much sought-after vocal and dramatic talents, Georgina was requested to premiere a newly composed Mass and to perform it in Chioggia, Italy. After receiving this request by telegram for the performance on October 29, 1898, Georgina accepted this grand honour.

The telegrams Georgina received read: "Your presence is indispensable at Chioggia. We count on your coming as soon as possible." Following that, "Orchestra and chorus refuse to practice without you. Everything in confusion, utterly ruined unless you come. Don't refuse." The third telegram read, "All is arranged. The Maestro Tacheo assumes direction of orchestra and desires that you only will sing his Mass. We await you anxiously. Telegram when we are to meet you."

On this "Night of Honour" in Chioggia, Georgina witnessed an incredible display of public ovation. Not only were there "heaps of choicest flowers" thrown to her from the opera box seats, but also "live doves and canaries" were concealed within the bouquets. This was indeed a significant night in Georgina's life, one that must have been a triumph for all her diligent work and sacrifice.

During this night of celebration, Georgina received grand testimonial in similar fashion to the one she had received in St. John's, Newfoundland, in 1895. This was bound in dark green velvet with gold lettering and presented in Italian. This piece of history is on proud display in the Twillingate Museum along with some of Georgina's other personal items and programs. Translated into English, it reads:

> To you young lady
> Marie Toulinguet
> Not the last of the chosen ones
> of which the art of aria honours
> who from the Italian stage and across the borders
> planted branches of laurel.
> We with heartfelt gratitude
> admiring and applauding
> consecrate this testimony to you.
> New triumphs we wish
> to this excellent artist
> gifted with such a beautiful voice
> who with intelligence and love

has been educated through severe laws
of harmony and sound
and now conquers and steals the hearts of the public
winning their admiration and applause.

Green velvet-covered Testimonial presented to Marie Toulinguet on October 29, 1898, at Chioggia, Italy, following a performance at the Ricordo Opera Hall, with photo and program (Author photo)

THE MOST FAMOUS PHOTOGRAPH OF GEORGINA was taken during this juncture in her career at Chioggia, Italy. It had been made into a postcard and viewed numerous times in newspaper articles. It then graced the cover of Amy Louise Peyton's book. On her own original postcard she sends season's greetings from Venice, Italy, in 1898 to the Linfield family back in Twillingate, signing her name as Georgie Stirling. I was thrilled to see one of these postcards in Georgina's private collection, which became the possession of Amy Louise Peyton and is now in the care of her daughter, Evelyn Peyton Murphy, in St. John's, Newfoundland and Labrador. We were invited to visit Evelyn's home in August 2018 while in St.

John's for the concerts and meet with three of the Peyton siblings—Evelyn, Carol Fitzpatrick, and Kent Peyton. This was a special visit for me and my grandfather.

There is a picture of Georgina's sister Lucy Stirling on the same kind of postcard format as that of Georgina's, which is shown on page 145 of Amy Louise Peyton's book. Lucy's picture is inscribed at the bottom, "F. Gavagnin—Chioggia," as is Georgina's, proving that Lucy had attended Georgina's performance in the new Mass. It is likely that their sister Janet from London also attended, but there is no picture to verify this.

Left: Georgina Stirling postcard, signed "Marie Toulinguet," Season's Greetings to family friends, the Lindfields in Twillingate, from Venice, Italy, 1898. Photo taken at time of her concert in Chioggia, Italy, October 29, 1898. (Courtesy of Vaughn Harbin)
Right: Lucy Stirling while attending Georgina's concert in Chioggia, Italy, October 1898 (Courtesy of Vaughn Harbin)

Georgina loved collecting, sending, and receiving postcards. Many of Georgina's postcards I had the honour of viewing were from Italy. They looked like miniature pieces of artwork, beautifully painted or featuring famous European scenes. Georgina had communicated consistently via postcards and written letters with her sisters, other family members, neighbours, and opera colleagues who had become good friends. She loved postcards.

During the height of her career in Italy, and after she had moved to Milan, the postcards seem to cease almost immediately after her friends, singer Boyd McQueen (stage name Tomaso Boyd) and his wife leave Milan in the fall of 1900 for an extended visit to Scotland and London. The McQueens write regularly, and soon with growing anxiety, because they receive no replies. Georgina's sisters in London were undoubtedly writing to her, as they had always done, but there is no record of a response from Georgina until September of 1901. In the latter part of that year, Georgina returned to London and for a while stayed with her sisters at the nursing station where Janet and Lucy worked and where they rented apartments.

What happened to Georgina in this year of silence, from fall 1900 to fall 1901, is shrouded in mystery. Perhaps the truth will never be known. The most common explanation is that she strained her voice or developed a serious throat ailment which led to depression and despondency and, eventually, as a way of assuaging the pain, to drinking.

Georgina seemed to descend quickly, from the dizzying heights of elation and significant career status, to heartbreak and emotional distress. She was experiencing an incredibly low and dark period in her life and career. As a tender and sensitive personality, this development—whatever it was—would have challenged Georgina's whole being.

What I have come to admire and appreciate about Georgina is her inner strength and determination to cope with great tragedy and loss. For a time it had overwhelmed her. She began to rebuild her life with a buoyant faith and a proactive desire to heal and rest herself, physically and emotionally. She needed time to heal the emotional trauma. There is a note of victory, even triumph, in Georgina's final years.

CHAPTER ELEVEN
BY TONIA EVANS CIANCIULLI

GEORGINA'S ARTISTRY AND HER HUMANNESS

"You are born an artist or you are not. And you stay an artist, dear,
even if your voice is less of a fireworks. The artist is always there."
— Maria Callas, Greek Soprano (1923–1977)

REFLECTING ON GEORGINA'S "DAYS OF DESPAIR," Amy Louise Peyton writes, "Periods of depression were taking a hold on her. Every singer dies two deaths, the first and the most painful is the cessation of one's singing activities. This was true of Marie Toulinguet and the trauma made a lasting impression in her life."

We may never really know what happened to the sweet voice of our Nightingale. Perhaps that mystery contributes to a lingering aura of the tragic romanticism and allure surrounding her life and legacy. The wondering keeps our hearts sympathetically tied to her. There will never be any denying that Georgina was an extremely gifted singer, musician, and artist. She made Newfoundland and the world abroad proud with her extraordinary talent and achievements. Knowing the real truth of what transpired with her vocal health, intimate personal life, and deep inner turmoil may remain a mystery forever. All we can do is respectfully surmise on the possibilities and be at peace with never truly knowing. We hold her talent and life in our compassionate hearts. Though her voice ceased to sing in grand opera, she never ceased to be an artist. Once you are an artist, you are always an artist. Georgina's art was expressed, took form, and continued to live on in other ways, as we soon shall see.

In the twenty-first century we are privileged to be able to instantly access any information we require. We can search the Internet or follow someone on social media and, for better or worse, find intimate details of someone else's life. We have exposure to people's greatest triumphs and strengths, and their failures and faults. This is especially true when it comes to the life of a celebrity, a title we can certainly attribute to Georgina. Her world was much different from the way the world is now, but as the saying goes, it's all relative. She was in the spotlight and was reviewed in global newspapers. She had grand goals and desires for her life. She was being held to the expectations of her day, her teachers, and colleagues, and most importantly, her own. Georgina was a trailblazer, living in a time when being a woman and taking on a career in the arts was considered very progressive. We see this in the instance of Mathilde Marchesi, whose disapproving husband, Salvatore, was not in favour of and even forbade her from pursuing a career in stage performance. Georgina Stirling, on the other hand, was living the life she envisioned and was privileged to have the necessary support of her father and sisters, and even friends, financially and emotionally, in order to strive for her dream career.

The modern-day luxuries that we enjoy were non-existent in Georgina's time. Immediate access to family and friends was not possible. Georgina's correspondence back and forth to family and friends would take weeks to reach its destination. She would have travelled and toured via steamer ship or train, journeys often taking a week to ten days arriving back and forth across continents. While this form of travel may have been at a slower and more relaxed pace than today, it was still tiresome and could often be lonely and treacherous on the ocean. On one such adventure in 1897, Georgina and mezzo-soprano Marie du Bedat were travelling for some twenty-five hours on the SS *Princess May* after a number of concerts in St. John's. Reported in the St. John's *Evening Herald* were treacherous waters on the sea during this voyage. "Miss Stirling's trunks, boxes, etc. had been placed on deck and covered with a sail, but the sea water penetrated everywhere and almost all her clothes, dresses, etc. were spoiled. The loss to her is a considerable one, and also serious if she has an engagement in New York for which costumes are required."

Much of Georgina's time was spent in solitude, working diligently on her music and travelling, with sometimes barely a moment to write home. This type of career comes with its moments of glory but is accompanied by hard work, isolation, and often loneliness. The life of a performing artist can be one of fulfillment as well as one of sacrifice. The presentation of opera looks glamourous and lavish. The audience arrives to experience a flawless and finely tuned product. Dazzling costumes or gowns along with polished sounds of singers and musicians present a stunning exterior. We read about the triumphant successes in newspapers or magazines. We assume because it all looks so perfect from the outside that it comes with ease. It can be taken for granted how much pressure, persistence, and even grief go into the production of these concerts and performances.

In a world of instant gratification, maybe it's one of those rare things in life that can be appreciated as a secret. That we simply adore Georgina for what she did, if only for a short time, to sacrifice for her art, her homeland, her country. Georgina contributed greatly to our unique cultural history. She profoundly impacted the hearts of those who heard her voice as they celebrated in her presence or through waves of international applause in the form of newspapers, telegrams, and letters.

What would have contributed to the loss of Georgina's voice? What voids might Georgina have been trying to fill? What heartache did she experience? What expectations did she feel she had to fulfill? To understand any of this, we need to know who Georgina was as an artist and not just as a woman.

JUST THE TIP OF THE ICEBERG

"If you want to be an artist be prepared to struggle. To sing is to live with daily struggles and at times suffer as we peel back the layers of the onion and discover our own individual voices."
— Manny Perez, Voice Teacher, Miami

I'D LIKE TO BRING A MORE INTIMATE ASPECT of being a singer into focus: the inner artist. Throughout my concert performances across Newfoundland, the sensitive topic of Georgina's use of alcohol was raised by some of the audience members. Some sympathetically wondered, and some were quick to judge. The rumours and lack of knowledge had marred her legacy for some.

It's important to me that people are educated on the elements involved in being an artist of Georgina's calibre. I'll share some information on alcohol and its effects on the voice, the physical consequences of performing heavy repertoire, performing too frequently without rest, and the pressures and expectations. I feel the judgment placed on Georgina was too harsh without proper understanding of her situation and actual proof.

Georgina was a jovial woman who enjoyed entertaining, cherished her time with family and friends, and celebrated life. Throughout her career she would have shared in wine or celebratory drinks after an evening performance, as many artists do. It's a common practice, especially at the end of a production, to celebrate with the other musicians and artists. It is possible, in an effort to drown her sorrows as a form of escape, to have overindulged. Based on her public successes, repertoire, and raving adulation on her public performances, I do not believe she combined singing and drinking. As we'll explore, this would have had a noticeable and visible effect on her ability to deliver. I'd like to offer you a big-picture look at the many aspects of the world Georgina lived in by sharing examples of other professionals, industry knowledge, and my own education and experience.

For years we have been witness to celebrities in many platforms of the arts who have had public struggles with alcoholism, drug addiction, and mental health. Many often go to great lengths to conceal or cope with the problem but are not always successful. Sadly, at times we find out when it's too late. We have high expectations of these artists. We prop them on a pedestal and think that because they have such incredible talent they must have superhuman strength. They do indeed have a certain amount of strength in order to do what they do, but they are, after all, human. To use a metaphor that many will understand, I like to think of the phrase, it's just the tip of the iceberg. On the surface the audience sees only a small tip, which can of course be quite large and stunning. However, under the water's surface lies the most stunning, gigantic, and truly impressive part of the iceberg. What is under the surface is the part that's not seen by an audience or by the public. Lying beneath the surface of this iceberg that we're calling a glamorous-looking career or production is hard work, competition, criticism from others and of oneself, tears, sacrifice, frustration, disappointment, and even depression.

The world has lost many talented icons to these demons. It is heartbreaking to see someone who is so wildly talented struggle through psychological pain and frustration or addiction. Some take their talent for granted and inflict harm on themselves, either knowingly or unknowingly. Some feel alone despite being surrounded by family, friends, and fans. With extreme access these days we can see behind the scenes of some of these celebrities' lives on TV documentaries, in movies, or in books. We realize that some of these artists gave so much of themselves in an effort to save themselves. Dancers dance, actors act, comedians tell jokes, painters paint, singers sing. If we don't pursue our art, we die inside. When we pursue it, we also die inside. Why? We are our own worst critics. Our inner critic never stops, and it's often not pretty. We hide the shame or dissatisfaction of our life with a beautiful artistic exterior, making everyone believe the character we are portraying in real life is as beautiful and perfect on the inside as it is on the outside.

I believe our art chooses us and it becomes our life's purpose to express and heal ourselves, and others, through that artistic expression. The life of an artist and a singer can be an emotional one, a feeling one, raw at times, and even torturous. There is a fear of being vulnerable even though, as an artist, that is one of the most powerful skills in our possession. Georgina was an instinctual artist from a young age. Proof of her artistic vulnerability was apparent, for to sing the type of music she sang, with the conviction in which she performed it, was a daily act of giving. We saw her vulnerability and sensitive soul in her generous acts of kindness and in her heartwarming personality. Regularly, Georgina had to access the pain from her past and present, and the anxieties of her future, in order to deliver the messages of the music she sang and the characters she embodied. Georgina understood the tragedy and longing of the music based on the tragedies she herself experienced.

Feelings weren't spoken about as freely in Georgina's day as they are today. Singing her woes would have provided her with the most natural outlet to heal the pain that lived deep inside her. She lost her mother at the young age of sixteen. She lost her sweet brothers at young ages, one to an accidental drowning, one to typhoid fever, and two others in their early childhood. Georgina coped with the heartache of what the family must have collectively mourned through. She lost her father when she was only twenty-three, at a most crucial point in her career and development as a young woman. Georgina dealt with the pressures and expectations of the world in which she lived. She dealt with the deep ache of losing her most prized possession and her purpose: her voice. We believe she must have suffered a catastrophic heartbreak, the details of which we may never truly know. We know that it must have broken her, broken her heart and broken her soul, for during a year of silence no one heard even a word from sweet Georgina, not even her precious sisters. What must she have gone through that silenced her, that she felt she could not even share with those who were closest to her?

AN ARTIST'S JOURNEY

"We don't present our voices to the audience, we resonate our souls."
— Thomas Hampson, American Lyric Baritone

BEING AN ARTIST IS OFTEN A MELANCHOLY existence. Another insightful sentiment my teacher Manny offered was, "We singers are a melancholy people. It can be a challenge because we feel so much and so deeply, and yet that is why we can do what we do." Perhaps it's for this reason, combined with the pressures of a professional musician, that I was not completely surprised when I found the results of this study published by Help Musicians UK. The study discovered that "musicians and music industry professionals may be more than three times more likely to suffer from depression than the general public." (Article published on November 2, 2016, written by Collin Brennan, www.consequenceofsound.net)

Thinking about being a singer in this way makes me present to the honour of this gift that can also be a curse, for it is a gift that comes with many strings attached.

In 2009, I had reached a pivotal point in my life as a woman, artist, and mother. I was home with my two babies, Sophia and Anthony; I was fulfilled as a mother but not as an artist. I was not singing at that point. Although motherhood fulfilled me wonderfully in one way, it drained me in others. It was impossible to train vocally or retain any consistency. I was also struggling with what felt like a deep depression; I felt a deep ache on an emotional level. I felt as though I was sinking, even though I was surrounded by a loving circle of family and friends. I kept a smile on my face and kept going on the outside, even though I felt like I was dying on the inside. Looking back now, I realize I wasn't fulfilling my artistic purpose in this life and as an artist; this was too much pain to bear. It's an internal torture, gnawing away. There was so much I wanted to achieve, and I had no idea where to start. There was so much I had to heal, with no idea how to find my way through it. I would sit and stare, cry and ache. I would look at my two precious children, thinking this should be the happiest time of my life, and yet I couldn't stop crying, feeling completely blank. The blankness I felt then had sometimes been there before, only it was magnified with having children. I knew I didn't want my children growing up seeing their mommy like this. I wanted them to know the real me underneath the pain and anxiety I was trying to hide. I've had a lot of painful experiences in my own life. We all have. No one is exempt from life's pain and struggles. Sometimes our pain comes from external factors forced on us by other people's decisions and actions. Sometimes, though, the pain is forced on us by our own selves, keeping ourselves locked in an emotional jail.

Since no one is exempt from pain and sadness in life, what makes us truly special is how we deal with it and what we do with it. I made a choice to become proactive about my own healing. I had a great support team with never-ending love and emotional support from my mother, a supportive husband, and encouraging friends who continued to buoy me up along the way. I met one of my best friends, Tanya Chernova, at this crucial point and joined her women's empowerment organization, Courageous Living (with partner Joanna Andros). I started on a journey of self-discovery and healing, reading every book and taking every course I could. As the clouds started to lift, I was empowered to take baby steps to move toward realizing my artistic dreams.

It takes courage to create real change in your life. Desire for change is only proven through action, not words. I realized that with my artistry, the vocal development would not proceed unless I did the emotional work. I knew that art was an emotional expression, and yet where was all the support for that aspect of being an artist? I had a short period in which I produced concerts and fully-staged operas with orchestra, under the name of Wish Opera. I felt fulfilled in the sense that I was offering other singers a platform to share their voices. I was becoming acutely aware of the lack of psychological preparedness in an artist's life, and lack of tools with which to cope. I wanted to have a positive impact on the artists in my community, and to continue my own inner work. I attained my certification in neuro-linguistic programming, the study of human perception, patterns, communication, and self-development. I developed a course for artists, of all genres, on the behind-the-scenes parts of being an artist.

I was starting to form a tribe of like-minded artists, called Wish Arts, and many of them have become close friends and confidants. In art, we need others with whom to journey and share. We need to feel comfortable with vulnerability and see it as a strength and not a weakness. Over the past ten years I have interviewed many Canadian artists, of all genres, about the psychological aspects of being performers and artists. Some of the Canadian opera singers I've interviewed for "The Artist's Spotlight" are: bass-baritone Brian McIntosh, Newfoundland's own tenor David Pomeroy, baritone Theodore Baerg, sopranos Irena Welhasch Baerg, Ambur Braid, and Miriam Khalil, and tenor Richard Margison. I have a series of self-reflective questions about their artistry and personal experiences. My goal is to inspire other artists, emerging or established, with insights into their personal experiences of being an artist. Sharing what motivates them, how they overcome their struggles, cope with anxiety, and how they psychologically prepare and persevere.

There was no easy access to self-help and development in Georgina's day. Much shame and judgment would have accompanied a struggle with an addiction, depression, or other mental illness. Georgina was said to have struggled with depression over the vocal and emotional challenges she experienced, and losing her voice would have been her worst nightmare.

I strongly feel, though, that she took refuge in more than what a bottle of wine could offer. I think she found refuge and channelled her pain into other hobbies and pastimes to which she devoted much time—one of which was a special love for cats and dogs, whose welfare she unabashedly championed throughout her life. She found solace in being kind and helpful to others. Her desire to heal and transform her pain into service and connection, despite what pain she must have carried throughout her life, was admirable.

THE PLIGHT OF AN OPERA SINGER

"I never step upon stage without asking myself whether I will succeed in finishing the opera. The fact is that a conscientious singer is never sure of himself or of anything. He is ever in the hands of destiny."
— Enrico Caruso, Italian Tenor (1873–1921)

THROUGHOUT HISTORY THERE HAVE BEEN MANY famous opera singers who have encountered struggles with depression, performance anxiety, and expectation. My search for examples of this in my field confirmed the sad truth. There is a great pressure and expectation that comes with having a career in the spotlight, being on the road away, and matching or improving upon one's last performance. Just as figure skaters are ruthlessly judged in a competition for their performance and ability to fulfill all of the technical requirements, an opera singer is under this same type of microscope. The competition is real and heavy. Like the saying goes, comparison is the thief of all joy. Opera singers will analyze with fierce judgment their every note, turn, and run. An opera singer will compare her/his high notes and trills to any singer they come in contact with. If the ego is not kept healthy and in check, it can easily become a destructive entity of its own. The pressure to be perfect, fear of getting sick and not being able to perform in peak condition, fear of rejection, self-doubt, and continuously having to show an upwards trajectory in a career of opera have produced destructive habits and behaviours similar to those in other genres of music.

Most would think this type of high-pressure environment is more believable in the world of competitive sports or in the pop and rock scene. Seeping into the high-class and fairy-tale world of opera, more frequently, are drugs in the form of beta blockers to ease the butterflies and stage fright, cortisol shots for inflamed vocal cords, antidepressants for depression and overwhelm, and plastic surgery and unhealthy weight-control tactics to keep up with the ever-growing demand to look perfect.

In addition to the normal stress of an opera singer and performer are now added stressors with more emphasis being placed on the glamour and fame of the industry. There is a pressure to stay "a favourite" in the eye of the public. Fortunately, singers and musicians are starting to speak out about the unrealistic demands, the pressure they feel, and ask for help. Ben Heppner is one of the most recognized and celebrated Canadian tenors of the twentieth century. In an article published on www.operawire.com, "The Wit and Wisdom of Tenor Ben Heppner" by David Salazar, Ben says: "When you first achieve success in your career, you want to take advantage of opportunity, because you feel like maybe it won't come again. At one point, I was traveling upwards of 300 days a year. . . . I realized that I was letting my career control me and that I wanted to have some control over the time I spent away. I gave myself permission to set limits."

I have had the honour of working in a master-class setting with renowned Canadian Soprano, Adrianne Pieczonka. In discussing this very topic with Adrianne during my research, she shared with me that, "pressure to perform at the highest level while looking glamorous creates pressure and stress. I find the opera business is more competitive than ever". In a *Washington Post* article in August, 2007, entitled, "Stressed Opera Singers Turn to Drugs'" by George Jahn, Adrianne Pieczonka, being a strong advocate for healthy singing habits and not succumbing to unhealthy expectations, speaks to this sad reality commenting, "It's become somewhat like a pop-star culture.'" And in the *Seattle Times* she is quoted, "The word that comes to describe this lifestyle is 'hideous.'" In this same article we hear from tenor Endrik Wottrich, who was harshly judged for cancelling a performance in Germany due to illness. He shares his frustration: "We are faced with the choice of performing and being attacked because we sing one false note, or being attacked because we are taking care of ourselves. . . . The real pressure is no longer good old stage fright but comes a new dimension that has penetrated opera—it now lives from glamour, and normal human mistakes are a disruption in such an environment." World-famous Russian soprano Anna Netrebko was also criticized for cancelling a performance with the Salzburg Festival in Austria due to laryngitis. Claims that she had been in perfect health a couple of days prior only fuelled the criticism. Cancelled or postponed concerts can come as the result of a variety of reasons, including physical illness, jet lag or fatigue from travelling, and even psychological distress. Audiences and directors can become enraged and unsympathetic, questioning singers who seemed perfectly healthy one day but are not able to perform the next, sometimes resulting in rumours or bad press. Having a career in the performing arts has never been as glamourous as it looks. Artists work painstakingly to carve out their legacy while working in an industry that does not come with the stability of a nine-to-five job.

Such unrealistic expectations placed on the art of singing by the industry, the audiences, and critics seem to have created a vicious cycle of unhealthy habits and resentment. These pressures were real in Georgina's performing days. It wasn't long before she realized this. Remember what she writes to her Papa from Italy: "Nowadays a great thing in a singer's success is, to make herself agreeable and liked, if you cannot do that, it does not matter how well you sing, you will never gain a footing with the public."

Expressing a unique aspect of being an opera singer in Georgina's era is the following passage from Charles Santley's memoirs, *Student and singer: The Teminiscences of Charles Santley.*

"The singer has a difficulty to contend with which does not affect any other artist, except, in a less degree, the actor. The singer's work is a picture painted on air. No sooner is it depicted than it is gone; while the poet's, painter's, sculptor's and architect's works remain, and can be examined and analyzed at leisure. Delicacy of treatment is the quality which is slowest to make an impression on the public eye or ear. The delicacy of a poem, a picture, a statue, or an edifice, though it may not strike at a first reading or view, will gradually impress itself on further acquaintance. The aerial picture of the singer, on the other hand, vanishes, and there remains nothing more than a dim shadow, insufficient to recall any real impression of its merit. Hence, almost unconsciously, in order to produce an immediate impression, the singer lays on strong, glaring colour and deep shadows where his artistic sense would suggest more delicate treatment.

THE VOICE AND THE DANGERS OF EXCESS

"Opera is an extremely disciplined art form, and every excess a singer indulges in has a direct effect on the voice."
— Beverly Sills, American Soprano (1929–2007)

INTERNATIONAL AMERICAN DRAMATIC SOPRANO Deborah Voigt wrote a book, entitled *Call Me Debbie*, about her experiences in the industry, her struggles with addiction and weight loss, and her recovery. Deborah would frequently be asked at auditions, "Why are you so fat?" It is public knowledge that she had even been fired from Covent Garden because of her weight. In 2012, she went to rehab for her alcoholism but said in an interview with the *Guardian*, US Edition (February 17, 2015), "I never drank on the day of performance, I never turned up for a rehearsal intoxicated. Nobody knew." I think she was brave for being so honest about her struggle, choosing not to suffer in silence, and in her choice to heal and recover.

In November 2017, my Facebook news feed was full of condolences and memories about the famous Russian baritone Dmitri Hvorostovsky. He was known for his striking looks, silver mane of hair, incredible breath control, stunning voice, and charismatic stage presence. The world lost Dmitri at the young age of fifty-five from brain cancer. He was also verbal about his struggle with alcohol, which could have destroyed his career. Unlike Deborah Voigt, his drinking had become a problem on stage. In the late 1990s, "His performances could be erratic—sometimes dramatically unfocused, sometimes vocally patchy. By his own admission, he was often arrogant with directors and colleagues. The main problem, it became clear, was his drinking." (*New York Times*, Anthony Tommasini, November 22, 2017) Experiencing artistic and personal-life struggles due to his drinking, he searched for strength and support in his family and found sobriety in 2001. Predating that article, on March 8, 2008, Anthony Tommasini asks Dmitri about these struggles and pressures. These few confessions give a sad insight into some of the defeating chatter and realities a singer of this calibre might have to face. "Who cares what I did last week? Yes, your name helps out and gets people's attention. But I have to prove myself every time." And about his broadcast of the opera *Eugene Onegin* with the Metropolitan Opera he said: "If something goes wrong from your point of view, it's so painful to see. I don't like myself really."

Before Dmitri passed away, he had managed to perform a limited number of shows, between treatments, at the Metropolitan Opera in their production of Verdi's *Il Trovatore* with his Russian colleague Anna Netrebko, and at Carnegie Hall, a poignant program of Russian music. The world was losing another Nightingale too soon. The *New York Times* prints one of Dmitri's final songs, Tchaikovsky's "The Nightingale," with lyrics by Pushkin:

Dig me a grave
In the broad open field
At my head plant
Flowers of scarlet.

THE PRESSURE FOR OPERA SINGERS to achieve stardom, to perform impeccably and frequently, is creating a harsh environment; however, it's not just in recent times. In an article called "Anna Netrebko: Criticized for not taking drugs?" Tobias Fischer writes, "Cases of classical musicians with an unhealthy habit of drinking have been known for centuries." Many composers and opera singers have struggled with the pressures of composing music and performance demands in the eighteenth, nineteenth, and twentieth centuries. Beethoven, Brahms, Liszt, Schubert, Schumann, Tchaikovsky, and Petrovich were some of the great composers who drank to improve their creativity and to silence the negative chatter in their sensitive artistic minds.

Swedish tenor Jussi Björling was one of the great voices of the twentieth century. I had heard of Jussi many times from my university teacher, Brian McIntosh, as one of his favourite opera singers. Performing internationally and for many years at the Metropolitan Opera, Jussi struggled with extreme paralyzation from nerves. He was told by his father on his deathbed that he had been a closet alcoholic. Details of this are outlined in an article called, "Jussi Björling—The Supreme Singing of a Shy Man," by Don Culp on his website www.diarci.com. Struggling with alcoholism himself, Culp shares some insights from Jussi's wife, soprano Anna Lisa Björling: "He rarely drank before a performance, in fact a full schedule of performance seemed to help him stay sober, and the alcohol never seemed to affect either his voice or his performance onstage. He was tortured by his alcoholism and its devastating effects on his family but the alcohol had no effect at all on his voice, no signs of aging, no deterioration of the voice or his amazing breath control."

Not only does alcohol have a considerable effect on a person's personality and behaviour, it has a direct impact on the voice and its production. If you weren't a singer, you might not consider how alcohol impacts your vocal production while singing. You would easily see the results of a couple of glasses of wine in your confidence and personality, and you would see the results of even more wine on your body and speech. One glass of wine could certainly "take the edge off" a performer while still allowing her/him to function normally; of course, one's body weight would be a contributing factor for determining this amount. Going past "taking the edge off" is where a singer enters a danger zone. While singers may feel that alcohol has a positive effect on their voice, making them feel more relaxed, open, and free, this is most likely just psychological. We saw this example with Dmitri Hvorostovsky being visibly affected in his demeanour and performance on stage.

I've read many articles and books on vocal health over the course of my career. Without getting too technical, I'll share a few of the most common effects of alcohol, and other external influences, on the voice. Dehydration is probably one of the biggest side effects of alcohol. A singer's body and delicate vocal cords need to be fully hydrated to retain flexibility. Many people are allergic to alcohol, which can cause inflammation of the sinuses and vocal cords, causing sneezing and congestion. When a singer's vocal cords lose hydration and are numbed from the effects of alcohol, there can be a tendency to force the voice in an unnatural way, causing the voice to become irritated and hoarse. The range of high notes a singer has access to can also become limited due to the inflexibility. Just as slurred speech occurs when someone drinks too much, a singer can also be impacted in this way when it comes to the enunciation of language, quick vocal reflexes, and any precise movements and interactions on stage. Singing repertoire of a fast tempo with coloratura passages would be greatly impacted because of a delay in the fast motor skills required to achieve these technically in a quality manner. Overall, alcohol would greatly impact a singer's ability to focus properly on breath control, sound production, and technique. It could, of course, even impact their personality in an unfavourable way among peers, colleagues, directors, etc.

The extent to which Georgina drank will never truly be known. It was a different generation with its own set of rules and etiquette. The definition of what was considered excessive consumption and "ladylike" conduct would have also been different. What would have been considered an alcoholic back then, especially by more conservative people, was referenced in Amy Louise's book when she quoted some of the Twillingate villagers saying Georgina "took wine with her meals and smoked the occasional cheroot." This seems overly judgmental and extreme, considering that Georgina had grown up in that same culture and lifestyle.

I feel strongly that Georgina's vocal production and performance ability would have been poorly reflected upon in her reviews should she have consumed an excessive amount. Based on everything I have come to learn about Georgina—her work ethic, technique, repertoire, reviews, what is known of her personal life and career, as well as the research I have done on the voice and how easily it can be affected—I believe that alcohol was not responsible for the demise of her voice. I also believe that any struggle with alcohol she experienced was as a sad result of her vocal sufferings and the emotional turmoil that would have come from a deep sense of heartache, loss, and loneliness.

SILENCE, A SINGER'S GREATEST FEAR

"I lost my voice immediately and it was the most frightening, terrifying experience ever."
— Denyce Graves, American Mezzo-soprano

THE UNIQUE INSTRUMENT OF THE VOICE is housed within the body. Unlike other instruments, it does not go back in a case after being used for a concert or opera. The voice is in use all the time; it is always with us. For a professional singer, the voice is their identity. Singers are sympathetic toward the fact that many of life's experiences and external influences will impact their sound, vocal freedom, and production. What they go through in their personal life could impact how they sound from day to day or month to month. It's no wonder singers need to take extreme caution over the care of their instrument.

In a singer's mind it can feel like a dramatic opera is taking place when it comes to the functioning of their voice and the paranoias that arise. When we understand the effects that a variety of external elements can have on the voice, it's no wonder opera singers can be very protective and, yes, even dramatic!

Besides the usual fear of getting sick before a performance, the voice can be harshly affected by endless factors: too much caffeine, yelling, crying intensely over emotional distress, dehydration from antibiotics and medications, inflammation caused by acid reflux burning the vocal cords, poor diet, eating late at night, hiatal hernia, as well as allergies from smoke, pets, or house mould. Singing while sick can cause great damage to the voice. Singers have to be their own best advocates in deciding what they're willing to do for the sake of a performance, their audience, and peers.

In the Canadian classical magazine *La Scena Musicale/The Music Scene*, November 1997, Joseph So interviewed tenor Ben Heppner. When asked about taking a break from singing for a few months the previous year, Ben shared what would be a scary situation for any opera singer. "I sustained an injury by singing with the flu during the second performance of *Andrea Chenier* in Buenos Aires. I was very sick, with chills and sweats, but against my better judgement I let them talk me into singing. Of course I gave the performance everything I had and my voice was hurt. It was scary at first, but fortunately there was no permanent damage. I just had to be patient and wait for the voice to return. It took six weeks of physical recuperation and it took time to recover my confidence as well."

Maria Callas was ruthlessly scorned in 1958 at a gala performance of the opera *Norma* in Rome before an audience of 3,000 people. Callas had even warned management that she was not feeling well and advised them to have an understudy fill in for her. She was told, "No one can double Callas." After being treated by doctors, she felt better on the day of the performance and decided to go ahead with the opera. Feeling that her voice was slipping away, she felt that she could not complete the performance, and consequently, she cancelled after the first act. She was accused of walking out on the president of Italy in a fit of temperament, and pandemonium broke out. Doctors confirmed that Maria had bronchitis and tracheitis, and the president's wife called to tell her they knew she was sick. However, they made no statements to the media, and the endless stream of press coverage aggravated the situation. (Callas 1958 Rome Walkout, www.eho.com.hr)

Understanding what the voice can handle, monitoring its progress and development, is crucial for singers of this calibre. Even experienced professional opera singers cannot be naive to the many demands on their instrument, including singing repertoire that they are not ready or meant to perform. In the above mentioned interview with Joseph So, Ben Heppner also discusses a variety of operatic roles he was preparing for the stage, the characters of *Siegfried* by Richard Wagner, and *Otello* by Verdi. When asked if it was the "right time to sing these roles," Ben replied, "By the time these plans reach the stage, I'll be in my mid-forties. I am looking four years ahead." Ben went on to explain his reasoning for cutting back on how many performances he did in a calendar year so that he had the time to fully prepare his roles, but this also gives us a confirmation of just how demanding some of the larger operatic roles can be on the body. He says, "It's difficult to sing my repertoire more than three times a week. *Gurrelieder*, for example, is a big workout." (*Gurrelieder* is a cantata by Arnold Schoenberg for five vocal soloists, chorus, and orchestra.)

Professional opera singers are considered vocal athletes. There are serious consequences and injuries professional singers live in fear of: vocal fatigue, nodules, even vocal cord hemorrhage. Many great opera singers have experienced vocal fatigue or some kind of vocal crisis in their careers. For opera and classical singers there has been deep-rooted shame around admitting to vocal damage such as nodes or hemorrhages. This ailment is not strictly limited to the pop and rock world. An example that made headlines in 2011 was British pop singer Adele. She had to stop performing mid-tour because of vocal cord hemorrhages, requiring microsurgery and months of vocal rest.

Vocal burnout can affect anyone. Opera and classical singers are not exempt from these same tragedies but seem to keep their struggles private and silent. America mezzo-soprano Denyce Graves speaks to the *Washington Post* (October 24, 2004, "After the Low Notes," by Nelly Tucker) about the non-cancerous polyp she had on one of her vocal cords, which was removed in surgery in 2001. She says, "It's taboo for opera singers to say they had vocal surgery, because if people know you've had it, they have an excuse to say, 'Oh, she's off,' or 'your performance is diminished.' I didn't want anyone to know." While Denyce was performing at Opera Delaware, she forced herself to sing even though she was ill, completing only the first half. "Just before the second set, I sneezed, and I had no voice," she says. She drops her voice to a stage whisper. "I don't mean I sounded like this. I mean I opened my mouth and no sound came out at all. I was bleeding from my vocal cords."

Natalie Dessay, French coloratura soprano, explains her heartbreaking experience in an interview with Rupert Christiansen (*Telegraph*, UK, "Trouble at the Top," May 2003): "It was at La Scala that I began to get really unhappy. Suddenly, I hated going on stage. I had to battle for every note, I couldn't do a pianissimo, I couldn't control my head voice, and I got tired quickly. No pleasure, only fear. I was spending too much time away from family, I had become a workaholic, and I was exhausted." Suffering from a node on one of her vocal cords, she too had to undergo surgery and a lengthy healing process. "I learned a whole new way of singing, on the basis that the voice is more fragile than I had ever realised." When your voice is your livelihood and your life's purpose, this kind of crisis would be traumatizing.

In Georgina's lifetime, many of the modern medical advances we've attained in the twenty-first century were in the early stages of development. In Roger Neill's book *Divas* (pages 14–15), he quotes Mathilde Marchesi's daughter, Blanche. She explains the wonderful discovery in 1854 by Manuel Garcia II, Marchesi's voice teacher. He had "attached a small mirror to a pencil, let it gently down his throat, and held a second mirror in front of his face and mouth. Whilst attacking a high note he suddenly saw the glottis—the two white vocal cords, in full function." The development of the laryngoscope was on its way to becoming a reality, but nothing was showing the great detail to which we now have access.

Most singers these days will have been to see an ear, nose, and throat specialist (ENT) and have seen their vocal cords. It's fascinating to see your own vocal cords flutter on the screen as you make certain sounds for the doctor. The laryngoscope, with its tiny camera, is slid down through the nose and into the throat. It's an awkward and uncomfortable process but an incredible advancement that allows us to monitor our vocal health. Many professional singers and actors will have an ENT they trust on hand should a vocal-related emergency arise.

During my graduating year of university, I was experiencing extreme swelling in the back of my throat after singing for short periods of time. I saw my ENT, and he told me there was a swollen lump in my throat, and when I was finished my graduation recital I would need laser surgery. He told me I'd have to undergo speech therapy and vocal rest. I was put on prednisone so that I could finish my year and recital. Something didn't feel right. I was terrified of the outcome. The medication caused extreme dehydration and insomnia. I was an emotional wreck, thinking, *How could this have happened to me?* I finished my graduation recital with the support of my studio teacher, Elizabeth Peters. A few weeks after I moved back home, the lump had disappeared. We discovered there was mould in the old house I was living in. I know this pales in comparison to what some of these singers have experienced, yet it made me realize how sensitive our vocal equipment can be.

So, what are these microscopic ailments, and how can they take a singer down? An opera singer's vocal cords undergo significantly more pressure than those of the average person speaking or lightly singing. Consider this amazing evidence about an opera singer's vocal production. Our tiny and oh so delicate vocal folds are only about 1.25 to 2.5 centimetres long, and yet a trained opera singer's voice can produce a volume of sound, and overtones, that can soar over an entire orchestra! These overtones are called "formants," or more commonly to singers, "squillo." A formant is the acoustics resonating from a singer's voice, which allows this increased vibrating or resonating. Squillo translates from Italian as "ring" and is responsible for the brilliance of the sound that rings out. Some professional singers can simply sing louder than others. However, taking advantage of proper technique, the overtones needed will carry the sound over an orchestra efficiently, regardless of the volume.

Our stretchy, moist, skin-covered vocal folds are small but mighty muscles. They vibrate together 100-120 times per second in an average speaking person. While an operatic soprano is singing, for example, these vocal folds will vibrate together some 2,800 to 3,400 Hertz (times per second). The air is channelled through the vibrating cords to produce intense volume, shimmer, and resonance. This allows the voice to be heard over an orchestra to the back of the theatre.

Vocal nodes and polyps are like calluses on the vocal cords, preventing the cords from meeting together evenly and properly, causing a raspy, unstable sound. As a performer becomes caught up in the whirlwind of career demands, they can appear over time if the voice is not properly cared for. The discoveries of these types of throat ailments were in their infancy during Georgina's era, with limited awareness and access to the education and medical advances. Marchesi consciously educated her students on vocal health to the best of her ability and knowledge.

Opera is an art form of high standards and technical requirements. It comes with its own set of elitist stereotypes. Singers can feel incapable of reaching for help. We can empathize in their fears of news spreading about an ailment and of not being rehired. Sadly, as the saying goes, the show must go on, and we've seen that there's a great deal of pressure on these professionals.

Empathy and support are needed to encourage the future health of opera—physically and emotionally. The human voice is just that: human. Regardless what genre a singer's profession is in, it can only withstand so much. No voice can escape the damage of repeated vocal stress, over-singing, or demanding performance schedules and repertoire. Having a long and successful career requires one to be proactive in ensuring the voice does not reach the point of damage and burnout. The brave vulnerability emerging from such singers as Denyce Graves, Ben Heppner, and Natalie Dessay allows for a more supportive and accepting atmosphere. I also feel that their willingness to be vulnerable makes them more compassionate and moving singers and human beings.

THE NIGHTINGALE'S VOICE AND DREAMS, HALTED MID-FLIGHT

I lived for art. I lived for love.
I gave the song to the stars, to the sky,
that make them more beautiful.
In this hour of pain, why, why do you reward me thus?

— Lyrics from the Aria "Vissi d'arte," *Tosca* by Puccini

MANY SOURCES DESCRIBED GEORGINA'S VOCAL CRISIS as happening "suddenly" or "almost overnight." She was performing strongly up until that point. Other rumours that circulated referred to an illness with diphtheria; also that when she experienced this vocal crisis it resulted in lowering of the pitch of her voice.

After Georgina's death, her cousin Jean (Stirling) Pratt in a 1955 CBC interview shared a recollection that Georgina's mentor and colleague, Charles Santley, had possibly foreshadowed this tragedy: "Santley told Toulinguet 'there's a fortune in your voice . . . but oratorio, ballad, and not opera' . . . and when he was told that Toulinguet had not been a success in some opera, Santley cried, 'The devil's cure to her . . . I told her not to go into opera.'" Perhaps Georgina confided in her cousin when she returned to Twillingate, reflecting on the end of her career as a performer. Santley would have certainly known Georgina's voice and its capabilities from being her teacher, touring and performing with her. He was well-respected as a teacher of voice and was a most eminent English baritone of the Victorian era. Knowing intimately the stress and lifestyle of a career in opera, he explains in his memoirs, "As I have said before, I found singing an opera every night fatiguing; not the physical exertion, though, besides the singing on a large stage like that at Covent Garden, the mere going through a long opera entails no small amount of bodily exercise, but on account of the expenditure of nervous force."

Georgina's cousin Jean continues her interview, saying: "The hall was packed. Toulinguet came on stage . . . a breathless hush waited for the first note, but the first note never came. In painful, sympathetic embarrassment the audience left. 'A little bit of nervousness' said one. 'A sudden touch of laryngitis' said another. 'They say she will never sing again.' . . . That horrible experience was the nightmare which haunts every singer. Whether the cause was physical or emotional that time, it signed the death warrant on Toulinguet's career."

The culmination of events leading up to such heartbreaking silence will never truly be known. Considering the facts, and looking behind the scenes in the opera world, we can be sympathetic to what might have happened to our dear Nightingale. With a busy schedule and desire to please her teachers, directors, and audiences, she may have started to suffer silently from what later resulted in a sudden vocal crisis. There were indeed periods when Georgina withdrew from her family and friends, and periods where she was instructed to rest her voice from being overtaxed. After rest, she performed again with great success. These could have been the early signs of vocal damage. Perhaps her voice was only capable of withstanding so much in a short period of time.

In my search for a modern-day opinion on what could have transpired with Georgina's vocal crisis, my teacher, Manny Perez, connected me with a well-respected and experienced otolaryngologist (head and neck surgeon) or laryngologist Dr. Richard J. Vivero in South Florida. Dr. Vivero received his training at Harvard and the University of Miami Miller School of Medicine. He specializes in procedures that manage lesions of the voice box and other vocal cord procedures. Also qualifying him is his advanced training in the "management of professional voice users including singers, actors . . . to produce the best vocal outcomes," focusing on the diagnosis and management of vocal cord nodules, hoarseness, polyps, cysts, vocal cord hemorrhage, paralysis, and even cancer of the larynx. I relayed what I knew of Georgina's situation to him, and he said, "From the limited information available (on Georgina), I agree with Manny. A vocal fold hemorrhage would result in an immediate change in voice and lower her pitch. She could have hemorrhaged with future performances (like Adele, the famous pop singer). Consideration should also be given to a vocal fold polyp or cyst, although I favour a hemorrhage."

Perhaps Georgina felt the strain of over-singing but didn't know exactly what was transpiring internally. Georgina would have had feelings of great despair, grieving the loss of full control over her beautiful voice. It's possible that Georgina suffered a condition similar to that of opera singers Denyce Graves and Nathalie Dessay—a sudden vocal cord hemorrhage. For Georgina, this could have led to her silence and long period of rest and recovery. A sudden scenario like this could indeed have thrown a compassionate artist like Georgina into a dark depression.

Suffering, Georgina eventually sought refuge in England at the Duxhurst Reformation Colony overseen by a compassionate humanitarian and female figure of the time, Lady Henry Somerset. From emotional trauma, loneliness, and pain in her own life, Lady Somerset was able to create, for women especially, an environment that encouraged healing and well-being; experiencing the simple joys of life. It was here that Georgina was able to find peace and solace, to heal much of her life's emotional pain, including the loss of her voice. We know from Georgina's correspondence that she embraced this fully and developed new talents and skills. In the quaint farm atmosphere, Georgina was able to lose herself in her love for horticulture and often mailed seeds home to her sisters Lucy and Rose in Twillingate. The community at Duxhurst must have fallen in love with Georgina's affectionate personality, for she was named "The Duxhurst Celebrity" and "The Lady of the Lavender."

Having rested again for some time in England with her sisters Lucy and Janet, Georgina returned with them to Twillingate for a visit in August 1904. She hadn't performed in St. John's for almost seven years, but she was requested to perform two "Grand Recitals" during her stay in what came to be hailed as brilliantly successful farewell concerts. The concerts were perceived as successful, but I feel Georgina was simply "holding on for dear life," singing for her adoring family, friends, and fans for what would be her final public performances. The *Evening Telegram* on October 25, 1904, wrote: "Could not sing: The grand vocal entertainment which was to have taken place in the College Hall last night, had to be unavoidably postponed, owing to the illness of Mlle. Marie Toulinguet. One of the largest audiences that ever attended to hear a singer in this city was present and though sorely disappointed at not hearing our native prima donna, they did not feel the disappointment more keenly than she did. She contracted a cold during the past few days and the condition of the atmosphere prevented her making a single note. She has the full sympathy of all who attended and are looking forward eagerly to Wednesday night when it is hoped that she will be fully recovered and treat our citizens to one of these wonderful exhibitions."

Keeping her audiences updated, a few days later the *Evening Telegram* writes: "Miss Marie Toulinguet is now almost completely recovered from her slight indisposition, and by Tuesday night, when her postponed concert is to take place, her voice will have regained all its former power and sweetness. The native prima donna is a fast favourite with the music loving public of the city, as was proved when her entertainment had to be postponed. Those who held tickets then can get new ones at Hutton's now."

As a singer, I was saddened to read Amy Louise Peyton's interpretation of the *Telegram*'s description on Georgina's "slight indisposition." I felt it jumped to the conclusion too quickly that it was alcohol-related. Likely, Georgina was experiencing the unreliability of her voice, accompanied by great nerves. Amy Louise writes, "Was the 'slight indisposition' referred to by the *Evening Telegram* really a cold or something else? If she had been suffering from a cold, surely there would have been an indication before curtain time, before a full audience had assembled. Was it not possible that she had been tippling and not fully recovered from it; seeking the consolation that she might have felt necessary, to allay her fears of voice failure?" With limited knowledge and education, this could have contributed to rumours and harsh judgment.

Once Georgina was well and gave her "Grand Recitals," the *Evening Telegram* wrote rave reviews of both concerts in November: "Rarely is such a large and representative audience seen at the College Hall, as that which attended there last night to hear Newfoundland's prima donna sing. It was a treat long looked forward to and was indeed one well worth waiting for. Since her first attempt to sing a week ago, when her medical advisers ordered a short rest, interest in Miss Toulinguet seems to have grown largely, and this is proved by the attendance being much larger last night than at that time. At the head of the audience could be seen His Excellency McGregor, Lady and Misses McGregor and suite, and in the different parts of the spacious hall sat all the prominent ladies and gentlemen of the city, who were thoroughly capable of appreciating or criticising such a musical performance. The opening was a difficult March from Tannahauser by Mr. LeSueur and then Miss Toulinguet made her first appearance on the stage amid loud applause. A most difficult aria from *Traviata* was sung amid the unstinted applause at the close, showed how well it was received. . . . *Never Weather-beaten Sail*, a song by Miss Louise Burchell, was then sung by Miss Toulinguet. It is a pretty piece of composition and was sung in a magnificent manner. The other numbers by the talented lady singer were *Ave Maria*, an aria from *Carmen*, the song *Oh that we too were Maying* and *The Indian Desert Song*, an aria from *La Tosca Centique de Noel* and *Rule Britannia*. The singer was enthusiastically applauded after each number and appeared time and again to thank her admirers. Her singing of *Norma* was so well rendered that the audience applauded to the echo, and a touching little song was rendered. Her *Rule Britannia* was sung in as brilliant a manner as was ever heard in the city before; and so loud and long was the applause that Miss Toulinguet had to repeat it. . . . At the close it was unanimously conceded that the concert was one of the most enjoyable and enthusiastic ever heard here."

Following Georgina's final concert in St. John's, the *Evening Telegram* reports: "Our native prima donna charms her audience. Miss Toulinguet Stirling's farewell concert at the Methodist College Hall last night was a brilliant success. The selections by the prima donna were rendered with taste and skill, and in a manner that charmed the audience, particularly in the rendition of *Killarney, For all Eternity, The Holy City* and *Newfoundland is Calling.* Miss Stirling was obliged to respond to calls for an encore when she sang *For all Eternity....* Miss Stirling we understand will be leaving Newfoundland in a few days. We extend her on behalf of the public, best wishes for her future success abroad and trust that the people of St. John's will again enjoy the pleasure of hearing her magnificent voice at no distant date."

Georgina left St. John's on November 17 with her sister Janet and travelled back to England. I hope that Georgina sailed away from her homeland on a musical high after giving such emotionally invested programs of music to her beloved Newfoundland.

Was England a place of escape from the pressures of performance for Georgina? Perhaps being in England allowed her a reprieve from the high expectations of the operatic hub of Italy and the whirlwind lifestyle of touring. Living in the places her audiences lauded her could have been a bittersweet reminder that her talents were slipping through her fingers. Georgina found solace in England. She immersed herself in the simple life at the Duxhurst Farm, spending her days gardening and reminiscing.

Janet and Georgina moved around in England and spent leisure and quality time with Ugo and Beavis. These two young men were of great significance in Georgina's life. Her sisters Janet and Lucy looked after the eight-year-old Ugo after he arrived in London, then with the help of their sister Susan, when Ugo enrolled in a school near Ticehurst, England. We may never fully understand Georgina's relationship with these boys. They seem to be connected with a hovering cloud of heartbreak in her life that, at one point, paralyzed her into deep sadness and inaction. In a separate chapter, Calvin Evans surmises and may shed more light on this perplexing development. Perhaps Georgina felt that God had given her more than she could humanly bear—the loss of her voice, a loss of love, the loss of her identity and purpose. Would she find her heart's song once again?

CHAPTER TWELVE
by TONIA EVANS CIANCIULLI

GEORGINA SERENADES HER BELOVED NEWFOUNDLAND

"I've discovered that the truly great singers are actually great human beings too, and through these role models I have gotten the ultimate proof that music refines the soul."
— Isabel Bayrakdarian, Canadian Soprano

THE MUSIC A SINGER CHOOSES to perform speaks to their characteristics as a musician and a human being. Many singers can be complimented on the beauty of their voice. To be moved by the voice *and* the singer's emoting is an even grander experience.

I'm reminded of the saying, "Our cracks are where the light shines through us." I imagine Georgina as an open vessel for her audiences, with her kindness and compassion shining through. She was full of love and generosity despite all that she had endured. She had been through enough tragedy in one lifetime that you wouldn't blame her if she decided it wasn't worth the struggle to work through her pain. She used music to deliver her light through her own humanness. Everyone loved Georgina, voice and person. She connected fully with her audiences and stirred their emotions. Georgina possessed this bittersweet blessing from a young age due to tragedies that came too early. She was a worthy servant of the music she delivered.

What a thrill it would have been to see her perform! To witness her audience being moved to tears, and to feel the deafening silence before an explosive applause erupted. Georgina sang for Newfoundland. They felt her palpable affection toward her homeland and the people.

On October 2, 1895, Georgina graciously lent her voice for the official opening of the new Synod Hall in St. John's, after the former Hall had been destroyed by fire. The *Evening Telegram* reported that the Lord Bishop of Newfoundland delivered an opening address expressing gratitude for Miss Stirling's goodwill: "Miss Stirling did not come to us as an outsider. She was a Newfoundlander, one of ourselves. 'She has nailed her colours to the mast.'

She owns up for Newfoundland. No such title as Mademoiselle or Senorita are hers by choice, but rather would she have Miss Twillingate Stirling, after her birthplace."

More praise for Georgina, voice and heart:

"The singer with the beautiful voice and the compassionate heart for the poor."

"Her nature was as angelic as her voice and this angelic nature shone through her personality."

"She sang this with much delicacy of expression and the occasion fully demonstrated Miss Stirling's abilities and was deeply appreciated by all."

"What shall we say of Miss Stirling, Newfoundland's star, whose voice, pure and sweet as her native air, has established for her continual fame."

"We have heard Parepa-Rose, Jenny Lind and Christine Nielsen at their best; but for those nobler characteristics of voice, manner and motive which appeal to the intellect, as well as to the emotions, we prefer our own Twillingate Stirling to all the prima donnas in the two hemispheres."

"Miss Stirling has laid St. John's under a debt of gratitude by this unstinted bestowal of her magnificent genius. She has been indeed prodigally generous, lending her exquisite talent to all who asked for it, and receiving no recompense but the plaudits and thanks of those whom she so delighted and moved."

I'VE WITNESSED PERFORMANCES OF TRULY CONNECTED SINGERS like Georgina and was left speechless and moved to my core. As a performer, I have felt the unique electricity between singer and audience when I've given a performance of benevolent love and service of myself. An audience wants human connection; this is one of the main purposes of music. Music is expressing the emotions of our heart and soul. When a singer who is in touch with these emotions sings for us, a healing takes place within them and in the listener. Georgina was a heart-expressive performer and a compassionate human being. She was generous with her time and talents, often even refusing to accept any financial compensation in support of charities and worthy causes. Her music complemented her generous heart and was internalized in the hearts of her Newfoundland audiences.

THE SONGS OF GEORGINA'S HEART

"If you knew what a sensation of the nearness of a higher power one instinctively feels when one is permitted to contribute to the good of mankind, as I have done, and still do! Believe me, it is a great gift of God's mercy!"
— Jenny Lind, "The Swedish Nightingale," Soprano (1820–1887)

GEORGINA WAS AN ARTIST who selected repertoire based on her "heart's obsession." Her rich family roots, her humble nature, and her faith in God influenced her greatly. Sacred solos, hymns, and songs held significant spiritual meaning for her. She had a special bond with the churches of Newfoundland. I imagine when she sang in those churches and halls she felt a nearness to God that brought her connection, love, and a sense of belonging. Her repertoire choices were greatly affected by this. "The Holy City" by Adams, Handel's "I Know That My Redeemer Liveth" and "He Shall Feed His Flock," Gounod's songs "Ave Maria," "From Thy Love As A Father," "Biondina Bella," "There is a Green Hill Far Away," "Nazareth," "Hear Ye, O Israel" from *Elijah* by Felix Mendelssohn, "The Lord is My Sheppard" by Smart, and "The Better Land" by Cowen. These are just some of the sacred pieces that Georgina was most known for in Newfoundland and were always favourites of her audiences.

". . . touching all hearts by her magnificent rendering of Handel's 'I Know That My Redeemer Liveth' and the beautiful song Jerusalem." — *Royal Gazette*, September 1895

"Needless to say she received an ovation." — *Evening Telegram*, September 1895

GEORGINA'S AUDIENCES WERE TREATED to the richness of this sacred music that filled their hearts. She also delighted them with the grand operatic sounds and repertoire that she was most known for internationally.

Rounding out her concert programs were such operatic arias as "Ombra Leggera" from Meyerbeer's opera *Dinorah*, "Ombra Mai Fu" from Handel's *Xerxes*, "O Mio Fernando" from Donizetti's *La Favorita*, "Ah fors' e lui" from Verdi's *La Traviata*, "Saper voreste" from Verdi's *Un Ballo in Maschera*, "Tacea la note placida" from Verdi's *Il Trovatore*, "O Patria Mia" from Verdi's *Aida*, "Divinite du Styx" from Gluck's opera *Alceste*, and Mascagni's "Ave Maria" from the opera *Cavalleria Rusticana*. Duets with Ireland's Nightingale, Marie du Bedat, in St. John's included Brahms's "Die Schwestern," "Mira O Norma" from Bellini's *Norma*, and "The Venetian Boating Song" by Blumenthal. With other church singers, "The Evening Prayer" from Hansel and Gretel by Engelbert Humperdinck, "O Lovely Peace" from Handel's oratorio, Judas Maccabeus and a vocal trio, Mendelssohn's "The Angels," also from the oratorio *Elijah*.

"Miss Stirling then sang her first solo, a scene from Verdi's Traviata and we think she never sang better. Her voice, if anything was richer and more mellow than before and every note clear and distinct. It was a thrilling performance and was tremendously applauded and encored. . . . The final duet between Miss du Bedat and Miss Stirling, familiar to most people as Hear me Norma was exquisitely sung and though at the end of it, it was getting to eleven o'clock, none seemed in any hurry to leave." — *Evening Telegram* concert review of Miss du Bedat and Miss Stirling, June 1897

"*The Better Land* and an aria from Dinorah, especially the latter, were masterpieces of the art. Loud and long applause followed, and of course, she responded to encores with her usual liberty." — *Evening Telegram*, September 1895

"She sang to the infinite delight of the crowded audience." — *Royal Gazette*, September 1895

Georgina also serenaded her audiences with the melodious, romantic songs that spoke to her family's proud Irish roots. She drew from the rich influences of both her grandfather and father's Irish ancestry. Having grown up in Great Britain's oldest colony, Newfoundland, Georgina's musicality was enriched by rollicking folk songs, sentimental Irish melodies, and British anthems of booming pride and strength. Her voice soothed hearts while she sang such Irish melodies as the traditional folk song "Killarney" by Balfe, "The Kerry Dance" and "Darby & Joan" by Molloy, "The Green Isles of Erin" by Bingham, and "The Wearing of the Green" (*author unknown*).

"*The Wearing of the Green* as sung by her is worth the admission money." — *Evening Telegram*, September 27, 1895

"Sentimentality was not wanting, for as Miss Stirling withdrew, every Irishman's son, or daughter, gave full vent to their pent up feelings." — *Evening Telegram*, September 28, 1895

"'The Green Isle of Erin" was one of the most adored by Georgina, who sang it frequently in Newfoundland and on tour in the United States. I included this stunning piece on my *Nightingale Sings* program. It perfectly alluded to the Irish instilled in her heart and blood. The Irish tenor John McCormack was later famous for singing it and recorded it in 1904.

When I sing these words, I imagine how Georgina must have felt. Georgina's experiences, memories, and relationships lived within her voice, culminating as the years passed to mark her a unique artist and human being.

THE GREEN ISLE OF ERIN

There is a voice in the silence, A voice ever calling
A voice like the song of a far distant sea
A music the soul the wanderer enthralling
It floats like a dream o'er the waters to me
I hear it with tears and a heart wildly beating
While far and alone in a strange land I roam
And I weep as I list and my prayers give it greeting
The green isle Erin, My country and home

Oh green isle of Erin, that waits for me yonder
Though fate may decree 'tis forever be part
Still exiled and lonely where ere I may wander
The green isle of Erin remains in my heart

There is nowhere a sea like the blue rippling ocean
That surges around and beside that dear strand

There's nowhere a star that looks down in devotion
So bright as are those that shine down on the land

With tears in my heart, tears beyond all controlling
I wake and remember an exile am I
And I pray tho' between us, the wide seas are roaring
To come home to thee, it is only to die.

— by Clifton Bingham

". . . when she stepped forward in response to an encore, holding in her hand a bunch of shamrocks green, the audience knew what the bouquet meant, and the deafening applause rang out for five minutes." — *Evening Telegram*, September 28, 1895

GEORGINA TRAVELLED TO DUBLIN, IRELAND, in April 1896 with Charles Santley for a concert that was quoted as being "one of the finest of the season." The *Freeman's Journal* of Dublin created great buzz around the Santley Concert, given at the Leinster Hall on April 9, outlining the success of not only Santley himself but the "lady artist'" Marie Toulinguet who was joining him. They generously singled out Georgina in their article, outlining her training in Italy with Vannuccini and in Paris with Marchesi, the "teacher of so many queens of song." Georgina was quoted as having sung "For All Eternity" by Angelo Mascheroni, which was also a favourite sung on her programs in Newfoundland. Undoubtedly, Georgina would have felt right at home in Ireland.

Georgina undeniably overwhelmed her audiences, "bringing the house down" countless times, with her renditions of their British anthems and songs. "Rule Britannia" by Thomas Arne, "Jerusalem" by William Blake, "Ye Mariners of England" by Thomas Campbell, and "God Save the Queen" (author unknown) always brought her audiences to their feet in standing ovations with "a storm of applause," with her ability to "simply electrify the people."

"All Miss Stirling's songs last evening were by special request. When she appeared to render the charming old and simple ballad *Ye Mariners of England* the enthusiasm of the assemblage burst forth in rapturous applause. She knows our likes and dislikes. Rule Britannia was Miss Stirling's encore song. Many a sturdy Briton's heart throbbed the faster while she sang." — *Evening Telegram*, October 4, 1895

"St. Patrick's Hall is packed to the door; all society there. Again last night the elite of the city attended in large numbers. . . . *Rule Britannia*, old, yet ever new, and soul stirring when sung in the presence of British subjects. An outburst of song found its way all over the hall. The audience was simply electrified by what they heard. The ovation which the talented artist received was deafening. She was cheered and applauded to the echo. As a matter of fact, her every appearance was a signal for tumultuous applause." — *Evening Telegram*, September 28, 1895.

THE POWER OF A SINGER

"We need you to remind us what empathy is by taking us deep into the hearts of those who are, God forbid, different than us—so that we can recapture the hope of not only living in peace with each other, but THRIV-ING together in a vibrant way where each of us grows in wonder and joy."
— Joyce DiDonato, American Soprano

MUSIC CAN HEAL THE WOUNDS of our soul in a way that nothing else can. All humans have throughout their lives heard particular songs or pieces of music that have in-filtrated their heart, leaving its impact on them their entire life. Music is a gift. Music lives forever, connecting and holding us together. As it crosses time, it gathers with it stories of love and heartache. I'll now highlight some of these songs, their stories, and the synchronicities that have strengthened my connection to my soul-sister songstress, Georgina Stirling.

Touching her audiences as a young lady, Georgina sang meaningful and appropriate songs in Twillingate. Some included "The Murmuring Sea" by Wilhem Ganz: *"The murmuring sea, ever wert thou sweet solace to me, oft when thy surging voices came . . ."* And the tender song "Daddy" by A. H. Behrend, at the Dorcas Society Concert in Twillingate in 1888. She was twenty-one years old. It would have been a most bittersweet song to sing with her father in the audience after her mother had passed away. I arranged for my daughter, Sophia, to perform this piece on my concert program to be representative of Georgina as a young singer. She was nervous but sang it ever so tenderly, bringing tears to both her mother and father's eyes. Georgina's father would have had a similar reaction, especially considering his health was declining. Here are the song's touching lyrics, which seem to have been written for Georgina and her daddy alone.

DADDY

Take my head on your shoulder Daddy, turn your face to the west
It is just the hour when the sky turns gold, the hour that Mother loves best
The day has been long without you Daddy, you've been such a while away
And now you're as tired of your work Daddy, as I am tired of my play.
But I've got you and you've got me, so everything seems right.
I wonder if Mother is thinking of us, because it is my birthday night.

Why do your big tears fall Daddy, Mother's not far away.
I often seem to hear her voice, falling across my play.
And it sometimes makes me cry Daddy, to think it's none of it true
When I fall asleep to dream Daddy, of home and Mother and you.
For I've got you and you've got me, so everything may go
We're all the world to each other Daddy, for Mother dear Mother once told me so

I'm sometimes afraid to think Daddy, when I am big like you
And you are old and grey Daddy, what you and I would do
If when we got up to heaven and Mother was waiting there
She shouldn't remember the two she left, so sad and so lonely here
But year by year still sees no change and so 'twill all be right
We shall always meet her in our dreams
Daddy good night, dear Daddy, good night

— by A. H. Behrend

"THE HOLY CITY" WAS WRITTEN BY STEPHEN ADAMS with inspired lyrics by Frederic Weatherly. It has long been a cherished piece and never fails to bring an audience to their feet in a standing ovation. Jerusalem is commonly interpreted as the "city of peace," and I believe this deeply moving song brings our hearts to search for peace and to be accepted no matter who we are. *"The light of God was on its streets. The gates were opened wide, and all who would might enter. And no one was denied . . . Jerusalem, Jerusalem, lift up your gates and sing.*

Hosanna in the highest, Hosanna forever more." Written in 1892, Georgina was the first Newfoundlander to perform this piece in concert, in St. John's during the summer of 1893 at the Methodist College Hall, less than a year after it was written.

Vaughn Harbin presents Tonia with Georgina's copy of "The Holy City." Georgina would have been the first person to sing this song in Newfoundland. (Author photos)

I grew up singing this piece in various churches across Newfoundland where my grandfather, Calvin Evans, ministered. It had already been a significant song in my life, and now having it on my *Nightingale Sings* program always brings such electricity, especially in Georgina's hometown of Twillingate. After the August 2018 concert in Twillingate, we had a family reunion at my uncle Neil and aunt Barb's home in Michael's Harbour. A touching moment came over us as we all sat around the kitchen table chatting. My dear aunt Leona was not able to attend the concert the day prior; she grew up singing in church choirs and latterly in the Cancer Survivors Choir in Grand Falls, so I knew she would have appreciated it. Sadly, she has Alzheimer's, and she didn't remember me when I saw her. We sat around the kitchen table reminiscing, laughing, and enjoying a big lobster feast. I quietly started singing "The Holy City" for her, and to everyone's amazement she started singing along. She knew all the words by heart. It touched us all so deeply that she was able to share that moment with us. Music is a universal language, and our gift doesn't always need to be shared with the entire world. Sometimes it means the world for that one special person who needs to hear it.

What happened later, though, truly cemented this song in my heart, connecting me to Georgina forever. In September of 2018 I had the pleasure of meeting a gentleman by the name of Vaughn Harbin. Vaughn is the first cousin twice removed of Maymie Roberts, Georgina's best friend. We initially connected on Facebook and messaged for almost an entire day back and forth about stories of Georgina that his "Aunt Maym" had passed down to him. I assumed Vaughn still lived in Newfoundland, but I was excited to discover that he lived only about twenty minutes from me in Toronto. Very shortly after, Vaughn and I met at a coffee shop and spoke for four hours that first day. Sophia and Anthony sat ever so patiently at the table next to us, occupying themselves with their iPads and snacks. Vaughn's lips quivered with emotion as he recounted story after story with great detail. I could appreciate the bond he had developed with his aunt Maymie, as it was so similar to the one I had with my uncle Brian. We both agreed that you don't have to know someone for an entire lifetime to create such a powerful bond; it can be for a brief stretch of time and easily have such a huge impact on your life.

Vaughn told me that he would sit for hours with Maymie as she showed him old photos and recounted stories about her own life and Georgina's life. He shared with me his own musical journey: he too had performed "The Holy City." Then he opened his briefcase and slid across the table a very old, stained, and tattered piece of sheet music. To my amazement, it was "The Holy City"! Vaughn told me that this score had belonged to Georgina originally and was passed down to her dear friend Maymie, and then to Vaughn. Yet another significant and serendipitous moment in which I had found myself holding a treasured piece of history. I'll never forget what happened next. Vaughn paused for a moment and then said, "I'd like you to have this. It doesn't belong in a museum or library, and I can't think of a better person to now own this than you." Well, then came the tears. I had *just* met Vaughn! I was overwhelmed with gratitude. Anthony stood by the edge of the table and cleverly commented, "Mom, this is so valuable, you have to frame it!" Vaughn said that Anthony, though young, was a pretty wise young man to recognize the significance of what I had just been gifted.

A feeling like no other comes over me when I sing "The Holy City." I'll never forget what one gentleman said to me after a concert. He insightfully told me he could tell when I sang that piece that I truly gave something of myself to the audience. "It really cost you something." This meant a great deal to me. The cost was truly worth the recognition I felt from the audience.

Another significant memory Vaughn recounted that afternoon was about the last time he saw his aunt Maymie in Newfoundland. Arriving one day to pick her up for a drive, he entered the house as she was playing "The Last Rose of Summer" on the piano and softly singing the words. As chance would have it, Vaughn handed Maymie the last rose he had found from a rose bush he passed en route to see her; they stopped often at this particular bush to pluck a rose. Vaughn's hands went up in the prayer position to one side of his sweet, smiling face as he imitated Maymie's reaction to seeing the rose. She had a heart attack that very day while making some rounds about town; she died in his arms after he pulled the car over.

Like many songs from Georgina's repertoire, "The Last Rose of Summer" had nestled its way into my heart over the years. The first time I heard it was during the committal service at Mount Pleasant Cemetery in Toronto as we committed the urn that held Uncle Brian's ashes into his plot in the wall, along with a dried yellow rose, his favourite. Georgina received glorious praise for this song across the United States. She nurtured her love of gardening in Twillingate until her dying days; it felt a suitable and poignant way to end my concert.

'TIS THE LAST ROSE OF SUMMER

'Tis the last rose of summer left blooming alone
All her lovely companions are faded and gone
No flower of her kindred, no rosebud is nigh
To reflect back her blushes and give sigh for sigh

I'll not leave thee, thou lone one, to pine on the stem
Since the lovely are sleeping, go sleep thou with them
Thus kindly I scatter thy leaves o'er the bed
Where thy mates of the garden lie scentless and dead

So soon may I follow when friendships decay
And from love's shining circle the gems drop away
When true hearts lie withered and fond ones are flown
Oh who would inhabit this bleak world alone?

— by Thomas Moore

I SAT WITH MY GRANDFATHER as we listened to Georgina's best friend, Maymie, in a radio interview archive with Hiram Silk, accompanied by the crackly sounds of an old record player. When Georgina returned to Twillingate for the last time, she could be seen tending daily to her spectacular garden on the Stirling property. She could be heard reciting over and over like a mantra a line from a Dorothy Frances Gurney poem: "One is nearer God's heart in a garden than anywhere else on earth."

Shortly after meeting Vaughn, I performed my *Nightingale Sings* concert at Wasaga Beach United Church in Wasaga Beach, Ontario, with my grandfather. When I sang "The Holy City" and "The Last Rose of Summer" that evening, I was overwhelmed with feelings of gratitude.

In the audience that night were Nicolina and David Anthony, the parents of my dear friend Andrea Rebello. They were so interested in learning about Newfoundland's "Nightingale of the North" that they made a lengthy drive to attend our concert. They were touched, and later that week Nicolina sent Andrea to my house with a special gift that brought tears to my eyes. Wrapped in a red plastic bag with pink ribbon was a single, tiny, and tightly closed red rosebud. It was the very last red rose from her garden. The sweet letter attached to the ribbon read: "Tonia, Thank you for a delightful evening! 'Tis the Last Rose of Summer. Put it in water and she will bloom. Love, Nicky."

These kinds of significant moments followed Georgina as well. This is what happens when we are living our purpose. We touch other people's hearts with our music, and the love ripples out from us.

In the fall of 1896, Georgina was asked to sing at the dedication service of Gower Street Methodist Church in St. John's. She graciously accepted and sang "Hear Ye, O Israel" for an audience of 1,700 people during the morning service and later that same evening for an audience that exceeded that number and the church's capacity.

"Miss Twillingate Stirling sang *Hear Ye, O Israel* in her own magnificent style. — *Evening Telegram*, October 1896

"Miss Stirling sang *Hear Ye, O Israel* in her own superb manner, the audience listening with rapt attention whilst the burst of melody held them spellbound." — *Daily News*, October 1896

MATHILDE MARCHESI HAD BEEN CLOSE FRIENDS with Mendelssohn, the composer of the oratorio *Elijah*, which "Hear Ye, O Israel" is from. He spent a great deal of time working with Marchesi studying his compositions. Perhaps this was one of the pieces in Georgina's repertoire in which Marchesi was able to convey the composer's direct intentions. It was a memorable experience when I performed this piece at Gower Street United Church during my first concerts in May of 2017 accompanied by Evan Smith. They gifted me a beautiful handmade bracelet that contained a piece of the original stained glass windows made by Linda Hogan, of the Gower Street United administration. This significant gift, in my mind, holds a little bit of Georgina in it.

That same week in October 1896, Georgina gave another concert at the College Hall and was gifted several special treasures. A poem dedicated to Georgina, written by Irish poet Mrs. F. F. Rogerson (pen name "Isabella"), was recited in front of the audience for her as a surprise, which was followed by enthusiastic applause. Georgina was then enveloped in a "silk scarf of native colors, that worn wound around the shoulders, hanging down, nearly reached the ground on either side." The poem of dedication read:

O 'tis only a Scarf: why it should be a Crown
For our own Queen of Song is she
And the glorious wealth of her voice of renown,
Se dispenses right royally.
Aye! And loyally, too! For she loves Newfoundland
No matter how far she may roam;

And on earth there is nothing more touchingly grand
Than the love of a patriot for home.
In the courts of our God we are rapt in amaze;
Caught up by that voice into heaven;
Till entranced we can hear the bright seraphin praise
Thro' the cleft air with melody riven.
O 'tis a wonderful gift for in Heaven with Love
It survives Faith and Hope: Aye, and Prayer.
Long may Twillingate Stirling praise God up above
With that God-given voice rich and rare.

— by Isabella, October 7, 1896

IN 1897, WHEN GEORGINA RETURNED HOME from the United States for summer holidays, she was in high demand to sing as part of the Queen Victoria's Diamond Jubilee celebrations for the laying of the cornerstones for Cabot Tower on Signal Hill and the Victoria Wing of the General Hospital. She was asked to sing our Royal Anthem, "God Save the Queen." As soon as I read this, I made an amazing realization. Exactly one hundred years after this occasion, when I was twenty-five years old, I was asked to perform at the 100th Anniversary of Guglielmo Marconi's first transatlantic wireless communication, at a gala in Toronto for his granddaughter, Princess Elettra Marconi. I delighted in sharing this story in concert with the audiences in Newfoundland before asking them to stand and join me in the singing of "God Save the Queen."

The *Evening Telegram* remarked on Georgina's great contribution to the week's festivities and concerts:

"Our native prima donna will always find a right royal welcome at the hands of a St. John's audience and her voice is even fuller, sweeter and clearer than we had the pleasure of hearing her sing."

"In the Hosanna the swelling on the high notes filled the hall with a flood of clear rich music that held the audience enthralled. She was loudly encored and gave another verse of the same hymn."

Left: Colourized photo of Georgina as a child, probably about age ten (Courtesy of Bruce Manuel and Brent English)
Right: Georgina Stirling headshot in blue gown. Promotional photo used for the Sofia Scalchi Opera Company Tour 1897–98. (Courtesy of Bruce Manuel and Brent English)

The night light which was gifted to Georgina somewhere in Europe, and given to Maymie Roberts by Georgina (Courtesy of Bruce Manuel and Brent English)

Left: Georgina with two of her travelling cats. Restoration and colourization. (Courtesy of Gerard Nash, The Photo Mender)
Right: Painting of Georgina by Kent Peyton, son of author Amy Louise Peyton (Courtesy of Kent Peyton)

Lorna Stuckless, who was curator at the Twillingate Museum 1973–1997 and who originally organized the Georgina Stirling exhibits (Courtesy of the Stuckless family)

Portrait of Georgina Stirling by artist Nina Keogh at Georgie's Restaurant in Twillingate. Seen with cake made and decorated by Catherine Sansome for a reception after the 2018 *Nightingale Sings* concert. (Author photo)

Tonia Evans Cianciulli filming the music video for Ron Hynes's "Marie" at Georgina's gravesite in Twillingate (Author photo)

Sophia Cianciulli singing "Daddy" by Behrend at St. Peter's Church, Twillingate, August 2018. Georgina Stirling sang this song at Twillingate in 1888. (Photo by Megan White Photography)

Tonia Evans Cianciulli singing at St. Peter's Church at Twillingate in August 2018, Georgina Stirling's home church (Photo by Megan White Photography)

Tonia sings "The Last Rose of Summer" in Georgina's home church, St. Peter's at Twillingate, 2018. (Photo by Kyle Greenham, the *Pilot*)

Gifting of a "last rose of summer" to Tonia after *Nightingale Sings* concert from Nicolina Anthony (Author photo)

Calvin D. Evans reading narrative from our new book, *The Heart's Obsession*, August 2018, Nightingale Sings concert at Gower Street United Church (Photo by Rich Blenkinsopp)

Tonia Evans Cianciulli, accompanied by Jason Locke, as she sings "Hear Ye, Israel" in August 2018 at Gower Street United Church, where Georgina Stirling sang the same song at the Dedication Service in October 1896 (Photo by Rich Blenkinsopp)

Tonia Evans Cianciulli at Gower United with her husband, Frank Cianciulli, and children, Sophia and Anthony. They love to travel together as a family for the *Nightingale Sings* concerts. (Photo by Rich Blenkinsopp)

Left: Tonia finds a heart rock at Twillingate for first *Nightingale Sings* concert in 2017, near Snelling Cove
Right: Tonia in Twillingate for her 2017 *Nightingale Sings* concert during Canada's 150th Anniversary, the same birth year as Georgina Stirling, 1867 (Author photos)

Georgina's bedroom furniture purchased by Charlie and Nancy Fendley in St. John's in 2019 and presently located at Twillingate (Courtesy of Charlie Fendley, Lupinfield Cottage, Twillingate)

A SONG I FEEL IS OF great significance to Georgina and adored by her audiences was "The Lost Chord" by Arthur Sullivan. It was most famously accompanied on the organ. With Georgina's great love for the organ, that she favoured this piece is undeniable. Arthur Sullivan wrote it in 1877 by his brother's bedside, five days before he passed away, set to the poem *A Lost Chord* written by Adelaide Anne Procter.

> *Seated one day at the organ, I was weary and ill at ease,*
> *And my fingers wander'd idly over the noisy keys;*
> *I knew not what I was playing, or what I was dreaming then,*
> *But I struck one chord of music like the sound of a great Amen.*
> *It flooded the crimson twilight like the close of an Angel's Psalm,*
> *And it lay on my fever'd spirit with a touch of infinite calm*
> *It quieted pain and sorrow like love overcoming strife,*
> *It seem'd the harmonious echo from our discordant life.*
> *It link'd all perplexed meanings into one perfect peace*
> *And trembled away into silence as if it were loath to cease;*
> *I have sought, but I seek it vainly, that one lost chord divine,*
> *Which came from the soul of the organ and enter'd into mine.*
> *It may be that Death's bright Angel will speak in that chord again;*
> *It may be that only in Heav'n I shall hear that grand Amen!*

In October 1895, the *Evening Telegram* reports:

". . . but in *The Lost Chord* the effect was sublime and grand beyond description. While the last notes trembled on her parted lips, as if reluctant to leave their natural abode, the fascinated multitude held its breath and when the climax was passed and the echo of her voice could no longer be heard, a storm of pent-up applause broke out that could only be allayed by her repeated appearance before the footlights."

"Then came *The Lost Chord*. The world loves this song; no matter when or where the words are echoed, they cause a feeling of sadness. At nearly every concert Miss Stirling has been prevailed upon us to sing it; the applause brought forth was deafening."

Singing her farewell to audiences on many programs was the traditional and well-loved folk song "Auld Lang Syne" by Robert Burns. Georgina was honoured with a jewelled bracelet and the aforementioned testimonial *Twillingate Stirling* poem in gold lettering during her 1895 storm of concerts in St. John's. After singing that final goodbye, the *Evening Telegram* most poignantly described her performance: "Miss Twillingate Stirling said it effectually by singing *Auld Lang Syne* with such pathos and feeling as to cause a flutter of tiny white handkerchiefs, and here and there amongst the audience might be seen a tear-bedewed eye. The thought naturally occurred to all present, when shall we see and hear her again."

"HAVE CHURCH"

*"Never forget to sing before the music is over. Never
forget to love before life says goodbye forever."*
— Debasish Mridha, MD, American Physician,
Philosopher, Poet, and Author

I'LL LEAVE YOU WITH A CONCEPT I believe Georgina was incredibly in touch with. I had read of this concept in Stephen Smith's book *The Naked Voice* and immediately associated it with Georgina. This is how I strive to feel and sing every time I perform. After all the singer's work is done, after all the notes are learned, the words are all memorized, and it's been practised to our satisfaction, it is then our job to walk out on stage and to be a vessel for our audience. One of Stephen Smith's students said you have to "have church." "Any time we sing for people, we've got to 'have church!'"

This is an extraordinary concept. I feel when Georgina was home in her beloved Newfoundland, she came to "have church." Her desire was to connect and to serve by offering the deepest part of herself to her audiences. She shared her heart and her voice, with all their joys and sorrows. More so than anywhere else on earth, Georgina felt this most poignantly in Newfoundland. I think Georgina's paradise on earth was Newfoundland. She filled the church pews to capacity. She stood at the front of the churches, just slightly above their eye level, not as a celebrity, not as someone who was superior to anyone else, but just simply as Georgina.

CHAPTER THIRTEEN
BY CALVIN D. EVANS

GEORGINA'S "FALL" AND THE LONG INTERLUDE IN HER LIFE

GEORGINA IS SAID TO HAVE CONTINUED singing in Italy after the fall of 1900, but no firm details are available. One source says that she experienced "continuous success," but there is no evidence to support that claim. It is stated by one source that she was singing again in Milan at the turn of the century, and this "probable fiction" is repeated by one or two other writers.

The mysterious gentleman "roto" continued to send postcards to "Mary" and "Marie" from various places in Italy—from Torino, Livorno, and Parma, for example—and Georgina is known to have kept all these in her postcard collection and later, from England, sent them to her sister Lucy at Twillingate, charging her to keep them all. Georgina and "roto" corresponded with each other, and in one postcard "roto" thanks her for her letter.

 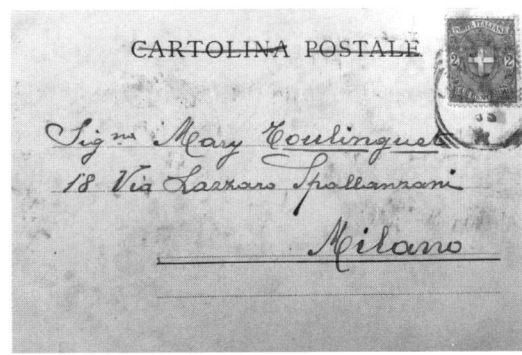

Postcard from "roto" to Georgina, proving that they corresponded. Was this a romantic liaison? "Received letter, Thank you—roto." Front and verso of postcard shown. (Courtesy of Amy Louise Peyton's children)

From the great heights achieved at Chioggia came the "fall." The accepted explanation has been either a strained voice or some kind of serious throat ailment, but that explanation does not seem for me to fit the facts, as we will consider them later. A grave emotional turmoil or catastrophe may be nearer the truth, but nothing can be concluded with any degree of certainty.

It cannot be determined exactly when the "fall" came. The crushing experience must have come very late in 1900 or early in 1901, but its effects carried through to at least September of 1901 before Georgina broke her silence, and then it was only to her two precious sisters in London. We have characterized this period elsewhere as "a year of silence." Whatever it was that happened to Georgina was a tragedy of gargantuan proportions.

Though friends and family tried painstakingly to contact her, she did not reply to their increasingly alarmed inquiries. Her good friends Boyd McQueen (who used the stage name Tomasso Boyd) and his wife had left Italy in the fall of 1900 to journey to Scotland and then to London, and they sent several communications to Georgina up until at least February 1901, by this time complaining bitterly of her refusal to answer and wondering if she had become so haughty with her successes that she no longer counted them as friends. Another of Georgina's friends, the decorated British baritone Charles Santley, who had become her third voice teacher, had told Georgina sometime earlier that "There's a fortune in your voice . . . but (in) oratorio, ballad, not opera." There were unconfirmed reports that she had not done well in some operas, perhaps the very difficult German operas in which Nellie Melba had strained her voice.

The "strained voice" scenario is still a hypothesis more than 100 years after the fact. Nothing has been proven or admitted. It is not known if Georgina sought advice and counsel from doctors in Milan, or whether she was advised to take a long rest or decided herself to take a complete rest. There is no indication that she tried to make contact with Madame Marchesi to seek help in determining what to do about a strained voice, which is most curious given the fine relationship she had developed with her famous and supportive voice teacher.

Though many sources list Georgina as one of Madame Marchesi's students, it seems rather strange that the famous teacher makes no mention of Georgina in her books on opera, especially since she had been so effusive in her praise of the young soprano (or mezzo-soprano) at her audition in 1891, and so supportive of Georgina through her period of voice training in Paris. Having developed such a close relationship with Madame Marchesi, it is passing strange that there is no comment on or recognition of Georgina in connection with a possible strained voice. The great silence may be pointing to something else, something which carried an aura of shame, an emotional "fall" that begged to be hidden. We shall pursue this possibility later.

Georgina's Milan address had been 18 Via Lazzara Spallanzani, Milano. She left Milan in late 1901 to join her sisters Lucy and Janet in England. She had been singing professionally for only eight or nine short years—eleven or twelve years, if the period of training and singing in Florence, Milan, and Paris and other European cities is considered.

A strained voice would have been a disaster for any singer, but for one who had been lauded as Georgina had been, whatever happened must have been a disastrous and devastating experience. Nellie Melba, during a visit to the Met in New York in 1896, had decided to sing Wagner against the strong advice of Madame Marchesi, and after only one performance as Brunnhilde in *Siegfried,* she declared with high emotion that she would never do this again. "It is beyond me. I have been a fool," she said. She was justly afraid of the damage that it would do to her vocal cords, and she withdrew from the performance. Melba went on to achieve worldwide fame after this wise decision. Such was not to be the case for Georgina. The fact that Georgina did not contact her famous and supportive voice teacher in Paris may suggest that it was not a strained voice that caused her despair and depression, but a serious emotional upheaval of some kind.

For her musical entitled *Georgie*, which Eleanor Cameron Stockley presented in Twillingate in 1997, the program carries these words: "Georgie passed a few Bohemian years in Italy before joining her nursing sister at Duxhurst Colony, a rehabilitation hospital in England." The statement is not quite accurate. There may have been one "Bohemian year," 1900–1901, in Italy and a few in England, 1901–1905, before she entered the Duxhurst Colony to conquer what had become her over-drinking problem. Janet left her nursing station in London to provide aid and comfort primarily to Georgina, but to others as well at Duxhurst.

Several writers suggest variously, without documentation, it seems, that 1900–1901 was a period of "degradation" for Georgina, that she was "near destitution," that she was soon in financial difficulties, and that she had to pawn her jewels to survive. In his usual exaggerated style, Hiram Silk writes, "With no work and too proud to ask her family for help she was soon in financial difficulties—after much heart break and degradation, she soon found her way home to Twillingate." It is true that her sisters sent her money from England in September

1901, but Georgina took accommodations in several places in London between 1902 and 1906, and sold property in Twillingate in 1906, but did not return to Twillingate until twenty-eight years after her "fall." There is so much conjecture and so little documentation that it seems impossible to determine the nature of Georgina's "fall."

When Georgina arrived in England in the fall of 1901, she stayed with her sisters Janet and Lucy, who were working at Janet's nursing station in London at 14 Bulstrode Street, and undoubtedly took a rest for a while. One writer suggested that "She was required to take an extensive rest," but no documentation for this could be found. It is possible that she may have received some medical attention from the Harley Street physicians who periodically visited Janet's nursing station. She may simply have shared an apartment with her sisters until she became settled, and soon found accommodations in a flat at St. Andrew's Mansions. It must have been a time of severe depression for Georgina. By late 1902 or early 1903, it appears that she had regained sufficient confidence to operate as a concert artist, meaning that she was helping to coach and sponsor other performers, and perhaps acting as an accompanist on piano or organ. One writer suggests that Georgina was assisted in these efforts by her two sisters, Janet and Lucy. She received encouraging correspondence from friends and family during the mid-1903 to early 1904 period, a few of them commending her on what seemed to be successful performances, and she is said to have corresponded with friends in Italy.

Then in 1904, Georgina and her sisters Lucy and Janet returned to Newfoundland, spending the summer in Twillingate and journeying in mid-October to St. John's, where Georgina had been invited to give two singing engagements at the Methodist College Hall, the first on October 24 at the express desire of her adoring fans in the city. They had not heard her sing since 1897 during the Queen Victoria anniversary celebrations. Over the next few days, the city's newspapers variously described Georgina's unspecified "illness" and expressed hope that she would soon have recovered and be able to sing. Both concerts were postponed and eventually delivered, on November 1 and November 15, and were acclaimed by the grateful audiences and lauded by the press.

The newspaper raved about the possibility "of hearing her magnificent voice at no distant date." Georgina left St. John's amidst calls for a quick return following this "brilliant success."

But Georgina would never sing again in St. John's. Though no formal and professional assessment seems to have been written about these engagements, Georgina must have been regarded, and possibly regarded herself, as a pitiful figure because of the long embarrassing preludes to these two performances. She probably genuinely felt that she had betrayed her various publics.

Though it is intimated that alcohol may have been a factor in the "indispositions" that caused the many postponements, it still seems more than odd that a badly strained voice was the real cause of her "fall." Alcohol seems not to have been her primary problem, but a sordid means of dealing with her problem. Was there some other deeper problem that had caused all this?

On November 17, 1904, Janet and Georgina left St. John's on the SS *Damara* for Liverpool, England. Sister Lucy had returned to Twillingate. By late 1904, Georgina was living in a house, presumably on her own, and making yet another attempt to cope with life.

It must have been a restful and invigorating winter for her because, in the summer of 1905, she writes to her sister Lucy at Twillingate informing her of their plan to attend evensong at Ely Cathedral "this evening" and their intention to leave for Cambridge "tomorrow morning." Obviously, she would be accompanied by her sister Janet. During August, she informed Lucy in a letter from Maidenhead that they were planning a picnic on the Thames River, that "I have closed the house for two weeks and we are living on a house boat and it is beautiful. Beabis and Hugo are coming, and we are going for a day's picnic up the Thames." A short time later, both Janet and Georgina request in separate communications to Lucy to "keep all the cards we send." Georgina later writes: "I have now arrived as far as Huntingdon and at 12 a.m. we start for St. Ives. I believe it is a rough passage. We shall have to pull our boat through the reeds and rushes. All the locks are closed on the river, so instead of going through, we have to pull her over a field and right over a gate. It is hard work but most enjoyable. Will write a long letter from Elys."

For two women aged thirty-eight and forty-four, this sounds like extreme physical labour. But for two young women from Twillingate, this would have been "all in a day's work." The Stirling girls had grown up by the sea. They used boats and understood them. They were accustomed to rowing and sculling a boat, bailing it out when it became filled with rainwater or wave action, tying it securely to a wharf, and hauling it up on a beach. They were no "wilting violets."

Georgina was still struggling with depression and thoughts of despair and taking refuge from her darkness by overindulging in alcohol. It was at this point, probably in late 1905 or early 1906, that she became a resident at the Duxhurst Farm Colony for Women and Children, where Lady Henry Somerset, "a driving force in the temperance movement," was totally engaged in the reformation of women inebriates and caring for the children of these women. In an Internet article entitled "Don't Mock the Victorian Do Gooders," it is stated, "Lady Somerset was not against the idea of people enjoying a drink in moderation, but she felt alcohol and drug use was the cause of many social problems . . . she was driven by her own religious convictions and by an empathy with women who were scorned by society because of their drink problems and subsequent behaviour."

Several women from the higher classes of English society were residents in search of sobriety. Some were "aristocratic ladies and stage celebrities suffering from alcoholism and narcotism." Ros Black, in her book about Lady Somerset, writes a paragraph about Georgina Stirling, and also mentions, as residents, Dr. Crippen's mistress, Ethel de Neve, and the well-known variety hall star, Cissie Loftus. "Cissie" may have been the Miss Marie Loftus, whose Grand Matinee at Leinster Hall in Dublin, Ireland, was advertised for the day following Georgina Stirling's appearance in the Grand Afternoon Concert in the same hall on April 6, 1896.

Early in 1906, Georgina's sister Janet left her "Surgical Home" nursing job in London and moved to Duxhurst to work in the Colony's hospital and to be near Georgina. Already having one nurse on staff besides herself in London, Janet would almost surely have hired a second nurse to replace her to keep the nursing station operating. She must also have retained her apartment at 14 Bulstrode Street for a very long time after that since, as late as 1923, her name, as a "friend," and that same address are given by a person who travels from England to the United States.

Part of the treatment for women with alcohol-related problems at the Duxhurst Colony was "to help them regain their self-respect" and then "to rid them of any bitterness embedded in their minds, thereby making it easier for each to regain their self-esteem," to use the words of Amy Louise Peyton, words which may have been garnered from the literature of the Colony. Here was therapy applied in a country setting to which Georgina was accustomed through her growing up in Twillingate, caring for hens and chickens, growing a variety of flowers and vegetables, and gathering seeds for the coming seasons. She now routinely sends seeds of all kinds to her sister Lucy at Twillingate and, later, to Rose when Rose moved home again. Georgina came to be known around the Colony as a celebrity and was dubbed "The Lady of the Lavender" because of her work gathering and drying lavender from the gardens.

In a letter to her sister at Twillingate, Georgina wrote on a picture postcard: "This is the cottage I am presently living in. The climbers, you see, are pink and yellow roses. You cannot think how pretty it is. I hope you got your flower seed, also spinach."

In addition to farm work for the women, there were other therapeutic activities such as sewing and weaving, basket making and pottery and making flags. The sewing activities would have reminded Georgina of Twillingate and the work she had done there in her youth with the creation of a Dorcas Society to sew clothes and blankets for the poor and impoverished families of her hometown.

One of the important features of Duxhurst was the Church of St. Mary and the Angels. John Norsworthy, a worker at the estate, wrote a fine description of the church. Since Georgina became an organist in this church, one of Ros Black's comments is of particular interest: "Most amazing of all, he spoke of roses growing in the church itself, on a trellis separating the sanctuary from the room behind the Lady altar which housed the organ. The organ was apparently a splendid instrument." The juxtaposition of roses and the organ would have made this a scene of great comfort and healing for Georgina. Lady Somerset caused much controversy as she became increasingly High Anglican and demonstrated this with the placing of statues and icons on the grounds and in the church, including a life-sized carved crucifix and the use of ten nuns to run the school. She introduced much direct Catholic teaching but was proud of the fact that their numbers included non-conformists and Romanists, and that there was a high degree of harmony among the residents. One wonders if this emphasis may have been a contributing factor in Georgina's decision to become a Roman Catholic, some details of which we will encounter in a later chapter.

On July 20, 1915, the Duxhurst Colony was taken over by the British War Office as a Red Cross hospital, and soldiers convalescing after battle injuries were cared for here. Janet stayed on as a nurse, and Georgina remained with her sister to do general work at the hospital. Displaying her good nature and zest for fun, Georgina dubbed two of the convalescing soldiers who helped her with general work at the Colony "The Heavenly Twins." For occasional breaks from the Colony, the sisters stayed at a place called "Wood Cottage" at Chorleywood, Hertfordshire.

It cannot be determined how long Georgina stayed at the Duxhurst Colony, but Amy Louise Peyton states that "her stays were intermittent over a long period." She was staying at "an elaborately landscaped forty-acre property" named Petwood at Woodhall Spa, Lincolnshire, in 1910, property which belonged to Baroness Von Eckardstein, according to a communication to her sister Lucy, but was soon "going back to Lady Henry." A postcard written in 1920 indicates that she was still at the Duxhurst Colony, as it had by then been vacated by the military after the war ended and Lady Henry would have continued her work there. It is likely that both Janet and Georgina returned permanently to 14 Bulstrode Street following the death of Lady Somerset on March 12, 1921. Janet would have resumed work at the nursing station and very likely continued this until her retirement about 1926. The Duxhurst Colony continued under new management and was formally passed over to the Holy Family Homes in 1929.

A striking likeness of Georgina as she is flanked by outline maps of her beloved Newfoundland and Labrador (Courtesy of Sylvia Ficken, Newfoundland artist, 1981)

After an absence of seventeen years, in the late summer of 1921, Georgina returned alone to Twillingate to visit her sister Rose. It cannot be determined how long the visit lasted. But the *Twillingate Sun* of October 15, 1921, noted that "a rare and thrilling treat was enjoyed by a large and appreciative congregation when Miss Georgie Stirling sang in her proficient and usual manner, ascending to the high notes and descending to the lower notes with much ease." The 1921 visit was further confirmed by Maymie (Roberts) Hewlett in a 1969 radio interview with Hiram Silk. Maymie reported that Georgina sang at the North Side Church, but she got the year wrong, saying it was 1922. Maymie also stated that on that occasion Georgina sang "The Holy City" and further stated that it was done in the North Side Methodist Church, rather than in the Church of England. Maymie may even have played the organ for Georgina because she too was a college-trained organist. This visit to Twillingate may have been precipitated by Lady Henry Somerset's death in England in March 1921 and may have been a "test run" by Georgina to determine whether she could indeed return to live in her old hometown permanently. Janet's death in Reigate, England, in 1928 must have confirmed Georgina's decision for a final return to Twillingate, and their sister, Susan Temple, had died in Kent, England, in 1925. Georgina appears to have arrived home in early 1929.

It is not certain when Rose returned to Twillingate, but the *Twillingate Sun* affirms that she was in Twillingate in early 1914. She may have returned unannounced only to discover that the Stirling house was occupied by the Church of England clergy and his family because the rectory had burned down. Lucy had died in Twillingate on March 18, 1913. We know that Rose had left Italy before 1911 because she was teaching in England that year. Only one issue of the *Twillingate Sun* for the first part of 1914 is available online, and it noted that sometime in January, Rose was leaving for St. John's "for the winter." Another issue of the *Sun* in December 1914 gives a similar message. Kate (Stirling) Putzki's children, Paul and Dorothy, came from the United States to visit Rose that summer, and Paul as a medical student was working at the Grenfell Hospital at Pilley's Island.

With the death of her two sisters in England, the stage was set for Georgina's final return to Twillingate.

CHAPTER FOURTEEN
BY CALVIN D. EVANS

GEORGINA'S LAST YEARS IN TWILLINGATE — TRIALS, MYSTERY, AND TRIUMPH

GEORGINA'S TWO SISTERS IN ENGLAND, Susan Temple and Janet Stirling, had provided the much-needed emotional support to Georgina during her most difficult years. Her sister Lucy had been in London from the time of Georgina's return from Milan in the late fall of 1901 until the three sisters—Georgina, Janet, and Lucy—returned for a visit to Twillingate in the summer of 1904, at which time Lucy decided to remain in the old Stirling home, and did so until her death in March 1913—except for one visit to London and Washington, DC, in 1907. The deaths of Janet and Susan in England seemed to have set the stage for Georgina's permanent return to Twillingate, where she would reside in the old Stirling home with her sister Rose. She arrived in Twillingate in early 1929.

At this stage in her life, the magic was gone, but she was determined to carve out for herself a very different kind of life. She was now a woman of mature years, aged sixty-two. Her new life would be a quiet one, in a hometown which had brought her so much joy as a child and young woman growing up in a secure family and community setting.

Twillingate had always been Georgina's lodestar and her continuous inspiration. She was never far away from home in her private thoughts, as reflected in her correspondence and her conversations. Twillingate anchored her and grounded her, and it was fitting that she would spend her final years here. Newfoundland in general, and Twillingate in particular, furnished the true, constant, and genuine inspiration for everything that Georgina accomplished

Georgina's life would have been an appropriate subject for a grand tragic opera, but there was no one to write it, no one to compose the music, no one to sing. So, the full opera remains unwritten and unperformed.

It should be noted that a musical has been written by Eleanor Cameron Stockley, at one time a teacher in the town and still a resident, and was performed in Twillingate in 1997 by a group of adults, youth, and children to honour Georgina Stirling's memory and her legacy in music and song.

Anne Morrow Lindbergh, to whom we referred earlier, would have been able to appreciate the tragic circumstances of Georgina's life as she contemplated "the shape of a woman's life." Her comments could readily have been applied to Georgina Stirling during the depths of her despair: "It is not the desert island nor the stony wilderness that cuts you from the people you love. It is the wilderness in the mind, the desert wastes in the heart through which one wanders lost and a stranger. When one is a stranger to oneself then one is estranged from others too. If one is out of touch with oneself, then one cannot touch others. . . . Only when one is connected to one's own core is one connected to others . . ."

We yearn to know more of what life was really like for Georgina when she settled in Twillingate in 1929. We know that she fell while on board ship during the voyage from England to St. John's and her broken arm was encased in a cast by the ship's doctor. Unable to manage her hair in the upsweep hairdo she constantly maintained, she asked the ship's barber to give her a "bob cut," which would almost maintain itself. That act alone denotes a woman who was very sure of herself and willing to live with necessity. She was experiencing the act of "getting in touch with herself," as Anne Morrow Lindbergh would phrase it in later years.

Amy Louise Peyton quotes comments made by some members of the Twillingate community about Georgina's "drinking," to her being a "drunkard," to "tippling," to carrying a "wee nip" in her purse. Perhaps some people of that day made a few references to such at the beginning, but those who had been her adoring fans in St. John's and elsewhere did not so much turn against her and reject her as they were embarrassed by this development and would have been uncomfortable in knowing how to relate to her. Besides, they were a coastal boat ride away from Twillingate, and their paths would never cross. They would not know how to reach out to her; they simply left her alone. But the people of Twillingate, her hometown, quickly accepted her as the woman she was or had become and knew instinctively how to relate to her. They became her friends and helpers and supporters, and even her voluntary servants.

Georgina's over-drinking had undoubtedly been a symptom of a far more serious problem, not the problem itself. Our attempts to probe beyond the act of conjecturing have borne some results, but much of what really happened to Georgina in the year 1900–1901 remains shrouded in mystery. More about that later. By the time she had returned to Twillingate, she had conquered the over-drinking habit, and some may even have looked askance at her "social drinking" because it did not fit with the morals of some people in the community at that time. But, as many others did, she demonstrated her independence and, being true to herself, she ordered wines and spirits through the local telegraph office, and these were delivered to her by the coastal boat. The sisters served wine at some of their entertainments, and Rose is said to have made blueberry wine which, at one point, was seven years old. People who knew Georgina best remarked that they had never seen any evidence of over-drinking during the last years in Twillingate.

Edward D. Moogk writes: "The local people had difficulty adjusting to Georgina, who, while in Europe, had a reputation for a bit of what was called 'loose living.' She had wine with her meals and smoked the occasional cheroot." What a curious comment from someone writing in 1975.

In 1971, Ed Manning of CBC London in a letter to Robert Walter Parsons had written similarly, so there must have been yet another source that both Manning and Moogk were quoting. Manning writes: "Twillingate, as I understand it, was very much inclined to hush up G.S. (Georgina Stirling) after she returned to the community to spend her years of retirement. She had apparently scandalized the Nonconformist conscience of the local folk by evidences of loose living (!) picked up in Europe; she regularly drank wine with her meals and occasionally went the length of smoking cheroot. . . . In consequence of all this, the people of Twillingate have been reticent to talk about her, and even historians of Newfoundland have done little in the way of research on her career . . . it's encouraging to know that among Canada's contributions to the world of fine music, and there were many, there was at least one colourful artist who drank wine with her meals, and occasionally smoked cheroots." My guess is that the "yet another source" was Hiram Silk, and we shall find out in the chapter on the controversial recording of Georgina's voice how that may have happened.

Ed Manning assured Robert Walter Parsons in his letter that "Research on G.S. will be an ongoing process" and also that ". . . your history of G.S. as outlined in your letter, seems a most complete one, and I shall be pleased to deposit a copy in the National Library, Ottawa, for their reference."

Robert Walter Parsons's letters in 1970 to the Library of Congress in Washington, DC, to the Biblioteca Comonale di Milano in Italy, to the Societe des amis de la Bibliotheque Nationale in Paris, and to the Library & Museum of the Performing Arts at the New York Public Library yielded only negative replies about the existence of any documentation on Georgina Stirling, and the response from the last one seems quite peculiar since Georgina is known to have sung in New York City and toured the United States with both Colonel J. Henry Mapleson and Madame Sofia Scalchi from 1896 to 1898. Their response reads: ". . . we were unable to find any reference to Mme. Toulinguet under either Georgina Stirling or Marie Toulinguet in the following places: the Music Division's clipping file, program file, picture collection of musicians, biographical file, the published annals of La Scala, Covent Garden in London, the Metropolitan, the Opera-Comique of Paris, the history of the opera houses of Bergano, Parma, and Genova in Italy, the autobiography of Colonel Mapleson, or the various Marchesi books." It seemed as if any reference to Georgina Stirling had been excised from all records, if they had ever been there. Perhaps a less than serious search of the records had been conducted. The response from the Library of Congress was a form letter that suggested the hiring of a researcher to find any available information.

The CBC Grand Falls interviews which appear later in this chapter and in Appendix Six will disprove the contention that local people had difficulty adjusting to Georgina and that they were reticent to talk about her. Of course Georgina had become accustomed to social drinking. It was part of the social scene in the late 1800s, as it is today. She was very probably gently introduced to wine by her father before she even left Twillingate at the age of twenty-one. No other reference can be found to whether Georgina ever engaged in the practice of smoking. The "cheroot" was "a kind of cigar having blunt ends and thicker at one end than at the other." Neither the social drinking nor the occasional cheroot could be described as "loose living."

Perhaps a further comment would be appropriate. There were two sets of moral expectations in Newfoundland for roughly the one-hundred-year period (say) between 1850 and 1950. In the Christian community represented by the Salvation Army and the Methodist/United Church there was a strict moral code that forbade unnecessary work and frivolous activity on Sunday and certain kinds of social practices such as dancing and the drinking of wines and spirits. Church of England and Catholic folk held a more liberal attitude toward the observance of Sunday and, when they attended the obligatory Sunday service, felt freer to resume regular activity for the remainder of the day—their moral code also allowed dancing and the consumption of wines and spirits. A certain amount of "judgment" may have been going on between the two groups, but having lived through part of that one-hundred-year period, my recollection is that the "judgment" was seldom overly serious.

Dr. Stirling represented the Church of England moral code in Twillingate, and he and his wife would have permitted their daughters certain freedoms that other Protestants in Twillingate would not have practised. This could hardly have been characterized as "loose living." Georgina may well have expanded her family's liberalism when she moved into the high social circles represented in the operatic world of Europe and the United States.

Dr. Stirling's record books for the 1880s show that he regularly ordered ale, even casks of ale, as well as wines and other liquors from merchants in St. John's. These would have been served to adult guests at the Stirlings' social evenings, times when the daughters, with their father, performed musical selections and singing for the guests. Undoubtedly, the daughters would be introduced to social drinking as they came of age.

If anyone in Twillingate ever "judged" Georgina for "loose living" after her return to her hometown in 1929, it probably would have been a few representatives of the Salvation Army or even the United Church communities. But this should not be taken too seriously. The people of Twillingate realized that they had a famous person in their midst, that she was one of their own, that she had achieved great honours in many countries, and that she had come home to stay. They loved her, and they appreciated what she was giving back to her community in tangible ways. Her humility and her caring actions were not lost on these people. These were part of who she now was.

THANKS TO A SERIES OF INTERVIEWS which Hiram Silk of CBC Grand Falls did with people of Notre Dame Bay and Green Bay from the 1950s to the late 1980s, we are able to gain new and fresh insights into and knowledge of the Stirling family, and in particular what life was like for Georgina after she returned permanently to Twillingate. Twenty-six interviews of twenty-three different people focus on the Stirlings and offer new information about Georgina's later years. Most of the tapes are of good quality, but in a few the audio is quite low and unclear. I have listened to all twenty-six of these tapes, several of them two or three times, and one in particular I have listened to five or six times because of the startling revelation which the reader will find near the end of this chapter.

Hiram Thomas Silk was the adopted son of Thomas William and Alfreda Silk of Grand Falls, Newfoundland and Labrador. The names of his birth parents are not known, though it is known that his father was from Green's Harbour, Trinity Bay, and his mother was from Grand Falls. His adoptive great-grandparents were Thomas Moore Silk of Bermondsey, England, and Grace Hannam of Leading Tickles, Newfoundland and Labrador. For many years, Thomas, Sr., held very responsible positions of lay leadership in the Church of England at Leading Tickles, acting as a lay reader and probably serving as the rector's warden or the people's warden.

Hiram Silk won an O'Leary Newfoundland Poetry Award in 1951 and came in third in the annual Peabody Institute of Music Competition. His instrument of choice was the organ, thus accounting for his particular love of church music. He was awarded a scholarship to the Julliard School of Music in New York but declined it and instead went to Ryerson University in Toronto to study broadcasting. At CBC Grand Falls, Silk hosted a program called *Looking Back*, in which he interviewed many Newfoundlanders about past years. He also hosted *Sounds of Faith* on Sunday mornings and recorded hymns, religious songs, and several church services. He was particularly impressed with the musical heritage and quality of singing and organ music in Twillingate. A third program that Silk hosted was called *Intermezzo*, and it specialized in classical music. It was on this program, probably in the very early 1960s, that Silk played the recording of what was believed to be of Georgina's song. This matter is dealt with in Chapter Fifteen of this book.

It is from Silk's *Looking Back* series of interviews that we garner much new information about what Georgina Stirling's life was like when she returned permanently to Twillingate. Several of the other Stirling sisters appear in the comments of the interviewees, and these are included here so as to present a truer picture of family members, particularly in the later years. There is a fair amount of repetition in the interviews, and some of this material is included so as to confirm general understandings of certain facts or conjectures about family members. To ensure that this is not tedious for the reader, most of the very general interviews have been moved to the appendices at the back of the book, and these appear in Appendix Six. Only selected and substantive interviews are summarized in this chapter.

In Amy Louise Peyton's otherwise fine book of research and writing, there is a disappointing lack of detail about what life was like for Georgina Stirling at Twillingate from

1929 to 1935. Peyton's Chapter 17, "Miss Georgie Returns Permanently to Twillingate," focuses too much on recalling the glories of Georgina's past and imagining what thoughts the boat trip from Lewisporte to Twillingate might have triggered in Georgina's mind. It is curious that Hiram Silk, when interviewing Amy Louise, seems not to have apprised her of many of the facts he had gathered and the knowledge that he had acquired during his many interviews. We know now that he was saving much of this for a book which he intended to write but never did.

It needs to be stated at this point that we owe a great debt of gratitude to Hiram Silk for the many interviews he did with older Newfoundlanders over a period of more than thirty years. Yet he appears to be ill-prepared for some of the interviews, sometimes gets his facts wrong as he prepares to ask the interviewees specific questions, and tends to over-prompt some of his interviewees.

Maymie (Roberts) Hewlett, taken sometime during the twenty-three years she was secretary/bookkeeper for Dr. John Olds at the Twillingate Memorial Hospital (Courtesy of Milton Anstey)

Two of Silk's interviews in particular consist of his conversations with Mary Annie Tucker ("Maymie" Roberts) Hewlett, who was "a near neighbour" of Georgina's from 1929 to 1935 (actually, Maymie lived across the road from Georgina, on the water side, and her father, Andrew's, house is visible in the picture of the Stirling house on page 52 of Amy Louise Peyton's book). Maymie was the secretary-bookkeeper of Dr. John Olds for twenty-three years and saw and interacted with Georgina "almost every day" during 1929 to 1935. Maymie was born in 1898 and was thirty-one years old when Georgina returned to Twillingate.

It cannot be determined where Maymie received her bookkeeping training. Maymie may have worked in one of the many merchant firms in Twillingate and may have been employed at the Twillingate Memorial Hospital from the time it opened in 1924, rising to the rank of secretary-bookkeeper to the medical superintendent in 1934 when Dr. Olds succeeded Dr. Charles Parsons.

The eminent Dr. Olds had first come to Twillingate in 1930 on a summer practicum and returned in 1932 to take up permanent residence. In 1934, when Dr. Olds presented his passionate case for increased government funding at St. John's and was flatly told that there would instead be a reduction in funding, he devised the "Blanket Contract" on his way home by coastal boat. This contract would require every subscriber to pay forty-four cents per year (or its equivalent). At first his hospital board had strong reservations but finally relented and gave Dr. Olds a one-year trial period. Dr. Olds needed someone smart and trustworthy to receive and convert to money the donations of fish, potatoes, other vegetables such as turnips and beets, as well as berries, firewood, hay, and whatever else people could give, and it appears that Maymie Roberts was selected to do this job. Dr. Olds must have had enormous confidence in the woman who would work for five successive business managers over a period of twenty-three years to keep control over the donations-in-kind. This contract was very probably the first instance of medicare in North America. Funds from the local Hustler's Club, an amateur theatre group formed by aides and nurses, supplemented the subscriber payments, and Maymie Roberts took a leading role in many of these stage productions. It is of interest that Georgina Stirling also sang and coached and directed both stage plays and singing during the years following her permanent return to Twillingate.

When Captain Andrew Roberts, Maymie's father, died without a Last Will on September 22, 1926, Letters of Administration from the Supreme Court of Newfoundland on January 31, 1927, granted all sixty-four shares in his fishing schooner *Hattie A. Heckman* to his wife, Maymie's mother, Lucy Roberts. On June 9, 1927, Lucy sold the vessel to her daughter, Mary A. T. Roberts, spinster—that is Maymie! Maymie held on to the fishing schooner for three years and sold it to the merchant firm Ashbournes Ltd. on February 17, 1930. This means that for three years Maymie would have been in charge of the vessel, hiring the crew, appointing the master of the vessel, supplying the vessel for the fishing season, keeping the books, assuring that the season's catch was sold to the merchant, and paying the crew members. This indicates something of the remarkable nature and qualities of this young woman—she was then between twenty-nine and thirty-two years old. This was one of only six instances of a woman selling her ship to another woman in the entire history of the nineteenth and twentieth centuries in Newfoundland. So, as an early businesswoman, Maymie was well-prepared for the job with Dr. Olds when she took over the reins of implementing the Blanket Contract.

Maymie left her job at the Memorial Hospital in 1957 when she married widower Gabriel Densolo Hewlett of Robert's Arm, a contractor for the Bowater's Paper Company of Corner Brook. It was a first marriage for Maymie, at age fifty-nine. It is as Mrs. Maymie Hewlett that Hiram Silk interviewed her in 1969 at Robert's Arm, just a year or so before her return to Twillingate. She died in Twillingate in 1984 at the age of eighty-six.

Because of her family background, education, work experience, work as a trusted employee of a brilliant long-serving surgeon, experience in her church and the community as a singer and church organist and involvement in concerts and plays, Maymie (Roberts) Hewlett must be regarded as a formidable witness to the details of Georgina Stirling's last years in Twillingate. Of all the people interviewed, Maymie stands out as the most knowledgeable and reliable source. The interviews portray her as an articulate, knowledgeable, trustworthy, no-nonsense, and quietly forceful person.

Added to this assessment is my extensive email correspondence in 2017 and 2018 with Pearl Legge of Howley, Newfoundland and Labrador, who was connected to both the Roberts and Hewlett families and had regular contact with Maymie during every summer from about 1962 to about 1971, living next door to her at Robert's Arm, and then corresponding with her regularly from 1971 until Maymie's death in 1984. Pearl, at eighty-one years of age, is a former teacher but a not-yet-retired bookkeeper with specific training in accounting at the college level, who established her own bookkeeping business in Ottawa and then in the Northwest Territories and ran it until she retired and moved back to Newfoundland in 2000. She described Maymie as "a force of nature," a memorable woman, loved and respected by all who knew her.

Over a three-month period in late 2017 and early 2018, I challenged Pearl (perhaps pestered is a better word) to try to recall every detail that Maymie had revealed to her about Georgina Stirling. Something mentioned in a general conversation would trigger a memory of Georgina for Maymie, and she would share something of this with Pearl. At first there was Pearl's recall of the great sadness that Maymie shared in her few conversations about Georgina. "Maymie was mainly thinking of Georgina's overall mental and physical health when she had those discussions with me," Pearl states. "Georgina's name came up when we were having a heart-to-heart conversation. She trusted me also. There was no idle chatter. She was above that." Pearl further states, "Maymie was absolutely credible, an honest and trustworthy person." Maymie was also a very well-organized person. She liked to fix problems and help people. These were the skills that Dr. Olds found in her and on which he depended when Maymie was his secretary-bookkeeper. With Maymie's experience at the hospital, interacting with a variety of people and problems, she would have found ways of helping Georgina and may have been instrumental in introducing Georgina to both Dr. and Mrs. Olds (who was a nurse at the hospital), and helping to include her in the social life at the cottage, the home of the Olds family, and persuading her to visit Dr. Olds when the cancer problem surfaced.

At one point, Pearl seemed to think that perhaps I doubted Maymie's credibility, and she took pains to persuade me that Maymie was no ordinary person. "I was wondering how I could explain Maymie. I wondered who I could compare her to in her demeanour, even her way of moving, speaking. I wondered what made her the way she was. . . . She must have been a girl of good breeding. She moved like the British actress Helen Mirren in her portrayal of Queen Elizabeth in the movie *The Queen*." Then Pearl further compared Maymie to Madeleine Albright: "She had perfect memory, spoke softly and quietly, and seemed to be a woman of good breeding, like Maymie."

Gary L. Saunders in his book *Doctor Olds of Twillingate* gives quotes, sometimes extensive quotes, from Maymie (Roberts) Hewlett. The quotes very probably came from another source, perhaps Jessie (Troake) Drover, who was a nurse at the hospital. Maymie had died by the time Saunders did the research for his 1994 book. The quotes portray a decisive, well-spoken, lively, no-nonsense person.

This serves as a fitting introduction to Maymie's testimony in Hiram Silk's interview of 1969. Maymie begins the interview with reference to Georgina's "kindly nature, her humility, her fame and her faults."

Maymie then proceeds to describe two gifts which Georgina gave her while they were living next door to each other in Twillingate. The first was the Testimonial, addressed "From Terra Nova to Twillingate Stirling" and printed in gold lettering on a blue satin background, which was (Georgina had told her) written by Georgina's friend Mr. Jardine of St. John's for that special occasion. (This was undoubtedly Frederick F. Jardine, journalist and antiquarian of St. John's and later Bell Island.) The Testimonial was presented to Georgina at the conclusion of the Grand Farewell Concert of October 3, 1895, at College

Hall in St. John's, along with a Letter of Appreciation and a jewelled bracelet which was to be given to Georgina when she arrived in London, England, in the next ten days or so. Maymie Hewlett reads the poem on Hiram Silk's tape. The first word of each line spells the name "Twillingate Stirling." *See Tonia Evans Cianciulli's Chapter Eight, Subheading "What's In a Name" for the transcript of the testimonial.*

THE SECOND GIFT THAT GEORGINA GAVE to Maymie Roberts was a domed night light that sits on a round metal piece, and at the centre is a brass candle holder which is surrounded by precious gems including amber, garnet, pearls, and emeralds.

The Testimonial is now housed at the Twillingate Museum and may be viewed by the public. The domed night light was given to Hiram Silk by Maymie just before she died and was subsequently given by Hiram to his friend Bruce Manuel.

Left: Maymie (Roberts) Hewlett, Georgina's best friend from 1929 to 1935, and Georgina's night light. China plate painted by artist Paul Putzki. (Courtesy of Vaughn Harbin)
Right: The night light which was gifted to Georgina somewhere in Europe, and given to Maymie Roberts by Georgina (Courtesy of Bruce Manuel and Brent English)

Pressed in the interview to describe what Georgina meant to her, Maymie said: "I loved her. That's the only way I can put it, really." Maymie was not at all reluctant to share her thoughts and her memories. Most people of that time had concluded that Georgina's sister Rose was eccentric, but when Maymie was asked if Georgina also was eccentric, she was quick to reply, "No, but she was different. She dressed differently. She spoke differently. She liked to be different in every respect. She was as humble as a child. She liked things that we might overlook. She loved everything of nature." Maymie continues to share her memories of Georgina, that she had learned botany while in England, that she had learned everything about flowers, trees, and shrubs, that she had studied horticulture, that the Stirling property at this time was rustic with fences and seats, that Georgina had animals—including cows, pigs, goats, and chickens—that "she was in her garden from the time the snow left until it came again in the late fall," that she grew a variety of vegetables in her garden and a profusion of flowers and all kinds of roses from which she made bouquets for neighbours and those who needed cheering up. When her roses were in bloom, she cut some every morning and gave these to people in the town. Amy Louise Peyton in her book names the flowers that filled Georgina's garden—bright red posies, blue delphiniums, orange and yellow calendula and marigold, tall hollyhocks, and foxglove, and scented mignonette. To these Maymie added the lilac bushes, both white and purple. All the flowers had come from seed that Georgina had sent home to her sisters in Twillingate during the years that she lived in London and in Surrey, England. Perhaps this was indeed part of Georgina's plan for a future back in Twillingate.

Maymie recalled that Georgina used to repeat often the lines:

> The kiss of the sun for pardon,
> The song of the birds for mirth,-
> One is nearer God's heart in a garden
> Than anywhere else on earth.

Maymie continued: "She was a real Christian at heart, kind and humble, a very humble person, for all the greatness and fame she had, yet she was so humble, a person who recognized things in others. She made everybody feel, she made me feel, that we were doing something wonderful. If someone just played the music for a hymn, Georgina made it seem wonderful for that person."

Maymie recalled that Georgina had once remarked that she had never, ever heard better male voices than in Twillingate. At this point Hiram Silk mentioned that the singing in the Twillingate churches had always been outstanding, that he had been very impressed by the quality of the singing and had recorded singing there several times. Georgina had once coached and helped a group which was putting on a play in the town, and at another time she arranged and coached a male singing quartet, including Mr. Hodge (almost certainly Arthur Harold Hodge, the merchant) and Mr. Edward Linfield (also a merchant), and on that same occasion Georgina had sung "Darby and Joan." Maymie was present to hear it. Mr. Linfield, she said, had a beautiful bass voice.

At this point Maymie interjects that Georgina had returned to Twillingate in 1922 (she had the date wrong; it was 1921) and that she sang "The Holy City" at the North Side Methodist Church on that occasion. This was briefly mentioned earlier. Maymie was then twenty-three years old, had done professional training in music at Mount Allison College in New Brunswick, and was one of the organists and a member of the choir in that church. Maymie may even have invited Georgina to sing, being unaware of all that had transpired in Europe, and Georgina, as usual, always found it difficult to resist such an invitation. Maymie may even have played the organ for Georgina's singing that day, as she did many times after Georgina returned to Twillingate, but she does not say so. No other source confirms that Georgina sang at that time. How could a woman who has such marvellous recall of events and is so articulate at expressing herself be wrong about this?

Maymie then begins to reminisce about an elderly woman who was still living (1969) at the age of eighty-seven and commented about her skill at playing the organ and singing. Her name was Mrs. "Minnie" Maley; her full name at birth was Mary Elizabeth Roberts, and she was born in 1882, so "Minnie" was a nickname. Georgina had once remarked to Maymie, "If Mrs. Maley had had the voice training that I had she would have topped the world." Even at eighty-seven, though "her voice was frail it had a rare, sympathetic quality, a sweet voice, like a bird." Mrs. Maley had been the chief soloist in the North Side Methodist church and the organist in that church for many years.

Maymie continued her recollections by stating that Georgina loved to read, that she was happy tending her animals, that she loved to cook—"she did everything with enthusiasm; she did everything well." Georgina entertained occasionally with dinner parties, serving full-course meals on ornate silver platters and with the Stirling family's monogrammed cutlery. Her puddings were her specialty and were served as a dessert. They were called the Queen Puddings. Garibaldi, her pet pig, named after a famed Italian painter whom Georgina had known, once almost knocked Georgina down as she was removing the pudding from the oven. Some of the guests at these parties were Dr. Parsons and Mr. and Mrs. Hodge. Maymie would also be invited to these events. Georgina's pet rooster was also a welcome guest in the house on occasion. I suppose one could conclude from this that she was a bit eccentric.

The reference to Garibaldi needs a bit of explanation. Giuseppi Garibaldi (1807–1882) was an Italian general and politician and played a key role in the Italian Risorgimento (the reunification or "resurrection" plan) for a new Italy, which began in the 1860s. It was such a vibrant period in Italy's history that it gave rise to an impressive array of art and painting, with the two brothers Gerolamo and Domenico Induno playing a significant role in this revival. Gerolamo Induno was a painter and soldier who lived from 1825 to 1890. Maymie (Roberts) Hewlett's reference to the name of the pig was undoubtedly in connection with Garibaldi the politician, and it must have somehow in her mind become associated with what was very probably Georgina's reference in a conversation about Italian art. She may well have known an artist who was familiar with the paintings of that crucial period in Italy's history. The naming of pet animals after famous figures was a reflection of Georgina's sense of good humour and not a sign of disrespect for the famous. One source states that Garibaldi, the politician, owned a Newfoundland dog, so this may have been the reason that Georgina attached the name to her pet pig.

Maymie comments that there were nine children in the Stirling family, seven sisters and "two brothers who died early in life." Amy Louise Peyton writes that there was only one brother, the boy who drowned, but we have already noted that there were at least three brothers and possibly four; in a later interview with Fred Manuel, he names two of these boys and furnishes some other details about them.

Hiram Silk questions Maymie as to whether Georgina died in poverty, as some people had suggested. Maymie considers that topic to be "ridiculous." She says that Georgina and Rose were surrounded by valuable antiques, any one of which could be sold for a high price. She also states that Georgina received income every month. Vaughn Harbin, whom we shall meet later in this chapter and who is a relative of Maymie's and spent much time with her in her last ten years, affirms that Maymie looked after Georgina's finances, including her banking, and her correspondence. "The sisters," Maymie claimed, "were well taken care of. I was there every day. Many friends and neighbours cared for them. Georgina's bed was changed regularly, and Dr. Olds attended her." I expect these last comments pertained to Georgina's final days as she struggled with cancer. Amy Louise Peyton had written that "She declined to visit the local doctor." We now know this was not true. Georgina was a frequent guest at the cottage, Dr. and Mrs. Olds's home. We know also from Gary Saunders's book that Dr. Olds made house calls. And during the summer of 1934, Georgina had a stay in the local hospital, where she was nursed by Jessie (Troake) Drover, with whom she had many long conversations when she could not sleep at night.

On the matter of financial support for the sisters, Maymie remarks that she was contacted as late as 1967 by a lawyer who was making a final settlement of the Stirling estate and wished to know if there were any living relatives. Maymie would have told them about the children of Kate (Stirling) Putzki, who were living at that time in the United States. We know also that in his Last Will, Dr. Stirling had made provision for an annual allowance to be paid to his daughters. Presumably, that continued for many years. His holdings in Newfoundland mines, especially at Tilt Cove and near Springdale, as well as his investments in the Dominion of Canada and the United States and properties held at Twillingate and St. John's, would have provided for his daughters for many years.

Maymie stated that Lucy Stirling had returned to Twillingate (that was in 1904) and "lived in luxury" in the Stirling house. Lucy seemed at last to have reached a level of peace within herself. She had come home to Twillingate to try to recreate for herself "a life as it once had been." She had conquered her brokenness and wanted to assure her community that all was well with her. She spent most of the next nine years at home in the Stirling house. However, we know that Lucy made at least one trip abroad. On December 7, 1907, she embarked on the SS *Lucania* at Liverpool, England, and arrived in New York on December 15, "intending to visit her sister Mrs. Putzki at Washington, D.C." The contact name given for the place from which she had come was "Miss J. Stirling, 14 Bolstrode (?), London West."

Maymie's personal journal reflects on this period when she was about seven years of age (in 1905) and would visit Lucy at the Stirling home. She writes, "My first recollection of the Stirling home was as a probably 7-year old child. . . . I went every Saturday and gathered roses with Miss Lucy. There were four beautiful rose trees in her garden, and she gathered the flowers each morning before the dew was off the trees. I suppose Miss Lucy at this time had returned from England to live at home. I was there quite often but not as much as with

Miss Rose and Miss Georgie when they returned. . . . Miss Lucy always kept a servant, who lived in, and entertained in great style. I used to like to go to her hall table and read the visiting cards, anyone who came, and Miss Lucy was out, left their little white card with name printed on a . . . little fancy plate . . . she lived there many years, living in splendour . . . latterly she became ill and spent a winter with Aggie and Will Peyton, cousin, and that is where she died." Later, in her notes, Maymie refers to "the grand style" in which Lucy lived. She recollects "seeing the beautiful Miss Lucy in her beautiful long dresses, and when the house was kept in Old English Style." "And I often carried baskets of roses from the big garden to her many friends, afterward being rewarded with a full basket for myself. I can see her now trailing down the lovely green field to cut these roses before the dew was off them. To me she was like a princess. She always kept a servant. Years before when she was tragically disappointed in marriage . . . her father settled a lifetime amount of money on her, and she returned to live in the old house."

Lucy Stirling became unwell in the fall of 1912 and spent the winter with her cousins, Will and Aggie Peyton, in Back Harbour, where she died on March 18, 1913. The Stirling house was subsequently rented to the Reverend Arthur Stirling, the incumbent of St. Peter's Church, and his family after the rectory burned down in 1913 and while a new rectory was being constructed, and just before Rose Stirling returned to Twillingate, probably in very early 1914.

MAYMIE REMARKED IN HER INTERVIEW that Rose was the "best educated person in the family," and states that Rose had accompanied Georgina to Toronto, where they lived for approximately two years. We know now that it was Kate who accompanied Georgina to Toronto in the fall of 1882. Maymie was mistaken about Rose accompanying Georgina, but is it possible that Rose went to Toronto later, (say) sometime in the period 1883 to 1885, and spent a year upgrading the teaching skills that she would have already acquired in Newfoundland where she had, very probably, been teaching previously? Rose may have been doing teacher training at the Toronto Ladies' College (or its precursor), whose curriculum included teacher training supervised by professors from the University of Toronto. There is nothing in Kate's letters which connects Rose to Toronto, but since Rose was sixteen years older than Georgina and Georgina's studies were being supervised by Mrs. Murray, it is just possible that Rose may have spent sufficient time in Toronto to receive teacher certification at a higher level than that offered at the time in Newfoundland, while operating quite independently of Georgina. How else is it possible to explain Maymie's statement that Rose was "the best educated person in the family"? This statement is affirmed by other sources as well, but it is suspect in view of the many years of vocal and instrumental training that Georgina had taken. Rose in Toronto is an unlikely scenario, but that would be to question Maymie's otherwise excellent memory.

Maymie also states that Dr. Stirling had sent Titus Manuel, a local carpenter, to Toronto ahead of the sisters to build a house in which the girls would live during their stay in Toronto. (This assertion has not been confirmed, though it is known that Titus Manuel did carpenter work in Toronto.) One would naturally conclude that Maymie had heard this information directly from Georgina herself, but it may simply have been hearsay around Twillingate. It is also noteworthy that Maymie specifically says of Georgina's time in Toronto "while they were studying there," which would not seem to refer to Georgina and Kate, since Kate had quickly moved on to Chicago, but rather to Georgina and Rose. These events all happened about fifteen years before Maymie was born, so that may account for what certainly seems to be an error. If, however, Rose studied at the Toronto Ladies' College, then Henry James Morgan may be partially correct—a Stirling studied there, but it was not Georgina; it may have been Rose. Yet another possibility!

Rose accompanied Georgina to Europe and stayed in Europe (for many years in Naples, Italy) for more than twenty years (other estimates given in these interviews are twenty-five and twenty-eight years; the latter is almost certainly accurate). Maymie asserts that Rose returned permanently to Twillingate "during the War," and that while living at Naples taught English to members of the Royal Family (undoubtedly the children). While in Europe, Georgina had sung with Caruso and Valacartier, another famous tenor (this name could not be found by Internet searches), and she had received frequent communications from someone named "roto." (We have examined many postcards sent to Georgina by "roto." The nickname "roto" was always signed with a high ascending but lower case "r.") Maymie stated that a member of the Royal Family, Prince Umberto, also wrote to Georgina. (As we shall see later in connection with Rose's many years in Naples, Italy, this Prince Umberto may have been a member of the Italian nobility rather than of the Italian Royal Family. There were two Italian kings named Umberto during this period, but it would certainly not have been one of these, unless it was simply a congratulatory letter in connection with Georgina's singing performances. It is asserted by one source that she sang before Royalty in Italy.)

When questioned by Hiram Silk as to whether Georgina talked very much about her glory days, Maymie replied "Not too much." At one time, however, she gave Maymie a program of her tour of the United States with Madame Sofia Scalchi. Maymie then states that Georgina's "first appearance in Italy was at La Scala House in Milan in 1897–98." This could have been in 1891, following her debut in the fall of 1890, when she had secured an engagement for the "coming season," or more probably in 1898–99 after Georgina had completed the Scalchi tour of the United States and when she was invited to come to Venice and later to Chioggia. Did that quote come directly from Georgina? There has been uncertainty in several records about Georgina singing at La Scala, and several researchers have sought in vain for confirmation. Georgina also talked about Nellie Melba, the Australian singer who had trained under Madame Marchesi, and Georgina described singing with her. Maymie also states that Georgina had sung at Albert Hall in London, England. Maymie then affirms that Georgina's cousin Will Peyton had conjectured that the reason Georgina's voice had changed was because of diphtheria and that "it had changed from soprano to contralto or mezzo-soprano."

Maymie then comments on the terrible April storm that had occurred at the time of Georgina's death on Easter Sunday of 1935 and continued until her burial on the following Wednesday. "The like had never been known before for April." The snow was so deep that the casket had to be hauled from St. Peter's Church to the cemetery by several men on a hand-cart. There was so much snow (six feet by some estimates) that it was difficult to find the burial plot. "It was like a snow house . . . it was just the way Georgina would have had it . . . so touching."

Hiram Silk entitles a separate tape "Maymie Roberts and Gabriel Hewlett Host a Tibb's Eve Party." Part two of this title consists entirely of an interview with Maymie and a focus on Christmas memories. Maymie describes the celebration of Christmas in her youth and young adulthood at Twillingate—the carolling from street to street and door to door on Christmas Eve, "a glorious night of singing," church choirs well-trained to the point where they often sang selections from Handel's "Messiah," including the "Hallelujah Chorus" at church services. Maymie remarks, "Twillingate was the home of good music and talented singers. When I played the pipe organ in church we had good training. . . . We had two ministers in our church. The assistant minister came from England and was a well-trained singer."

Maymie then mentions the Dorcas Society and their major efforts at sewing to supply clothes and blankets to the poor and needy in the town. This remark leads immediately to a further discussion of Georgina Stirling, and Maymie says: "She was very kind to anybody who was poor—she would make sure the poor had a lovely Christmas, especially the children. I knew her better in the latter years than anyone else. . . . Almost every day she came to our house. . . . She sang for us. . . . She preferred the organ over the piano. . . . In England she played the organ regularly at Lady Somerset's chapel. . . . I loved her, she was humorous, kind and good, a little eccentric at times . . . if she disliked you she could put on quite an act to make you feel uncomfortable . . . once you knew her you would never forget her . . . she was so different . . . she sometimes made her own dresses." At the end of the tape, Maymie comments on the Stirling house, which apparently was built originally as a double house with two entrances, two sets of stairs, and a separating wall. She affirms that the house was constructed by two brothers from England. Another source affirms that these were the Murphy brothers (one of them was William J. Murphy), who were brought over from England to build St. Peter's Church of England, whose construction was completed in 1845. The brothers then built what would become the Stirling house, and the younger brother sold it to Dr. Stirling, who is believed to have come to Twillingate as early as 1843 and who was living with his family on the South Island until about 1852. Another source says that Dr. Stirling bought the house from the Slade brothers, a merchant family.

These are just some of Maymie's comments gleaned from this interview. The two interviews with Maymie Hewlett give us the most fulsome picture of what Georgina Stirling was like during the last seven years of her life in Twillingate. There are other important interviews which we will look at presently, but the testimony from this intelligent, articulate local woman forms the basis for an entirely new assessment of Georgina Stirling's last years. Maymie alludes occasionally to the underlying sadness of Georgina's life but portrays for us a strong woman who is determined to make the very best of her lot.

In a separate conversation with Maymie Hewlett, Hiram Silk asked her: "What was Georgina like in her last years in Twillingate?" Maymie replied, "She was tall, a heavily built woman. She carried herself well, even towards the end of her life, when she was cripple. She had a wonderful carriage. Of course, she was trained to that on the stage, and she often said that she never fell in the many times she was on stage. She could prove it herself, almost on her toes, and still stand up straight. She was a good actress, too." The reference to "cripple" is alluded to elsewhere in the interviews, very probably in connection with "the Stirling bandy feet," or possibly gout.

IN SEPTEMBER 2018, WE HAD THE GOOD FORTUNE to meet Vaughn Harbin, a retired teacher with family roots in Twillingate and also a third cousin once removed of Maymie (Roberts) Hewlett. Vaughn spent much concentrated time with Maymie from about

1975 until her death in 1984, mostly at Twillingate but also at Grand Falls, where Maymie died in his arms with a heart attack. She was Vaughn's grandfather's first cousin. During his times with Maymie, Vaughn acquired a great deal of information about Georgina.

Vaughn has a background in voice training and singing, and thus a unique sympathy with Georgina and other singers. He is a lyric tenor and studied in Newfoundland with Natasha Roth and Rosalind Bonia, in Florida with Bernie Kovacs, and in Montreal with Huguette Touangeau. In Montreal he sang briefly with l'ensemble vocale d'orchestre symphonique de Montréal. He describes himself as only an amateur.

Vaughn describes Maymie in this way: "She was an intelligent, articulate, refined woman, possessed of a rare wit and keen insight. She rather reminded me of Dame Maggie Smith's character, Violet Crawley, in *Downton Abbey*. She was indeed a character in search of a play."

Georgina at one point gave Maymie a Satsuma vase which Maymie subsequently gave to Vaughn, and he has now donated it to the Twillingate Museum. Practically all of Georgina's other mementoes that Maymie acquired were given to Hiram Silk, both because he wanted them and because he stated that he intended to write Georgina's biography. Maymie had told Vaughn that she had no confidence that Hiram would ever write the biography. She knew him well. Vaughn states in an email: "She shared many details of Georgie's life with me, some in confidence, and some not, and was always concerned that people often seemed more interested in the sensational and overlooked Georgie's many acts of kindness and charity. . . . She (Maymie) was a stickler for detail and scrupulously honest, as well as clear and sharp of mind until the day she died." Maymie had begun to write a mini-biography of Georgina in the last year of her life, which she had entitled "The Stirling Saga for Vaughn," but her sudden death ended that initiative.

Continuing in his description of Maymie, Vaughn writes: "She always had a mischievous twinkle in her eyes. . . . From Aunt Maym's reminiscences I gleaned that Georgie was a very interesting person, capable of being theatrical, flamboyant, imperious, passionate and fun-loving, as well as kind, thoughtful, artistic, patient and caring."

Maymie attended Mount Allison College in Sackville, New Brunswick, during World War I and studied music there; she was probably away from Twillingate for about two years during the 1914 to 1918 period and would have been away when Rose Stirling returned home, probably in early 1914. Mount Allison seems to have been a finishing school for young ladies at that time. Maymie's mother, Lucy Roberts, would have known Rose; in fact, they attended the same school in Twillingate when they were young girls.

Maymie was one of the organists at the North Side Methodist Church at Twillingate and played the pipe organ there for many years. She used to play for Georgina to sing both at the Stirling house and at Maymie's home when Georgina came to visit, as she frequently did. It is virtually certain that Maymie would have played at the North Side Methodist Church when Georgina sang "The Holy City" during a visit home in 1921.

An example of Georgina's playful and flamboyant manner is found in an incident that Maymie related to Vaughn about a dinner party at the Stirling house where the people have gathered and Maymie is playing the piano and Georgina appears at the top of the stairs clad in a long black silk gown, with a red rose clasped in her mouth, and glides gracefully down the stairs and sings something appropriate for the gathered guests. Being a very private person, Rose generally chose not to attend such events. She chose to be elsewhere in the house.

Maymie presents quite a different assessment of Rose, much more measured and sympathetic, than is shown in several of Hiram Silk's CBC interviews. Rose was an educated woman, very private and reserved, having worked as "an English governess for the Italian Royal Family and living in a palace in Milan," as Maymie stated to Vaughn. We examine that particular claim later in the book. If this is so, she would have had years of living in a very cultured environment, amongst well-bred people, and after returning to Twillingate she may have kept her social contacts to a minimum, and thereby given the impression of being very aloof. She hired help to do the chores on the Stirling estate, purchased animals and practised husbandry, including maintaining a garden where she grew vegetables for her own needs. As she aged, she seems to have become more withdrawn, perhaps even "cranky," as some have testified, and possibly quarrelsome, as others have stated. Several have also used the word "eccentric" to describe her conduct, but at least one person used that term to describe Georgina. It is a dismissive word often used when people don't know how to evaluate a person. Rose appears not to have had close friends in Twillingate after her return; she interacted mostly with the Hodge merchant family, made regular visits to the Manuel family, and visited her neighbour Aunt Ide (Ida) Stuckless, usually at night and always carrying a lantern, as a granddaughter recalls. She also sometimes sent written notes to Aunt Ide, requesting her to come down to the house. In the early years after her return to Twillingate, Rose also made regular trips to St. John's. Georgina did not.

Another incident described by Maymie gives us some insight into Rose's character. One rainy evening, Georgina appeared outside Maymie's house, holding an umbrella and a basket and rapping on the window to get Maymie's attention; Maymie then went to the door and was presented with the empty basket and told by Georgina, "Maymie, for God's sake take this basket in to Dr. Wood and get it filled with books for Rose to read." Rose was such a voracious reader that she must have read everything in her father's extensive library and thirsted for more.

Rose and Maymie sorted carefully through Georgina's things after Georgina had died, and it may have been through this activity that Maymie acquired other mementoes of Georgina that she passed on to Hiram Silk and Vaughn Harbin.

Over time, as Vaughn Harbin disclosed, Maymie had written a series of journals relating to various aspects of Twillingate's history, probably some of it covering what she called "The Stirling Saga." These had been compiled following the publication of Amy Louise Peyton's book. It is believed that the journals were given to her niece Phyllis Loring in Nova Scotia.

Roy Manuel and Fred Manuel were the sons of Alfred Manuel and the grandsons of Titus Manuel of Twillingate and the great-grandsons of Thomas Manuel. At the time of Roy's undated interview, he was living in Springdale. Roy was the older brother, and he and Fred had followed their father, Alfred, in the undertaking business, and Roy later moved to Springdale to set up the undertaking business there.

Roy Manuel spent three years sometime prior to 1937 training in Toronto with a funeral director and returned to Twillingate to continue in the business which his father had started. They constructed caskets in the family carpenter shop and covered them with a special cloth (velour) in at least three colours—black, purple, and white. Roy joined the Newfoundland Rangers for a time but resigned from the Force following Confederation in 1949, and then moved to Springdale to set up the funeral business there and worked at that business until shortly before his death at age seventy. Fred remained in Twillingate and continued the funeral business there. He died in 1989 at the age of seventy-eight.

As a young man Roy remembered Georgina in her garden, among her rose bushes and walking her pet pig on a leash. He once took part in a play for which Georgina was doing the coaching, and she took strong issue with Mr. Hodgkins, a teacher who was the director of the play. Roy was acting as a policeman in the play. When asked if Georgina and Rose were desperately poor, he replied that they were not in need, that the people of Twillingate would not have allowed it. He recalled that Georgina used to wear unusually big earrings and tied her hair up in a red bandana. Roy's grandmother had lived with the Stirling family in the early days, probably as a maid or a housekeeper, and in the later period Rose visited the Manuel house regularly. Both sisters came to visit Roy's mother when she was sick. Roy had heard that

Rose had been a governess at one time. Rose had promised to leave him some of her books, but he was not at home when she died. (The Stirling library and all books from the Stirling house were later offered for sale at the Linfield shop after Rose died.) Roy stated that Georgina was well-respected in Twillingate, and he recalled hearing her singing from behind a screen at some event. "Singing behind a screen" is mentioned by other interviewees and appears to have happened only in her last public appearances after she had become crippled either with gout or through what some have called "the bandy Stirling feet."

Georgina also once served as chair of a political meeting for the election of Norman Gray and stoutly represented him; he was subsequently elected to a conservative government that opposed the reigning Liberal government of Sir Richard Squires, which was defeated in the election of June 11, 1932. This would have been the election in which Georgina supported Norman Gray. The political party in which Gray served from 1932 to 1934 was named the United Newfoundland Party, under the direction of Frederick C. Alderdice. His short-lived government was succeeded by the Commission of Government appointed by Great Britain.

Roy stated that Dr. Stirling had a lot of shares in the Tilt Cove copper mines, and he and a Mr. Manuel held property in Springdale from which copper ore samples had been taken.

Will Peyton of Back Harbour, Georgina's cousin, made all the final arrangements for Georgina's funeral in 1935, and the Manuel brothers were engaged to make the casket in their carpenter shop. Roy assisted his brother Fred in "laying her out" for burial. Rose told Roy that Georgina had converted to the Roman Catholic faith, and she handed Roy a set of prayer beads to be placed in Georgina's hands in the casket. This fact, I think, has never been made public.

When asked about the monument that had been erected in Georgina's honour, Roy stated that he didn't think Georgina would have liked that at all, despite knowing that Hiram Silk, the interviewer, had played a major role in this action. Roy concluded his remarks by stating that there is still no headstone for Rose and he would be happy to contribute to a fund to correct that oversight.

Fred Manuel, in his interview, confirmed the fact that he had helped to construct the coffin in which Georgina was buried. He stated that Georgina had left very specific directions for her burial. She wanted the casket to be covered with white velour cloth; the colour white was usually reserved for children. She also had strongly affirmed that she wanted to be buried on Burnt Island, where the sailor with smallpox had been buried in 1885 in order to avoid a possible spreading of the disease to the local population. (Georgina's father, as the town's doctor, would have had to examine the body and sign the pronouncement of death, so it would have been a story shared in the Stirling family.) Fred stated that Georgina "had no fear of dying, or of anything." (Amy Louise Peyton had stated that some people had said "perhaps jokingly" that Georgina had expressed an intention to be buried on Burnt Island, but it seems clear from Fred's comments that this was an idea seriously entertained by Georgina.)

Then Fred disclosed something that had never been made public, that Dr. and Mrs. Stirling had had two sons, not one as Amy Louise Peyton states in her book, that the boy who was accidentally drowned in the puncheon of water was named Edward and that the other son was named John Peyton Stirling and died with the measles. Fred said that both boys were buried in the churchyard cemetery near where Thomas Lyte was buried. (Thomas Maximillian Lyte had been an early merchant at Twillingate and died in 1850 in his forties. Thomas was the brother of Henry F. Lyte, author of the well-known hymn "Abide with Me.") As we learned earlier, Maymie (Roberts) Hewlett confirmed in her interview that Georgina had told her that there were nine in the Stirling family, seven sisters and "two brothers who died early in life." We have seen already that, in fact, there were at least three Stirling brothers and possibly a fourth. The two older brothers had died as infants (one only a few months old and the other at three years), several years before Georgina was born, so it is possible that she was never told about these. Fred, in this interview, would have been trying to recall the information on the headstone marker in the St. Peter's churchyard cemetery, but he got it wrong. The marker lists three brothers. He was probably thinking about the name John Mayne Stirling and the boy who was drowned whose name does not appear on the marker, and whom he calls Edward. Another source says this boy's name was Peyton, so this unfortunate boy may have borne both names—Edward Peyton Stirling. Amy Louise Peyton states that the name Peyton Stirling is recorded in the Stirling birthday book, which seems to have disappeared.

Contradicting information supplied by several others, Fred affirmed that Georgina's funeral brought out a very large attendance. Fred also said that he had heard Georgina sing when he was a young boy.

Elsie Hodge was a well-spoken, well-educated woman and was married to Arthur Harold Hodge, who with his brother Cyril Leonard Hodge owned the Twillingate merchant firm Hodge Brothers. Arthur Hodge had married Elsie Balsan Wood, an American woman. This couple and Arthur's brother Cyril and their sister Mabel were especially close to and supportive of the Stirling sisters, as their parents, Richard Dorman Hodge and Grace Helen (Purkis), had been to Dr. and Mrs. Stirling. Grace Hodge died in 1932, just three years before Georgina died. The interview with Elsie Hodge is undated but must have been after 1970 and was probably in the 1980s. Elsie had moved to Twillingate in 1925. She is extremely careful in her responses to questions during the interview, not wanting to leave any false impressions. She referred to Georgina's five cats, one of whom was named "Felix." She affirmed that Georgina was a wonderful gardener, that she was an attractive woman, "not like the ordinary person . . . she was really famous, a good woman." Elsie had heard her sing at a concert. "She refused to come out, she sang behind a screen." This is a slightly different interpretation from one presented earlier. "She really could sing . . . she was a trained lyric soprano." Mrs. Hodge (Elsie's mother-in-law, Grace) "was very impressed with her . . . she had an autocratic manner." I think Elsie must have meant "aristocratic." She affirmed also that her husband's sister, Mabel, was a specialist in music, and also served as organist at St. Peter's Church. In fact, Elsie B. (Wood) Hodge is also listed in the St. Peter's Church history as church organist.

Elsie had visited the Stirling house several times for "suppers" (the Newfoundland term for dinners, evening meals). Members of the Hodge family were frequent visitors. "They entertained beautifully, they were always beautifully gowned. Georgina was a good hostess." This also contradicts the statements of some others. Georgina talked about her career in music. She talked about Madame Marchesi. "Mrs. Hewlett (Maymie Roberts) and Mrs. Roberts (Lucy, i.e. Mrs. Andrew Roberts) came often." These two women lived just across the road from the Stirling house, and Maymie Roberts can be said to have been Georgina's "best friend" during these years. At that time she was Maymie Roberts, and when her husband died at Robert's Arm, Maymie moved back to Twillingate as Mrs. Hewlett.

Elsie states that she went to visit Georgina three days before she died, and Georgina requested Elsie to make some custard for her. Elsie described the day of the funeral. "We walked on top of six feet of snow . . . the grave was in a very deep hole because of the snow . . . it was a very large attendance."

Elsie would often go to the Stirling house to help Rose. "When Rose needed help, I would go . . . and do a few jobs for her. . . . I didn't visit Rose as much after Georgina died." When Hiram Silk asked Elsie if she had heard that Rose had been a governess for the Italian Royal Family, she replied, "Yes, and I believe it." She would have heard this story from her mother-in-law, Grace, who stoutly defended the veracity of the story. Grace must have heard this story directly from Rose, who had been living back in Twillingate at least eighteen years before Grace died.

Elsie commented briefly on Kate (Stirling) Putzki, Georgina's sister, who came to visit in the summers. She described Kate as "a grand dame." Kate once presented Elsie with two lovely watercolour paintings that Mr. Putzki had done. Some of his paintings were hanging in the Stirling house.

Hiram suggested that Georgina did not lose her voice because of diphtheria, as some had suggested. Elsie curiously did not comment on this. Silk then raised the issue of Georgina's drinking. Elsie affirmed that "I never saw her under the influence." Hiram asked if the sisters had received a pension of any kind. Elsie replied simply, "I don't know." Hiram suggested that they had a great deal of pride, and mentioned the pride of the Peyton clan. He then claimed that, in his interview with Dr. Olds, the physician had stated that the condition of Georgina's teeth seemed to have indicated that she had taken drugs over a long period. "She was immune to narcotics because she had taken so much," Dr. Olds had stated.

(Did this habit, I wonder, begin with Georgina's initial depression? Remembering that her father, a doctor, had administered opium to her mother in order to deal with the despair and depression from which she suffered after losing her little son in the tragic drowning accident, did Georgina self-administer opium in order to deal with her own depression? If opium was still present in her father's dispensary, did she take it in order to deal with the advancing cancer in its last stages? Again, we are left only with questions.)

Continuing to probe in his interview with Elsie Hodge, Hiram raised the issue of quarrels between the two sisters. He said he had seen a picture of Georgina and Rose taken in Naples in 1898; they were both beautifully dressed and stood very close together and looked very happy. Elsie did not comment. Hiram then said he had heard that Rose had had an unfortunate love affair that ended in a breakup and that was the reason that Rose wore only black ever after. Elsie did not comment. (See more on this later.) Elsie did reiterate the story that Rose had been a governess with the Italian Royal Family. Silk then closed the interview with the statement that he had heard that someone was writing an opera based on Georgina's life. Elsie did not know about that. Silk was at his most assertive, almost abrasive in this interview.

THIS MAY BE A GOOD PLACE to deal with the story of Rose Stirling having possibly been an English governess to the Royal Family in Italy. F. C. Farr after his encounter with Hiram Silk in 1969 put it this way: "One of her (Georgina's) sisters became governess to the children of the Italian royal family . . ." Several people in the interviews refer to this matter and to the fact that Rose was regarded as "the most educated" of the Stirling sisters.

Rose accompanied Georgina to Italy in 1888. Georgina's two letters to her father from Florence, Italy, in 1889–90 disclose that Rose is living with her and taking drawing lessons twice a week, thus adding to her skills as a teacher. Some sources state that Rose routinely acted as a travel companion and chaperone to Georgina.

Since Georgina went directly to Italy after leaving Twillingate in October 1888, then Rose would have attended her and helped her to get settled, and then after two years, when Georgina went to England, would have begun to look for employment for herself. She had formal training as a teacher and experience working in a hospital, and she was about thirty-six years old. She would therefore have been eminently employable. She almost certainly lived with Georgina in Florence for the first two years and then began the search for employment.

Vaughn Harbin informed us that Maymie (Roberts) Hewlett clearly stated that Rose had been employed as an "English governess with the Royal Family and that she lived in a palace in Milan." Having known Rose during the period 1929 to 1935 at Twillingate, and possibly having been at least acquainted with her for several years before Georgina came home, we have to take Maymie's claim seriously. The "palace in Milan" should probably be interpreted as "the palace in Naples." There were many royal palaces in Italy as well as the palaces of the nobility. We must not forget the stoutly defended claim by Mrs. Grace Hodge, the merchant's wife, that Rose was an English governess in Italy, and such a claim must surely have come from Rose herself, who knew the Hodge family very well and saw them often.

While I have the highest respect for Maymie's testimony in every regard, I would question her interpretation of what she had heard, of what she had been told about this matter, that Rose had been a governess to the Italian Royal Family. In what follows I try to develop a more likely scenario of what Rose was doing during her "more than twenty years" in Italy.

It is known that Rose lived in Naples, Italy, not in Milan. Postcards from Naples confirm this. She would have visited Georgina in Milan; she may even have lived there in the early period. Correspondence from Rose to her sisters in England confirms the "more than twenty years" in Italy since Rose was back in Twillingate by January 1914. She would have spent about twenty-five years in Europe.

If the story of Rose being an English governess in Italy is true, and there does seem to be some basis for this claim, it is much more likely that she would have been a governess to families of the Italian nobility rather than to the Royal Family. There were many families of nobility in Italy before Reunification occurred in 1861, and these continued beyond that period. In the middle of the seventeenth century in Rome alone there were about fifty families of nobility which had existed for at least 300 years, about thirty-five families of nobility which had existed for about 200 years, and about sixteen families of nobility which had existed for about 100 years. Many of the families of nobility in Italy had the authority to grant titles to their offspring, such as prince, princess, duke, marquis, count, baron, etc.

Rose was uniquely qualified for the role of governess with her training and experience as a teacher, with the new artistic skills which she had acquired in Florence, and with her experience working in a hospital. In her capacity as a governess, Rose is also credited with arranging for Georgina to sing before Queen Margherita of Italy, who was a great patron of music. The Queen had a particular interest in Wagner's music, but it is not known if Georgina ever sang Wagner, even though she visited Germany either for a concert tour or additional vocal training about 1895. The source for this information about Georgina being invited to sing before the Queen is Hiram Silk, who is not always the source of reliable information; however, he had a special relationship with Maymie (Roberts) Hewlett, Georgina's best friend in Twillingate during 1929 to 1935, and it ought to be considered that he may have acquired this information directly from Maymie.

Queen Margherita of Savoy lived from 1851 to 1926. She married Umberto, her first cousin, in 1868, becoming the first lady of Italy at the time of her marriage. They settled in Naples at first, and subsequently moved to Rome. It seems highly likely that Queen Margherita periodically visited her former palace home in Naples, and it may have been here that Georgina sang for the Queen. Naples was only about 150 miles from Rome. It seems less likely that Georgina and Rose would have been invited to Rome. The palace in Naples was very likely where Rose was employed as an English governess.

Rose is listed in the 1911 Census of England as being a teacher, aged sixty years, and a boarder in the household of a widow, Annie Coruner in Southborough, Kent. She had evidently left Naples sometime after 1905 and was in 1911 teaching near where her sister Susan (Stirling) Temple was living in Kent. Rose very probably continued to teach in England until her return to Twillingate in early 1914.

Now, here is a zinger! A most reliable source has disclosed that "Rose was reputed to have been a mistress to Prince Rupert" for several years. Another version says that it was with "the Crown Prince," which, I think, can be dismissed. If the mistress story is true, there may well have come a point where the relationship was severed by family decree or voluntarily by her suitor, and this may have precipitated both Rose's move to England in or before 1911, where she is listed as a teacher, and her decision to wear only black ever after. It may also have caused a bitterness in her disposition that led to a reclusive and very private lifestyle after her return to Twillingate.

AMY LOUISE PEYTON WAS INTERVIEWED briefly by Cathy Porter of CBC Radio and more extensively by Hiram Silk, probably in 1984 or 1985—a year or so after her book was published. Amy Louise affirmed that she wanted to write the book because she felt that Georgina Stirling had been forgotten and people needed to know the full story of her life and her accomplishments. "She was ahead of her time . . . a celebrated and loved person." Georgina was respected and loved by all the people who had ever heard her sing and especially by the people of Newfoundland. Amy Louise affirmed that she did not know anything about Rose having been a governess to the Italian Royal Family. She dismissed as a rumour that Titus Manuel had been sent by Dr. Stirling to Toronto to build a house for the Stirling sisters when Georgina began her musical and academic training there in 1883. She affirmed that Georgina travelled alone and that Rose did not act as her chaperone.

Most sources affirm that the sisters seemed to feel it their duty to travel with their youngest sister and be helpful to her. The only time, it seems, that Georgina travelled alone was on short train trips in Ontario during her training and one trip to Chicago and her brief visit home to Twillingate in 1921. Her sister Kate had accompanied Georgina to Toronto in the fall of 1882 and assured that she was settled there under the supervision of Mrs. Murray. Rose accompanied Georgina to Florence, Italy, in the fall of 1888 and remained with her for about two years. Janet and Lucy travelled with her from England to Newfoundland when she came home for a rest and presented many concerts in Twillingate, Harbour Grace, Whitbourne, and St. John's.

Amy Louise commented in the interview on the Testimonial that was printed in gold lettering on a blue satin background and presented to Georgina on October 3, 1895, after the Grand Farewell Concert in St. John's, and she noted that the phrase "Thrice gifted daughter" recognized Georgina's performance as actress, singer, and pianist. Amy Louise commented on Charles Santley's conclusion that Georgina should have confined her performances to oratorio and ballad rather than to opera, and referred very briefly to Georgina's recording of "Lo, Here the Gentle Lark."

Twillingate was always a musical community, Amy Louise said. And Georgina lived a simple life after her permanent return to Twillingate. "She was absorbed in her garden." She helped young people with their plays, etc. in the town. And "she was always the first person to make a pot of soup and take it to the sick."

Though Georgina sang for charities in all of her Newfoundland performances on her many return visits to Newfoundland, Amy Louise revealed that Georgina was once paid $250 for a single performance in Boston, which was a substantial amount in 1896.

Amy Louise shared a charming story about Georgina's performance at the Roman Catholic Cathedral in St. John's when the snow was so deep that the horses could not proceed through the drifts, and a group of young men pulled her sleigh all the way to the hotel where she was staying. It seems that could only have been in late November 1892, the latest time she had remained in Newfoundland during her visits.

Hiram Silk did not, in my judgment, probe sufficiently in interviewing this author who had painstakingly gathered so much primary material from various sources for her book *Nightingale of the North*. As we have seen through the very extensive series of interviews Silk had already done, he had acquired a great deal of information that he declines to share with Amy Louise in the interview. We are left to wonder why he did not disclose this information and why he did not challenge some of her conclusions in this crucial encounter. Had she acquired new information after the book was published? Was there significant feedback from those who had already read the book? As with this interview, Silk appears not to have prepared himself sufficiently for several of the interviews and does not always probe carefully to extract vital information.

There is another probability; Hiram Silk may well have resented the fact that Amy Louise Peyton had pre-empted him in writing the book on Georgina Stirling. This had been his intention, as he had stated to Maymie (Roberts) Hewlett, to write Georgina's biography and to tell the story of her remarkable life. Maymie knew him well and was confident that he would never write such a book.

There is an intriguing story in Amy Louise Peyton's book about Georgina being present at St. Peter's Church at a little blind girl's funeral. The friend with whom she was sitting in the church pew was suddenly called by the minister to play the organ, since the regular organist was not present. The organist then began to play the hymn known as "Olivet." Because of what the hymn may have meant to Georgina, it is worth repeating here in full. It appears that she was not familiar with this hymn; perhaps she was hearing it for the first time.

'Tis midnight and on Olive's brow
The star is dimmed that lately shone;
'Tis midnight in the garden now,
The suffering Saviour prays alone.

'Tis midnight and from all removed,
The Saviour wrestles lone with fears—
E'en that disciple whom He loved
Hears not His Master's grief and tears.

'Tis midnight and for others' guilt
The Man of Sorrows weeps in blood;
Yet He that hath in anguish knelt
Is not forsaken by His God.

'Tis midnight and from ether plains
Is borne the song that angels know,
Unheard by mortals are the strains
That sweetly soothe the Saviour's woe.

Amy Louise states that Georgina went to the organist's house after the funeral service "to familiarize herself with the tune." My guess is that it was not the tune that gripped her attention, but the words. The hymn must have "spoken to her" in a deep way. The little blind girl may have been from one of the families that Georgina assisted through the Dorcas Society. But when the congregation pealed out the words "The star is dimmed that lately shone," Georgina must have heard that as applying also to her (she had been a "star") and what she had endured in recent years. The words "wrestles lone with fears" would have stabbed at her heart. "Not forsaken by His God" might well have given comfort to Georgina in her pain. "The song that angels know" would have reminded her that her many fans had often said that "she had the voice of an angel."

And the fact that all this took place in a garden would have confirmed what Georgina already knew, that her garden with its profusion of flowers and shrubs and trees was a scene of solace and healing. *See Appendix Six for summaries of important points in Hiram Silk's CBC interviews from the 1950s to the late 1980s with several other people of Twillingate.*

I HAVE LEFT THIS SECTION UNTIL LAST because of the surprising, startling news it bears. On the tape of the interview with Herb and Edna Burton, Mr. Fifield, and Frank Curtis, Hiram Silk also interviews Stan Curtis, Frank's brother and the brother of Bessie (Curtis) Barnes. As indicated earlier, this interview is undated but probably occurred in the late 1970s. Stan's mother and father had once worked for the Stirling family, and now Stan worked for Georgina and Rose—shovelling snow, bringing water, and doing other odd jobs. He noted that Georgina was always more generous than Rose in her payments for work done. He was working at the Stirling house every day, sometimes two and three times a day. He noted that the two sisters "would fight quite a bit." Usually he would walk out when they quarrelled; it would be embarrassing for a young man. Stan was between fourteen and twenty years of age during the time that Georgina lived in Twillingate, 1929 to 1935. Stan died in 1981 at the age of sixty-six, so Hiram Silk very probably interviewed him in the mid- to late 1970s. One of my recent correspondents in Twillingate assured me that Stan was an honourable and trustworthy person.

Stan was invited to have many meals with the two sisters. He stated that they had a good garden and "grew stuff" for their own use. He noted that they were not particular as housekeepers and used the words "shabby" and "not clean" to describe them, but he didn't mention the presence of the pet pig or the rooster in the house; perhaps that is what he meant. Yet he noted that they entertained a lot. Stan had heard Georgina sing at one of the community concerts; the song he remembered especially was "The Rio Grande." He had seen Dr. Stirling's surgery and observed the human skull and the skeleton, which he had found a bit scary. He knew also that Rose had been a governess in Italy.

More than once Stan had heard Rose and Georgina quarrel. Hiram asked Stan at this point, "Did she ever mention her brother who was drowned?" Stan replied, "No, no, but her son." Instead of waiting to hear what else Stan would say, as a good interviewer would do, Hiram interjected: "She had a son, a child. His name was Hugo Vincent." He then asked Stan: "Did she ever tell you she had a son?" Stan replied, "Yeah." Hiram asked, "What did she say about him?" And Stan said, "Not much." I would interpret Stan's responses to mean that he must have overheard Georgina talk about the son to Rose, not to him—unless it was

Georgina's attempt to explain their quarrels to Stan. Hiram had obviously heard the story previously, but he does not mention this in any of the many other interviews. He said he had heard that Rose often accused Georgina of having had a son, that she would say, "At least I never had a child like you, never married." And Georgina would respond, "You never knew the love of a man."

How can this quarrel possibly be explained? Was this the real reason for the despair and depression into which Georgina sank in 1900 to 1901, rather than the straining of that astonishing and glorious voice? Perhaps none of the other explanations fit the facts—an ailment, a serious throat ailment, a strained voice, strained vocal cords, neuritis and nodules of the vocal chords, diphtheria, etc. Amy Louise Peyton introduces most of these concepts in her book but wrestles with the lack of clear documentation. It is impossible to draw clear conclusions from the one-way correspondence from Lucy in London to Georgina in Milan. We have none of Georgina's letters from this period. Ever since the publication of Amy Louise's book in 1983, most writers have simply accepted the scenario of the strained voice.

If we accept too easily the possibility of a strained voice, it may cloud our exploration of other possibilities. Who was the Prince Umberto who wrote to Georgina, as Maymie Roberts had affirmed? Was he the same person as "roto"? Was "roto" the royal personage whom some have intimated he was? It should be noted that "roto" always used a high ascending but lower case "r" and not a capital letter when he signed his cards. Curious! Little can be concluded from the many cryptic notes on the postcards he sent to Georgina from several locations in Italy, but in those times, people seldom expressed affection on postcards. Most cards from "roto" were signed simply with "Saluti," "Remember me," and "Kind regards." Once, however, he did write "Received letter. Thank you. roto." So, she corresponded with him while in Italy. And note this: Though there are many postcards from "roto," none can be found postdated after 1900.

Did Georgina convert to the Roman Catholic faith in anticipation of a marriage to "roto" or to some other gentleman in Milan, perhaps a member of the Italian nobility? Did she have an affair with him?

We have probed, and probed deeply, attempting to discover the truth of what happened to Georgina in Italy. What follows is the result of our probing. We leave it up to the reader to decide how successful we have been in our endeavours. I take full responsibility for the conjecturing that is done in this section.

From the research of our Newfoundland colleague Milton Anstey we have been able to confirm that Ugo Angelo Vincent did indeed exist. "Hugo" is the English form of the Italian "Ugo." Vincent may have been an anglicized version of his family name, and it may have been "Vincente," and pronounced "Vin-chen-tay." Hugo Vincent is listed in the Census of England and Wales on March 31, 1901, as an eight-year-old "Pupil boarder" in the home of Julian A. K. Gildes of Milward Crescent in Hastings, St. Mary in the Castle, Sussex, England, near Ticehurst, where Georgina's sister Susan Peyton (Stirling) Temple was living. Susan's daughter, Marion Stuart Temple, was a teacher in England for several years, and her parents moved from Saint Pierre to England, probably about 1900. It is possible that Ugo was placed in the school where Marion Temple was teaching. It is also of interest that the other "Pupil boarder" in that home was Richard Mariner, aged thirteen, who was from Marylebone, London, Middlesex, which is where Janet Stirling was living during that same census in 1901. Hugo Vincent and Ugo Angelo Vincent is undoubtedly the same person, as Hugo's estimated birthdate was given as 1893, though his birthplace in this record is curiously given as "America Nk F S," for which searches of the Internet yield nothing. That may simply be a way of indicating Hugo's connection with the Stirling sisters from North America, since an eight-year-old boy possibly just recently come from Italy whose English was not yet perfect may have had trouble communicating accurate information, or the adult members of the household knew only of the North America connection. These adult members of the household could have been responsible for anglicizing Ugo's Italian name. Ugo Angelo's full name was found in the 1911 Census for England and Wales when he was listed as a "visitor" with Janet Mary Stirling, Georgina's sister, who is also listed as a "visitor," when they were spending time at the home of Susan Peyton (Stirling) Temple of Ticehurst, Surrey, in England. Ugo was then eighteen years of age, and the Census record shows that he was born in Italy and his occupation was now "Railway Clerk." So, it is clear that he was connected to the Stirling sisters and, at this time, both Georgina and Janet were living at the Duxhurst Farm Colony for Women and Children, Georgina as a resident recovering from alcoholism (more likely having already recovered, since she entered the Colony in late 1905 or early 1906), and Janet transferred to the Colony as a nurse at the facility. Since children of inebriate women were only admitted to Duxhurst in the later years, it seems highly unlikely that Ugo would have been there from the time of Georgina's admission.

Ugo could not possibly (in my judgment) have been the natural-born son of Georgina Stirling. Thanks to Milton Anstey's research, we know that Ugo was born on May 28, 1893, in Milan, Italy. Between June and October 1892, Georgina and Janet had been visiting Twillingate and St. John's, and they left St. John's on November 22, arriving at Liverpool about

December 1. Georgina probably spent December with Janet in London and travelled in late December to Paris to begin the second year of her studies with Madame Marchesi.

If Georgina had a "lover" who was an English businessman living in London and working in Italy (or a member of the Italian nobility, working in England), *and if* Georgina had met him in London immediately upon arriving back from Newfoundland near the end of December, *and if* she had become pregnant immediately, she could not possibly have had a five-month pregnancy and delivered a baby prematurely in Milan, *but* this was her last year of vocal studies with the acclaimed Madame Marchesi in Paris. The pregnancy would not have gone unnoticed during the year of study and could have been a reason for dismissal from the École Marchesi— and, besides, she made her debut in Paris—probably in the spring of the year—at almost the very time when she would have been delivering a baby in Milan. Not very likely!

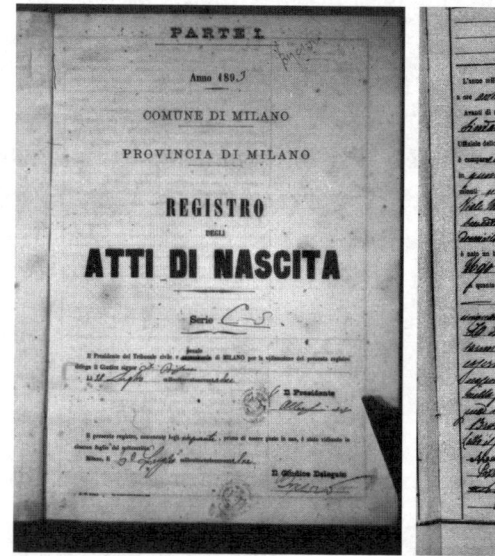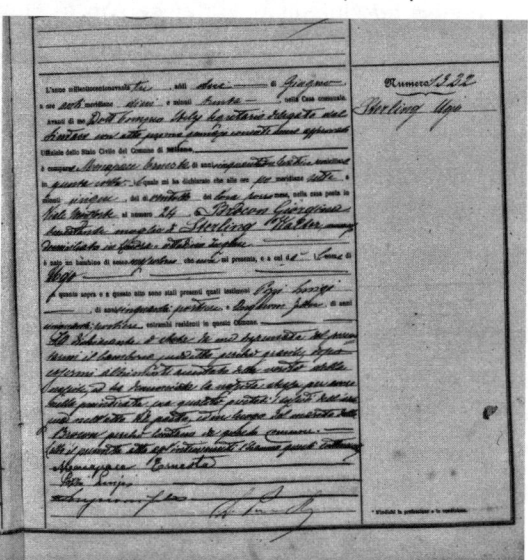

Birth registration for Ugo Sterling, born on May 28, 1893, in Milan, Italy
(Courtesy of Jeff Golden)

Before the reader dismisses the idea of a possible pregnancy, please consider a comment made in Ed Manning's February 1971 letter to Robert Walter Parsons in which he is passing on information about Georgina: "Like many another famous singers, we could mention Nellie Melba here; it was apparently established that in her heyday in Europe, she had been involved in at least one liaison, when a son was produced. The father was reputed to be connected with the Royal House of Savoy." Note the words "apparently established." Nellie Melba was a world-renowned Australian singer, a graduate of École Marchesi a few years before Georgina, and a good friend and strong supporter of Georgina early in her career.

As with many conjectures, this one can apparently be explained by reference to Jim Davidson's 1986 article in the *Dictionary of Australian Biography* and other sources. Before she left Australia, Nellie Melba had married Charles Armstrong and had a son by him, George Armstrong, born in 1883. The marriage lasted for only two years, and when the child was only three years old, Nellie's mother died, and Nellie moved to England with her father and the child. Her husband also moved to England, and when Nellie enrolled in École Marchesi, he often visited his wife and son in Paris. Beginning in 1890, Nellie apparently developed an undefined relationship with the Duke of Orleans, Philippe, heir of the Bourbon pretender to the French throne, and in addition to being seen together in London, Paris, Vienna, St. Petersburg, and Brussels, they once occupied a box seat at the opera. Rumours flew, and Charles Armstrong filed a petition for divorce, the Duke went underground, Nellie was devastated at the scandal, and Charles took his seven-year-old son to America, returning to England after his divorce from Nellie in 1900, and remarrying. In addition to this scandal, Nellie Melba was plagued for years by unfounded stories of an over-drinking problem.

Curiously, there is no mention of this "apparently established" possibility in Roger Neill's book on Nellie Melba and Madame Marchesi, but Neill does supply some information about Nellie's marriage and her son.

Since this relationship with the Duke of Orleans developed after Nellie's graduation from École Marchesi, there would have been no penalty assessed by Madame Marchesi in terms of bringing shame on the school. If something similar had occurred to Geor-

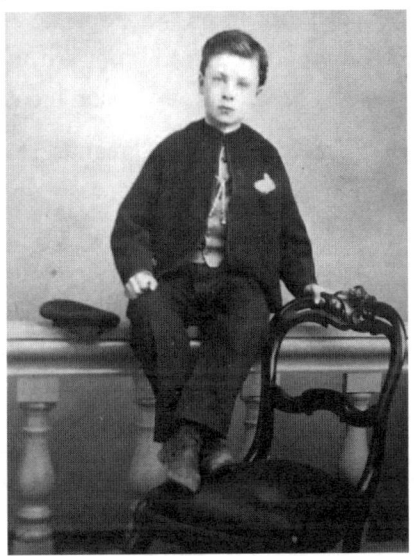

This is thought to be the photograph of Ugo Angelo Vincent which Maymie Hewlett queried Rose Stirling about in 1935 and was told it was Georgina's son. (Courtesy of Bruce Manuel and Brent English)

gina in 1892, in the midst of her two years with Madame Marchesi, it is hard to imagine that she would have been permitted to continue her studies while being pregnant and delivering a baby about the same time as she was making her debut in Paris. If Georgina had become pregnant, it must surely have been at a later date, (say) 1900–1901, or possibly at an earlier date, (say) 1893–95, when she was doing concert tours in England, in Ireland, and in Germany—and making two trips to Newfoundland! Again, not very likely!

If Georgina had gone directly to Italy after her arrival in England at the end of December 1892 from Newfoundland to meet a "lover," there is no way that she could have become pregnant and had a child by May 1893. More travel time would have been involved, and an even shorter pregnancy period. She would not have left a small baby in Milan (unless she was forced to, by "royal decree" or some such). We are familiar with Georgina's sensitive nature, her caring for children, her loss of three (possibly four) little brothers; she could hardly have sustained the total mental disruption that this scenario entails and at the same time progress with her singing career as she did so gloriously on the European and North American stages from 1893 to 1899. Her singing career progressed steadily onward and upward from 1888 to 1900, nothing interrupting the flow, no sign of anything wrong, and then collapsed in a severe and devastating emotional breakdown.

The "printed edited manuscript," to which we referred earlier, comments on two periods of "illness" which Georgina suffered, the first in the spring of 1895 in England, when her medical advisers recommended a six-week rest. She spent the summer in Twillingate and then gave eighteen concerts in St. John's in a sixteen-day period, returned to England by mid-October, and became ill again, undoubtedly as the result of exhaustion from the concerts. Neither of these periods can be construed as a pregnancy or as a delivery; only a miscarriage would have been possible, it seems.

So, Ugo was not Georgina's son by birth (in my judgment). Could he have been her son by adoption? If she had developed a romantic relationship with a royal personage or a member of the Italian nobility—a widower, perhaps—and if that person had died suddenly, it is possible that Georgina, in her grief, may have adopted the child and sent him to England sometime before March of 1901 to be close to her sister Susan (Stirling) Temple, and possibly registered in the school where her niece, Marion Temple, was teaching. We can only conjecture. With a broken heart from the loss of a lover, Georgina may well have felt obligated to adopt the child. She may even have been prevailed upon by her dying lover to adopt him. Or, she may well have made arrangements through the local authorities to adopt the boy and send him to the security of her sisters in England. It seems natural from what we know of Georgina that she would "fall in love with a little boy" as she might have "fallen in love with a man."

About a year elapsed between the "late fall" of 1900, when Georgina's friends the Mc-

Queens left Italy, and September 1901, when Georgina finally reached out to her sisters in England, and curiously not to her sister Rose in Naples, Italy. Little can be inferred from the McQueens' regular communications to Georgina from several places on their journey from Italy through Europe to Scotland and then back to London and up until February of 1901. From Paris in December 1900, Boyd McQueen wrote, "We hope everything is turning out to your satisfaction and that you are not feeling too lonely." The McQueens, husband and wife, were her good and supportive friends. Their comment seems to mean that her singing engagements were still progressing well when they left Milan in the late fall, and one would expect that kind of comment as Christmas approached. In his January 1901 communication McQueen accuses Georgina gently of being a "lazy girl" for not writing and exclaims, "Do write." In his February 1901 letter, he is obviously exasperated at the lack of any response from Georgina and mentions "the gnawing anxiety that is eating at our hearts."

Amy Louise Peyton states that toward the end of January, Georgina "was singing in Milan," but again it is impossible to confirm this, and it seems most unlikely. If it were so, why would she not have been answering the regular correspondence from the McQueens? Accepting this date of January 1901, David Macfarlane in his beautifully written book *The Danger Tree* quotes the newspaper *Evening Telegram*, but gives no date, and links Georgina's singing at the La Scala Opera House at the same time as the famous Italian composer Giuseppe Verdi was dying. Macfarlane writes, "There, earlier that month, a great man had suffered a stroke and the streets outside his curtained windows were covered with straw so that passing carriages wouldn't disturb his rest. The entire city seemed silent, as if under a blanket of snow. Marie Toulinguet was singing at La Scala when, in a hushed room in an elegant hotel, Giuseppe Verdi died." As with much of Macfarlane's writing in this book, it is difficult at times to separate historical fact from imaginative reflection.

Whatever happened to Georgina seems to have happened very quickly, but we still have no firm clue. If Macfarlane and Amy Louise Peyton's January 1901 date is factual, then whatever happened to Georgina in Milan took place between February and August, or possibly as early as Christmas 1900, an appropriate time for loneliness and love to intersect. But the fact that Georgina did not respond to the regular correspondence coming from the travelling McQueens means that this whole scenario of Georgina singing and enjoying "continuous success" up until the end of January 1901 is suspect.

Following what seems to be a year of total silence from the fall of 1900 to the fall of 1901,

Georgina sends a letter to her sisters in London, but we have only Lucy's postcard response of September 4, stating in part: "Glad to hear so far all is well. Do hope you won't have trouble." A postcard of September 13 from Lucy states, again, in part: "However things go with you to-morrow, let us know. We are thinking of you all the time. . . . Do keep up heart. We know what you must feel." These seem to be curious comments to describe a strained voice. Postcards sent by Lucy over the next two weeks could possibly refer to vocal problems in comments such as: "We are delighted and proud of your success. . . . We hope everything is still going all right," but the fact that Georgina had sent only one newspaper (no date given) and two letters up to this time may refer to a year-long absence from singing and that she was desperately trying to make a comeback. If Georgina had indeed strained her voice, why would she not have explained this earlier to her sisters in London? Why the need for secrecy between her and the two sisters with whom she had such a perfect relationship? Why is there no record of visits to a doctor? Why did she not contact her mentor, Madame Marchesi, as her good friend Nellie Melba did when she suffered a voice problem after singing Wagner against Madame Marchesi's advice? Why did Georgina go totally incommunicado for an entire year? She moved back to England in late 1901 and stayed for a while at the nursing home/surgical facility where her sisters Janet and Lucy rented space and also occupied at least one apartment.

The fact that the McQueens and Lucy's several correspondences to Georgina from the fall of 1900 to September of 1901 are still preserved would seem to mean that Georgina's apartment at 18 Lazzara Spallanzani, Milano, was being maintained and that she was not "on the streets," as one source has implied.

We can only conjecture. There is a mystery hidden here. The quarrels between Rose and Georgina at Twillingate should not be lightly dismissed as "little spats" only, as Amy Louise Peyton suggests. The radio interviews seem to reflect regular contention between the two sisters. Perhaps they had been on better terms when they lived apart. Rose's letter from Naples to Georgina in England in late 1901 was a loving, sisterly communication. It read: "Just a line to wish you a good, prosperous and Happy New Year. Why don't you write me sometime? I am always so pleased to get a letter from you. Now goodbye for this year. I will write again soon. Your loving sister. Rose." In other communications in 1902 and 1904 Rose signed herself "your affectionate sister" and "to dear Georgie with love." If Georgina was keeping a deep, dark secret from Rose, that might explain the letters, but it was her sisters Lucy and Janet (and less likely Susan) to whom Georgina had turned, not to Rose. Travel from Naples to Milan required only part of a day.

From Naples, Rose continued to write to her sister Georgina in England, expressing affection but also exasperation at the lack of communication. There were letters sent by Rose from Naples between 1901 and 1904, and one card was sent from Hyeres, France, in 1904, but the month cannot be discerned from the postmark. Rose must have been vacationing in France; she was known to be a traveller. She must by this time have received a letter from Georgina. Rose's response, written on the back of the card, is terse and telling: "So many thanks for letter *but explanation—not to my mind.*" (italics mine) Rose was not impressed with the explanation Georgina had given her. For what? For what had happened to her in Milan? Rose was a perceptive and exacting sister. She had spent much time with Georgina—being the chaperone for her travel to Italy, and living with her in Florence, Italy, for about two years, and along with her imbibing the Italian social environment; now she wants a clearer comment than Georgina had given in her letter. It sounds a bit like the request "Tell it like it is." Was she rejecting Georgina's "explanation" as a strained voice and suspecting something more serious than over-drinking to quell her anxiety? She would not have been happy if only Janet and Lucy knew the truth.

If it is true that Rose had acted as an English governess to children in the Italian Royal Family or in the Italian nobility, and that Georgina had taught music and singing to members of that same family (as some sources affirm), would Rose have felt betrayed and compromised by a possible sexual impropriety by Georgina because of Rose's long service to that family in Naples and because of the relationships of trust she had established over time with them? However, that would not be so if, as already mentioned, Rose had become the mistress of a Prince Rupert (or of the Crown Prince, far less likely) in the castle where she lived. What a tangled web!

Let us at least assume that Stan Curtis's testimony is reliable. It would mean that Georgina did indeed have a romantic attachment in Italy and that a child was somehow involved, a child who was not her own but who, for some reason, she sent to England, to the care of her sisters. A possible scenario that seems to make sense is that the child's mother was not still living, that Georgina's "lover" may have died suddenly or unexpectedly, and that she had made a promise to look after and take responsibility for the boy who was seven years old in 1900. This possible relationship, broken by her lover's death, could have been the reason for her despair, her depression and her desperation and possibly for her over-drinking, as a way of deadening the pain of the loss.

That could also more clearly explain why, during her trip home to Newfoundland in 1904, she was so inconsistent in her singing performances in St. John's. What was the real reason for Georgiana's inconsistencies? We may never know, but now we have one more reason to consider.

This new information could also explain Georgina's determination to be buried on Burnt Island, where the sailor who had died with smallpox on board ship was buried at the captain's direction for fear of spreading the disease among the local population. Georgina's father, Dr. Stirling, would have been asked to visit the ship anchored just outside the harbour to examine the dead sailor. I was told by a resident of Twillingate in August 2018 that the dead sailor was buried in Surgeon's Cove or Sergeant's Cove on Burnt Island. The cove is visible from the Stirling property. The doctor, presumably Dr. Stirling, was said to have been immune to smallpox perhaps because he had had chickenpox previously, or perhaps he had been vaccinated as a result of Dr. John Clinch's vaccination work which had originated at Trinity, Newfoundland, in 1798. The Twillingate doctor was said to have moved the coffin up the beach in a zigzag fashion by lifting one end at a time until he reached the hole which had been dug by the ship's crew. Dr. Stirling would have shared this news with his family. Georgina stated to the local funeral director her desire to be buried on Burnt Island as she made preparations for her funeral. Perhaps this was a kind of admission of failure, what she may have interpreted as a flaw in her own character, rather than seeking refuge in an explanation that involved a strained voice. Indeed, a strained voice seems to me to carry no sense of failure or shame (but I am not an expert in this area); perhaps she had lived with that story for too long.

Another explanation for her wanting to be buried on Burnt Island may have to do with the fact that Georgina had abandoned her Church of England faith and become a Roman Catholic. There was no Catholic church in Twillingate, nor one close by, and Georgina had told the funeral directors that she did not want to be buried in the Church of England cemetery. She must have realized later that there were few alternatives available.

There is still another intriguing development. During August 1905, nine months after Georgina's interrupted and personally disappointing performances at St. John's, despite the positive public accolades, she writes from England to her sister Lucy at Twillingate that "We have all come for a picnic on the Thames. I have closed the house for two weeks and we are living on a house boat and it is beautiful. Beabis and Hugo are coming, and we are going for a day's picnic up the Thames." Georgina addresses her sister Lucy in Twillingate as if Lucy is familiar with the two males, and she would have been, since she was living in England during the period 1901 to 1904 after Georgina had returned from Italy. The name Beabis is almost certainly a misspelling; it was probably meant to be Beavis, a male name, which a search on the Internet confirmed, and perhaps Amy Louise Peyton misread the handwritten "v" as a "b," an easy mistake to make. And the fact that Georgina wrote "they are coming" affirms that Ugo at twelve years of age "was being brought" by Beavis. Was Beavis Ugo's father, perhaps, and a person with whom Georgina was romantically involved? Did Beavis follow Georgina to England and bring his son with him? Or was he Ugo's guardian? Or was he, perhaps, Janet's "friend"?

Thanks to the avid research of our friend Milton Anstey, we have discovered in the 1907 Electoral List for London, England, the name Thomas Henry Bevis Vincent, who was a lodger at 26 Doddington Grove, Battersea Park Road, S.W. London, in a one-room furnished apartment. It has been confirmed that he was still there as late as 1911. Complicating matters further is the "Name and Address of Landlord or other Person to Whom Rent is Paid"—this is L. Vincent, same address. Five of the ten furnished rooms at this same address were being rented by women whose first names are given, but we are left to guess whether L. Vincent was female, or whether it was Bevis's father, mother, or some other relative. The scarce information given in this record would seem to indicate that Beavis was a single man, possibly recently arrived in England (from Milan?) or at least unrooted at this stage.

A search of the Internet indicates that the name Beavis is a variant of Bevis and, according to the Multilingual Translation Dictionary, the name Beavis is common in Spanish, Italian, Latin, and Polish, but the forenames Thomas Henry certainly are English. Again, we are left to wonder whether the name Vincent had been anglicized from the name Vincente, which would have been Italian. And why does Ugo Angelo have what appears to be the English form of the surname?

There is no denying a strong connection between the Stirlings and the Vincents. There is too much here to be coincidence—Ugo being in a school in early 1901 near where Georgina's sister Susan Temple lived and prior to Georgina's return from Milan, Ugo having been born in Milan, Beavis and Ugo joining Georgina and Janet for a picnic on the Thames River in 1905, Beavis being a single lodger in London from 1907 to 1911, Ugo giving Janet Stirling's name as his "friend" when he travels to the United States in 1923, etc.

When we first discovered Beavis (Bevis), it seemed that it was possible that he was the "person of interest" in Georgina's life, and possibly her "lover." While we were searching for the possible causes of the turmoil in Georgina's life at this stage, we considered that the emergence of Beavis might be a contributing factor to the enormous change in Georgina's fortunes. That would also be consistent with the explanation that a catastrophic emotional turmoil had occurred in her life in Milan and that the strained voice scenario was the most convenient or acceptable way to explain what had happened. Of all the scenarios that we had considered, this one seemed to be most consistent with the data that we had so far compiled.

In spite of our conjectures thus far, it soon became obvious that Beavis (or Thomas Henry Bevis Vincent) was not "the person of interest" in Georgina's life. His name could not be found in any of the Census Records for England and Wales during this period, but a record was found in the England and Wales Birth Registration Index for the first quarter of 1884 for Thomas Henry B. Vincent, presumably the same person. If this is an accurate dating of his birth, he would have been seventeen years younger than Georgina and only nine years older than Ugo. We may conclude from this that Beavis was Janet's young friend and that he was acting as a guardian of Ugo Angelo.

So, this information takes us back to "roto" (the prince? the Umberto who had written to Georgina, according to the information gleaned from Maymie (Roberts) Hewlett? and possibly a member of the Italian nobility? or an English or Italian businessman or government representative working in both countries who was enthralled with Georgina's singing (and her person?). "roto" had been consistently attentive to Georgina, and his frequent, abbreviated communications with her were by postcard, but all this could be interpreted as "pursuing" her in a gentlemanly manner.

Only a great novel, painstakingly and sensitively written—with no trace of the outrageous—could do justice to this likely scenario and this remarkable woman. Peter Worthington of the *Toronto Sun*, after a visit to Twillingate in 1999, and hearing the story of Georgina Stirling for the first time, wrote: "Does this not have the makings of a poignant movie, or story? For a girl from the fishing outports of Newfoundland to make it to the opera stage and be the darling of Europe, is the stuff of Hollywood complete with fame, misfortune, recovery and inspiration."

Ugo may have been taken to England by Beavis in or before March 1901, perhaps by an undisclosed arrangement with Janet, and placed in a school near where Georgina's sister Susan Temple lived, and possibly in a school where Susan's daughter Marion Temple was teaching. Georgina arrived in England in late 1901, lived with her sisters Lucy and Janet for a period of much-needed rest before moving to St. Andrew's Mansions (probably in 1902 or 1903) while she tried to make a comeback as a concert artist, which obviously failed, then made the trip to Newfoundland in 1904 with her sisters Janet and Lucy.

In late 1905 or early 1906, Georgina became a resident of Lady Somerset's Duxhurst Farm Colony for inebriate women. Georgina remained at the Duxhurst Colony for several years, possibly until Lady Somerset died in 1921, in the later years as a helper to her sister Janet, the nurse, and when she returned to Twillingate in 1929 her "son" would have been about twenty-eight years old and independent.

Again, there is no certainty here; we are left with questions only. The sole additional reference to "Beavis" after 1911 is in 1912, when "Thomas Henry Vincent" (no mention of Bevis in his name, but very likely the same person) is listed in the Polling District of Tollington as occupying a dwelling house at 1 Gladstone Street. If the birth record mentioned previously is accurate, he would then have been twenty-six years of age. All other attempts to find Beavis or Thomas Henry Bevis Vincent in the English records have proved fruitless to date in spite of the painstaking and diligent research of our friend Milton Anstey.

According to the Hertfordshire County Council in England, Ugo started his employment as an apprentice clerk on April 29, 1909. He was designated as a "Railway Clerk" in 1911. He visited the United States in 1923, leaving Liverpool, England, on May 12 and arriving via the SS *Baltic* on May 21 at New York. He was then twenty-nine years old, was single, was described as having a "dark complexion," and his height was given as five feet eleven inches. It is stated that his occupation was clerk, that he had been born in Milan, Italy, and that his last permanent address was London, England. Ugo came to the United States for a "business purpose," his fare was paid by his employers, and he was intending to stay for four or five months, and his contact in New York was a friend, John Pairman (?), whose address was 200 Fifth Avenue. The name and address of the friend in the country from which he came was given as Miss Janet Stirling of 14 Bulmoor (?) Street, London West. This address should be Bulstrode Street, as we have verified from other sources. At some point Ugo returned to England. He obviously remained in the railway business, because at one time he is listed as a "British Railway inspector." When he attended Susan (Stirling) Temple's funeral in England in 1924, Ugo is named as her "nephew." Ugo died at Dacorum, Hertfordshire, on April 13, 1983, at age ninety, and his body was cremated. He probably would not have visited Twillingate while in North America, because that might have raised questions. Janet died in England in 1928, and Georgina returned to Twillingate in early 1929. Ugo was now a man at age thirty-five.

Based on all the data compiled from these many sources and this extensive "body of evidence" and some natural and necessary conjecturing, we are now in a position to suggest what may be "a likely scenario." I take full responsibility for presenting this as a "possibility," but a strong possibility nevertheless. Tonia Evans Cianciulli will develop a parallel "possibility" as, in one of her chapters, she examines the hypothesis of "a vocal problem." She is much better qualified to reflect on this than I am. Let the reader consider both.

According to what I call "a likely scenario," Beavis and Ugo are brothers, more likely stepbrothers—both sons of an English or Italian man who had business or government interests in both countries and with whom Georgina had developed a romantic relationship—Beavis born in England in 1886 of an English mother who died, and the father moved (or moved back) to Italy to continue his business or government interests, remarried—this time to an Italian woman who was the mother of Ugo Angelo, born in 1893, and who was responsible for giving him the Italian names, since mothers generally take responsibility for deciding on the names of their children. By the same token, the English names given to Beavis were very probably chosen by his mother, and the name Beavis, being more common in Italy than in England, may have been the father's contribution and may suggest that the father was indeed Italian, working initially as a businessman or government representative, possibly even a member of the Italian nobility, in England. His original family name may have been Vincente and been anglicized to Vincent.

Let me introduce another zinger! This may seem far-fetched to the reader, but please bear with me. After I developed "a likely scenario," I began to search for clues to some hidden meaning in the nickname "roto." Roto in Latin means "wheel," and so in Italian. Could this "Italian businessman" or "English businessman working in Italy" possibly have been involved in the recently spawned process of "rotogravure," which "uses intaglio printing, in which cylinders are etched, forming recessed printing 'cells' to hold the ink"? The process was co-founded by the Englishman William Henry Fox Talbot and the Czech Karel Klic in the early 1890s. An Internet article states that "The process is still used today in high quality photographic reproductions of original artwork." The process was also used in the printing of illustrated books and also in art and photographic magazines.

For marketing this new and exciting product, what better place could there be than beautiful, cultured Italy?

It is entirely possible that the cylinder seen—holding up a window—in the Back Harbour home of Will Peyton, Georgina's cousin, was one on which Georgina's voice was recorded at St. John's either in 1896 or in 1904. Or, it may have been one that Georgina had brought back to Twillingate from Milan as a memento of her love relationship. Kent Peyton, Amy Louise

Peyton's son, had seen this cylinder in the window, and his memory was affirmed by Robert Walter Parsons in Toronto, a descendant of the Peyton family of Twillingate.

After Rose Stirling died, some of Georgina's costumes, her postcard collection, photos, and other memorabilia were taken to Will Peyton's house, at that time occupied by Will's twin sister, Edith. When Ernest Peyton, Amy Louise's husband, bought the house (sometime after 1946), these items were found stored there. In her 1981 letter to Robert Walter Parsons, Amy Louise stated, "It has been most helpful in my research. Also, most interesting." These items were later donated to the Twillingate Museum by Amy Louise and Ernest when Lorna Stuckless was the curator. The cylinder apparently remained in the Peyton house and was probably discarded as being of no significance. Fortunately, the record (thought for a time to be of Georgina's song) was left in the attic of the house, and Hiram Silk found it there about 1960.

What I have called "a likely scenario" suggests that Ugo's mother had also died, and Georgina was being wooed by a widower with two sons. The widower may have become familiar with Georgina as a singer during his stay in England, or he may have become aware of her astonishingly great voice after his return to Italy. But how can we explain the grave emotional turmoil in Georgina's life that followed her achievements of such stunning success in the world of Italian opera? The one year of silence, from the fall of 1900 to the fall of 1901, was sufficient time for Georgina to become pregnant and have a baby which died. Having been so close to, and dependent on, her two sisters in England, Janet and Lucy, it is otherwise very difficult to explain Georgina's curious incommunicado for almost an entire year.

Yet another death is conceivable in this scenario—that of the person with whom Georgina may have been having the romantic relationship. This is the only conceivable explanation for how the two "brothers"—Beavis and Ugo—were able to leave Italy and move to England, with the father's pre-arranged approval, a move that occurred prior to March 31, 1901, which may have been the approximate date at which the father died. There may not have been a pregnancy at all; the death of her lover may have been sufficiently traumatic to unleash in Georgina a period of despair and depression for which she sought temporary refuge in overdrinking. It may also be the reason why Georgina may not have sought medical help in Milan and apparently did not reach out to Madame Marchesi in Paris. Shame can be a harsh teacher.

My one other contribution to this scenario is that something far more serious than "a strained voice" is involved here. Of course, a strained voice might well precipitate a long period of depression and despair but less likely the experience of "sinking to the very depths," as one of Georgina's friends suggested, and as Hiram Silk blithely accepts. In fact, Hiram states, "She (Georgina) was rescued from this sad existence by an English lady of high degree who was travelling in Italy and had heard of the plight of the former opera singer. The good lady had Georgina sent to England and then to a Convalescent home." This is a most unlikely explanation of what happened. The correspondence dating from September 1901 between Georgina in Italy and her sister Lucy in England resulted in Georgina leaving Italy in the late fall of 1901 and moving back to London, where she resided with her sisters Janet and Lucy in the "Surgical Home" or "convalescent home" that Janet, the nurse, was operating. The "English lady of high degree" was probably Lady Somerset, who did not meet Georgina until late 1905 or early 1906, when Georgina entered the Duxhurst Colony, along with several other "ladies of high degree," to seek professional help for their over-drinking problem. Hiram seems to have periscoped his information into a chance encounter. He even suggests that Georgina was operating in Italy as a governess (to make ends meet?), "in those days the only profession open to an educated woman." At least one other source maintains that Georgina had previously taught music and singing to children of the Royal Family, more likely to families of the Italian nobility. Again, Hiram's suggestion seems to be out of context. He simply accepts the notion suggested by others, that her beautiful soprano voice had unalterably changed because of a serious throat ailment.

A romantic relationship, resulting in a possible pregnancy, a possible death of the child, the possible death of her lover, would much more likely create the conditions for a total breakdown and the seeking of refuge in the excessive consumption of alcohol. I hesitate to call Georgina an alcoholic; alcohol seems not to have been her problem but a way of attempting to deal with a far more serious problem. In 1901, Georgina was a "broken woman," but broken by what? The love scenario seems to make more sense; there would have been more shame attached to it according to the Victorian morals of the day than to a strained voice and over-drinking. And shame seems to have been the motivator for Georgina to "open up" to the funeral directors and the female Salvation Army brigadier in Twillingate as she made preparations for her death and funeral.

If Georgina had lost her ability to maintain "a variety of trills, runs and scales to display a singer's skills," she might well have sunk into deep depression for a time, but there was no shame attached to this, and yet for a full year she did not reach out to her precious sisters in England—Janet and Lucy. She maintained silence. When she moved back to England in the late fall of 1901, after a rest in her sister's convalescent home, and possibly some medical attention from the Harley Street physicians who sometimes visited Janet's nursing station, she attempted to make a comeback as a concert artist, arranging concerts for other singers and probably participating herself—this appears to have been during the period 1902 to 1903 or even to the spring of 1904; the comeback appears to have failed, but there were many encouraging messages received from friends throughout that period.

The two magnificent concerts which Georgina presented in St. John's on November 1 and November 15, 1904, included "a difficult March" and "a most difficult aria," and many other vocally demanding songs. So, the question must be posed: How could a singer with "a strained voice," a singer who had "lost her coloratura," who had not performed publicly since late 1900, except for an unsuccessful trial as a concert artist, make such an astounding comeback? With the encouragement of her sisters and a mighty resurgence of her own strong will, she was able to perform in what her faithful audience in St. John's regarded sincerely as an astounding performance. The "strained voice" scenario does not make sense to me (but again, let me say, I am not an expert).

Consider this possibility, before we ask the experts to comment: Try to imagine the situation of a young woman who is in the midst of a love liaison, becomes pregnant, has a miscarriage or the baby dies, her lover dies, and she has been prevailed upon to adopt his son (and possibly care for a second son) and she is alone, considering her future. The crying, weeping, screaming, and protracted wailing may have caused a vocal breakdown. This possibility fits with "a likely scenario" that has been outlined above.

A final comment on "a likely scenario": *If only there had not been a "son." If only.* I could consider "the strained voice scenario" as the strongest possible explanation for what happened to Georgina in 1900–01, *if only* there had not been a "son." But there *was* a "son." So, it appears that Georgina may have maintained the strained voice "explanation," even during her many years at the Duxhurst Colony. Yes, she had a problem with over-drinking and the problem was out of control for a few years—but for a powerful reason—perhaps the love liaison. Among the many "sins" short of murder to which Georgina seems to have admitted, she may well have been haunted by the deception which she had maintained for almost thirty-five years.

Even if Ugo Angelo Vincent was not Georgina's natural-born son, how did an eight-year-old boy born in Milan come to be in England in 1901, then and forever after associated with the Stirling sisters?

Georgina Stirling, unlike the great and tragic Maris Callas, overcame her despair and depression, with expert help from a professional, caring Lady Henry Somerset, but also with an inner strength gained, and now regained, through her family upbringing, from the two sisters who were closest to her, Janet and Lucy, and from the support of her faith in God. Georgina triumphed at the end, carving out a very different life in Twillingate, a life of help and service to the poor, to neighbours, friends, and her community. It was not at all a cloistered life but outward-looking. That astonishingly great voice that had touched so many hearts never fully returned, but she had aged and now selected her public songs more carefully. However, her kind acts and loving service to others will never be forgotten by the people of her hometown.

We do not know from whom Hiram Silk acquired the information about Georgina Stirling's "son." Were there multiple sources? In addition to Stan Curtis, the man who attempted to moderate the quarrels between the two sisters (almost certainly Martin Stuckless, who died in 1944) must have surely heard the story. The funeral directors of Twillingate, with whom Georgina had shared a great deal of personal information, knew.

What is most curious is that Georgina's "best friend" during the last years in Twillingate, Maymie (Roberts) Hewlett, found this out only after Georgina had died as Maymie and Rose were sorting through Georgina's personal effects. It seems strange indeed that Georgina did not share the information about her "son" with Maymie, her best friend. It is certain that Georgina's two closest sisters in England, Janet and Lucy, also knew—and that her sister Susan would have been told something in order to explain the presence of the boy Ugo but may never have been told the whole story. There may well have been an agreed-upon "conspiracy of silence" among the three sisters in England not to share anything about the matter and to leave no record. It is probable that the news was never shared even with their sister Kate in the United States. In a letter written to a lawyer in England in December 1928, Kate observed, "I have known little or nothing of the situation with my sisters in England . . ."

There is another intriguing possibility as a source for this information about Georgina's "son." Philip Anstey of Back Harbour, Twillingate, was born in 1865—two years before Georgina—so he was a schoolmate of Georgina at St. Peter's School. In fact, in the high school mid-summer examinations of 1880, Philip achieved the same mark as Georgina in the subject of geography—65 out of a possible 90. Philip married his sweetheart, Annie Selina Tucker, in January 1897, and she died in May of the same year. She had contracted tuberculosis and supposedly said that she would not die happy unless she married Philip. He "had been abroad" prior to his marriage (the country is not known for certain, but since he was a singer he very probably had travelled to Italy, knowing that his friend Georgina was there), and shortly after his wife's untimely death in 1897, he left Twillingate and moved to Italy and is said to have been living there about the time that Georgina was in Milan. Philip possessed one of those "great male voices," which Georgina herself had lauded to her friend Maymie (Roberts) Hewlett. If Philip had made a prior visit to Italy and been exposed to the music and singing and culture of this great country, he may well have yearned to return. A nephew of Philip had affirmed that during his time in Italy, Philip had "performed before Royalty." The Anstey family of Twillingate produced many fine musicians, including Philip's nephew, Frank Anstey, who was the organist at St. Peter's Church for more than forty years, and his great-niece Hilda (Anstey) Manuel sang in the choir for more than seventy years; other members of the Anstey family also served as choir members. All the affirmations above give substance to the possibility of Philip having been in Milan and singing before either the Royal Family or, more likely, before the families of the Italian nobility, with whom both Rose and Georgina were apparently associated. When he became ill in Italy, Philip returned to Twillingate and lived with his sister until his death in 1921. It is quite possible that Philip brought back with him some details of what had happened to Georgina during that terrible period which we have called her "fall" and shared these details with someone who later divulged them to Hiram Silk in a radio interview.

One other factor needs to be considered: These interviews by Hiram Silk were recorded to be broadcast over CBC Radio to all of Newfoundland and parts of Labrador. People must have heard this interview with Stan Curtis, so this so-called "shocking" information is probably already out there in the public domain. Many of the people who heard this interview will have died by this time, but some will still be living.

Perhaps this particular interview was never broadcast. The people of Twillingate at least appear to have graciously kept the matter secret during Georgina's lifetime, and perhaps it has disappeared from the public memory. I have discussed the matter in confidence with a few residents of Twillingate, and the answers range between "I never heard of it" to "I seem to have a memory of having heard something about it." Perhaps it did not bother Georgina that much, but she would have been sufficiently discreet not to have made it a matter for public knowledge. She appears not to have kept her "indiscretion" a big secret from those in her immediate circle in Twillingate; otherwise there would be no knowledge of it at all. She was remorseful and repentant for her past conduct, as her good friend Maymie (Roberts) Hewlett affirmed, but she still carried the weight and the burden of something she had done in the past. She had lived through it and triumphed over the tragedy that had befallen her, whatever it was. She proved to be a woman of great inner strength, and she must have deeply appreciated the support she received from her community.

What may have been shocking to an audience in the 1930s and also in the 1970s will be much less so today; contemporary hearers will be much more sympathetic to the plight of an extraordinarily gifted young woman who once "slipped" from the moral expectations of the day and knew "the love of a man" and the heartache involved in being responsible for the "son" while she herself was attempting to deal with the attendant despair and depression, and for a time taking refuge in alcohol, from which she was eventually delivered. In her brokenness she seems to be closer to us, and we find ourselves more sympathetic to her despair.

In his 1969 article in *The Canadian Statesman*, F. C. Farr reports further on his conversation with Hiram Silk to the effect that Georgina "having committed, she said in an interview, every sin in the book except murder." What are we to make of such a statement? My best guess is that this "interview" must relate to information that Hiram Silk had gained from his interviews with the funeral directors at Twillingate with whom Georgina seems to have shared some of her innermost thoughts during the preparations for her funeral, including her desire to be buried on Burnt Island; or it may have come from another local source, for example information shared with someone by Philip Anstey, referred to earlier. The three funeral directors knew Georgina in her most open and vulnerable moments, and she must have felt some relief in sharing her thoughts with them. One of the funeral directors had said in later years that there were things about Georgina that were "better not talked about."

In that same article, F. C. Farr also writes that "She (Georgina) was buried by the Salvation Army; only they, she said, would have the compassion not to condemn her." This statement is most curious and is undoubtedly based on a radio interview that Hiram Silk did with Brigadier Jones of the Salvation Army, who had visited Georgina three or four times before Georgina died. It is likely that she met Georgina while visiting her in the Memorial Hospital. It is not known for certain if she visited Georgina at home. Memorial University has the digitized radio tape with this interview. Brigadier Jones told Hiram that she would not share with him what was disclosed to her in confidence during the visits. She also stated that it was a hard death, probably describing the pain that Georgina endured due to the cancer that took her life. Georgina was not buried by the Salvation Army. She was buried from St. Peter's Church, where she had begun her singing and musical career about fifty-four years earlier.

It was reported by one source that when Georgina was once reminded that she had had "the voice of an angel," she retorted, "Yes, and the face of a devil." Even in her last years in Twillingate she was referred to by some people as a beautiful and refined woman; she seems to have reached peace within herself by this stage. So, the harsh retort may have referred to an earlier stage, what we have called her "fall"—a period of self-loathing or self-condemnation for whatever it was she had done that caused her such pain. There are depths here that we cannot plumb.

Georgina appears to have totally unburdened herself only to her two beloved sisters in England, Janet and Lucy. She had concluded that the Burnt Island burial site was the most appropriate place for her to be buried, to cover her shame. In the distant past, people who were judged to have committed terrible sins were buried outside the cemetery fence and not in "consecrated ground." Georgina would have known this. If there had been a Catholic priest nearby, Georgina would have gone to the confessional.

Instead of a Burnt Island gravesite, God gave Georgina a "magnificent snow and ice castle" in the Snelling Cove Cemetery as His way of saying that all confessed sins are truly forgiven and covered. Her good friend and long-time supporter, and the author of the Testimonial which was presented to her at the Grand Farewell Concert in St. John's on October 3, 1895, wrote a beautiful and fitting tribute to her, which was published in the *Evening Telegram* and reprinted in the *Twillingate Sun*.

The *Twillingate Sun* of April 27, 1935, carried this terse description of Georgina's death and funeral: "Died, Toulinguet Stirling—Nfld's Prima Donna. On Easter Sunday at about 3.30 p.m., Georgina, youngest daughter of the late Dr. and Mrs. Wm. Stirling, at 68 years, passed away after an illness due to cancer. Funeral was held at St. Peter's on Thursday, Rev. Butler officiating. She leaves to mourn at home Miss Rose E. Stirling, and Mrs. Putzki (Kate) in Washington, D.C., and many relatives. (No obituary, by request)." The note in brackets must have been entirely at Georgina's firm direction through a pre-arrangement.

With a few other close family friends and supportive neighbours, Maymie had sat by Georgina's bedside every day until her death. A few days after the funeral, Rose and Maymie sat together in the Stirling house and sorted through Georgina's personal things. As they looked at the photographs in Georgina's collection, Maymie asked, "Who is this little boy?" Rose answered, "That is Georgina's son." Maymie was astounded; she had never heard this startling news before. Rose was definitely under the impression that Maymie knew, that Georgina had shared this news with her, as she had shared so much other news. It is beyond curious that Georgina, who had told Maymie a great deal about her "fall," about "sinking to the very depths," did not share the story of her "son," and about a possible romantic relationship—unless the two were unconnected. Hearing this story from Rose, for whom Maymie held the greatest respect since she was "the best educated sister" in the Stirling family, she would not have questioned its veracity; she would simply have accepted Rose's version of the story and sought no details. Why would she not?

A story has been circulating of late (2018) that Georgina came back to England from Milan (in 1901?) and had a baby which was then put up for adoption. While that seems most unlikely, it is possible, I suppose, that "the little boy" in the picture was Georgina's natural-born son, and not Ugo Angelo Vincent. If Ugo Angelo has not entered Georgina's life until (say) 1901—as an adopted son—he would hardly have been "a little boy" at eight years of age. So, the little boy may have been Georgina's natural-born son, and the picture may have been given to Georgina by the adoptive parents. It is yet another "possibility."

Did Rose ever get from Georgina the "explanation" that she sought in her postcard of 1904 from Naples to Georgina in England, referred to earlier? See page 194 of Amy Louise Peyton's book for the front and back of the postcard. Is it possible that Rose did not ever know the whole truth, that Georgina withheld some information about what happened in Milan?

Perhaps the two sisters—Rose and Georgina—were withholding information from each other. If the conversation (quarrel) which Hiram shared with Stan Curtis is accurate, it now seems possible that both sisters were indeed not telling each other the whole truth. Rose reportedly said "*At least* (italics mine) I never had a child like you, never married." That could be construed as meaning, "I may have had a sexual relationship (with Prince Rupert?), but a child was never produced." If something of this nature happened to Rose in the palace in Naples, it would have been after Georgina had left Florence and gone to London and Paris. Perhaps Georgina had never been told the story of Prince Rupert, was not aware of that possibility. That almost seems to be implied in Georgina's response to Rose: "You never knew the love of a man."

We have already dealt with the sheer impossibility that Ugo could have been Georgina's natural-born son; time and place make it impossible. Every record that we have for Ugo Angelo Vincent affirms that he was born in May 1893. So, the very fact that Rose thought Ugo was Georgina's "son" proves that she did not know the whole truth. Georgina must have allowed Rose to believe this "fiction." What was she covering up? The love liaison of 1900–1901? This may be one of the factors that kept the relationship between the two sisters simmering and resulted in their occasional (or frequent?) quarrels.

It is obvious now that Georgina did not share all the details of her life with Maymie, her best friend of at least seven years and possibly of fourteen years (dating back to 1921). The fact that Maymie did not know about Georgina's "son" proves that Georgina did not share the whole truth with her best friend. Why did she withhold the story of her "son"? Why was Georgina so selective in telling only parts of her story? What was she trying to hide? Why was Rose surprised at this? Just for self-protection, it may well be that Georgina had resolved to keep certain secrets from both her sister and her best friend. It was not living a lie. It was simply withholding the whole truth from both of them. The "cover story" seemed to have worked for years. Reminiscent of the book/movie *A Bridge Too Far*, this may have been "the story too far" which could only be described by a phrase which she purportedly used, probably with the funeral directors of Twillingate, that she had committed "every sin in the book but murder." The strained voice scenario could have been used by Georgina as a convenient cover for what really happened in Milan in 1900–1901. Here we have a riddle within a mystery.

There is nothing in the extensive interviews with Maymie to indicate that Georgina's problem had been a strained voice. However, Maymie may simply have been discreet on the subject, knowing that these interviews would be publicly broadcast. Vaughn Harbin, Maymie's cousin, says that during the period 1975 to 1984, when he visited her many times in Twillingate, Maymie had disclosed to him that "Georgie did indeed develop a throat ailment from which she recovered and went on to sing afterwards. However, her voice was never quite the same as before the ailment." While I have the greatest respect for the person and the extensive testimony of Maymie, there is something too neat about that summary. Her statement could possibly be interpreted to mean simply that this is as much as Georgina was prepared to disclose to Maymie, having already decided not to disclose the information about her "son." Maymie was simply and sincerely repeating what she had been told.

We now know that Maymie had shared the information about Georgina's "son" with at least three of her cousins and had suggested to two of them that they "keep it hidden." As the years passed, there seemed to be less reason to keep the matter secret, and a certain amount of fiction has been added to sensationalize the story. We have tried to keep our conjecturing as close as possible to revealed facts.

What Maymie may have told Hiram Silk about Georgina's vocal problems is unknown. Hiram takes it upon himself, in a rambling introduction to his intended remarks at the unveiling of Georgina's monument (for some strange reason he did not attend), to declare that ". . . she is finished as a singer. It was a severe throat ailment that had cut short her brilliant career. Her beautiful soprano voice, after the throat ailment, had changed to contralto . . . and apparently not a good contralto at that." That sounds like a mix of Will Peyton's random comment that Georgina had developed diphtheria and Amy Louise Peyton's sincere attempt to diagnose the problem. Amy Louise Peyton introduces the strained voice as a possibility and gradually begins to accept it as the reality, but still seeming somewhat uncertain. Other writers, too, try to be content with "whatever it was" that happened to Georgina. No one knows for sure.

The "strained voice" scenario may have been Georgina's initial explanation for what had happened so quickly to her in 1900–1901 in Milan; she may only ever have told the whole truth to her two sisters in England, Janet and Lucy, and not the whole story to her sister Susan in England, not to Rose, and certainly not to Kate in the United States. Holding such a secret from anyone close to her would have caused her more grief and pain.

Georgina must surely have known that there were cures for a strained voice, if that was her problem. There is no clear indication that she saw a doctor in Milan. Even medical assistance in England, if she received it from the Harley Street physicians at her sister's nursing home, did not effect a cure.

Possibilities! Possibilities! Somewhere in amongst all these is the truth, the whole truth, and nothing but the truth. But it seems we will never know for sure. Yet we cannot but guess.

By way of summary: As one soberly considers all the known and unknown factors concerning Georgina Stirling, all the evidence and the possibilities, and all the conjecturing, it is impossible to escape the conclusion that something is deliberately hidden or camouflaged or undisclosed here, and that even in her last days, Georgina "controlled the narrative," that there were things she wanted no one to know. So, after all our conjecturing is ended, we have to let it go, let it lie, "rest in peace."

In the midst of her despair, Georgina felt a true penitence for what she had done, but her penitence was beautifully balanced with a strong determination to give back to the community which had given so much to her. She truly triumphed over what she must have felt were the depths to which she had plummeted. We feel such empathy with this woman in her struggle. How much was hidden in Maymie Roberts's comments about Georgina's "fame and her faults"!

AFTER DEVELOPING WHAT I HAVE CALLED the "likely possibility," new and startling information has surfaced about Ugo. A handwritten birth registration from Milan was found in the Mormon Church Records which matches exactly the birthdate of May 28, 1893. The record was found in 2016 but only translated into English very recently.

The English translation reads as follows (with some unnecessary parts edited out): "2 June 1893 at 10.30 a.m. at the town hall before me Dottore (illegible first name) Cosigno, Secretary delegated by act of the Mayor . . . there appeared Ernesta Menapace, age fifty-two, a midwife living in the city (Milano), who presented a child of the masculine gender and declared that he was born in a house on Viale Monforte, number 24, at 7:05 p.m. on the 28th of the previous month (May) to Giorgina Bracon (my reading, CDE, or Brown—another source), well-off, wife of Walker (I read it as Walter, CDE) Sterling (with an "e") (illegible occupation), a resident of London and an English citizen. The child was given the name Ugo. The declaration was made in the presence of Luigi Pozzi, age fifty, a porter, and Felice Angaroni, age fifty-three, a porter, both residents of the town. The declarant presented the same child to me and attested to the veracity of the birth in her position (as midwife) in assisting the birth. She did so in place of the husband of Bracon (looks more like Brown this time, CDE) because he is far away from the town. I read this act to all involved and we signed it." Four signatures follow this entry.

What are we to make of this? Is it an elaborate and deliberate cover-up to shield "our Georgina" from public disgrace as she approaches the pinnacle of her operatic training? Is it an incredibly amazing coincidence? Or is it genuine? Are these real people or pretenders?

There is no doubt, I think, that Ugo Sterling and Ugo Angelo Vincent are the same person, but considering all the data we have compiled on Georgina Stirling's activities for 1892, I think that Giorgina (note the Italian spelling) is not "our Georgina." Georgina would have had to become pregnant while she and Janet were in Newfoundland between late June and November 22 when they left St. John's, and specifically about August. They were both still at Twillingate until about mid-October. Amy Louise Peyton, on page 85 of her book, writes of a young lawyer who was rumoured to be in love with Georgina (believed to be William Henry Horwood, who later became Chief Justice of Newfoundland), but this has been described elsewhere as a platonic relationship based on their mutual love of music, and Georgina is said to have dismissed any sign of affection from the young lawyer with the comment, "And what would I do with you, young man?"

It seems quite impossible that Georgina would have carried a child through her second and final year of vocal training with Madame Marchesi in Paris, escaped the scrutiny of her teacher and classmates, faced the possibility of dismissal from École Marchesi, the rancour of the press, and made her debut (probably in June 1893) or rushed off to Milan, had the baby, and returned to Paris for the debut. The exact date of the debut is unknown, but since it would have been at the end of the second year of studies, June of 1893 would seem to be most likely.

And the way Georgina's operatic career soared from 1893 to 1900 in England, France, Ireland, Germany, the United States, Canada, and Italy seems "to give the lie" to the possibility of her having borne a child. If Ugo was Georgina's child, why would she have referred to him as "Hugo" in her 1905 letter to her sister Lucy?

But the situation was quite different for Janet Stirling. As early as 1884, Kate Stirling in a letter to her father from Chicago expressed her frustration about a letter she had received from Janet (who was still at home in Twillingate) and this "rubbish" about Charlie Newman. It seems to have had the makings of a love relationship. If Janet had left Twillingate in 1890, as is conjectured, coming back home after only two years may have fanned the flames of an old relationship. Charlie was three years her junior; she would have been thirty-one, and he would have been twenty-eight. Charlie left Twillingate in 1896 and moved to British Columbia, marrying a Twillingate girl in November of that year. Or Janet may have met some other young man in Twillingate, or one visiting the town. It would still be four years before Janet enrolled in the School of Nursing in London, so she must have been doing general work in that city for that long period, unless she had enrolled in the school and took a long leave to have a baby and regain control of her life. Being knowledgeable about the city of Milan, Georgina would have shared relevant information with Janet, who would probably be accompanied by her sister Lucy and with Georgina's support and empathy. Yet another consideration: from the picture of Georgina with her sister Rose taken in Florence or Milan in or about 1890, Georgina is a slim young woman. Janet, on the other hand, was as Amy Louise Peyton affirms, "tall of stature . . . and of sturdy build," which is confirmed by the picture that Amy Louise supplies on page 47 of her book and by the graduation picture which is almost surely that of Janet. A pregnancy for Janet could have been more easily concealed. We also know that Janet had visited Italy, since when Rose received a letter from her friend at Florence in 1916, she sends "regards to Janet." Janet had very probably also attended Georgina's concert in Chioggia in 1898 with her sister Lucy.

If this conjecture fits the facts, Janet would have arranged for the adoption of the child in Milan by the Vincent (or Vincente) family, which added the name Angelo. Janet would then have returned to London, either waiting four years before she enrolled or possibly re-enrolled in the School of Nursing. It cannot be determined when Ugo Angelo Vincent was brought to England; it may well have been before we find him enrolled in a school in March 1901. It should be noted that in all the discovered records it is always to Janet that Ugo relates, never to Georgina. In her existing correspondence she makes only one reference to Ugo, in the planned picnic up the Thames in 1905. Since Janet moved to the Duxhurst Colony with Georgina in 1906, this may have been an act of gratitude for what Georgina had done for her in 1892.

Since the boy who was brought to London from Italy sometime before March 1901 is the same boy who was born to Giorgina Bracon (or Brown) and (the fictional?) Walter Sterling, it is impossible to deny that he was uniquely connected to the Stirling sisters in England.

Georgina did not *take* Ugo to England. She left Milan in late fall 1901, and by that time Ugo had been registered in school in England for at least seven to eight months, so he may well have been taken there several months, even years, before that. So, Ugo was *taken* to England by someone else, possibly by his brother (?), Thomas Henry Bevis Vincent, as I have suggested earlier, or possibly by Janet Stirling, in the event that Ugo's adoptive mother had died. The so-called English father of Ugo is almost certainly fictional, and possibly part of a cover-up. Yet another point to consider: There was a four-year period for Janet, between 1892 and 1896, for which there are no records—a period in which she could have recovered from a birth ordeal, travelled back to London, found a job with the support of Mrs. Sheppard, and began the process of entering the nursing school, which she did not do until 1896—six years after she left Twillingate, which is a very long time for a young woman to settle into a profession. There was no such quiet period for Georgina—from 1893 to 1900 was a busy, active, at times frantic period of travel, continuing vocal lessons, participation in numerous concerts in at least eight countries—nothing in the way of a year-long rest was possible, adding further mystery to the "year of silence" in Milan, 1900 to 1901. Also, the fact that sister Rose believed up until 1935 that Ugo was Georgina's son may have meant that Georgina was still keeping what may have been Janet's secret.

In this book of "possibilities," this is one more possibility that is worth consideration. But, once again, there are more questions than answers.

WE RETURN TO GEORGINA IN TWILLINGATE in the 1930s. We must remember and applaud the woman who scaled great heights and triumphed in the end, not the woman who "fell" and despaired of life. I have developed such enormous admiration for Georgina as I have reviewed all the documentation pertaining to her life.

When Hiram Silk interviewed Amy Louise Peyton sometime after her book appeared in 1983, he does not mention the incredible possibility that Georgina could have had a romantic relationship which could have produced a "son." The interview with Amy Louise was probably done in 1984, or 1985 at the latest, I would think, a year or two after her book was published. Silk would very probably have interviewed Stan Curtis sometime in the 1970s. We have already noted that Stan died in 1981. The last recorded interview in Silk's entire production was 1988, and the earliest in the 1950s, so he already knew about the story of the "son" when he interviewed Amy Louise, even though he did not understand the full context. Why did he not share this story with her? Perhaps she could have shed some light on this complex and mysterious scenario. Was Hiram saving this and other information for his own proposed book on Georgina? Hiram was very possessive about the data he had compiled on Georgina. For example, when he discovered in 1980 that Marilyn Pumphrey was writing a play on Georgina for CBC Radio in St. John's, and that she had travelled to Twillingate to interview Maymie (Roberts) Hewlett about it, Hiram accused Marilyn of being "unethical," since he was writing a book on Georgina. Marilyn simply laughed at his retort.

The picture of Georgina Stirling from 1929 to 1935 that emerges from these several interviews is quite different from some of the impressions that have been put forward and have gained some credibility in the common imagination. Georgina comes home in 1929 broken but unbowed and with a strong determination to make a life for herself in her former hometown, to contribute to the musical and cultural life of the town, and to regain some semblance of a normal life.

Using the seeds she had been sending to her sisters in Twillingate, Georgina creates a beautiful and varied flower garden with a special emphasis on a variety of roses. The community soon took notice of the profusion of flowers in her amazing garden. Georgina must have modelled her flower garden on the beautiful English gardens to which she had become accustomed; she had rustic garden furniture built and low fences constructed around sections of the flower garden which enclosed varied species of roses.

Rose would have restarted the vegetable garden, out of necessity, because her financial resources appear to have been limited. Both sisters now would have been cultivating the vegetable garden, reviving the tradition of their parents, because they were both accustomed in their early years to growing both vegetables and flowers on the one-and-a-half-acre lot. Dr. Stirling's meticulous records show the purchase of "garden seeds," this phrase indicating a variety of seeds, turnip seed and flower seeds through the 1880s. Georgina had the more recent experience of growing a variety of vegetables and flowers at the Duxhurst Colony, where she had resided intermittently for about fifteen years.

Georgina Stirling's vanity box with perfume bottles, hairpins, brooches, etc. (Courtesy of Bruce Manuel and Brent English)

Both Georgina and Lucy were fascinated with the beauty of roses and regularly shared the beauty with friends and neighbours—and Georgina faithfully and regularly cheered up the sick and shut-ins with her flowers. She created bouquets as a medicine for those who needed it, as well as for weddings. She found such pleasure in the garden that one worker noted that she was forever humming when she worked there. She quoted verses from Dorothy Frances Gurney's poem "God's Garden" more than once to visitors.

Dorothy Frances Gurney was an English poet and hymn writer who lived from 1858 to 1932, almost the same years as Georgina did. Gurney lived near London, where Georgina lived for several years before she moved in late 1905 or early 1906 to the Duxhurst Farm Colony at Reigate, Surrey. Could the two women possibly have met? The poem is worth repeating in full:

The Lord God planted a garden
    In the first white days of the world,
And He set there an angel warden
    In a garment of light unfurled.

So near to the peace of Heaven,
    That the hawk might nest with the wren,
For there in the cool of the even
    God walked with the first of men.

And I dream that these garden-closes
    With their shade and their sun-flecked sod
And their lilies and bowers of roses
    Were laid by the hand of God.

The kiss of the sun for pardon,
    The song of the birds for mirth,—
One is nearer God's heart in a garden
    Than anywhere else on earth.

For He broke it for us in a garden
    Under the olive trees
When the angel of strength was the warden
    And the soul of the world found ease.

DOROTHY FRANCES GURNEY'S HUSBAND AND FATHER were Church of England priests. Dorothy left her church and converted to the Roman Catholic faith in 1919, and her husband followed her. Could it possibly have been through such an influence that Georgina also became a Roman Catholic, as the funeral director at Twillingate stated in an interview that she had done; and he had heard this directly from Rose? With their shared interests in gardens and flowers and hymns and music, it is just possible that Georgina and Dorothy Gurney may have met and shared thoughts.

The Duxhurst Colony, where Georgina lived intermittently between 1906 and the death of Lady Somerset in 1921, was a facility for Protestant women, so it does not seem likely that this is where Georgina converted to Catholicism. However, in the spiritual environment of Duxhurst there may well have been a small cohort of Church of England women who were pondering the same set of circumstances that led Dorothy Frances Gurney away from her former faith to join the Catholic Church. We have already noted that Lady Somerset was becoming increasingly High Anglican in the later years and had introduced much direct Catholic teaching. Again, Georgina may well have converted to Catholicism while still in Italy, as already conjectured.

Gurney's poem was inspired by Lord Ronald Gower's exquisite garden at Hammerfield Penshurst. Gurney penned it originally in Lord Gower's Visitors Book.

Continuing with the theme of what life was like for Georgina after she returned permanently to Twillingate, it is recorded that Georgina and Rose hired maids and other workers to assist with the heavy work around the large property, and they were commended by many neighbours and visitors for being hard workers themselves. Insights garnered from Maymie (Roberts) Hewlett's journal furnish a more complete picture of what life was like on the Stirling estate for the two sisters. Their sister Lucy had lived in the house from 1904 to late 1912, but she appears not to have done any vegetable gardening; she instead focused her energies on flowers, especially roses, as Georgina would later do. Maymie recalls that "Miss Rose came . . . to stay, and soon had things in ship shape. She bought a cow, a pig and hens and ducks. The stable was white-washed inside. She had help all the time, sometimes there were two women and a man there doing gardening, attending to the animals and cleaning, especially in the spring. She didn't live the grand style like Miss Lucy did, everything was done to make it pay, and apart from the little help she got from her sister, her animals kept her, and she could certainly drive a hard bargain. She was a very clever business woman and though she didn't mind owing money, one could be sure eventually, when she sold a pig or a calf, etc. it would be paid. That could be said of both Miss Rose and Miss Georgie, but with Miss Georgie, if a merchant bugged her too much for payment, she made sure he waited the longest." The two sisters appear to have settled on "a division of labour."

Georgina contributed to the community by giving children and young women piano, organ, and voice lessons. She assisted high-school students, both male and female, with French lessons. She sang at the town's churches and at the Hustler's Club, supporting their efforts to raise funds for the Memorial Hospital. Georgina coached people for dramatic plays. She coached at least one male quartet singing group. She read a great deal, and the Stirling library was well-stocked. She renewed her interest in the local Dorcas Society and participated in sewing clothes and blankets for the industrious poor and needy of Twillingate. She cooked and baked. She entertained at the Stirling house with dinner parties.

It is worthy of note that neither Georgina nor Rose went to church regularly. When sister Lucy lived back in Twillingate from 1904 to 1913, she attended church regularly, and people remember the rustle of her silk dresses as she walked up through the church and took her seat. Georgina appears to have gone to church only when she was asked to sing or to attend special events, for example the little blind girl's funeral. Elmo Baird, working at the Stirling house from the time he was a young boy until the age of fifteen, was also a bell ringer at St. Peter's Church and regularly pumped the pipe organ, but today—with a very sharp mind and memory at age ninety-nine—has no recollection of either Rose or Georgina attending church, yet he had heard Georgina sing twice at the Orange Hall. Even in the 1930s, according to her best friend, Maymie (Roberts) Hewlett, Georgina "could almost stand on her toes, glide down the staircase in the Stirling house," and pirouette for her guests before breaking into song. Perhaps Georgina's irregular attendance at St. Peter's had to do with the fact that she had converted to the Catholic faith while still in Europe.

The way Georgina conducted herself in Twillingate in those final years was not a case of a great woman condescending to the poor and needy around her. Georgina was "in her element" in Twillingate. Her actions were firmly planted in her nature—to be among those in need, to bring comfort and help where needed. She was a truly humble woman. This must have been what Maymie Hewlett meant by her comment, "She was a real Christian." This kind of service she had learned at St. Peter's Church in her youth, and in her family, and was reflected in the great hymns and songs she sang which resulted in many accolades and caused countless joyous tears.

Hiram Silk had recorded these words of Maymie (Roberts) Hewlett: "She (Georgina) was a very kind person, and often did without things herself to give to those less fortunate. I have seen her take off the clothes that she was wearing to give to a poor woman who came to her door." The *Twillingate Sun* of December 1898 drew attention to what was a Stirling trait in Georgina: "She has always, in common with the Stirling family, been very considerate to the poor and many instances were mentioned of her kindly care of the sick to whom she has often taken nourishment and other necessaries."

Georgina remained true to herself in her last years. Her best friend during those years, Maymie (Roberts) Hewlett, focused on Georgina's humility, a startling characteristic of a woman who had reached such heights of acclaim in many cities on two continents. But even in her last years, this scarce virtue of humility was balanced with an incisive ability to bring the haughty and the proud "down a buttonhole or two," to use a favoured Newfoundland saying. She saw through every false veneer and responded appropriately.

Georgina neither sought nor would tolerate the pity of the people of her hometown but she was supported and respected and loved by them. She was an independent woman, superbly in control of her life and facing life with a steely determination and an upbeat attitude. She was now fulfilling the words of Anne Morrow Lindbergh: "One has to come to terms with oneself not only in a new stage of life but in a new role."

ONE FINAL COMMENT on the seven Stirling sisters: Three of the sisters married—Eleanor in 1877, Susan in 1881, and Kate in 1886. Three of the four sisters who remained unmarried appear to have had tragic or shattering romantic relationships—Lucy, the eldest sister, was jilted by her lover even as all the preparations had been made for the marriage at Twillingate, and the groom was expected to arrive by coastal boat but did not, this occasion probably happening in the early 1870s; Rose, the third sister, is reputed to have been the mistress of Prince Rupert in either a royal palace or, more likely, in a palace of the Italian nobility. If the rumour is true, this would have been in Naples, where she had lived for many years, and the relationship may have come to an abrupt end. It is said that she then vowed to wear only black ever after—long black dresses, black shawls, black beads, etc.; and Georgina, whose conjectured shattering romantic relationship has been described above.

If our conjecturing above is true, not even Janet escaped the tragedies of the heart. In 1884, sister Kate in Chicago feared that her three sisters back in Twillingate would all become "old maids." At that time, Janet was twenty-three years of age, and the "rubbish" referred to in Kate's letter seems to be referring to an infatuation Janet had with Charlie Newman. Janet was the sister who later protected and sheltered sister Lucy from life's hard blows following her jilted heartbreak, and who carried the major responsibility for helping in Georgina's rehabilitation from over-drinking, and for assisting Ugo to build a normal life in a new country. Her amazing strength and support were crucial to helping Georgina rebuild her own life.

It was always to Janet Stirling that Ugo seemed to relate. For the picnic up the Thames in 1905, it is Janet and Georgina who take him. In the Census of 1911, Janet is visiting her sister Susan and has taken Ugo along. In 1916, he is noted as living at 14 Bulstrode Street, Janet's apartment. In 1923, he gives her name as his "friend" when he travels to the United States. One may have thought that it would be to Georgina that he would especially relate.

CHAPTER FIFTEEN
BY CALVIN D. EVANS

GEORGINA'S VOCAL RECORDING
— THE SEARCH CONTINUES

FOR SOME TIME NOW there have been doubts expressed about whether the recording of "Lo, Here the Gentle Lark," which is regularly played for visitors at the Twillingate Museum, is actually that of Georgina Stirling's voice.

There now seems to be a growing consensus that the recording is that of an Italian singer, Amelita Galli-Curci. Galli-Curci was born in Italy in 1882, arrived in the United States in 1916, and made her debut at the Met in 1921. She signed a contract with the Victor Talking Machine Company shortly after arriving and made records exclusively for this company until 1930. She died in 1963.

A tape of the original recording was presented to the museum by Hiram Silk sometime after he discovered it about 1960 in the attic of Will Peyton's house in Back Harbour, Twillingate, where many of Georgina's costumes and mementoes were stored following her death. Amy Louise Peyton states that "Georgina Stirling did not live in the age of discography, for it was only at the end of her career that the recording machine was invented. It is believed that the only recording of her voice was made in 1904. This recording, 'Lo, Hear (sic) the Gentle Lark,' was the first recording made by a Newfoundlander. Her operatic voice then was not as it once had been."

However, there is good news on that front. An article in the *Newfoundland Quarterly*, Winter 1987 (Volume LXXXII, No. 3), provides quite a different picture of early recordings. Brian Wadden, father of the celebrated Newfoundland journalist Marie Wadden, is the author of this article, which is entitled "Early Demonstrations of the Phonograph in Newfoundland." Thomas Alva Edison invented a speaking machine, a phonograph, as early as 1877. E. Berliner developed the first flat record in 1895, but the phonograph was first exhibited in St. John's on May 11, 1891, according to H. M. Mosdell's book *When Was That?* which was published in 1923. This assertion by Mosdell cannot be independently confirmed. However, A. A. Urquhart arrived in St. John's on October 29, 1891, stayed for "over six weeks," and demonstrated the phonograph, at the first event playing several New York operatic songs, recording a local political speech, an address by a clergyman, and "a cornet solo" which became "the very first recording made in Newfoundland." At that time, Georgina Stirling was immersed in her third year of voice training and performances in Paris, France. Mr. Urquhart charged a small fee for those wanting to "use the tubes of the machine." From St. John's he journeyed to Harbour Grace, Carbonear, Heart's Content, Upper Island Cove, Spaniard's Bay, Bay Roberts, Brigus, Placentia, and Whitbourne before returning to St. John's, where he gave the final demonstrations on December 20, 1891.

D. F. Nolan visited St. John's on December 4, 1893, with the Edison's Phonograph, but problems with the machine at Harbour Grace caused a quick exit from the island. But he returned with his brother P. J. Nolan on February 21, 1894, and they demonstrated with great success the facility of the machine at various venues in St. John's and one in Whitbourne until August 15, 1894. Yet another visitor, C. C. Carlyle, arrived that year, about the middle of March, using the phonograph primarily to reach people who would agree to work and settle on the Canadian prairies, but he stayed only for about two weeks.

The date that interests us the most in connection with Georgina Stirling is August 1896. R. Chappell brought his Graph-O-Phone to St. John's during the month of August, and it was introduced at the B.F.B. Grand Exhibition on August 26, 1896. His machine was called the Tainter and Bell, and it was regarded as stiff competition for the phonograph. Though this was the first visit of these recording machines that was covered by the local newspapers and over a thousand people attended the exhibition, nothing in particular was written in the local newspapers about the success of the machines. The machines were now getting to be such commonplace features that journalists of the day did little in the way of coverage.

Brian Wadden then writes: "The very first Newfoundland Amateur Athletic Association sports day was held that year in Llewelyns Field off Forest Road and Mr. Chappell's Graph-O-Phone was placed at Woods refreshment pavilion and for the price of 20c, it could be seen and heard. I have no evidence, but there was a possibility that a Newfoundland prima donna, Miss Twillingate Stirling, *who was visiting at this time* could have made recordings into this machine. She was at the height of her career and sang at the R.C. Cathedral and the Presbyterian Church *that week* as well as at a concert at Whitbourne. Those who still have cylinder records take note."

Brian Wadden seems to be incorrect in his dates, since the *Daily News* of October 5 indicates that Georgina was at Whitbourne on October 2, 1896.

However, in connection with R. Chappell's visit to St. John's, we have only this one firm date—August 26—but these visits often extended for months until the novelty wore off after about 1898, when people were able to purchase their own machines. Georgina and her sister Lucy had spent the summer of 1896 at Twillingate, and Georgina planned to sail from St. John's to New York in October for singing engagements in that city. According to Amy Louise Peyton's calendar of events for Georgina Stirling that year, she sang at Fr. Browne's Church at Whitbourne on October 2, at the Dedication Service of the Gower Street Methodist Church on October 4, at the Grand Sacred Concert of St. Andrew's Presbyterian Church on October 6, at the Ladies' College Aid Society's "At Home Musicale" at the Methodist College Hall on October 7, at the Grand Concert at St. Patrick's Hall on October 8, at the Grand Complimentary Concert for Mr. Hutton on October 12, and at Gower Street Methodist Church College Day with no date mentioned, but from Amy Louise's narrative it appears to have been October 5.

Because of damage to the ship on which Georgina intended to sail from St. John's to New York, the SS *Portia*, Georgina took the train to Harbour Grace and sailed from that town on the SS *Coban* sometime after October 12.

Brian Wadden is correct to raise the possibility of Georgina visiting one or more of the venues in St. John's where the Graph-O-Phone was being demonstrated and making a recording of "Lo, Here the Gentle Lark," as well as of other songs. Georgina was in St. John's for at least eleven or twelve days with no events scheduled from October 9 to October 11, and the Graph-O-Phone may well have been available for recordings at other locations in the city during that period. It is interesting to speculate. There was a noticeable excitement about the recording machines among the St. John's populace. The Graph-O-Phone was "all the rage."

The source of Amy Louise Peyton's statement on page 12 of her book cannot be determined—"It is believed that the only recording of her voice was made in 1904." We must, therefore, agree that Amy Louise may have been right, that sometime in that confusing and heartbreaking visit to St. John's, more likely when Georgina had recovered from her "indisposition," and perhaps between the two successful concerts on November 1 and November 15, she had agreed to make such a recording. The recording machine was no longer in its infancy, and almost surely Georgina's voice had been recorded elsewhere in the period (say) between 1891 and 1900. A suggestion by her hosts to make a recording of her voice would almost certainly not have been regarded as unusual by Georgina, and she would not have rejected the request after the acclaim accorded her following the performance of November 1. The newspaper next day had commented on the "magnificent manner" of her performance, the enthusiastic applause of the audience, and that Georgina on stage had "appeared time and again to thank her admirers." The article had concluded with the comment: "At the close it was unanimously conceded that the concert was one of the most enjoyable and enthusiastic ever heard here." These comments seem to form a favourable prelude to the recording of a song by Georgina. As Brian Wadden suggested in his article, there may well be "cylinder records" somewhere in St. John's containing recordings of Georgina's voice.

As a footnote to the above, it should also be noted that F. C. Farr, writer for the *Canadian Statesman*, following two visits with Hiram Silk in 1969 at St. John's and Grand Falls, wrote: "The Silks have in their possession a rare copy of the only record that Twillingate Stirling ever made—that soprano show-piece of her era, 'O Listen to the Gentle Lark.' Its reproduction, of course, is not high fidelity, but as we listened, we knew why Hiram Silk—musician, Christian gentleman and lover of Newfoundland—wanted his countrymen to remember her." Of course, Farr would have been listening to the tape that plays at the Twillingate Museum.

Paul Butler, writing in the *Evening Telegram* of October 16, 2004, states: "Sadly, the only actual recording of Marie Toulinguet was made in 1904, after her great voice was damaged. . . . Even though the singer is past her prime and the recording crackles, her voice is still remarkable." Likewise, Butler would have listened to the tape at the Twillingate Museum.

James B. McPherson, writing about Georgina Stirling in the *Canadian Encyclopedia* in 2013, states that "The only recording (Milan ca. 1904), surviving in a private collection, reveals a high soprano of great brilliance and agility." The suggested city and the date are certainly incorrect. Georgina's singing career ended probably in early 1901, and she left Milan and returned to England in the late fall of 1901 to be with her sisters Janet and Lucy. McPherson quotes his research sources as Amy Louise Peyton's book and the National Library of Canada, Music Division Vertical Files. He states that Georgina "enjoyed a successful concert and opera career in France, England, Germany and the United States and particularly in Italy . . ." and mentions her performance in Montreal.

Edward B. Moogk was for many years head of the National Library of Canada's Recorded Sound Section. His impressively large book *Roll Back the Years* is "a national collection of records of Canadian performers and composers." Unfortunately, he provides a very slim bibliography and does not note the sources for his extensive bibliographical notes. Nevertheless, his brief comment about Georgina Stirling's recording is significant. "She is believed to have made just one recording, possibly for an Odeon label, in 1904—the title is unknown." This comment would support my earlier suggestion that Georgina made a recording between her two public concerts at St. John's, sometime between November 1 and November 15. From other sources we have heard that the title of the song was "O, Listen to the Gentle Lark" and "Lo, Hear the Gentle Lark," both of these titles slightly incorrect.

An Internet search determines that the correct title is "Lo, Here the Gentle Lark," the words written by William Shakespeare and the first four lines set to music for soprano, flute, and piano by Sir Henry Rowley Bishop. It was a song favoured by Nellie Melba, one of Georgina's fellow graduates from the École Marchesi in Paris, and one of Georgina's best friends in the early years. The first stanza reads as follows:

> *Lo, here the gentle lark, weary of rest,*
> *From his moist cabinet mounts up on high,*
> *And wakes the morning, from whose silver breast*
> *The sun ariseth in his majesty:*
> *Who doth the world so gloriously behold*
> *That cedar-tops and hills seem burnish'd gold.*

THERE SEEMS TO BE MORE SUPPORT from sources for Georgina having made a recording on the 1904 date, but we ought equally to consider the importance of October 1896, since visits by the recording promoters lasted for months at a time, and R. Chappell was in St. John's from August of that year. The song was written originally for soprano, flute, and piano.

Roger Neill in his appendices notes the number of recordings that had been made by Madame Marchesi's pupils, though he does not list Georgina in this group. There were three recordings made by Marchesi's pupils in 1880, one in 1881, one in 1882, two in 1886, two in 1887, two in 1889, one in 1891, three in 1892, one in 1896, two in 1899, two in 1900, one in 1901, one in 1902, one in 1903, three in 1906, two in 1907, one in 1908, and two in 1909.

This is probably not an exhaustive list and serves little purpose except to indicate that recordings were being made by Madame Marchesi's pupils during the very long period of her professional teaching career, which lasted from 1854 to 1910.

Kent Peyton, Amy Louise Peyton's son, informed us in 2018 that he remembers having seen a recording cylinder in Will Peyton's house in Back Harbour, Twillingate, which at that time was occupied by Edith, Will Peyton's twin sister. Edith was noted as being somewhat eccentric, and Kent clearly remembers that the cylinder was used to prop up the window to allow the wind to blow through the room. Robert Walter Parsons of Newcastle, Ontario (and formerly of Grand Falls, Newfoundland and Labrador), a descendant of the Peytons, remembers having heard that story as well. For those who are unfamiliar with this object, this type of cylinder is defined as "on a printing press, a roller carrying the printed plates or the part receiving the impression." Did this cylinder contain a number of songs that Georgina had recorded, and had she brought it back from England or did it come from St. John's? Brian Wadden in his article refers both to cylinders and tubes that may still exist in private collections in or around St. John's.

Clyde Gilmour of CBC Toronto did an appreciative excerpt in one of his radio programs in October 1970 about Georgina Stirling and played the recording of "Lo, Here the Gentle Lark." Robert Walter Parsons heard Gilmour's program and wrote to him, requesting additional information about the recording of what was said to be Georgina's voice, and Gilmour referred Parsons's letter to Ed Manning of CBC London. Writing from the *Toronto Telegram* office on January 6, 1971, Gilmour's handwritten note states, "Dear Mr. Parsons. My apologies for the delay in answering your October letter. On thinking it over, I've decided to send it to Mr. Ed Manning of CFPL-TV in London, Ont., a computer-like authority in such biographical matters. If he cannot trace your operatic ancestor, he may be able to tell you who can. Best wishes. Clyde Gilmour."

Throughout Ed Manning's long typed response, dated February 18, 1971, which deals with other topics related to Georgina Stirling, he consistently refers to her as "G.S." Manning wrote: "It has been suggested that the record to which you refer, may have been made by Fonotipia. I could either verify, or dispute this, if I could see the record personally. But as this is not possible, I will continue my efforts to find listings of this double-sided disc, 'Lo, Here the Gentle Lark' and a Bellini aria (?), and others if possible. The fact that G.S. recorded so early (1904), was very complimentary to this young singer. On being questioned in later life, G.S. maintained that she had recorded only the one record. She recalled that she had to sing down a long horn and being told to turn her head away when she came to loud notes." This last comment may support, as already suggested, the earlier date of 1896—rather than 1904— as the time of recording. In a margin note on his typed letter, Manning had written "labels are not intelligible." It cannot be determined where Manning acquired the information about Georgina's comments "in later life," and having made "only the one record," about "a Bellini aria," and "having to sing down a long horn." Perhaps this information is in the National Library of Canada's Music Division Vertical Files, to which James B. McPherson refers as one of his sources. Robert Walter Parsons thinks he may have heard about "singing down a long horn" from Amy and Ernest Peyton, or possibly from Hiram Silk.

A depiction of Georgina making a recording by "singing down a long horn," possibly in St. John's, in 1896 or 1904 (Courtesy of Sylvia Ficken, Newfoundland artist, 1981)

Ed Manning also referred to a double-sided disc, almost certainly the one that Hiram Silk found in the attic of the Peyton house in Back Harbour. If that is so, then the disc is housed somewhere in a secure vault in Grand Falls, Newfoundland and Labrador, placed there by Hiram Silk, who is now deceased. All attempts to get access to the original record have proved fruitless. Robert Walter Parsons was living in Grand Falls when he heard Hiram play the recording on his *Intermezzo* program of classical music on CBC Radio. He acquired a copy of the tape, and when he visited London, England, shortly afterwards, he, at Hiram's suggestion, visited the Sound News Productions at 10 Clifford Street, New Bond Street, London, W.1, and they put the recording on vinyl for Robert. The vinyl is played at 33 1/3 rpm. Ed Manning had promised to get back to Robert, but he never did.

My guess is that most of the information that Ed Manning reveals came either directly or indirectly from Hiram Silk. Hiram trained in broadcasting at Ryerson University in Toronto and very probably came to know Clyde Gilmour at that time. He may have known Ed Manning and would have come to know several other CBC staff. Hiram must have shared a copy with either Clyde Gilmour or Ed Manning, more likely Manning. Hiram would have cautiously shared information about Georgina Stirling, probably in the early 1960s, with fellow broadcasters, and this may have been the catalyst for Clyde Gilmour's 1970 broadcast. Hiram first played the recording on CBC Grand Falls in 1962 and would have shared a copy with one of his Ontario colleagues following that date. He would have been careful not to reveal too much, since he would have been saving the choicest parts of Georgina's story for his own intended biography of the Nightingale of the North. This may be the way the information found its way into the Vertical Files of the Music Division of the National Library of Canada.

The British writer of the "printed edited manuscript" to which we referred earlier, after conversing with Madame Mathilde Marchesi in Paris in 1892 about her young pupil, Georgina Stirling, states that Georgina's "voice compass ranges from the lower G to the upper C" and noted that Madame Marchesi had said, "That pretty girl possesses the finest mezzo-soprano voice I ever heard. It is a marvellous voice, and I predict a great future for her."

In Georgina's letter to her father, "My dear Pa," of December 1, 1889, she writes "when I take a very high note (such as this)" and then draws the note on the scale and later writes, "The compass of my voice now is nearly three octaves" and then draws a musical scale to indicate the range. She follows it with a comment, "If you do not understand, Janet (her sister who is at home in Twillingate with her father) will explain it to you." Tonia Evans Cianciulli comments that Georgina's voice range went up to a high D, and the sketch she draws for her father shows a D above the staff.

Edward B. Moogk suggested that the recording may have been made for an Odeon label, and Ed Manning suggested that it may have been done on a Fonotipia record. I would suggest that these are both wild guesses. Fonotipia Records was established in 1904 in Milan, for the express purpose of recording celebrity opera singers and classical violinists. Its records were lateral needle-cut of the usual kind and were played at or near the speed of 78 rpm. Odeon had been founded as early as 1897 by Carl Lindstrom, and Fonotipia later became part of the Carl Lindstrom Company. The name of Georgina Stirling could not be found in Fonotipia's catalogues. During 1904, Georgina was living in England, having attempted and failed to make a comeback as a concert artist, and still grappling with the problem of over-drinking. She and her sisters Janet and Lucy arrived in Newfoundland on August 24, and Georgina and Janet returned to England on November 17, following two successful concerts in St. John's on November 1 and November 15.

On May 15, 2019, we took our questions and queries to an expert in the person of Stephen R. Clarke, chair of the board of *Opera Canada* magazine, who has been collecting recordings for over fifty years. Clarke is the custodian of the renowned Stratton Collection of vocal recordings who is also a tenor and a former pupil of Howell Glynne, Elizabeth Benson Guy, and Greta Kraus. He has dedicated most of his life to the study of singers and singing styles of the past. An avid educator, he shares his extensive expertise and resources through regular classes with artists of the Canadian Opera Company Ensemble Studio and students in voice and opera at the University of Toronto Faculty of Music.

I quote from one of his responses to us: "I have listened many times to the recording on the video which you (Tonia—of the Italian soprano Amelita Galli-Curci) sent me and observe first that the recording is of soprano, flute and orchestra. The presence of an orchestra suggests very strongly that it cannot be a recording made at a public display of early recording equipment and also suggests that it is not a private recording but a studio recording done at some expense. Now if there is no outside evidence of the identity of the soprano singing on the recording in the video, I have to say that I lean to thinking that it's a poor transfer of the Galli-Curci recording. The tempo and manner of the delivery of the coloratura is really the same in both recordings, in spite of the obvious difference in the sound quality. Galli-Curci was not a Marchesi pupil and neither her recording nor the mystery recording sounds like the singing of a Marchesi pupil. There is, of course, a recording of the song by Dame Nellie Melba. It sounds quite different. In some ways, I regret that I feel sure about all of this as I would rejoice if the recording was indeed Georgina Stirling who clearly was an exceptional singer and had a fine career. The great soprano Jessye Norman has been searching for a recording of the first black soprano to sing at Carnegie Hall whose name was Sisseeretta Jones but so far, no luck. The record-collecting world has been looking for a hundred years for two published Fonotipia recordings of the great Polish tenor, Jean De Reszke, who we know made two recordings, but to date nothing has been found, even though the recording appeared in a Fonotipia catalogue. . . . I wish that I could be more encouraging but I don't think that the case for Stirling has yet been successfully made."

From such an eminent person, that seems to settle the matter—the record found by Hiram Silk, a copy of which plays at the Twillingate Museum, is not that of Georgina Stirling. Experienced voice professors Darryl Edwards, Brian McIntosh, and Manny Perez agree.

Why, then, was this record found amongst Georgina's memorabilia, which had been taken for safety (and for posterity?) to the Peyton house after her death in 1935? Almost certainly because of the sentimental nature of what the song meant to her. She had been a lark herself, a nightingale, and when she heard this recorded song in or after it had been recorded in 1919, she may have purchased it as a personal treasure to remind her of what once had been. The presence of the flute would have reminded her of her father, and it is just possible that Georgina may have sung that song at home with her father on the flute and her sister Lucy at the piano. Sir Henry Rowley Bishop had written the song sometime in the 1840s.

It is just possible that when Hiram Silk visited the Peyton house at Back Harbour, he should also have taken the "cylinder record" that Edith Peyton was using to hold up her window. But it was such a useful object for her purposes that Hiram would have had a much more difficult job persuading her to surrender it than the double-sided record. This would fit with an 1896 recording at St. John's by R. Chappell, and Brian Wadden would have been right. It would also fit with Georgina's comment "in later years" that she had made only one recording and that she had to "sing down a long horn." How easily great treasures are lost to posterity!

So, no one now living knows what Georgina's voice sounded like, but that is not important. She had such an astonishing and beautiful voice, such a stellar, though short, career, had developed such a broad and varied repertoire, and was lauded by ecstatic audiences in so many countries, that she is deserving of our continuing adulation and our greatest respect.

We would encourage readers and archivists and those who search attics and basements to be on the lookout for ancient cylinder records in the event that one of these may contain the song(s) of Georgina Stirling. We are pleased to be able to state that since we began our research in May 2017, several items belonging to Georgina have been found, including her vanity box, her laptop organ which she carried on all her travels, her jewelled night light, her bedroom furniture, and her piano. Hopefully there is more to be found.

CHAPTER SIXTEEN
BY TONIA EVANS CIANCIULLI

GEORGINA'S ETERNAL LEGACY, A HEARTFELT GOODBYE

Twillingate's a million miles away
The orchestra's in tune and waits to play
Send a horse-drawn carriage straight away
For Marie Toulinguet

I don't feel like I belong, some days I'm not that strong
Everything's too fast for a young girl
So far from home, so far from home

Better watch out for what you wish
I can't believe I used to dream of this
Now I dream for what I miss
Now I miss my home, now I miss my home

And the name upon the marquee isn't mine
It's a stage name, to complete a grand design
But it swells a small-town singer to sublime
Like warm Italian sunshine

I am just Georgina back at home
Not so special, not famous or well-known
Just a Stirling girl from Twillingate
That a tiny twist of fate, smiled upon
Fate smiled upon
Twillingate's a million miles away . . .
— "Marie," by Ron Hynes

THE MOMENT I FIRST HEARD RON HYNES'S song "Marie," its melody and lyrics were profoundly imprinted on my heart. Its tenderness speaks to the pride of Georgina's birthplace and calls out to the striving wanderer whose origins are intimately there. It's a humble nod to her peaceful and idyllic hometown. I feel "Marie" was heaven-sent to me. It's become a favourite request at bedtime from my son and has impressed upon both my children and my audiences a precious, compassionate, and accessible insight into Georgina's emotional life and career. Georgina's life started and ended with her first love, Twillingate.

The deeper I ventured into this journey—the writing of this treasured book—the greater my joy. With both Georgina and my grandfather, Calvin D. Evans, leading the charge, it came as no surprise that life has unfolded with such staggering synchronicity. Newfoundland for Georgina was a lighthouse always guiding her back. I felt confident that Georgina had become my lighthouse . . . to beckon me back home to my treasured roots and to have me tell her story. I thank God when I think back to the gentle nudge from my sweet cousin Jody and the inspired notion to crack the spine of the dear book *Nightingale of the North*. I will never forget that moment.

No one knew the significance of home more intimately than two of our province's most talented singers, Georgina Stirling and Ron Hynes. In my journey to connect deeply to my Newfoundland roots and my homeland, I am forever grateful to the cascading series of events that have come together, linking me irrevocably to them over ocean waves and time, through the most poignant form of expression—song. The obsession of our hearts is deeply ingrained in the art and expression of our love for music and of our native homeland. It has led me to the honour of sharing with the world and, more intimately, with Newfoundland, what a blessing we had in our sweet native songstress. I believe this is resulting in a most heartfelt and timely reunion of current and future generations to the significance of our roots and home.

How is it that Ron Hynes was able to delve so deeply into Georgina's psyche? His artist's empathy, which gave him access to all forms of humanness, must have had a special affinity for Georgina, whose emotional intelligence was so near to that of his own. They had in common their love and emotional connection to their home, Newfoundland.

I reflect on my most emotionally charged moments of performance. The most memorable is my performance of "Marie" and other repertoire of Georgina's in her hometown church, St. Peter's, at Twillingate. I reflect that I also am at home, and I am deeply moved by my own sense of "place." Georgina's energy still resides there, and it instantly connects me to my own heart's obsession. As a child of Newfoundland, I have come to experience it and recognize it as one of the most significant places I've ever known. It is a place that delights in the retelling of its prideful and splendid history, the childhood stories, the unique culture, and sense of community. When I visit Newfoundland, I affectionately nod in delight as I sit opposite aunts, uncles, and cousins at their kitchen tables. Every visit is full of retelling. They're all storytellers; they tell these stories frequently to keep the memories alive and fresh in their minds, to stay connected to their "place." They never get tired of the retelling, just as singers never get tired of singing the songs that mean the most to them. Inside the songs are sweet memories and stories that ring even more vividly and tenderly because they are set to music and sung by the human voice. The stories and memories are tied intimately to our hearts and emotions. Home is not just a physical place. It is also a feeling—of warmth, of belonging, and of connection to who we really are.

The proverb "Home is Where the Heart Is" originated more than a century ago, in 1870, in the story of Davy Crockett by J. J. McCloskey when he wrote, "Well, home, they say, is where the heart is." Both Georgina Stirling and Ron Hynes shared both this sentiment and love of home so beautifully with their music; this is why I've developed an equal connection to them despite the genre differences. They were both storytellers who never ceased to be rooted in their provincial home in the music they chose to sing and write and for which they became known. Georgina's repertoire, when she was home in Newfoundland, was the more classical version of Ron's heartfelt lyrics about home, but they are both so connected to "place."

Newfoundlanders had a sentimental tie to Georgina. When she was home, she settled right into her beloved roots. It may not be too much to claim that a sense of place means more both to Newfoundlanders and to those whose home is an island. The juxtaposition between land and sea is another powerful factor in defining the sense of connectedness, of identity, of memory, of belonging that an islander feels strongly. "Place" defines one's roots, one's situation, and even the purpose of one's life. No matter where we live in the world, Newfoundland is always home.

Georgina Stirling was as "rooted" to the sea as she was to the land; it was a powerful facet in the shaping of her voice and her life. Calvin D. Evans shared this noteworthy recollection with me after he read the book *A History of Architectural Conservation*, author Jukka Jokilehto: "If we want to learn anything from the past . . . and we have any pleasure in being remembered in the future, we need memory, we need something to which we attach our memories." Memory is one of the key factors in the Newfoundlander's sense of place, and it is this which accounts for and produces the fine art of storytelling and the fine music and songs of many genres which blend into one to keep us grounded to our island home. I think Georgina would say "Amen" to that.

THE LAST ROSE OF SUMMER

"It sometimes seems to me that one of the strangest things in this world is the realization that there is never time to perfect everything in us; that we carry seeds in our souls that cannot flower in one short life. Perhaps Paradise will be a place where we can develop every possibility and become our complete selves."
— Sofia Scalchi, Italian Contralto (1850–1922)

OH MY, IS IT EVER HARD TO SAY GOODBYE! I know you will agree. The afternoon I stared to write this chapter, I was speaking to my grandfather over the phone. Prior to us hanging up, I sensed he wanted to share something else, and when I asked him, he said: "I just have so much on my mind that I want to say and share that I find it hard to say goodbye." I giggled and told him how much I loved him before hanging up the phone. I then recalled the anticipated moment in which I closed my *Nightingale Sings* concert in Georgina's church at Twillingate, with "The Last Rose of Summer." Tears welled up in my eyes, and I felt a knot in my throat as I paused to sing the final refrain. The final line of music I would utter that evening was, *"When true hearts lie withered and fond ones are flown, oh who would inhabit this bleak world alone?"* Georgina had experienced so much loss over the course of her life—the loss of parents, brothers, loved ones, and the loss of her voice. She had moments of bleakness but also moments of splendour. Georgina did not "inhabit this bleak world alone." She was loved dearly by her family, friends, her international audiences, and most of all, Newfoundland.

Thinking back on the journey we've shared over these pages, you can surely understand what a tearful moment it was for me and the audience. Pausing, I could tell my pianist, Jason Locke, also sensed this. He took a last deep breath along with mine. Standing where Georgina stood, singing what Georgina sang, I felt overcome. It is these songs, Georgina's stories and the retelling of ours, that will forever keep us connected to home and our great sense of "Newfoundland place."

As our retelling comes to an end, I am reminded of a story that Maymie Roberts frequently told Vaughn and had shared in an interview with Hiram Silk. It was of the last times Georgina played the organ. Vaughn shared: "We had invited her over to dinner, and after dinner she asked me to play, and I said, 'Which would you rather I play, the organ or the piano?' She said, 'The organ.' She was very fond of organ music and sacred music. I played something for her and then asked her to play and sing to which she replied, 'Maymie, I shall never sing again.' But she got to the organ and she played and played, as if it were her last time, and it proved to be her last time. It was the last time she ever crossed over the road from her house to ours. She went back home that evening and I don't think she was ever out again. Shortly after that she was bedridden and very shortly after that, she died."

THE NIGHTINGALE RESTS HER VOICE AND SOUL

"Last but not least, the gift to guide pupils, characters and natures; to help to change them in necessary cases, and to show them a high ideal. If one could, one would try also to wake in them the love of God. This will make certain people smile, but in Art whether it be painting, sculpture, or music, love of beautiful things, love of human beings, and love of God is perceptible in the work exhibited and elevates it to the highest realms."
— Mathilde Marchesi, Georgina's Voice Teacher and Mentor (1821–1913)

ON EASTER SUNDAY, APRIL 23, 1935, Newfoundland lost its Nightingale. Georgina's celestial voice was stilled. She was surrounded by her roses and her many beloved pets at her Twillingate home. Her sister Rose and her best friend, Maymie Roberts, were by her side.

Georgina's talents, voice, and heart were first heard and shared in St. Peter's Church at Twillingate. Her church had witnessed and cradled the sounds of sorrow, joy, of stories told and memories shared, and reflections embraced and felt. And now this church witnessed her passing with a silent remembrance, for the voice that once filled its walls and soaring ceilings was no longer to be heard. Georgina's cousin Jean (Stirling) Pratt wrote, "Perhaps the glorious voice of Toulinguet was heard again that day in the celestial choir. For on earth they had said 'She had the voice of an angel.'" (*Sunday Miscellany*, 1955)

Sadly, there was no "horse-drawn carriage" to carry our provincial songbird to her final resting place, overlooking the ocean at Snelling Cove, on the sad and snowy day she was laid to rest. In true Newfoundland fashion, there was no spring in sight when Georgina passed on that snowy Easter Sunday. Up over the small hill from St. Peter's Church, Georgina was drawn in her casket by Twillingate gentlemen, carrying the body, heart, and voice of Georgina Stirling, Newfoundland's Nightingale of the North, to her grave. A few weeks after Georgina passed, Fred F. Jardine, who had written the Testimonial which was presented to Georgina in 1895 at St. John's, sympathetically wrote in honour of her for the *Evening Telegram* on May 16, 1935. Here are a few more of his words:

> "On Easter day a life ended, a voice was stilled and a great heart entered into rest. . . . To all lovers of real music that passing brings back beautiful memories, and although tinged with sorrow, they are beautiful to look back on. To look back to that shining star of the musical firmament of dear Newfoundland, Georgina Twillingate Stirling.

> "How fragile indeed is the fabric of fame? Yet, lesser lives have been perpetuated and lesser names engraven on the altar of the fatherland. Who in those days that knew her and heard the glorious voice, the vibrant timbre, the musical culture, that issued in those magnificent arias, from the throat of the gifted daughter of Twillingate and Newfoundland . . . can forget her? To know Georgina in those days of her triumphs, in her glorious singing days, was to know a splendid unspoiled type of artiste. Kind, affable and willing, to her native land she gave something that in that era was a most valuable thing: the service of her glorious voice. The touch of a famous diva, fresh from the hands of a famous molder of operatic stars; the real touch that had enthralled those that had heard her.

> "Georgina Stirling's striking figure and physique and the glorious quality, richness and roundness of her voice, electrified her charmed audience. . . . Now that heart and voice is stilled forever. . . . May the earth lie lightly on the body of Georgina Stirling. She was a very lovable woman and a great lover of her native land. She is survived by her sister (Miss Rose) whose devotion to her sister (Miss Georgie) is proverbial. This country's sympathy is with her, especially all lovers of good music, that Georgie Stirling knew so well."

ON THE BEAUTIFULLY WARM SUMMER DAY of July 19, 1964, Marie Toulinguet received the long-awaited praise for her life and achievements of which she was so deserving. How divinely fitting and serendipitous that my grandparents, Goldie and Calvin Evans, and my great-grandparents, Minnie (Waterman) and Gordon Locke, were in attendance that day to remember sweet Georgina. Droves of people gathered in Snelling Cove cemetery, overlooking the ocean, where Georgina had been lowered into her grave almost thirty years before. The only sunshine that would feel as sweet on Georgina's face besides that of Italy was that of Twillingate. The sun was shining down on her that day as people from across the island gathered to honour her. Also in attendance that day to mark the important occasion were Archdeacon L. Norman, to represent the Bishop of Newfoundland, and Constable Reeves of the RCMP, representing the State. Reverend A. R. Brett delivered a touching tribute:

> "My fellow Newfoundlanders, we are gathered here in the historic Church of St. Peter's to pay our respects to a great and historic Newfoundlander, Miss Georgina Stirling, 'our prima donna, the Songstress of Newfoundland.' It was in this church, which is now one hundred and twenty-two years old, that Miss Georgie's voice was first aired in public. I know very little about the personality or ability of Miss Stirling, but I hope that this assemblage today will make us all the more informed and appreciative of this outstanding Newfoundlander. I hope to portray for you some of the admiration and love that those who knew her, for her ability, had for Miss Georgina. I propose to do this by giving you some extracts, which I have taken, from the writings of those who have conveyed to me their appreciation for the contribution Miss Georgina has made to our history."

GEORGINA WAS THE HEROINE OF HER own opera and her own life. She poured her heart and soul into her passions. She lived for her art. Georgina soared to the "dizzying heights of fame," and she felt and endured every heartache of life that no human can escape. She shared her love and her light by example. She struggled in her humanity, and she triumphed in her healing. She lived a richly textured life in spite of her passage through some deep valleys, giving of herself in service to others and through the myriad of gifts she possessed.

Georgina lived the hero's journey. Georgina has become my hero, my muse, my example of what's important in this one life we have to live. Georgina lived her "heart's obsession," and isn't it something by which we can all be inspired? I, too, echo the words of Georgina's best friend, Maymie Roberts: "Her humility, her fame, and her kindly nature and her faults. I loved her. That's the only way I can put it, really." Dear, sweet Georgina, rest in peace and in song. Your life and legacy will never be forgotten. You voice will be carried forth and reborn in this retelling for generations to come. Brava!

NIGHTINGALE SINGS

Hear her cry 'midst the gulls . . . where wild waves roar . . .
'Neath the grave, songs unsung, come rise up.
Whispers recalled, forget-me-not
Gentle Lark, sing your prayers.

Drawn to rest forever more, this voice is still.
Heavy heart, precious Lark, pray peace comes.
Over the waves, live your songs, carry your heart back to life.

Odi il pianto suo fra i gabbiani . . .
ove selvagge le onde urlano . . .
Sotto il sepolcro, si innalzano non celebrati i canti.
Nobili: il suo cuore e la sua voce,
in quiete, rimarranno in eterno.
Divine, possano le sue melodie
essere udite sull'oceano d' onde
per le quali ella era solita cantare.
La gemmea voce dell'amabile Lark
eternamente, vivrà nel rimembrar nostro.

English translation of Italian lyrics:

Drawn to her final resting place, on a horseless carriage,
The Nightingale of the North is now at peace with the rest of the world.
Her great heart and voice is stilled forever.
May the earth lay lightly on her body where faded flowers grace a mossy floor.
May her celestial melodies be heard dancing on the ocean waves she so often sang to.
The voice of this gentle Lark so fair, live on in our memories forever.

— Original Song in Dedication of our "Nightingale of the North" by Tonia Evans Cianciulli

ACKNOWLEDGEMENTS
BY CALVIN D. EVANS

WHEN WE BIRTHED THE IDEA of writing a new book about Georgina Stirling, while sitting together in the Centre for Newfoundland Studies at Memorial University in May 2017, it had been as a result of finding three new pieces of information about Georgina which were not in Amy Louise Peyton's book, *Nightingale of the North*. We could not possibly have had any idea at that time of the amount of material that would almost immediately start coming our way from multiple sources. Soon the trickle became a flood, new material arriving up to the day before we submitted our manuscript to our publisher. We are enormously grateful to the many people who helped us put this book together. We could not have done it without your generous help.

NEWFOUNDLAND, AS A WHOLE, and Twillingate in particular, owe an enormous debt of gratitude to Amy Louise Peyton for her book on Georgina Stirling, entitled *Nightingale of the North*, and we as authors echo that strong sentiment. We are grateful for the enormous amount of research Amy Louise completed and the many sources she identified. Thanks to that book, Georgina Stirling will never be forgotten—which was Amy Louise's intention in writing it. We hope that our efforts will meet the desire of many new readers to know more about Georgina Stirling, and complement what Amy Louise has already accomplished through her research and dedication toward assuring that Georgina would be forever remembered. Because of our additional research, and through the help of many new researchers and unselfish helpers, we are fortunate in being able to add much new material not previously identified and to correct or elaborate on statements made by Ms. Peyton.

We have met with the children of Amy Louise and Ernest Peyton—Kent Peyton, Carol Fitzpatrick, and Evelyn Peyton Murphy—during our visit to St. John's in August 2018, and we have kept in touch with them by telephone and email since then. They have been generous and diligent in responding to our requests for additional help and clarification of several issues.

We acknowledge with much gratitude the enormous contribution made to our project by Milton Anstey, a retired Royal Canadian Mounted Police officer and Provincial Security Manager with Sobeys Group Inc., an ardent examiner and long-time researcher of Newfoundland and Labrador history and genealogy, particularly respecting the early inhabitants of Notre Dame Bay. He is truly an intrepid and thorough researcher. Quite independently of our project, and driven by an enormous curiosity, he has compiled a body of unique information that would benefit any Newfoundland researcher. The key phrases of his research are "hard evidence, credible records, and physical evidence."

We are enormously grateful in retrospect to Hiram Silk of CBC Grand Falls for the interviews which he did with the people of Twillingate and Notre Dame Bay from the 1950s to the late 1980s and which provide much additional material about Georgina Stirling's last seven years in Twillingate. The twenty-six interviews which we reviewed provide many new perspectives on what life was like for Georgina after she returned to her home from Europe.

A very perceptive real estate agent in St. John's, Chris O'Dea, when selling a piece of property for Karen Stirling of St. John's (who spends half of each year in the United States), just happened to mention that he and his wife and other family members had just returned from an operatic concert presented by Tonia Evans Cianciulli in Twillingate in honour of Georgina Stirling, and would there be a possible connection to that Stirling family of Twillingate? There was, in fact, and Karen Stirling, a descendant of Dr. William Archibald Stirling (Dr. Stirling, Sr., Georgina's grandfather, through his fourth son, Edgar Charles Thomas Ridley Stirling), said that she actually had several letters that Georgina and her sisters had written to their father in Twillingate in the 1880s. She told Chris O'Dea that she would be prepared to share these documents with the people who were writing the new book on Georgina Stirling. Thus, the material came to us, scanned, indexed, catalogued, and transcribed by the Stirling family of Newfoundland. We were given access to the material by Chris O'Dea and Karen Stirling in October 2018, and we are supremely grateful for their generosity in sharing these valuable documents with us. Excerpts from these letters and documents are included in this book. Our correspondence with the Stirling family of Newfoundland has continued through to February 2019.

We are also grateful to Robert Walter Parsons, formerly of Grand Falls, Newfoundland and Labrador, and for many years working in Toronto and now living in Newcastle, Ontario, for sharing valuable information on the controversial recording which many have maintained for years is the voice of Georgina Stirling. Robert is a descendant of the Peyton family, a great-grandson of Thomas Peyton, who was the son of John Peyton, Jr. Robert has pursued a long-time interest in Georgina Stirling and has done diligent research over the years, particularly on the subject of the controversial recording. Robert's document on Georgina Stirling, written in the early 1960s, has been deposited in the National Library of Canada in Ottawa by Ed Manning of CBC London. Robert is a retired social work consultant and for many years served in that capacity with what is now the Toronto District School Board. His contribution is included in the chapter on the Georgina recording.

Twice in August 2018, during our visit to Twillingate, we met with Lorna Stuckless, who for twenty-four years was the curator of the Twillingate Museum. She was the curator when, on a special day in her life, Amy Louise and Ernest Peyton arrived with several bags full of costumes and memorabilia which had belonged to Georgina Stirling and which had been

safeguarded in the Back Harbour home of Will Peyton, Georgina's cousin. It is largely through the deep interest and expertise of Lorna that this material is now on display in the Twillingate Museum. Several other gifts and donations from the public have been added to this, and all materials are beautifully displayed in three rooms at the museum. Though Lorna is long since retired, it is evident from two afternoons spent with her in the summer of 2018 that her enthusiasm for "things Georgina" has not slackened. In recognition of her enormous contri-

Tonia takes a selfie with Georgina Stirling in the Twillingate Museum during her first visit in 2017. (Author photo)

bution to preserving valuable aspects of Twillingate's amazing history, Lorna was recently presented with the Queen's Jubilee Award. Sadly, Lorna died in late 2018.

We are grateful for the assistance given to us by Beverly (Compton) Warford of Point Leamington, Newfoundland and Labrador, recently retired public/school librarian, in helping us identify family connections in Notre Dame Bay and referring us to Jill Marshall, to whom we are likewise enormously grateful for searching her voluminous database on the Notre Dame Bay area, for sharing a photo of Maymie Roberts, Georgina Stirling's neighbour and "best friend" during the period 1929–1935, and for introducing us to Pearl Legge of Howley, Newfoundland and Labrador. And we are grateful to Pearl Legge, a former teacher and at age eighty-one years a trained and not yet retired bookkeeper with working experience in Newfoundland, Ottawa, the Northwest Territories, and Nova Scotia, in which province she is presently the bookkeeper for a medical firm which is owned and operated by her son. Pearl has a youthful attitude toward life, the avid curiosity of a serious researcher, and an energy that knows no bounds. Pearl had a summer home at Robert's Arm and was the next-door neighbour to Maymie (Roberts) Hewlett there from about 1963 to 1971 and corresponded with her faithfully until Maymie's death in 1984.

We acknowledge with gratitude the contributions made to our project by the staff at the Memorial University of Newfoundland Archives Division, and the Centre for Newfoundland Studies, and in particular to Colleen Quigley, Bert Riggs, Paulette Noseworthy, and Linda White. They worked tirelessly and enthusiastically to identify relevant material for our project and photocopy the identified materials during our short but frenzied visits during two summers.

We offer our thanks to local Twillingate people who have helped us with tracing family connections, including connections to the Stirling family and Georgina Stirling in particular, supplying photocopies of local events connected with Georgina Stirling, referring us to people who had additional information, identifying local trails and other sites which the Stirling sisters and their cousins in Back Harbour would have traversed in their youth, and identifying the prevailing winds at Twillingate at various seasons of the year and the directional locations of other sites. We mention in particular Deborah (White) Bourdon, Eleanor and Alfred Manuel, Linda Blondin, Irene Pardy, and Eric Waterman. We are grateful also to Elmo and Eleanor Baird, formerly of Twillingate, but now residing in St. John's, and their daughter Margaret (Baird) O'Dea for supplying additional information on the Stirlings, and about other Twillingaters with whom the Stirlings interacted.

We appreciate additional information supplied by Margo (Margaret Drover) Evans, daughter of Jessie Troake and Ted Drover. Margo's mother nursed Georgina at the Twillingate Memorial Hospital when Georgina was a patient there in 1934. Troy Mitchell, now of St. John's and formerly of Durrell, Twillingate, has provided us with a picture of the Stirling root cellar on the former Stirling property in Twillingate. This root cellar may date from the 1850s, when Dr. Stirling settled on the property. The root cellar was undoubtedly used by Georgina and Rose Stirling, because they, like their father, were avid gardeners, dependent on the root cellar for securing their food through the long winters. Troy is involved with international food security and is a board member for Ottawa-based USC Canada—thus his interest in root cellars as a traditional method of securing food. He has built a website that indicates the location of more than 230 roots cellars on Twillingate's North and South Islands. The work was done in 2008;

photographs were taken by the late Otto Sansome of Twillingate, and his widow, Louise Sansome, mapped each root cellar location. There are more root cellars in Twillingate than in Elliston, Trinity Bay, "the root cellar capital of the world." Root cellar enthusiasts from as far away as Norway have come to view the Twillingate sites and talk to local people.

We are enormously grateful to Jeff Golden of Minnesota, USA, great-grandson of Kate (Stirling) Putzki—Georgina's sister—for material which he has shared with us through the fall and winter of 2018–19, particularly excerpts from many of Kate's letters which affirm the fact that she moved to Chicago almost a year earlier than was thought (very probably early in the New Year of 1883). Kate's letters also make clear that she and Georgina had left Twillingate together by mid-fall of 1882 and Georgina began her music and vocal studies in Toronto in January 1883, rather than in September of 1883, as previously believed. Kate's letters seem to suggest, but do not conclusively prove, that Janet almost certainly did her nursing training in England, and not in either Toronto or Chicago, as well as correcting several other conclusions which we were in danger of drawing because of the scarcity of reliable documentation.

These letters of Kate's are a mine of solid and reliable information. Kate was a remarkable young woman, trusted at age twenty-two by her father to be his reporter from the mining sites at Betts Cove, Newfoundland, and other mining sites nearby, trusted to take the fifteen-and-a-half-year-old Georgina to Toronto and get her settled there under Mrs. Jessie Murray's general supervision, trusted to be his go-between with Mrs. Murray in all affairs concerning Georgina's music and academic studies and reporting regularly to him, as she did very fully and faithfully over the two-and-a-half-year period that Georgina was studying in Toronto. Jeff Golden had made two trips to Twillingate, in 1980 and 1984, met with Maymie (Roberts) Hewlett both times, met Hiram Silk of CBC Grand Falls, as well as Amy Louise and Ernest Peyton, shortly after *Nightingale of the North* was published. Jeff has a continuing interest in operatic performances and now has the

The Stirling family root cellar at Twillingate, where Georgina and Rose preserved their vegetables during the winters (Courtesy of Troy Mitchell, Twillingate Root Cellars)

links to Tonia's various websites, as well as an interest in Twillingate and in fashioning an authentic history of the Stirling family.

Georgina's piano, gifted to her about 1878 by her father, and constructed by Broadwood & Sons in London, England. Repurchased from an auctioneer in St. John's in 1979 and presently located in Calgary, Alberta. (Courtesy of Keltie Matthews)

In August of 2018 we were contacted by Keltie Matthews of Calgary, Alberta, informing us that she had purchased Georgina Stirling's piano from an auctioneer in St. John's in 1978 when she and her family lived there for one year only. She was informed by the auctioneer, Carl Sterrett, that it was indeed the piano of the opera singer Georgina Stirling. The piano has been in Keltie's possession ever since, even as they have moved around the world in various jobs. Keltie is still in the process of authenticating that the piano did indeed belong to Georgina. It is a Broadwood piano constructed in London, England, by a Scottish craftsman, very probably in the 1860s. Dr. Stirling would have bought the piano for Georgina when she was about ten or eleven years of age, (say about 1878), and it is not known whether it was a new or used piano at that time. All the furnishings in the Stirling house were sold under the direction of Edward

Linfield, a local merchant, shortly after Rose Stirling's death in November 1937. Sterrett would not have been the first owner of the piano following the sale. He came to Newfoundland in 1966 from Belfast, Ireland. Perhaps someone will come forward with details as to who previous owners were, so that the piano can be authenticated as belonging to the Nightingale of the North. We are ever so grateful to Keltie for sharing her extensive research on the brand and, most recently, sending us a picture of the piano.

We express our thanks to Bruce Manuel and Brent English of Avondale, Newfoundland, for providing us with pictures of several of Georgina's artifacts which were given to Bruce by his friend Hiram Silk, especially the lap organ that Georgina carried with her on all her travels and the resplendent domed night light which had been gifted to Georgina somewhere in Europe. Bruce and Brent operate an antique shop in Holyrood.

Dr. Lynn McDonald, professor of sociology and anthropology at the University of Guelph in Ontario, came to our rescue in early February 2019 in helping us to access the London Metropolitan Archives and identify where Janet Stirling had done her nursing training. Professor McDonald is a specialist in Florence Nightingale Studies at the university. We had found an entry for Janet in J. Abbott's Names List at the University of Guelph but were unable to interpret the abbreviations and acronyms, and Professor McDonald did the interpretation for us.

We are especially grateful to Stephen R. Clarke of Toronto, who has dedicated most of his life to the study of singers and singing styles of the past and who, as an avid educator, shares his extensive expertise and resources through regular classes with artists of the Canadian Opera Company Ensemble Studio and students in voice

Georgina's lap organ with bellows, which she carried on all her travels (Courtesy of Bruce Manuel and Brent English)

and opera at the University of Toronto Faculty of Music. His generosity of knowledge and time to help us assess the authenticity of what had been thought to be a recording of Georgina Stirling's voice is very much appreciated.

We would also like to thank Breakwater Books for permission to use quotes from Gary L. Saunders's book *Doctor Olds of Twillingate* and Amy Louise Peyton's *Nightingale of the North*.

ACKNOWLEDGEMENTS
by TONIA EVANS CIANCIULLI

WHILE SOME HAVE BEEN MENTIONED and praised throughout my writing, and by Calvin Evans, I would like to express my deep gratitude to these integral people who helped me bring this labour of love to life.

In acknowledgment of my precious grandfather, Calvin D. Evans. It has been a once-in-a-lifetime privilege to share this journey with you as you guided me in finding my voice as a writer. I thank you and my grandmother, Goldie, for being adoringly supportive of my singing and now writing. Goldie, thank you for supporting us *both* with your patience and love throughout our tireless research and writing.

Frank Cianciulli, my husband and knight in shining armor. Thank you for believing in me, for all your support and love as I bring my musical dreams to fruition. And to our children, Sophia and Anthony, for being Mommy's biggest fans, always checking on me backstage, even singing by my side. I am so blessed to have the best family ever. The best is yet to come!

Joanne Evans, my mom, you have been with me every step of the way. You're my greatest example, mentor, cheerleader, and best friend. Thank you for being a huge part of this particular journey as you travelled back "home" with me each time, being the loving, doting, and supportive mom I needed. Snowballs, homemade bread, and Newfoundland beach walks forever!

Jody Locke, thank you for being my artistic soul sister across ocean waves, always inspiring and believing in me. You planted the precious seed of nurturing my Newfoundland roots and have encouraged me every step of the way. I've cherished sharing this journey with you.

Tanya Chernova, for your loving support and treasured friendship. I am grateful to you for physically being by my side, encouraging me, as I neared the finish line, for all our late nights of fine-tuning and editing while our children played, and "birthing" yet another vision together!

Artist Pandora Topp, you joined us on this cherished journey in September 2017 in preparation for the second round of *Nightingale Sings* concerts in August 2018. Your artistic and extensive experience performing on the life and music of Edith Piaf was invaluable to us. You assisted us in creating the poignant flow of music and narrative that weaved throughout our program, helping us to create the perfect partnership in the churches of Newfoundland as we portrayed Georgina's music and life's legacy.

Maestro Kerry Stratton, you've been a valued mentor and friend for many years and a beautiful example of what a true entrepreneurial Canadian artist is. I am also grateful for your significant support in crafting *Nightingale Sings* and your poignant foreword.

My dear friend Anna Bateman, for your support and guidance training Sophia to perform the *Nightingale Sings* concerts with me and on the Georgina Stirling companion album.

My high school English teacher and treasured friend, Laurie Laughlin-Hillier, your trustworthy council and encouraging voice is forever in my ear as I write.

My friend and colleague Dann Mitton, many thanks for your valued contribution as you put your doctoral of vocal pedagogy to good use!

Thank you Eric Alper, my publicist, for your passion and expertise in helping me share Georgina Stirling and Ron Hynes music across Canada.

My voice professors, teachers, and mentors—Brian McIntosh, Manny Perez, and Darryl Edwards. You've worked tirelessly to help me reach my full potential as a performer and singer and to interpret the music and essence of Georgina in my Nightingale concerts. Also, thank you for your wise counsel and for sharing your expertise throughout my research.

We are incredibly indebted to Vaughn Harbin of Toronto, and previously of Grand Falls, NL, for his generosity of time and the large amount of material that he supplied to us on Georgina Stirling through his cousin Maymie Roberts, who was Georgina's best friend in Twillingate during the years 1929 to 1935. Vaughn's gracious gifts of photos, sheet music, and descriptive material have enriched and enlarged our knowledge of Georgina.

Daphne Wheeler-Anstey, Linda Gaye Blondin, and Lorna Stuckless, such amazing ladies! Thank you for your contribution in passionately preserving Georgina's memory at the Twillingate Museum. And thank you for your energetic support as I join forces with you to share in this recollection and preservation of our Nightingale of the North.

Flanker Press, thank you for believing in us and for taking a chance on me, a brand new author. Your support is integral in keeping the legacy of Georgina Stirling alive.

Coast to coast, to my entire treasured family and supportive friends, thank you for ALWAYS believing in me!

APPENDICES ONE TO SIX
BY CALVIN D. EVANS

APPENDIX ONE: BRINGING GEORGINA STIRLING INTO THE TWENTY-FIRST CENTURY

THE TRIBUTE STATEMENTS THAT FOLLOW should be viewed primarily as a tribute to Georgina Stirling herself, her music and her songs, because they form part of the amazing legacy that she has left to her community of Twillingate, to her island home of Newfoundland, and to her many audiences on two continents and in many cities and towns throughout the world. We all pay tribute to her astonishing and beautiful voice which comforted, uplifted, and deeply moved so many grateful publics.

Following are some of the recent testimonies connected with Tonia Evans Cianciulli's attempts to revive Georgina Stirling's repertoire of songs and hymns and to establish the enduring quality of the songs themselves and to recapture the effects that these songs must have had on Georgina's original audiences. Even these recent comments should be viewed as a further tribute to the songs and music and legacy of Georgina Stirling.

* * * * * * *

Comments on Tonia's singing of Ron Hynes's song "Marie"
A comment from David Pomeroy, world-renowned Newfoundland opera singer who is presently residing in St. John's. David is the grandson of the celebrated Newfoundland musician and music professor Ignatius Rumboldt. David returns to St. John's to present concerts on occasion and is a sometime-teacher of vocal master classes at Memorial University of Newfoundland: "After viewing Tonia's version of 'Marie,' I was transported back home to my loving province of Newfoundland and Labrador and all the wonders it has to offer. As an international opera singer from the province and listening to stories as a child from my grandfather about Madame Stirling, I was delighted to learn that Tonia had done something special in the renowned soprano's honour. When Tonia combines

her beautiful voice and spirit with the legend of Ron Hynes's music it becomes transcendent. I hope this song and version reaches many hearts from Newfoundland and beyond as it did mine."

A comment from Charles MacPhail, for many years the manager of Newfoundland singer/songwriter Ron Hynes, before Ron's death in 2016: "The first time hearing Tonia's rendition of 'Marie' I was flooded with emotion, the goosebumps led the way to tears and the memories of Ron writing this hauntingly beautiful piece. I am sure Mr. Hynes would be smiling to hear your lovely voice deliver his lyrics and music in such an exquisite way."

A comment from Chris LeDrew, Newfoundland singer/songwriter, and close friend and colleague of Ron Hynes: "Tonia Cianciulli's beautiful rendition of Ron Hynes's 'Marie' brings to life the longing and emotional power of this story as told through Hynes's poignant lyrics. Cianciulli's operatic mastery adds a majesty to Hynes's finely crafted song and brings us that much closer to feeling what Marie would have experienced in her own life as a world-renowned opera singer."

A comment from actor and author and Order of Canada recipient Gordon Pinsent on receiving a copy of the video of "Marie": "Love it. Carried me away. Mother of all goosebumps. I'm going to say: Sure, I knows her!! x Gordon"

A comment from William Brenton, a friend of guitarist Glenn Simmons, who played for Ron Hynes on his final album just before Ron died with cancer: "Can you hear that? The remarkable sound of Ron leading the world beyond in a standing ovation for Tonia! Your rendition nails the beautiful words, the haunting melody, and Ron's tremendous talent as one-of-a-kind wordsmith. Thank you so much for this outstanding performance and Hats Off to the excellent piano played by Evan Smith, and to the videographer. A marvellous musical production. Tonia, the world awaits your extraordinary talent."

A comment from Tony Ploughman of Fred's Records (music store) in St. John's, Newfoundland and Labrador: "Tonia, thank you for sharing this blissful video with me and everyone else. It's one of the jewels of the crown on Ron's final album. I was left pondering the soulmate factor Ron may have held with Georgina Stirling the first 3 or 4 times I heard his recording and I'm glad to say you and your associates have embraced the essence of the song in this lovely homage. Cheers, Tony."

A note from a former resident of Twillingate, Bruce Roberts, on "Marie," Tonia Evans Cianciulli and Evan Smith's Ron Hynes cover: "I was born in Twillingate. I left there to move to Toronto at age 20; that was back in 1967. I have often heard the story of Georgina Stirling but, I confess, I never found it to be that interesting. I expect it was mostly because I never really thought about it. But this video has really given the story a new life in my mind. A well-written song, sung beautifully, against the backdrop of Twillingate scenery, has created a great interest in me in the character Marie Toulinguet. Is this her beautiful ghost strolling the hills of our hometown? It all makes me homesick. Bravo to all involved in this creation!"

* * * * * * *

Comments on Tonia's singing of her own composition, "Nightingale Sings"
Linda Blondin, curator of the Twillingate Museum, 2000 to 2017: "Tonia, greetings from Twillingate. I was so excited when I returned from St. John's to receive your new song and video. It is so beautifully haunting!! I watched it and didn't realize until the end that I had tears rolling down my face; it is amazing!! When I think of Georgina's final return to Twillingate, there was none of the former fanfare, and then the number of years she lay in an unmarked grave it always made me so sad for her, but now you have changed all that. You are bringing her back to new generations and to the world. Thank you so much for keeping her memory alive. Keep in touch. Love, Linda."

* * * * * * *

Comments on Tonia's Concerts
Chad Stride, music director, organist (Wesley United Church, St. John's, NL), conductor (Cantus Vocum Chamber Choir): "Newfoundland and Labrador history reveals a vibrant palette of colourful personalities. It is with thanks and admiration we see Tonia Cianciulli recount the success and contribution of our celebrated opera great, Georgina Stirling. Tonia's work enables all to enjoy an uplifting addition to our history pages. Additionally, Tonia's voice is a testament to our musical wealth."

Hedy and Julius Lis, now living in Montreal, were present at Tonia's concert at St. Peter's Church in Twillingate on August 25, 2017. Both are avid opera lovers who travel the world, attending the opera seasons at the Met in New York, La Scala, Opera D'Montreal, etc: "On our first day in Twillingate we were informed of Tonia's upcoming concert at St. Peter's Church and we immediately made reservations to attend. We truly enjoyed Tonia's performances, an absolutely wonderful experience in Twillingate. Tonia is a beautiful lady with a voice to match. We were so glad to have been there. Tonia's connection to and love of the late Georgina Stirling provided a beautiful and unexpected evening. Bravo, Tonia! The next day we visited the Twillingate Museum, where two whole rooms are totally dedicated to the memorabilia and costumes of Georgina Stirling and where one can listen to one of her recorded arias. This gave us a fuller understanding of this lady's past and her love of opera. And it was at the museum that we again had a few wonderful moments with the beautiful Tonia."

A comment by Dr. Douglas Dunsmore, Director of Choral Music at Gower Street United Church in St. John's, Newfoundland and Labrador, and retired professor of music at Memorial University of Newfoundland (following the August 19, 2018, concert at Gower Street): "Thank you for a job so well done yesterday. Your singing was beautiful and your presentation (musically and dramatically) was magical indeed! Jason's accompaniments were beautifully done and the combination of Calvin's spoken word and your artistry as a singer and actress combined to recreate Georgina before our very ears and eyes. We were all transported to another time and place! It was lovely! Thank you all so much."

A testimonial from the Very Reverend Dr. Marion Pardy, 37th Moderator of the United Church of Canada, Minister Emeritus of Gower Street United Church in St. John's, NL, and summer resident of Twillingate:

"A six-foot monument stands erect in St. Peter's Anglican Church Cemetery, Twillingate, NL in perpetual memory of Georgina Stirling (1867–1935), known also as Mlle Marie Toulinguet, Songstress of Newfoundland, Nightingale of the North, Miss Georgie, and Georgie. This international-renowned opera singer is described as one who 'entertained royalty with her voice and the poor by the kindness of her heart.' Mlle Toulinguet's legacy is now a 'living' memory. Opera singer Tonia Evans Cianciulli, with her Newfoundland birthplace roots, meshes past with present as she transcends the years with her soaring soprano voice and by her 'Georgina' music research, resulting in this book, *The Heart's Obsession: An Intimate Biography of Newfoundland Songstress Georgina Stirling*, to evoke a yearning within for that which is eternal. Her deep commitment to her cause resonates in her voice and in her writing. Those who have had the privilege of listening to Tonia as she graced us with her passionate, engaging re-enactment, blending her own voice with that of Georgina Stirling, Mlle Toulinguet, have been doubly blessed."

An excerpt from the Gower Street United Church fall newsletter 2018 in a column entitled "The Nightingale of the North Returns": "Tonia's voice made that August service one of the highlights of our year; it rang out clear and strong, filling the acoustically friendly confines of Gower with an incredibly joyous sound. Jason Locke's piano provided the perfect degree of accompaniment for Tonia's pure and haunting voice and Calvin's erudite commentary on Georgina's life brought a unity that blended effortlessly with the rest of the service. The spontaneous applause after each of the numbers and a standing ovation at the end were indicative of the delight and inspiration that Tonia and her Georgina Stirling persona brought to the Gower congregation and the many guests who attended the service."

Following are comments from all three of Amy Louise Peyton's children following Tonia's concert at Gower Street United Church on August 19, 2018. Amy Louise Peyton was the author of the book *Nightingale of the North*.

From Kent Peyton: "As I sat in the church (Gower Street) where Georgina Stirling actually sang, I was truly amazed at the power and beauty of Tonia's soprano voice, and I kept looking high up in the ceiling thinking how my mother would have loved to hear that great performance."

From Evelyn Peyton Murphy: "Tonia Evans Cianciulli gave an outstanding performance of songs from Georgina Stirling's repertoire. Her hauntingly beautiful voice and strong stage presence were her own, but gave a fitting and touching tribute to Marie Toulinguet, the Nightingale of the North."

From Carol Fitzpatrick: "As Tonia's beautiful voice filled the historic Gower Street Church with selections from Georgina Stirling's original programs, I felt that I was being transported back in time to the heyday of Georgina's career. The setting and performance combined to create the sense that I was in attendance at one of her magnificent concerts. It was a memorable experience! What better way is there to honour Georgina's memory than through beautiful music and song?"

A comment from Daphne Wheeler-Anstey, manager and curator of the Twillingate Museum since 2017: "As I sat in my seat in St. Peter's Anglican Church, the place where our Nightingale Georgie started her singing career, I felt transported in time as the magnificent Tonia started to sing. Her voice wraps itself around you like a soft breeze! The combination of story and song are fairly mesmerizing, it fills your heart!"

A tribute to Tonia Evans Cianciulli by Phyllis Wareham Langdon, who over the years had a full career teaching, including children's choirs and music festivals in Newfoundland

and Montreal: "I had heard that Tonia was visiting Twillingate to do a concert in memory of Georgina Stirling. A day or so later, I heard that Tonia would be coming here to sing at the Sunday service. To my surprise Tonia phoned me and said she would be singing three numbers—*Lead Kindly Light*, *It is Well With My Soul*, and *The Holy City*, two of which are my favourites. She showed poise and a high degree of skill and her voice had a professional quality. I found her performance uplifting and inspiring. I was sure the congregation felt as I did, and I saw a number of people wiping away tears. I had to focus hard on the music sheet or I may have done the same. It was wonderful to be given the opportunity to hear those old songs from years gone by and have them sung by such a talented person."

APPENDIX TWO
TRANSCRIPT OF KATE STIRLING'S LETTER
OF OCTOBER 1, 1884

DEAR PAPA

Just a few lines respecting Georgie. I will quote from Mrs. Murray's letter. "I am glad to say Georgie seems quite interested in her studies and happy. I hope this pleasant state of things will last. She spends <u>four hours</u> and sometimes more a day in music practice. She has begun singing with Mrs. Bradley & is much pleased both with her teacher & her prospects of singing. Her organ practice is arranged, she gets her first lesson next Saturday. Martens thinks one lesson a week should suffice, as she is pretty well drilled in the theory. We have made a beginning at French and History & she is to have some special instruction from a good teacher in Arithmetic. I will write from time to time & will prompt Georgie to keep up her correspondence as she should. She is going to write from copies you sent her."

When here I made Georgie write a little every day & I found she could copy my hand-writing nearly exact. Her own writing at its best was very scratchy and uncharacteristic so I thought it better as she found it so easy, to let her adopt my style. Of course, there are many little peculiarities which she need not follow. Before she left I set her a number of copies. Mrs. Murray did not go into details. Of course, there are other studies she will take up. You have a general idea of how she spends her time and to my mind this ought to be quite satisfactory.

Grace was up last night, and we had a long talk together. They have a new girl as correspondent and she is no good. Skills well but ideas limited & does not suit Mr. Dean at all. Another old girl (Mrs. Weir) left on Saturday so Grace reigns supreme.

Had a letter from Janet last week. She does not seem to be very favorably impressed with St. Pierre.

Lizzie Clegg promised me that she would telegraph before leaving Toronto so that I might meet her here, but although I have not heard I'm sure she must have gone on, because I wrote her at Toronto last week and as yet have received no answer. Will write soon again.

Yours, Kate

APPENDIX THREE
THE CHILDREN OF DR. WILLIAM C. STIRLING AND ANN (PEYTON) STIRLING AS COMPILED BY MILTON ANSTEY

SINCE THERE ARE DISCREPANCIES in various sources regarding birthdates, names, and even the number of Stirling children, and since the church records were destroyed by a fire in the rectory in 1913, we have turned to a careful and consummate researcher in the person of Milton Anstey, a retired Newfoundland Royal Canadian Mounted Police officer who has practically made a profession of researching the families of Notre Dame Bay, Newfoundland and Labrador. We are grateful for these results of his painstaking research. We present here only the most basic information about each of the children. Additional information is disclosed in several of the chapters.

Lucinda (Lucy) STIRLING, born about 1847 (the birthdate of October 3 is written in a birthday book of one of Lucy's friends in 1897), did not marry, lived and worked in Chicago, USA, and London, England, and died at Twillingate at age sixty-five on March 18, 1913.

David Orestes STIRLING, born about 1849, and died the same year. His name is one of three sons of Dr. William and Ann (Peyton) Stirling on a headstone marker in St. Peter's churchyard cemetery. Added to this is an excerpt from the diary of Reverend Gordon Elliott (See Appendix Six) quoting "Source: an old diary in Twillingate" that one of the Stirling sons had drowned in a water barrel.

Eleanor Emma STIRLING, born in 1850, married Reverend Alfred S. Hill Winsor in 1877, died on January 12, 1925, at age seventy-four and was buried at Douglassville, Berks County, Pennsylvania, USA.

Rosetta Elizabeth Crosse (Rose) STIRLING, born about 1852, did not marry, lived in Italy and England for about twenty-eight years, died at age eighty-five on November 14, 1937, at Twillingate.

John Mayne STIRLING, also born about 1852, died at age three years July 1855, his name also appears on the headstone marker. It cannot be determined whether he was a twin with Rose.

Susannah Peyton STIRLING, born about 1856, married Reverend Thomas William Temple in 1881, died in 1924 at about age sixty-eight in Bromley, Kent, England, and was buried at Ticehurst, East Sussex.

Kate Stuart STIRLING, born January 25, 1859, married Paul Adolphe Putzki in 1886 at Chicago, USA, lived in Chicago, Indianapolis, and Washington, DC, and died April 3, 1941, at age eighty-two.

Janet Mary STIRLING, born 1861, died at age sixty-seven in 1928 in England, where she had worked as a professionally trained nurse for about thirty years. An ancient journal by a careful Twillingater records, "Mrs. Stirling confined of a daughter" on July 31, 1861, so this must be the record of Janet Stirling's birth.

Thought to be William Archibald Stirling about age seven or eight (Courtesy of Bruce Manuel and Brent English)

William Archibald STIRLING, born about May 1, 1864, died with typhoid fever at age ten years and four months on September 1, 1874. His name also appears on the headstone marker. Dr. Stirling was so ill at the time of his son's death that he was unable to attend the funeral; he recovered subsequently.

Georgina Ann STIRLING, born April 3, 1867, died at Twillingate April 21, 1935, at sixty-eight years of age. Georgina had lived in Toronto, Florence and Milan (Italy), Paris (France), London (England), and toured the European continent and the United States in many operatic presentations.

A possible fourth son named Peyton STIRLING (who is recorded in a Stirling birthday book, according to Amy Louise Peyton), who was very probably the toddler who accidentally drowned in the family's water barrel. He may have been born about 1871 or 1872 and was still living when the headstone marker was erected in the churchyard cemetery, and dealing with the tragedy of his death after losing three other sons may have naturally postponed the erection of yet another headstone marker. Another name, Edward, is suggested from some sources, so this boy may have been named Edward Peyton Stirling. Amy Louise Peyton asserts that the toddler's is one of the graves in the Stirling family plot, the others being Dr. Stirling, Ann (Peyton) Stirling, and Lucy Stirling.

It should be noted that Milton Anstey is reluctant to accept the existence of a fourth son because of the lack of "hard evidence." The same is true of Jeff Golden.

The picture of Lucy Stirling holding a small boy on page 36 of Amy Louise Peyton's book purports to be that of the boy who accidentally drowned, Georgina's "only brother," according to Amy Louise. The boy seems in the picture to be about two years old.

The testimony of Edna Burton (Appendix Six) must be considered very seriously. Edna asserts that it was her Grandfather Stuckless (John B. Stuckless) who discovered the body of the toddler at the bottom of the water barrel. John B. Stuckless was the father of Martin Stuckless, who worked for Georgina and Rose in the 1920s and 1930s, and who was born in 1882—the year that Ann (Peyton) Stirling died. John B. Stuckless lived from 1852 to 1916. These dates would have coincided with the events already outlined. Added to this is an excerpt from the diary of Reverend Gordon Elliott (See Appendix Six) quoting, "Source: an old diary in Twillingate" that one of the Stirling sons had drowned in a water barrel.

Curiously, when Kate (Stirling) Putzki made notes from the Stirling Family Bible during her visit in 1937,

Found in the Stirling family album, this could possibly be a picture of William Archibald Stirling and the elusive Peyton Stirling, shortly before Peyton's death by drowning. (Courtesy of Bruce Manuel and Brent English)

she made no mention of Peyton (Edward) Stirling—so we have only Amy Louise Peyton's reference to Peyton's name in the Stirling Birthday Book and of the fact that the boy who drowned was buried in the family plot along with his father, mother, and sister Lucy. We have also, as mentioned, the weighty testimony of Edna Burton about her Grandfather Stuckless.

This list of Stirling children is noticeably different from Amy Louise Peyton's list in her book *Nightingale of the North*. Lucy is actually the eldest daughter, Eleanor is the second daughter, and Rose is the third daughter. Amy Louise lists only one son—the elusive Peyton Stirling—whereas there were at least three and very likely four.

If we accept the premise that the Stirlings had eleven children, born to Dr. Stirling and Ann (Peyton) Stirling between about 1847 and (say) 1872, they would have been born over a period of about twenty-four years. This would have been a long birthing period for a woman, but many large families were produced in Newfoundland, and this conjecture is worth consideration.

APPENDIX FOUR
TRANSCRIPTS OF THE CONCLUSION OF GEORGINA'S FIRST LETTER AND THE TWO LAST LETTERS FROM FLORENCE, ITALY, 1889–90.

First Letter—Conclusion

A transcript of the first part of Georgina's first letter from Florence, Italy, to her father in Twillingate is given in one of Tonia Evans Cianciulli's chapters. The letter was started on December 1, 1889, and continued on December 4 and concluded on December 5. It is virtually certain that a line is missing between the first part of the letter and its continuation with the "gambling" theme, the card-playing, and the winning of "several pennies."

* * * * * * *

Conclusion of the First Letter

Dec. 5th. Last night we spent the evening at the big villa & amused ourselves by playing a game of cards, called twenty-one, can't say it was interesting. All their games are just meant to play for money, there is no <u>play</u> in them. Rose and I are both . . .

. . . one (won?) several pennies. I do not think though that we shall become gamblers through this success. I am very glad you have disposed of mink (?). Rose seems very well satisfied with the bargain. Do you know, I think my spelling gets worse every day and I account for it in this way, the difference in the pronunciation of the letters of the alphabet in Italian to the English, & of course all day long, I am practicing Italian. Janet tells me Tiga (probably the name of a dog, CDE) is very lame, now I do not believe Jan understands his appetite. I remember when I was home she used to think a little plate full was enough for him. She should boil lots of potatoes with the old fish tails & old meat bones that are no (so?) good.

For some time past the dog of the gardener has been ill. The young signor told me last night that he saw him in the yard dying & that he had not eaten any thing for some days. After Rose and I came into our house, I put on my coat and went down to look for him in the yard. I found him under an old part of the house not able to move, so I brought him up & gave him some warm bread & milk & kept him in all night, this morning he seems much better than he did. I would love to flog all the people who ill treat dumb beasts. When I am rich I shall found an asylum for poor cats and dogs. I think I like them better than I ever did & of course everyone laughs at me but I don't mind.

I am sending you an Italian almanac. I hope you will understand it (Dom Sunday) (Lun Monday) (Mar Tuesday) (Mer Wednesday) (Gio Thursday) (Ven Friday) (Sab Saturday). In full they are Domenica, Lunedi, Martedi, Merdcoledi, Gioredi, Venerdi, Sabato. I would have sent you an English one, but it was impossible to get a small one.

You will find the said article in a newspaper, hope it will reach safely.

Rose is waiting to go to the post, so I must close with much love.

Georgie

Note by CDE: It is intriguing to think that the "said article" may refer to an article printed in the *Twillingate Sun* (no date found yet) entitled "A Newfoundland Singer in Florence," in which Georgina is noted as "this promising debutante" who "rendered a soprano aria . . . with such distinction as completely to captivate even the critical taste of an audience in the second musical city of Italy." Or check the third letter on which the newspaper article may be commenting.

Second Letter
 Via Panconi
 Piano 2do
 San Gallo
 Feb. 28, 1890
 My dear Papa

You will no doubt think me very lazy, etc. because I have not written so long, but Rose can tell you that for the last month & a half, I have hardly had time to eat and drink, practicing for so many concerts. On Sunday I am singing in another concert—this time the Coutralls—all the people compliment me and tell me I have a most beautiful voice & with more study will become a <u>great</u> <u>artist</u>. There are three old professors who are specially delighted with my voice.

I make myself also very agreeable at the rehearsals telling funny stories, etc.—so that the people are always glad to see me. I have two practices and one lesson this evening so have only time to say good bye with much love to all.

Georgie

My son Cosimo sends his love.

Third Letter

Same address
March 28, 1890
My dear Pa

This morning we received your letter saying that you are much better which of course makes us much more comfortable. Today is as warm as any summer day I ever felt home. I only wish you were here to enjoy it.

On Monday night last I sang at a concert of a pianist, sang very well indeed & at the end of the evening was presented with an immense basket of flowers. The newspapers also spoke well of my singing next day. I am sending you one of the notices that they put on the walls, for the concert of the Violinista Torricelli. I also sang pretty well that night, but was not very well, so did not do as well as I should have done. The week after next I sing at another concert & next week "Holy Week" I sing the Contralto solos in a Stabat Mater to be given in the Spanish Chapel of Santa Maria Novella. Then I shall sing for the first time with an orchestra. I do not know how I shall get on I am sure because singing with fifty or sixty instruments is quite different to singing with a piano or organ. When I receive the beautiful flowers at these concerts I always think of Mrs. Hodge, also I had presented to me a bouquet "very large" of <u>double</u> <u>pink</u> Hyacinths. I thought if only Lethbridge could have seen them. The morning after the concert I always divide my flowers among my friends because I can never find enough vases to put them in. One day I had to put a lot in the Po (chamber pot?) I thought the servant would die laughing when she saw them.

My master has decided that—I am to go to Milan to study Dramatic. If I can manage it I should be there by the 1st of May. Vannuccini leaves Florence for London on the 28th of April. One night a little while ago we were invited to a private concert in the Palace of a gentleman here. I sang two operatic solos, a celebrated Violinist played once & the most distinguished Harp Professor in Italy played two solos on the harp, this composed the concert, afterwards there was a supper & a ball. Rose danced. I did not.

In the autumn I am to make my grand debut in opera, I believe in Milan. This letter is most dreadfully written but I have only a sharp pen to write with. I am just off to a rehearsal of the Stabat Mater so must close with much love to all my sons. My Italian son is in the country for a week.

Your loving daughter
Georgie

Note by CDE: "Lethbridge" must have been William Lethbridge, lay reader of St. Peter's Church in Twillingate. Note also that in the first letter Cosimo was referred to as "she." In this third letter Cosimo is her "son."

APPENDIX FIVE
TRANSCRIPT OF THE "PRINTED EDITED MANUSCRIPT"
MISS GEORGINA STIRLING

IN 1892, WHERE WE WERE IN PARIS, Madame Marchesi, a celebrated teacher of singing, directed our attention to a charming young lady who had just finished her lesson. "That pretty girl," said she to us in French, "possesses the finest mezzo-soprano voice I ever heard. It is a marvellous voice, and I predict a great future for her."

The young lady of whom she spoke was Miss Georgina Stirling, whose voice compass ranges from the lower G to the upper C. She was born at Twillingate, in the extreme north of Newfoundland, and is the only singer from that country who has ever been enterprising enough to come to England professionally. Much of her early life was spent in the open air and on the sea, and this freedom of existence gave strength to her body as well as to her voice. Such latitude and freedom was permitted to her that although the daughter of a physician of considerable standing in his profession she has been known when but a mere child to go twenty miles from land with a rope and knife to kill her seal and tow it home in triumph! To all her sports singing was an accompaniment, and long before she knew a note of music she charmed the air with vocal melody. On one occasion, on one of his frequent trips round the coast, Sir Edward Blake (sic; it was Sir Henry Arthur Blake), then Governor of Newfoundland, accidentally heard her sing. He was enraptured with her voice, and insisted upon her friends permitting her to study. At this time she was receiving an education to fit her for the position of an organist. On permission being given her to study singing, *hey presto, away* flies the lady to Florence, where she studied for opera under Vannuccini. After a time she made her *debut* at the Opera House at Borgo, in San Donini, just outside Parma, where she sang in "Trovatore" and "La Favorita."

Having thus tested her strength she came to London and was advised to go to Paris and study under Madame Marchesi, which she did for two years. She then returned to London and sang for Vert and Santley, the latter gentleman taking considerable interest in her. Amongst other good services he rendered he wrote a recommendatory letter for her to Sir Augustus Harris, which, however, she had no opportunity of presenting as she had accepted an engagement for Berlin. This was in 1893. She soon afterwards fell ill, and was compelled to return to Newfoundland in order to recruit her health. She stayed there for six months, again came to England and once more fell ill. This was particularly unfortunate for her, as no less than three engagements for oratorio were offered to her by Vert, which she was unable to accept. She gradually recovered her strength, and on April 28th last made her first London appearance at the Portman Rooms at Mr. Santley's concert. This function was a huge success. Miss Stirling made a great impression on the public, and as a result she has secured a multiplicity of engagements for the next four seasons. This was the more gratifying as Miss Stirling at this concert was a stranger in a strange land relying solely on her vocal abilities, and with not a friend present in the audience to give her countenance. She deserves success, for she is a plucky woman to come among us to try her chances. After the concert at the Portman Rooms she sang at Madamoiselle (sic) Pozzio's matinee on June 27th, and on the 28th sang at the Carmelite concert at the Queen's Hall. In that month she also sang at Mr. Henry Bird's concert at Kensington Town Hall. On July 3rd she appeared at Signor Tito Mattei's concert at the Queen's Hall.

Madame Melba has proved a most kind friend throughout the whole of Miss Stirling's career, and Miss Stirling is particularly grateful for the interest thus taken in her. We have heard that Miss Stirling accepts engagements for "At Homes," concerts, &c. If this be so we have no doubt her services will be constantly in requisition. Those who desire a successful "At Home" could not fail to achieve society distinction for themselves if they secured the services of this most accomplished singer. She is equally proficient in Italian, French or English, and we would add that Miss Stirling is a wonderful improvisatore, but although numerous offers have been made to her by continental and English publishers she will not under any circumstances allow her compositions to be published. Miss Stirling resides at 23, Sandwell Park, West Hampstead.

APPENDIX SIX
SUMMARIES OF IMPORTANT POINTS IN HIRAM SILK'S CBC INTERVIEWS FROM THE 1950s TO THE LATE 1980s: THE WITNESS OF GEORGINA'S COUSINS

GEORGINA (SCOTT) BUCKINGHAM WAS INTERVIEWED at Corner Brook in April 1987 when she was ninety years of age. She died in 1994 at age ninety-seven. Georgina Buckingham's mother, Annie, was the eldest daughter of Thomas and Mary Ann (Pearce) Peyton. Georgina Scott was, therefore, a cousin of Georgina Stirling but was thirty years her junior, born in 1897. Her father, William J. Scott, was a magistrate at Twillingate and was himself a singer of note; their fine house in Twillingate was called "Normount," a large house with four bay windows, four fireplaces, and six bedrooms. Georgina Scott's sister, Margaret, was also "trained in voice" and took music lessons in St. John's. At some point, though the dates are not given, Georgina Stirling gave singing and organ or piano lessons to the eldest Scott sister, Eleanor. That was probably on return visits from Europe or possibly the United States. Eleanor eventually went to Toronto and continued her music lessons at the Royal Conservatory of Music. Georgina Scott had heard her cousin, Georgina Stirling, sing at their home in Back Harbour, and the one song she remembered vividly was "Listen to the Mocking Bird." She commented, "You would swear the bird was right there." (This popular American song was written in 1855 and depicts a young man mourning the loss of his sweetheart as the mockingbird to which they had listened in the happy days of their courtship now comes and sings over the grave. Yet it has a somewhat lively tune and was even used as marching music during the American Civil War. The author was Septimus Winner, and he wrote under the pseudonym "Alice Hawthorne.")

Georgina Scott stated that Rose acted as a chaperone for "Miss Georgie" when they travelled. She stated that Rose returned from Europe in 1914. Different sources give different dates for the year of Rose's return, but we know she was in Twillingate by January 1914. Georgina also said that Rose was a governess with the Italian Royal Family and that Mrs. Hodge (undoubtedly Grace, wife of the elder merchant Richard Dorman Hodge) had told her this. The other Mrs. Hodge (this would almost certainly be Elsie, wife of Arthur Harold Hodge, a son) had told her during visits to Twillingate that Rose and Georgina looked very different from each other; Rose was short and Georgina was much taller. She stated further that Maymie Roberts, a "near neighbour," was also a good friend to Georgina Stirling.

Margaret (Scott, Blackmore) Goodyear was interviewed by Hiram Silk on April 24, 1987. She was then ninety-one years old, a well-spoken, articulate woman. She was a sister of Georgina (Scott) Buckingham, and a cousin of Georgina Stirling. Having grown up in nearby Back Harbour and being familiar with the Stirling house, she noted that there were always six large water barrels kept in the Stirling house between the porch and the kitchen, and the young Stirling boy had drowned in one of these. The mother, Ann (Peyton) Stirling, was so distressed by this terrible event that she was administered opium, undoubtedly by her husband, to help her deal with the tragedy. Margaret, in an offhanded way, remarked that Georgina also took opium in later years. She affirmed that Georgina had given her voice lessons, "a few lessons," and taught her the scales on the piano. Margaret followed this up with voice lessons in St. John's with a Professor King.

Margaret stated that Georgina had "lived with Royalty in Italy. She even taught Royalty." She also mentioned that "Sir William Horwood came to visit Georgina" (presumably in St. John's), that "he admired her as a singer" and that "he was very much in love with Georgina . . . they thought that Georgina and Sir William would be married."

Margaret also stated that Rose had been a teacher, that Mrs. Hodge's (Elsie's) mother-in-law (Grace, wife of Richard Dorman Hodge, merchant and best friend of Georgina) affirmed that Rose had been a governess to the Italian Royal Family, and that Rose "could tell you all about Royalty."

Margaret had completed training as a nurse at the General Hospital in St. John's and had done private nursing with the Knowling merchant family and had even been a nurse for Lady Squires, wife of Sir Richard Squires. When Margaret married businessman Pierce Blackmore, she moved to Pilley's Island and became the nurse at the "Mine Hospital," a cottage hospital which was supported by the Grenfell Association of St. Anthony. She later moved to Robert's Arm as a widow and subsequently remarried.

There are two undated interviews with **Eleanor Peyton** when she was eighty-six years old. She was living in Grand Falls at the time. She was the daughter of either James or Elias Peyton, though it should be noted that Thomas and Mary Ann (Pearce) Peyton also had a daughter named Eleanor, but her married name was Roberts. These are Eleanor's recollections and memories of the four sisters. During her years at Twillingate, Eleanor had known Rose, Lucy, Kate, and Georgina. She affirmed that "Miss Lucy was beautiful, she was my favourite." She remembered sitting in St. Peter's Church and hearing the rustling of silk dresses as Miss Lucy strolled up through the church to take her seat. When "Miss Lucy" was living at the Stirling house after returning from England in the fall of 1904, the house was beautiful; Lucy died at Twillingate in 1913. After Rose returned to Twillingate in 1914—in fact, Eleanor said, "Both Georgie and Rose came back after the War," i.e. 1918 or 1919—the house soon became unkempt and disorganized.

Eleanor noted that "Mrs. Putzki" came home for summer visits and said she was "very high and mighty," which was probably her way of saying that she was very sophisticated. Eleanor also affirmed that Rose was the intellectual of the family, "a very learned and educated person," and that she had been a governess. Rose travelled extensively—to Ireland, France, Italy, etc. Rose was also very brusque; in the later years she once invited a woman to dinner, but the woman did not come because she was concerned with Rose's untidiness at the Stirling house. When Rose saw her later, she questioned the woman about not coming, and the woman, caught unawares, made a lame excuse, and Rose retorted, "You won't be invited again."

About Georgina Stirling, Eleanor said that she never boasted about her career, and she "felt perfectly at ease in Georgina's company." Georgina, she said, "enjoyed the simple things, a cup of tea and a slice of toast." Georgina looked very nice when she first returned to Twillingate in 1929, but soon "she began to dress like a gypsy, wearing loose dresses and wearing a red bandana around her head." Georgina and Rose did a lot of gardening, and the outside "stores" were well-kept and tidy. Georgina dressed well when she sang at church, and Eleanor remembered Georgina singing "The Holy City" at church and Mrs. Dr. Wood played the organ for this performance. Georgina also sang at the Peyton house in Back Harbour. Eleanor said that she never saw Georgina's beautiful gowns and that Georgina gave away a lot of things in the Stirling house, beautiful things.

Eleanor also stated that Mr. Horwood, presumably one of the magistrates or possibly the Chief Justice of Newfoundland—W. H. Horwood, a personal friend of Georgina's—had arranged "some sort of pension" for the two sisters. This may have been in connection with Dr. Stirling's investments in the Newfoundland mines and his investments in the Dominion of Canada or from the sale of his properties in St. John's. This may have been done through the same legal firm which contacted Maymie (Roberts) Hewlett in 1967 about settling the Stirling estate.

Eleanor was one of the people sitting with Georgina when she died. Hiram Silk questioned her about Georgina's death, as to whether it was a painful passing or a quiet death, and Eleanor said that she died very peacefully. Hiram remarked, "A quiet ending to a turbulent life." Eleanor agreed.

Edgar Baird, whose mother was Thomas Peyton's daughter Louisa Isabella, and whose father was William W. Baird, manager of the Horwood Lumber Company pulp mill at Campbellton when they were married in 1901 and were living at Angle Brook, Glovertown, in 1934, in a 1960 interview with Hiram Silk said that he was about thirteen or fourteen years old when he came with his mother to visit the two Stirling sisters at Twillingate. Louisa Isabella (Peyton) Baird was a cousin of Georgina and Rose. Edgar's mother asked Georgina how she liked being back in Twillingate, and Georgina replied that she was delighted. She expressed to Edgar's mother the fact that she had trouble finding women's shoes large enough for her feet and that she was presently wearing loose men's shoes. Edgar recalled a boyhood memory that she seemed to be suffering from gout. He remembered her as a large, buxom woman. Edgar was uncomfortable with the way the sisters had mounted their father's old surgical instruments on a wall in commemoration of their father's life as a doctor in Twillingate. It was startling to the boy because he had never seen such a thing before. Though he does not mention it, his discomfort may also have been heightened by the skeleton which Dr. Stirling had left in his surgery. Edgar commented on the beauty of the house and compared it to large beautiful houses that he had seen during his travels in later years in the New England states. He recalled that the carpenters who built the Stirling house had come from Poole, Dorset, in England, that they had first built St. Peter's Church and then several other houses in Twillingate.

Elmo Baird is a cousin of Edgar Baird and is about ten years younger. He is presently living in St. John's at Tiffany Village Retirement Homes, having moved there from Gander in 1996. I interviewed Elmo and his wife, Eleanor, by phone on March 27 and 29, 2018, and again in October. Elmo had just recently celebrated his ninety-eighth birthday. His mind is clear, and he possesses a fine sense of humour. I discovered just before the interview that he is my cousin. His mother, Dinah J. Manuel, was the daughter of Job and Sarah Manuel of Northern Arm (my hometown), and his father, Harold Baird, had come to Northern Arm from Twillingate to work as a blacksmith for Job Manuel, a merchant-shipbuilder. Elmo was born at Northern Arm on March 7, 1920. Job Manuel's sister was my grandmother—Maria Jane Manuel. Harold Baird may have come to Northern Arm as early as 1907 and may have worked on Job Manuel's 120-ton three-masted schooner *Nina*

L. in that year, and then went to Norris Arm to work with Job, who was the master builder for the Martin Shipbuilding Company between 1917 and 1919 in the construction of four large three-masted schooners.

When Elmo was ten months old his mother died, and his father moved back home to Twillingate in 1921 with his six children and took over his father's blacksmithing business. His father, Samuel Baird, had been a blacksmith in Ireland and emigrated to Newfoundland when it became apparent that he was going to be forced to make shackles for prisoners. Because Elmo was a baby at the time the family returned to Twillingate, he was raised by his grandmother, Catherine (Britt) Baird, and they lived at the top of the hill near St. Peter's Church. Elmo's father soon remarried and lived across the road from St. Peter's Church.

When Georgina Stirling returned to Twillingate in 1929, Elmo was nine years old, and he was fifteen years old when Georgina died. Every Saturday morning from the age of twelve to fifteen years, he was sent down to the Stirling house by his Granny Baird to help the sisters in any way he could—he spent much time chopping and sawing wood for their stoves and fireplaces, feeding the pig, gathering up and carrying away trash, and doing all kinds of household chores under the sisters' direction. Both sisters took turns giving him orders.

Eleanor, Elmo's wife, also from Twillingate, told a story about Mrs. Tuffin, who was a housekeeper for the Stirling sisters. She had been charged by Georgina never to enter Dr. Stirling's surgery. It was a sacrosanct area of the house and important to the sisters' continuing adulation of their adored father. The sight of accumulating dust in the surgery caught Mrs. Tuffin's eye as she was passing by the door one day and, unable to restrain herself, she entered the room and began to clean it. Georgina caught her in the act and tipped the pail of water over Mrs. Tuffin's head.

* * * * * * *

A SOMEWHAT LENGTHY "ASIDE" is worthy of description in connection with this incident, which must have occurred in early February 1933.

The merchant Arthur Hodge sends a communication to Georgina on February 14, 1933, that must have been in response to a telegraph that Georgina had already sent. In an envelope which bears the words: "About Mrs. Tuffin from Per H. to keep safe." Inside is a written copy of the Chief Justice of Newfoundland, Sir W. H. Horwood's telegraph to Georgina on the same date which reads: "To A. H. Hodge. Girl should be ordered to leave say within an hour, failing compliance she should be put out by anybody whom Georgie may employ for that purpose, care to be taken that no more force be used than is necessary to affect her removal. Sgd. W. H. Horwood."

Mr. Hodge then appends a note to Georgina: "If Miss Rose is determined to keep Mrs. T. on, I hardly see how you can act. Might be better consult the magistrate first, if I were you. I write now, as no doubt you are expecting to hear from Sir William. I wish matters could be amicably settled of yours and regret your trouble. Yours sincerely, Arthur Hodge."

The matter was not immediately settled, and on February 28, 1933, Georgina sends another telegraph to Sir William Horwood, with whom she had been personally acquainted for many years; the telegraph reads, "Rose better, quite out of danger. Woman did not give me notice and refuses to go. Can Rose engage her under these conditions? As she has not given me notice, is she not still in my employ? Please answer me personally immediately. Much distressed. G. Stirling." The chief justice responds immediately to "Miss G. A. Stirling. This woman being your servant can be dismissed and ejected by you. If her presence interferes with your enjoyment of the house, you can refuse to allow her to re-enter though engaged by Rose. W. H. Horwood."

This was yet another incident which caused friction between the two sisters. It cannot be determined what happened to Mrs. Tuffin.

Sir William Horwood, chief justice, had communicated to Georgina and Rose by advising them about Dr. Stirling's mining interests and transactions, and letters written by him in 1910–12 and in 1928, now in possession of the Golden family in the United States, attest to this. A letter of Kate's dated January 20, 1938 (an almost exact copy of which she saved), affirms that Sir William had accepted responsibility to sell the house after Rose's death, but according to a letter Kate received from Edward Linfield, the merchant who had organized the sale of all remaining items in the house, Sir William missed an opportunity to sell the house by setting the price too high when Mr. Linfield's cousin had expressed interest.

Amy Louise Peyton affirms that Kate and Janet had provided money for Rose's upkeep, presumably after Rose had returned to Twillingate in 1914. She states that when Janet died in England in 1928, Rose wrote, "Dear Kate has promised to keep me since Janet's death." Rose's spending seems to have been totally out of control, for in the ten-year period between 1928 and 1937, Kate paid Rose's bills to the tune of $5,000 and, when she returned to Twillingate in 1938, discovered that Rose still owed $500, which Kate then paid. Kate shared this information with Sir William so that he would understand her reluctance to spend more money on the Stirling house in preparing it for a possible sale.

Years before this, as Kate revealed to Sir William, Georgina and Rose had conveyed their interests in property at Wild Cove to her, "knowing my love for the place & gratitude for the assistance I had given them from time to time." Kate had fond memories of playing and picnicking at beautiful Wild Cove when she was a child. The Golden family still possesses the Deed of Gift dated 1931. It is sad to think that this may have been the same piece of property that Kate sold in Twillingate to provide further financial assistance to Rose after Georgina had died.

* * * * * * *

TO RESUME THE INTERVIEW WITH ELEANOR BAIRD: Eleanor also spoke of the many superior male singing voices in Twillingate and particularly praised the singing of the funeral director, Alfred Manuel. She also said that Granny Baird had been the president of the Dorcas Society of Twillingate for twenty-five years, which would have endeared her to Georgina, who had been one of the founding members of the society in her youth.

Elmo said it was the pig that Georgina had named Garibaldi, not the goat as Amy Louise Peyton had stated. He remembered Martin Stuckless and Stan Curtis working around the Stirling estate, and several other people. His Granny Baird regularly visited the sisters, and Georgina would often come to visit his Granny.

Elmo also remembered Maymie Roberts regularly being at the Stirling house. Elmo had never been inside Dr. Stirling's surgery, so he had never seen the surgical instruments and the skeleton that his cousin Edgar had found so frightening.

Elmo commented that Georgina and Rose were very different from each other. He said they didn't get along very well, and they never went out visiting together. In fact, he said that, "If one of them came in the front door, the other went out the back door." This could have been a remembered comment from an adult. Some have said that the sisters used different staircases in the Stirling house. This may have been simply to get access to their own private quarters and was misunderstood by adults who had seen it happen. The sisters seem, however, to have sometimes entertained together, though Georgina appears to have done the cooking. Elmo thought that the word "cranky" would be a good word to describe Rose.

Elmo's father, Harold Baird, was often called on to do jobs at the Stirling house, such as repairs, fixing or replacing stovepipes, etc. As a blacksmith, he was a handyman and his skills were often needed. Elmo remembered the berry bushes on the Stirling estate—black and red currants, gooseberries—and the flowers and trees.

I asked Elmo if Rose and Georgina attended St. Peter's Church. Elmo took turns pumping the pipe organ in the church and regularly ringing the bell, but he has no recollection of having seen either of the sisters at church. We know from other sources that Georgina occasionally sang at St. Peter's Church and that she attended the funeral of the little blind girl, but she seems not to have been a regular attendee. Elmo recalls that she would walk to the Orange Hall, which was a short distance from her house.

Elmo had heard Georgina sing twice in the Orange Hall, but he could not remember the names of the songs. When I asked him if she sang behind a screen, as some have stated, he said, "No, she stood out on the stage." He had no recollection of her singing around the house or in the garden. He did not attend Georgina's funeral in 1935.

* * * * * * *

Observance of the Forty-eighth Anniversary of Georgina's Death

In 1983, Hiram Silk arranged a radio broadcast to recognize the forty-eighth anniversary of the death of Georgina Stirling. He read from the diary of Steven Loveridge of Twillingate. The diary noted the extreme winter-like conditions of Easter Sunday, April 23, the day of her death, and the two days before Georgina's burial on April 25.

Then follow two interviews with people who had known Georgina. **Rev. Gordon Elliott** was now aged ninety-four, and he had been married to Lily Stirling, a cousin of Georgina's from Conception Bay. His family had lived on Kenna's Hill in St. John's, and Georgina used to visit the family home when she was doing her performances in the city in the early 1890s. He observed that Georgina possessed a wonderful sense of humour. At that time, she had "a famous Persian cat which she carried with her everywhere." The cat was named Marchesi. When Georgina would return home from a performance or an outing, she would call for the cat, "Marchesi, Marchesi, come to Mummy," and the young men gathered there would mimic the cat's meow in order to confuse Georgina, and she was always quick to "turn the tables" on them when she got the chance. When the young man Herbert Stirling came to visit the house one day, he called out in jest, "Marchesi, Marchesi," and Georgina, standing on the upstairs balcony above his head, poured a large pitcher of water over him. Herbert Stirling later became the very accomplished organist at St. Thomas' Church in St. John's and was invited to Twillingate in 1897 to put together the new Norman & Baird pipe organ which had just arrived, and then he played for the service and gave a half-hour recital, to the delight of the congregation of St. Peter's Church.

The *Twillingate Sun* of December 1898 reported on what must have been a second cat named Marchesi. This one—"a black cat, sleek and glossy"—had been presented to Georgina in Italy.

Georgina spent a lot of time with Hon. William H. Horwood in St. John's during those years, but Mr. Elliott affirmed that it was a purely platonic relationship, based on their mutual love of music. Other sources affirm that she was being pursued in a romantic attraction. Mr. Elliott and his wife had also visited Georgina and Rose at Twillingate shortly before Georgina died. He said that at this stage her body was racked with cancer and she was no longer careful about her appearance. He said she took drugs and alcohol to deal with the pain, that he excused her for this and that hers was now "a spoiled life." Other sources differ with this statement. Mr. Elliott's statement seems to be lacking in a depth of understanding and sympathy that one might expect from a Christian minister. The evidence shows that Georgina's was not "a spoiled life" but one redeemed by struggle and suffering and faith and eventually triumph.

Rev. Mr. Elliott's diary (no year given, but the dates are December 1 and 2; it was written sometime after 1937) gives a summary of Georgina's life. We touch only on a few points in this summary. He says that Georgina was trained in London, Vienna, and Rome, that ". . . she became famous as an operatic singer in the capitals of Europe. . . . She often stayed with W. R. Stirling (my father-in-law) who was her cousin as his father and hers were brothers. She and Sir Wm Horwood the Chief Justice were great friends drawn together by a common interest in good music, but I think this was on a strictly Platonic level. Her physical appearance in her prime was imposing—tall, dark and well-built, but as she grew older her appearance changed and she became shy in appearing on the concert stage and in one or two in her later years, she would only sing if allowed to do so behind a screen." Mr. Elliott added that, "When she died, there were mountains of snow and it was above the heads of those who stood at the graveside."

Mr. Elliott commented on Janet Stirling and said that "she had a nursing home in Harley Street, London." He also stated that the Stirlings had two sons "who died at an early age, one of which was drowned in a water barrel. Source, an old diary in Twillingate." He closes his comments on the Stirling family by noting that "Putzki (meaning Paul Adolphe Putzki, Kate's husband, an accomplished artist) decorated a dinner service, some parts of which are still in Twillingate, as it was dispersed with her possessions after Rose's death." The Putzki family returned from the United States and lived in the Stirling house for the year 1896–97.

A second interview to recognize the forty-eighth anniversary of Georgina's death was with **Mrs. Minnie (Patten) Smith**, aged ninety-three. Her father had been a policeman in Twillingate in the 1890s, Sgt. Patten, and she spoke of the Stirling sisters walking to church and around the town, all of them carrying colourful parasols. She had heard Georgina sing "in her heyday" and also at the concert at Pitts Memorial Hall in St. John's. Mrs. Smith recalled the gala balls that would be held whenever the Supreme Court made a visit to Twillingate, and stated that Georgina was there on at least one occasion, "dressed in her finery, a black silk dress with long white gloves and an ostrich feather." Mrs. Smith's late husband had once met Georgina and her sister Janet in Portugal when he arrived there by steamship, and the sisters, happening to be in the town where the ship had docked and hearing that there was a Newfoundlander on board, Mr. Smith, asked if they could come on board and meet him. Their request was granted, and they were taken to the saloon, where there happened to be a piano, and Georgina sang there for the entire afternoon. Mrs. Smith also observed that Dr. Olds had bought much of the fine furniture from the Stirling home when the sale was organized after Rose's death.

* * * * * * *

Witness of Workers at the Stirling House, Neighbours and General

These interviews are presented here in no particular order since many of them are undated. I have tried to give a brief summary of what each person said without using the specific colloquial language.

In an undated interview, **Herb Burton** recalls that as a young boy with his two dogs and a slide (sled) he was passing the Stirlings' gate when the dogs made an unexpected turn toward "Miss Georgina" coming out through the gate with a large bag of apples. The dogs knocked Georgina down, and each dog grabbed an apple and proceeded on down the road. It took Herb a few moments to get control of the dogs, and he turned them around and went quickly back, thinking "I knocked down an old lady." He quickly apologized and asked if she was "hurt-ed" (the old Twillingate way of saying "hurt"), and she replied "No, but I got a big surprise." Herb started to pick up the apples and realized the bag had burst open, so he ran to a nearby store to get a good bag and explained to the lady in the store what had happened, and she gave him a suitable box for the apples. When he returned to Miss Georgina, she was laughing the incident off, but she said to him, "Those dogs are wonderful naughty and they don't obey." (It is worth noting what seems to be an apparent contradiction; "wonderful" in this context is simply the Newfoundland way of expressing emphasis, and it carries the meaning of "terrible.") Herb determined that he would not tell his parents about the incident when he got home or else he would get a "trimmin'" (a beating) for knocking down an old lady. Herb often delivered parcels to the Stirling home and described Georgina as "a blocky woman, heavy-framed and built like a man. . . . I knew she was a singer. I heard her sing a few times but always behind a screen . . . they were good songs, she sang well and in good harmony . . . that's all gone out now." The reference to "singing behind a screen" happened in Georgina's later years when she was having trouble with her feet and had to wear men's loose shoes.

Edna Burton said that her Grandfather Stuckless used to do chores for the Stirling family when the children were growing up. This could not have been Martin Stuckless who was born in 1882 and died in 1944 but must have been Martin's father, John B. Stuckless, who lived from 1852 to 1916 and who must have worked for the senior Stirlings. Edna stated that one of Grandfather Stuckless's chores was to make sure that the water barrels (seven of them, according to one source) were kept filled. One day the young Stirling boy (a toddler) went missing and the sisters were looking for him for hours. When Grandfather Stuckless brought the last "turn" of water for the day, he discovered the boy drowned at the bottom of one of the barrels (said by one source to have been a large puncheon). Edna noted that Martin Stuckless, who must have been her father, helped milk the cows and get wood for the stoves for Georgina and Rose.

When Miss Lucy Stirling was jilted and her lover did not arrive on the coastal boat as he had promised and all the preparations had been made, the cake ready, the wedding party dressed, St. Peter's Church ablaze in lights, Dr. Stirling was heard to say that he would have killed the scoundrel if he could have found him, especially after finding his daughter lying prone on her bed in her full wedding regalia. The large room which had been prepared for the wedding banquet was kept closed for a whole year.

Grandfather Stuckless affirmed that the Stirling family were all hard workers, and they would often share with him the cream taken off the cows' milk.

Ella Burton was interviewed on October 17, 1986. She was a young girl when she used to visit the Stirling sisters in the 1930s. They lived "just down the road from them" (the Stirlings). She said that Georgina loved her flowers and talked a lot about them. She did a lot of humming when she was working in the garden. The sisters had thirteen cats; five belonged to Georgina, and seven were Rose's. (Ella got the total wrong.) Georgina taught Ella and her sister organ lessons. Their father, who worked there with the animals, brought the family organ over to the Stirling house so that Georgina could teach his daughters. Georgina told Ella that she was "fast to catch on." The organ was eventually returned to Ella's house, and Georgina would play the organ there during her frequent visits. "I liked the both of them," said Ella, but later in the interview she affirmed that "I liked Georgina the best." "I heard her sing many times . . . in the sitting room upstairs . . . she had a wonderful voice . . . she told me she was a singer." Ella had been invited up to the sitting room many times. Georgina wore long dresses "down to her feet" and wore a cape around her shoulders.

Georgina had a favourite dog, which she once brought with her to Ella's house. Ella was intrigued because she knew that her father would not allow dogs in their house. When Georgina sat at the table for a cup of tea, she said to the dog, "Lie down, Chip." And the dog obeyed immediately. When a slice of toast was given to Georgina, she said to the dog, "What do you want, Chip?" The dog came to Georgina's place at the table, sat, and extended his paw. Georgina placed a piece of bread on his paw, and he sat and ate it.

Ella affirmed that Rose and Georgina quarrelled many times. "Father tried to pacify them in their quarrels," Ella stated. "Dad knew of her drinking." Georgina would go occasionally to visit the Manuel family at Exploits Islands, and Rose would often go to St. John's for visits. Both sisters would sometimes spend the weekend at Back Harbour visiting their cousins. They had two girls (maids) live with them in the later years.

The man who witnessed these quarrels between Georgina and Rose and tried on occasion "to pacify them" was almost certainly Martin Stuckless, Ella's father. It cannot be determined how he was related to Edna Burton or Herb Burton.

Bessie (Curtis) Barnes was interviewed by Hiram Silk in September 1985. Bessie was a sister to Frank Curtis and Stan Curtis. We have read of Stan Curtis's interview in a previous chapter. We shall read Frank's testimony presently. The Curtis family lived just up over the hill behind the Stirlings and could look down on their house. Bessie worked at the Stirling house when Georgina and Rose were living there, not as a maid but simply helping out. Bessie helped with milking the cows, making butter from the milk, washing the dishes, fetching capelin for the sisters' meals, and delivering butter to the Hodge merchant family. She affirmed that there were a lot of "stores" and barns on the Stirling property. She said also that the sisters had two cows, and Georgina would get mad when the calves took most of the milk and there was less for them to drink and make butter. Bessie affirmed that Rose had worked in the St. Anthony Hospital, that she was a teacher, and that she had spent twenty-five years in Italy. Rose loved all her animals and had given names to all of them; she also wore men's long johns in the cold weather and had made blueberry wine that was now seven years old. Rose routinely scolded visiting children for tormenting the dogs. Georgina went to the nearby Curtis home almost every day for a cup of tea and would say, "This is the best cup of tea in Twillingate." Bessie was enthralled with the marble-top tables in the Stirling home, especially in the dining room. She also affirmed that the live-in maid slept in a bedroom on the third floor of the Stirling house, obviously the servants' quarters. Georgina had once given Bessie the iron saucepan in which her father, Dr. Stirling, always sterilized his medical instruments. Bessie stated that Georgina was good-looking, that she had heard her sing, and that she seemed to favour "songs of the British Empire."

Mr. Hodge's servants would occasionally come with horse and carriage and take the sisters for rides around town. The sisters also invited doctors and nurses from the Memorial Hospital over to their house for social evenings. And Bessie's sister, Margaret, was one of the women who sat with Georgina when she was dying.

Frank Curtis, in an undated interview, but likely in the 1980s, recalled Georgina as a tall, red-faced woman. He remembered her as being very nice and kind and hard-working. He lived just up over the hill from the Stirling house and as a young man cut the grass there and fed the pigs. He said Georgina loved her animals and gave them all names. He said the two sisters entertained quite a bit, and two of their frequent visitors were Mr. and Mrs. Hodge, of the merchant family. The sisters also went out to visit in the town. He remembered Rose as "being on the cranky side" but Georgina was "not like that." He also stated that "she had her money come from somewhere." **Frank and Stan Curtis** and their sister **Bessie (Curtis) Barnes** were the children of Thomas Curtis.

It is of interest that the December 31, 1892, issue of the *Twillingate Sun* states that Frank Curtis was "Best in all" in the Standard V at St. Peter's School examinations, a school which had recently been reorganized on the latest academic principles by Mr. S. C. Thompson, a new teacher.

Delcy (Hynes) Gillard, in an undated interview, said that she had started to work for Rose and Georgina as a maid when she was only twelve years old and stayed with Rose for almost two years. Obviously, Rose had hired her. It is curious that Delcy does not disclose a lot of information about Georgina, so one wonders if she worked at the Stirling house for two intervals—once when she was twelve years old, and again during Georgina's last years. Delcy mentions Georgina briefly as being present but curiously makes no mention of her death. Delcy may have been excused from her work during this period with so many relatives around to carry the workload. Most of her time at the Stirling house was under the control of Rose, though Delcy was slyly getting long evenings out by secretly putting the clocks back so that Rose would be unaware of the late hours she sometimes kept. Rose, she said, was a hard taskmaster, and Delcy, who occupied an upstairs bedroom, would have to get up every morning and clean out the Waterloo stove, bring water from the barrel, and make meals and also tend to the animals, though someone came to milk the cows and bring the milk into the house—she complained that all her labour gained her just $3 per month. She noted that all of Georgina's gowns and other personal things were packed away in trunks, but her shoes and hats were still out in sight.

Delcy affirmed that the two sisters "always fought" and sometimes Georgina in frustration would walk over to Mr. Stuckless's house and say, "Martin. I can't get along with my sister."

During the latter part of Delcy's two years of service, Rose was spending most of her time in her room but still giving strict orders. This must have been after Georgina's death. The Peytons from Back Harbour came to visit occasionally, but very few other people visited. Martin Stuckless was the only man around, doing chores and tending the animals; others came to milk the cows. If the outside door was left ajar, Rose's favourite hens would enter the house and would sometimes hop up the stairs and enter Rose's bedroom, and Rose would shout to Delcy to "get them out of here." (This would have been a difficult time in Rose's life; her sister was gone and she was now alone; overwhelming frustration was setting in.) She was even losing patience with her pets. Rose always dressed in black, Delcy stated, and wore black shawls routinely, and she had a lot of trouble with her feet, perhaps what some called "the bandy Stirling feet." "Bandy" means bent or curled outward. In another context, Hiram Silk describes Rose in the later years as "a semi invalid," undoubtedly a reference to her difficulty in walking.

Delcy was also aware that Rose had once been a teacher. Having learned the strict discipline of schools in those day, the result was that "everyone was scared of her." Rose talked a lot about her father, Dr. Stirling. He had been the inspiration for all the family members.

Rose's sister Kate Putzki, during one of her summer visits from the United States, sold land in Twillingate, undoubtedly land that Dr. Stirling had owned, and gave Rose the money, "lots of money," in Delcy's words. Delcy also stated that Rose had "thousands of money." Remember that Delcy was only about fourteen or fifteen years old at this time. Rose complained at one time that there was a man in the house who wanted all her money. This turned out to be a man who was arranging to place her money in the bank, probably a relative and possibly her cousin Will Peyton. However, Rose managed to keep money in the house. She may have felt insecure about depositing money in the bank, as many older people did in those days.

Asked by Hiram Silk if she thought the house was haunted, Delcy replied that she sometimes heard doors banging when she knew that all the doors had been closed for the night. She stated that the Spracklin family, the new magistrate, had occasionally heard things that could not be explained. This would have been sometime after 1942, when the Stirling house was refurbished and rented to a series of magistrates

When Delcy left the Stirling house as Rose's maid, she acquired a job of the same kind in Merritt's Harbour for $10 a month, but it must be said in her favour that she returned on occasion to visit Rose. Presumably, another maid had replaced her.

There were lots of beautiful things in the house, Delcy said. The sisters never threw anything away, so this would account for a lot of clutter. After Rose died in 1937, a sale of all the significant items in the house was organized and carried out. It was after Rose's death that Kate Putzki came and took back to Washington, DC, some of the finest furniture and the family's monogrammed silverware. (Other items had already been taken to the Peyton houses in Back Harbour when Lucy Stirling moved there in 1913, including a large four-poster bed. Some of Georgina's gowns and memorabilia from her travels in Europe and the United States were taken to the Peyton houses, and later presented to the Twillingate Museum by Amy Louise and Ernest Peyton.)

Harris Rideout, aged eighty-five, originally from Twillingate but at the time of the undated interview living in Seal Cove, stated that his father used to work for Dr. Stirling, especially cutting grass on the large one-and-a-half-acre lot. This was undoubtedly done with a scythe and the grass "made" and stored in the barn for Dr. Stirling's animals. Harris remembered the Stirling sisters as big women, nice-looking, always beautifully dressed, and he would see them riding in their father's horse and buggy. He had heard Georgina sing in St. Peter's Church, though he regularly attended the Methodist Church, where he usually pumped the pipe organ. Hiram Silk's interest in ghost stories, the occult, and strange happenings eventually teased out of Harris an unusual dream that he had had when he was a boy. In his dream his father came and took him down to Dr. Stirling's garden with an armload of lumber, hammer, and nails; in the dream his father made three Crosses, dug three holes, and then nailed his boy to the centre Cross. When the father lifted the Cross up it fell with a heavy thud into the hole and the boy woke up from his dream with a start. He commented: "It took my parents a long time to console me after that dream." Perhaps the dream had been associated with a Good Friday commemoration of the death of Jesus on the Cross; or possibly with the story in the Book of Genesis of Abraham and his son Isaac on Mount Moriah.

In **Arthur Fifield's** interview of 1985, we are told of a winter incident in Georgina's young life when she was hauling a slide (sled) home after a visit to her cousins at Back Harbour. At the top of Church Hill, she decided to ride down the steep incline. At the same time, Mr. Fifield's grandfather, Simon Warr, was walking up the hill on his way to Back Harbour. Whether Georgina tried to avoid the elderly man or lost control of the slide cannot be determined, but the slide went one way and Georgina went another, ending up in a large snowbank by the cemetery fence. Mr. Warr ran to her aid and asked if she was "hurt-ed." "No," she said, "but I got one hell of a flice." The *Dictionary of Newfoundland English* defines a "flice" as engaging in rough-and-tumble play or a sudden quick gesture or movement. I guess the Stirling family was not unaccustomed to the use of salty language. (Note once again the old Twillingate way of saying "hurt.")

Arthur Fifield, who lived from 1907 to 1987, also described Dr. Stirling's herb garden where he grew a variety of plants for making medicines. Dr. Stirling had planted trees all along one side of his garden, including dogberry trees. This line of trees is visible in the picture of the Stirling house on page 52 of Amy Louise Peyton's book. One of the houses on the opposite side of the road belonged to Captain Andrew Roberts, the father of Maymie Roberts, Georgina's "near neighbour" and best friend from 1929 to 1935.

Mrs. Florie (Parsons) Burton was originally from Trout River on Newfoundland's west coast and moved to Twillingate in 1926 with her Twillingate-born husband, so she was in Twillingate when Georgina was living there. She had visited the Stirling house and encountered the many cats and a few dogs around the place. She noted that the cats had scratched the beautiful furniture. The Burtons later bought some of the furniture when a sale was organized after Rose's death. The sisters got their water from wells on the property. Florie remembered Georgina in her garden with the red kerchief tied around her head. She also met Georgina at church and heard her sing at a concert in the Orange Hall, where she wore a beautiful dress and hat. She said that Georgina was pretty and that she was very quiet (reserved?). When she heard Georgina sing at church, Florie refers to her as "hauling out those hymns" and said that "she was a real nightingale." She noted that the Hodge brothers and their wives (however, only one was married) were good friends of the Stirling sisters.

Mary "Polly" Anstey, who was eighty-plus years old at the time of her interview, knew that Georgina was an accomplished singer from Twillingate, but she could not remember if she had ever heard Georgina sing. She knew, however, that Mrs. Manuel accompanied Georgina on the organ when she sang, and that Miss Mabel Hodge, sister of two local merchants, was an accomplished organist and very probably accompanied Georgina also. Miss Hodge was also a music teacher in the town. At the age of eighty, Mrs. Anstey, because of problems with her sight, had to cease playing the organ herself after many years of being a church organist in Twillingate.

Nathan Penney was a Newfoundland Ranger and was posted to Twillingate for a nine-month period in early 1942. He was interviewed by Hiram Silk on November 23, 1988. He had no stories to share about Georgina Stirling, but he was involved as a government representative in the disposition of what was left in the Stirling house and for preparing it as a residence for an incoming magistrate. He observed that it had taken four years (from Rose's death in 1937?) "to clear up the estate," which would seem to indicate that there still were funds left from Dr. Stirling's investments, and this is further confirmed by Maymie (Roberts) Hewlett's story of being contacted in 1967 by a lawyer about the final settlement of the estate. The Stirling house was purchased by the Commission of Government, through the Department of Works. Penney visited the house on May 4, 1942. The place was in shambles. After Kate Putzki had taken away some of the finest furniture following Rose's death in 1937, there had been a sale of all other items in the house, and many local people, including Dr. John Olds of the Memorial Hospital, had purchased furniture. Dr. Olds's furniture had been lost in the fire that destroyed the old cottage, the home of the Olds family, in 1940.

Penney felt that the house had been abandoned for some time and that it had been totally ransacked, and what was left was of no value. He described the dirty, torn costumes (the remnants of Georgina's glory days), scores of programs from her many concerts, and colourful posters advertising her singing engagements. There were many old jars of ointments and medicines—undoubtedly from Dr. Stirling's active days of preparing medicines from his herb garden. In the doctor's dispensary the shelves were well-labelled and still displayed a semblance of order. None of what lay scattered on the floor was worth saving because of the woeful condition left by people who must have been searching over time for anything of value. All of this clutter was thrown out and destroyed through government action.

Magistrate Beaton Abbott soon came to the town as magistrate and moved into the entirely renovated Stirling house. The wallpaper at the house showed good taste, stated Mr. Penney. Structurally the house was still sound and the old building showed great character; the ancient timbers would last for a long time, observed the Ranger. Nathan Penney left Twillingate before Christmas 1942.

Hiram Silk interviewed **Jessie (Troake) Drover** on February 25, 1983, but curiously he did not question her about Georgina Stirling; perhaps he did not realize that she had nursed Georgina in the Twillingate Hospital, or perhaps there is another tape that has not yet surfaced.

The following information is not contained in the Hiram Silk interviews but in Gary L. Saunders's book *Doctor Olds of Twillingate*. Jessie Troake had been a worker at the hospital since 1926, and Dr. Parsons must have seen the promise in this young lady and arranged for her to go to Montreal to be trained as a nurse, loaning her money for the three-year commitment. She returned to Twillingate in 1933 with her RN. Up until that time all the nurses at the hospital had come from Johns Hopkins University in the United States. Almost immediately after Jessie's return to the hospital, Dr. Parsons requested her to take a posting to Carmanville because of his concern about the lack of nursing care along the coast once navigation closed in the fall. Jessie was there from December 1933 until the spring of 1934, and then returned to the Twillingate Hospital until fall, when she was posted to Musgrave Harbour. Sometime during this interval (spring to fall), Georgina Stirling spent time in the hospital, and Jessie was her nurse on occasion. This quotation of Jessie's words from Saunders's book is of particular interest: ". . . Miss Georgina Stirling, the retired opera star, coming to Sunday tea at the Cottage . . . her blouse was on inside out; she knew but wouldn't change it—bad luck. She was a patient later when I was on nights. She couldn't sleep and we had some interesting chats . . ." The fact that this quotation is followed in Saunders's book by four periods must mean that Jessie had shared other things about Georgina Stirling. We would love to know what these "interesting chats" were all about. It is also confirmed here that Georgina was regularly invited to the cottage as a guest of Dr. and Mrs. Olds.

In the 1983 interview with Hiram Silk, Jessie Troake confirmed what many other sources have affirmed—the high quality of singing in Twillingate. Of her Grandmother Troake, Jessie said: "She had a lovely voice." The Troakes were noted singers in Twillingate, and many of them sat in church choirs. Two Troake brothers, Peter and Lewis, and their families lived in a double house in Durrell, separated only by a thin partition. When one family would begin to sing, the other family would join in and they would sing together "for hours" the old hymns of the church. Passersby would frequently stop outside the Troake gate and gather in small groups to listen to the singing.

During March–April 2018, I talked to **Margaret "Margo" (Drover) Evans**, Jessie (Troake) and Ted Drover's daughter, and we subsequently corresponded by email. She shared a most interesting story that her mother had related about Georgina's stay in the hospital in the summer or fall of 1934. There was only one private room in the hospital, and Georgina was the occupant; it was on the second floor. Jessie had "a funny feeling" about Georgina one night, so instead of working at her desk, as was normal, Jessie took her paperwork and stationed her chair just outside Georgina's door so that Georgina would be aware of her presence. Later, Georgina told her, "If you had not been there I would have been out the window. My Chinese friends were down below the window calling to me and I wanted to jump but I knew you wouldn't want me to."

The condition that Georgina was experiencing at that time may well have been occasioned by the severe pain of the growing cancer that would take her life early the next year, and also by the fact that she may have been self-administering opium to deaden the pain. It is said that Dr. Stirling administered opium to his wife after the tragic death of their fourth son to help her deal with her grief. Dr. Stirling may have left a supply in his surgery which Georgina was now using. Dr. Olds had stated in an interview that the deteriorating condition of Georgina's teeth was very likely caused by the use of drugs. We do not know if this was the only visit that Georgina had made to the hospital, but we do know from one source that Dr. Olds had visited her at her home. Amy Louise Peyton's statement that Georgina "declined to visit the local doctor" is incorrect, unless she was referring only to the very late stages of the growing cancer, and Georgina probably knew that even the doctor could not help at this point. There is another possibility, of course. Perhaps Georgina's hallucination was caused by drugs which were being administered by the doctor or hospital staff, or she may have been temporarily delirious from a fever.

BIBLIOGRAPHY

Bennett, Chad. "Georgina Stirling, 'The Nightingale of the North.'" Newfoundlandia, In the *Overcast.* October 7, 2018.

Black, Ros. *A Talent for Humanity: The Life and Work of Lady Henry Somerset.* Chippenham and Eastbourne, England: Antony Rowe Publishing, 2010.

Burry, Dean. "Great Canadian Musical Figures: Georgina Stirling 1867–1935." In *Opera Canada*, Vol. 39, no. 1, Spring 1998.

Butler, Paul. "Newfoundland's Nightingale" in the *Evening Telegram*, St. John's NL, October 16, 2004.

Coish, E. Calvin. *Central Newfoundland.* Grand Falls–Windsor: College of the North Atlantic, 1997. Book 3 of Basic Hitch-Hiker Series.

Davidson, Jim. "Dame Nellie Melba 1861–1931." In the *Dictionary of Australian Biography*, Volume 10 (MUP), 1986.

Dictionary of Newfoundland and Labrador Biography. St. John's: Harry Cuff Publications, 1990.

Dictionary of Newfoundland English. Toronto: University of Toronto Press, 1982.

Edward, Joan. *This is Our Place: This is Our Home.* St. John's: Breakwater Books, 2005. A short section on Georgina Sterling (sic).

Encyclopedia of Newfoundland and Labrador. Vol. 5. St. John's: Newfoundland Book Publishers (1967) Ltd., 1994.

Evans, Calvin D. *Silk Sails; Women of Newfoundland and Their Ships.* St. John's: Breakwater Books, 2008.

Farr, F. C. "Confederation Plus 20." In the *Canadian Statesman*, Bowmanville, Ontario. August 6, 1969, p. 5.

Georgina Stirling—Marie Toulinguet. Memorial Erected to Famous Newfoundlander. Author not designated. In the *Advertiser,* Grand Falls, NL. July 20, 1964.

Gilmour, Clyde. Letter to Robert Walter Parsons dated January 6, 1971.

Gimlette, John. *Theatre of Fish: Travels Through Newfoundland and Labrador.* London: Hutchinson, 2005. Pages 170–174.

Hiscock, Pamela. *A Report on the Development of Two Instructional Units on Women of New-foundland and Labrador entitled "Mary Southcott" and "Georgina Stirling."* A Report submitted in partial fulfillment of the Requirements for the Degree of Master of Education. St. John's: Division of Learning Resources, Department of Education, Memorial University of Newfoundland, 1981. Watercolour illustrations by Newfoundland artist Sylvia Ficken, 1981.

Hiscock, Philip. Book Review of Amy Louise Peyton's book *Nightingale of the North*. In *Newfoundland Quarterly* 80, no. 1 (1984): 36.

Industries of Canada: Historical and Commercial Sketches of Toronto and Environs; its Prominent Places and People; Representative Merchants and Manufacturers; Progress and Enterprise. Toronto: M. G. Bixby, 1886 (OCR Reprint).

Kallmann, Helmut. *A History of Music in Canada, 1534–1914*. Toronto: University of Toronto, 1960.

Lindbergh, Anne Morrow. *Gift from the Sea*. 50th Anniversary Edition. New York: Pantheon Books, 1975 (1955).

Macfarlane, David. *The Danger Tree: Memory, War and the Search for a Family's Past*. Toronto: Macfarlane, Walter & Ross, 1991. Page 40.

McPherson, James B. "Marie Toulinguet." In the *Canadian Encyclopedia*. Edmonton: Hurtig Publishers. Article published 07/30/07. Last edited 12/15/13.

Memorial University of Newfoundland. Digital Archives Initiative. Hiram Silk Collection. Interviews of Newfoundlanders done by Hiram Silk from the early 1950s to the late 1980s.

"Monument to Singer Unveiled." In the *Evening Telegram* July 20, 1964.

Moogk, Edward B. *Roll Back the Years: History of Canadian Recorded Sound and its Legacy. Genesis to 1930*. Ottawa: National Library of Canada, 1975. (Georgina Stirling pp. 154–155).

Morgan, Henry James. *The Canadian Men and Women of the Time: A Handbook of Canadian Biography*. First Edition. Toronto: William Briggs, 1898. p. 972.

Morgan, Henry James. *The Canadian Men and Women of the Time: A Handbook of Canadian Biography*. Second Edition. Toronto: William Briggs, 1912.

Neill, Roger. *Divas: Mathilde Marchesi and Her Pupils*. Sydney, Australia: New South Publishing: University of New South Wales Press, 2016.

Peyton, Amy Louise. *Nightingale of the North*. St. John's: Jesperson Press, 1983.

-------. Letter from Amy Louise Peyton to Robert Walter Parsons, dated October 6, 1981.

Riggs, Bert. "Nightingale of the North." In MUN *Gazette* November 26, 1998. Revised and published in Newfoundland and Labrador's National Post, Famous Players Reeldeal, The Telegram Online, April 4, 2001.

St. Peter's Anglican Church, Twillingate. One Hundred and Twenty-five year History. 1845-1970. And in Addition, Early History of the Church from 1813. Foreword written by (and booklet prepared by) Edith M. Manuel. 1970.

St. Peter's Anglican Church, Twillingate, A History. From the Nineteenth to the Twenty-first Centuries. 1st edition. Prepared for the St. Peter's Anglican Church Women by Dr. David J. Clarke, 2012. Made in the U.S.A., Charleston, SC, 14 June 2012.

Saunders, Gary L. *Doctor Olds of Twillingate; Portrait of an American Surgeon in Newfoundland*. St. John's: Breakwater Books, 1994.

Sawler, Harvey. *One Man Grand Band; the Lyrical Life of Ron Hynes*. St. John's: Breakwater Books, 2016.

Seary, E. R. *Family Names of the Island of Newfoundland*. St. John's: Memorial University of Newfoundland, 1977.

Silk, Hiram. "Newfoundland bits and pieces" about Georgina Stirling, in the *Advertiser*, Grand Falls NL, December 22, 1966.

-------. "Newfoundland bits and pieces" – More about Georgina Stirling. Photocopy undated, in the *Advertiser*, Grand Falls, NL.

-------. "Newfoundland bits and pieces" – about Lucy Stirling and her sisters. Photocopy undated, in the *Advertiser*, Grand Falls, NL.

Smith, W. Stephen with Michael Chipman. *The Naked Voice: A Wholistic Approach to Singing*. New York: Oxford University Press, 2010.

Wadden, Brian. "Early Demonstrations of the Phonograph in Newfoundland." In *Newfoundland Quarterly* 82, no. 3 (1987): 44–48.

Worthington, Peter. "The Rock's Unsung Opera Star: The Nightingale of the North is one of Canada's many forgotten heroes." In the *Toronto Sun*, October 19, 1999.

Many Internet articles including Census of England and Wales and articles on the Italian Nobility, the Italian Risinamento and the Risorgimento, modes of travel in Europe in the 1880s, vocal hemorrhaging, and the tracing of book titles.

Soprano **TONIA EVANS CIANCIULLI** was born in St. John's, Newfoundland. She is honoured to have embarked on this passionate journey to revive the life and legacy of the late Newfoundland Nightingale, Georgina Stirling, alongside her grandfather, Calvin D. Evans. She has toured her concert program, *Nightingale Sings*, across the province of Newfoundland, and in cities such as Toronto, Ottawa, and Miami and beyond. In 2018 she was awarded a Canada Council for the Arts grant for this significant and historical work, and she is now a proud member of both the Writers' Alliance of Newfoundland and Labrador and The Writers' Union of Canada.

Tonia is a multi-faceted concert artist, performing her signature programs across North America and for niche events and fundraisers to rally support and encouragement within communities. She performs a wide variety of music, from opera to her own original music, and celebrates her roots covering the music of Newfoundland's late folk hero, Ron Hynes. Praised for the work she does to shine a spotlight on two of her province's most talented musicians, Georgina Stirling and Ron Hynes, Tonia has been featured in numerous interviews with CBC, SiriusXM, and Eastlink TV. Represented by Newfoundland's record label, Citadel House, Tonia will be releasing two tribute albums paying homage to Georgina Stirling and Ron Hynes, to coincide with the launch of this book. *The Heart's Obsession* companion album highlights repertoire most beloved by Georgina Stirling's Newfoundland audiences, and *Beckon Me Home* is reflective of the love and connection to our island home that shines through the poignant lyrics and melodies of Ron Hynes. Both albums will continue to feature spectacular music videos that highlight the stunning landscapes in Newfoundland and its beloved culture, filmed by Twillingate drone artist Julian Earle, like that of her video of Ron Hynes's "Marie."

In 2010, Tonia founded Wish Opera/Arts, a non-profit organization and community of supportive artists, in collaboration with Maestro Kerry Stratton and the Toronto Concert Orchestra. She has produced multiple fully-staged theatrical productions, concerts, and niche events that feature Canadian opera singers and artists.

Tonia shares behind-the-scenes aspects of being an artist in her "Artist's Spotlight," an interview series that shines a spotlight on leading Canadian artists to inspire and motivate others within their industries. Passionate about supporting artists to embrace their gifts and talents, she obtained her certification in Neuro-Linguistic Programming as an NLP practitioner and developed "An Artist's Journey," which offers programs, workshops, and performance series to artists of all genres, guiding them to develop and excel at achieving success and confidence throughout their artistic careers.

Tonia holds a Bachelor of Voice Performance from the University of Western Ontario. She trains vocally with Manny Perez in Miami and Brian McIntosh in London, Ontario.

With her husband, Frank Cianciulli, Tonia lives between Toronto, Ontario, and Miami, Florida. They are blessed with two beautiful children, Sophia and Anthony, which she homeschools while pursuing her musical endeavours.

Tonia returns to Newfoundland often to visit family and perform, and she never misses an opportunity to search for heart rocks on her favourite Newfoundland beaches. She encourages you to look for hearts in your everyday life. You can post pictures of them on Instagram and hashtag them #TheHeartsObsession.

You can find Tonia on YouTube: **Tonia Cianciulli Wish Arts**; Instagram: **@toniacianciulli**; Facebook: **Tonia Evans Cianciulli Soprano/Author**; Twitter: **@WishTonia**; and her website: **www.wisharts.ca**. You can contact Tonia directly at **tonia@wishopera.ca** for music or performance inquiries. Her albums will also be available online through all major streaming sites and available to order from Fred's Records: www.fredsrecords.com.

CALVIN D. EVANS retired from dual careers as a university librarian and a United Church minister. He has lived and worked in six of the provinces—Newfoundland, Nova Scotia, Quebec, Ontario, Saskatchewan, and Alberta. He is the author of six books: *For Love of a Woman: The Evans Family and a Perspective on Shipbuilding in Newfoundland* (Harry Cuff Publications, 1992); *Soren Kierkegaard Bibliographies* (McGill University, 1993); *Silk Sails: Women of Newfoundland and Their Ships* (Breakwater, 2008); *Master Shipbuilders of Newfoundland and Labrador* (Breakwater, Volume One 2013, Volume Two 2014). He has also written several articles on library science and has been a contributing writer for the *Dictionary of Canadian Biography* (seven biographies) and for the *Encyclopedia of Newfoundland and Labrador*. In 2005 he wrote the biographies of fifteen Newfoundland women for the Grand Falls–Windsor Chapter of the Council on the Status of Women. This document is available on an Internet site. In 2018 Calvin's booklet *Major Sidney Cotton's Aviation Adventures in Newfoundland and in the Two World Wars* was printed by Morgan Printing of Bishop's Falls, Newfoundland and

Labrador, under the sponsorship of the Botwood Heritage Society. Calvin is a member of the Writers' Alliance of Newfoundland and Labrador and of The Writers' Union of Canada. In 2009, Calvin was awarded the honorific title of Librarian Emeritus of McGill University. Calvin now lives with his wife, Goldie, in Wasaga Beach, Ontario. They have three children (plus one deceased), six grandchildren, and nine great-grandchildren. They have spent the past ten summers at a cottage in Pleasantview, Newfoundland.

INDEX